REVELATION, SCRIPTURE AND CHURCH

How does God's involvement with the generation of Holy Scripture and its use in the life of the Christian church figure into the human work of Scripture interpretation? This is the central question that this book seeks to address. In critical conversation with the influential hermeneutic programs of James Barr, Paul Ricoeur and Hans Frei, Topping demonstrates how God's agency has been marginalized in the task of Scripture interpretation. Divine involvement with the Bible is bracketed out (Barr), rendered in generic terms (Ricoeur) or left implicit (Frei) in these depictions of the hermeneutic field. The result is that each of these hermeneutic programs is less than a 'realist' interpretative proposal. Talk of God is eclipsed by the terminal consideration of human realities. Topping argues for the centrality of doctrinal description in a lively theological understanding of Scripture interpretation for the life of the church.

ASHGATE NEW CRITICAL THINKING IN RELIGION, THEOLOGY AND BIBLICAL STUDIES

The *Ashgate New Critical Thinking in Religion, Theology and Biblical Studies* series brings high quality research monograph publishing back into focus for authors, international libraries, and student, academic and research readers. Headed by an international editorial advisory board of acclaimed scholars spanning the breadth of religious studies, theology and biblical studies, this open-ended monograph series presents cutting-edge research from both established and new authors in the field. With specialist focus yet clear contextual presentation of contemporary research, books in the series take research into important new directions and open the field to new critical debate within the discipline, in areas of related study, and in key areas for contemporary society.

Series Editorial Board:

Jeff Astley, North of England Institute for Christian Education, Durham, UK
David Jasper, University of Glasgow, UK
James Beckford, University of Warwick, UK
Raymond Williams, Wabash College, Crawfordsville, USA
Geoffrey Samuel, University of Newcastle, Australia
Richard Hutch, University of Queensland, Australia
Paul Fiddes, Regent's Park College, University of Oxford, UK
Anthony Thiselton, University of Nottingham, UK
Tim Gorringe, University of Exeter, UK
Adrian Thatcher, College of St Mark and St John, UK
Alan Torrance, University of St Andrews, UK
Judith Lieu, Kings College London, UK
Terrance Tilley, University of Dayton, USA
Miroslav Volf, Yale Divinity School, USA
Stanley Grenz, Baylor University and Truett Seminary, USA
Vincent Brummer, University of Utrecht, The Netherlands
Gerhard Sauter, University of Bonn, Germany

Other Titles in the Series:

Pentecostal Theology for the Twenty-First Century
Engaging with Multi-Faith Singapore
Tan-Chow May Ling

Neopragmatism and Theological Reason
G.W. Kimura

Revelation, Scripture and Church

Theological Hermeneutic Thought of James Barr,
Paul Ricoeur and Hans Frei

RICHARD R. TOPPING
*The Church of St. Andrew and St. Paul,
Montreal, Canada*

LONDON AND NEW YORK

First published 2007 by Ashgate Publishing

Published 2016 by Routledge
2 Park Square, Milton Park, Abingdon, Oxon OX14 4RN
711 Third Avenue, New York, NY 10017, USA

First issued in paperback 2018

Routledge is an imprint of the Taylor & Francis Group, an informa business

Copyright © Richard R. Topping, 2007

Richard R. Topping has asserted his moral right under the Copyright, Designs and Patents Act, 1988, to be identified as the author of this work.

All rights reserved. No part of this book may be reprinted or reproduced or utilised in any form or by any electronic, mechanical, or other means, now known or hereafter invented, including photocopying and recording, or in any information storage or retrieval system, without permission in writing from the publishers.

Notice:
Product or corporate names may be trademarks or registered trademarks, and are used only for identification and explanation without intent to infringe.

British Library Cataloguing in Publication Data
Topping, Richard R.
    Revelation, scripture and church : theological hermeneutic thought of James Barr, Paul Ricoeur and Hans Frei. - (Ashgate new critical thinking in religion, theology and biblical studies)
    1. Barr, James, 1924–2006 2. Ricoeur, Paul 3. Frei, Hans W. 4. Bible – Hermeneutics
    I. Title
    220.6'01

Library of Congress Cataloging-in-Publication Data
Topping, Richard R., 1960–
    Revelation, Scripture, and church : theological hermeneutic thought of James Barr, Paul Ricoeur, and Hans Frei / Richard R. Topping.
        p. cm. – (Ashgate new critical thinking in religion, theology, and biblical studies)
    Includes bibliographical references (p.   ) and index.
    ISBN-13: 978-0-7546-5802-3 (hardcover : alk. paper)
    1. Bible – Hermeneutics. 2. Bible – Evidences, authority, etc. 3. Bible – Inspiration.
4. Barr, James, 1924–2006 5. Ricoeur, Paul. 6. Frei, Hans W. I. Title.

    BS476.T66 2007
    220.601—dc22

                                                                                    2006030602

ISBN 13: 978-1-138-31182-4 (pbk)
ISBN 13: 978-0-7546-5802-3 (hbk)

To Amy Susan, my wife
and Karl and Paul, my sons

Contents

Foreword by John B. Webster	ix
Preface	xi
Introduction	1
1 Revelation and Biblical Interpretation: Divine Disclosure and the Constitution of Faith	9
James Barr: Cumulative Tradition and Its Soteriological Function	9
Paul Ricoeur: Manifestation and the Hermeneutic Constitution of Faith	31
Hans Frei: Apologetics, Christology and Anthropology	53
The Birth and Shape of Modern Doctrines of Revelation	55
2 The Bible as Holy Scripture: Construal and Authority	79
James Barr: The Bible as Faith-Structured Classic Model	79
Paul Ricoeur: The Bible as Polyphonic Intertext that Names God	104
Hans Frei: The Bible Read 'Literally'	130
3 The Church and the Bible Critically Read	157
James Barr: Critical Biblical Research and the Listening Church	158
Paul Ricoeur: Suspicious Hermeneutics and Submissive Communities	176
Hans Frei: The Critical Primacy of *Sensus Literalis*	194
Conclusion	213
Bibliography	217
Index	235

Foreword

Theological interpretation of the Bible enjoys high profile at present for a number of reasons. In part it indicates the maturing of protest against the apparent theological impotence of critical 'history of religions' study of the biblical texts: rather than satisfying themselves with polemic, theologians and theologically-minded exegetes have begun to take responsibility for shifting the interpretation of the Bible to a more fruitful orientation. Further, the renewal of theological interpretation stems from a recovery of interest in classical, especially patristic, biblical exegesis—initially, at least, largely on the part of Roman Catholic theologians like Jean Daniélou and Henri de Lubac, but now much more widely shared across the Christian confessions. This recovery was, of course, itself stimulated by the centrality of 'church' in much theology in the second half of the twentieth century; the expansion of ecclesiology affected not only ecumenics and dogmatics but also hermeneutics, especially when allied with philosophical theories of the communal character of human interpretative activity.

This provocative study identifies a lacuna in these developments, namely the need to root what is said about the Bible and its interpretation in Christian teaching about God. Theories—sometimes complex theories—of communities of interpretation and their interpretative acts and ends are surely necessary to any adequate theological hermeneutics. But they do not prove sufficient, and require grounding in a theology of divine action. More specifically, they have to be located in the wider context of theological claims about God's communicative and saving activity as revealer and reconciler. If this kind of grounding is necessary, it is in the end because only in that way can theology offer effective resistance to the instinctive naturalism of a good deal of modern hermeneutical theory and exegetical practice, which handles the Bible as an immanent field of human communicative acts. It matters little which acts are highlighted (authorial, redactive, canonical, interpretative): the result is a mislocation of thinking about the Bible as it is moved from its proper habitat in talk of God and God's communicative presence. Whatever else the notion of Holy Scripture may mean, it means at least that the production and reception of the biblical writings has to be accounted for by appealing to God's activity with a measure of directness. Hence the theological realism of the argument which follows: "properly to attend to the nature and function of the Bible and biblical interpretation, is to attend to the agency of God both in terms of the formation and use of 'Holy' Scripture."

The argument gently but unremittingly detaches its readers from habitual naturalism by working through three doctrinal topics—revelation, Scripture and church—and their treatment by three magisterial figures in modern biblical interpretation: James Barr, Paul Ricoeur and Hans Frei. Each chapter is an exercise in critical theology, modestly and respectfully accomplished and yet reaching some penetrating theological judgements about the matter in hand. Yet the end of the exercise is constructive, namely, to suggest that theological hermeneutics has a good deal to profit from appeal to divine action, and that it will remain disordered unless it makes this appeal both in its self-articulations and in its practice. This appeal means—to simplify the argument conducted here with considerable sophistication—that interpretation and interpretative communities are functions of the notion of Holy Scripture; that notion is in its turn a function of revelation, which is itself an extension of the doctrine of God. To have recovered that insight, which was second nature to much of the classical Christian tradition but from which modern theology has allowed itself to become estranged, is not the least of the virtues of this work, from which exegetes and dogmaticians may learn a great deal.

John B. Webster
University of Aberdeen

Preface

This book would never have come to completion without the help, encouragement and generosity of the Church of St Andrew and St Paul, whose Session and congregation gave me an extended leave of absence to finish it. By the initiative of the Clerk of Session, Dr Lawrence Hutchison, and the generosity of a most kind group of congregants, I was able to give my full attention to academic work free from ministerial duties. I am also grateful to J.S.S. Armour, Minister Emeritus of the congregation, for returning to work from which he had retired, much to my delight and that of the congregation.

The Reverend Professor John B. Webster was a constant source of encouragement. His kind and thorough attention over the duration of the project, his confidence that the topic was important for contemporary theological hermeneutic reflection and his cheerful friendship made the work a pleasure. Professors David Demson, John Vissers, Gordon Rixon and Joseph Mangina all offered helpful and insightful comments on the text, which has, no doubt, greatly improved the finished product. My friend James Dickie gave careful editorial attention to the manuscript and made incisive comments on it as did Philip Hillyer. I am grateful to Sarah Lloyd and Sarah Charters of Ashgate Publishing for their support and guidance throughout this project. Any infelicities that remain are my own.

I have no doubt that my interest in the interpretation of Holy Scripture for the life of the church is the result of the influence of my parents, Paul and Norma Topping. My wife Amy was so very supportive and patient over the too long a time that it took me to complete this work. I am grateful to God for her love and strength and friendship. My sons, Karl and Paul, showed no little interest in this project, but granted their father the quiet he needed. They did wonder when I would finish my homework. This completed homework is dedicated to them, my family, with gratitude and love.

Richard R. Topping
Ordinary Time 2007

Introduction

Argument

In contemporary biblical-theological hermeneutics there has been a proliferation of methods developed to depict the hermeneutic situation of the church and to discern the meaning of the Bible for the life of the church.[1] Three important methods operative within the contemporary interpretative landscape are historical-critical, hermeneutic-poetic and a retrieval of the classic figural and Christocentric reading of the Bible. These three strands of biblical interpretation, in the examples we examine, share a common deficit: each of them fails adequately to depict the hermeneutic situation of the church and the nature of the Bible in terms of their common implication within God's communicative and salvific action. While each of them is attentive to texts, interpreters and communities as human and historical phenomenon, they fail in their interpretative proposals to offer an account of how these same factors acquire specific attributes in their relation to God, that is, each is insufficiently realist in its account of the nature, function and critical reading of Holy Scripture as it is implicated in God's revelatory action.

Historical-critical interpretation of the Bible continues to be an important and dominant option within the academy. One important strand of this approach to biblical interpretation, represented by James Barr, encourages interpreters to bracket out theological constructs, like revelation and Holy Scripture, for the sake of critical interpretation in the life of the church. Interpreters who are truth-seeking work with freedom from theological belief and ecclesial context in order to let the text speak against received doctrine, which may be and often is an imposition upon the text. Concepts like revelation, inspiration and Holy Scripture are held up against the scrutiny of an empirical examination of the use of such terms within the Bible and of the human and historical reality of the people of God, including the socio-intentional world, which lies behind the texts of the Bible, and in effect generated their inscripturation. In the attempt to maintain some account of divine action in relation to human action, Barr tends to render divine action immanent within human performance in the inscripturation and formation of the Bible. Where theological doctrines of revelation, Holy Scripture or church operate in a fundamental fashion to provide a map of the interpretative terrain and of the nature of the Bible in its relation to the salvific work of God, such doctrines are regarded as obstacles to be overcome since they frustrate the freedom of the historical critic to follow research wherever it may lead.

The dominance of the historical-critical approach to interpretation, which consigns the primary locus of textual meaning to a world "behind the text," has

---

1 Thomas Long gives a brief overview of the proliferation of hermeneutic options and their effect on the location of meaning in contemporary biblical interpretation. See "Committing Hermeneutical Heresy," *Theology Today*, 44/2 (July, 1987): 165-167.

2   *Revelation, Holy Scripture and Church*

been challenged, and in some instances modified, by "hermeneutic" models, which shift meaning away from sources and authorial intention and toward the reader or the interpreting community as the primary locus. Where biblical interpreters in the dominant traditions of Western Protestantism after the Enlightenment once began with historical "excavative"[2] work, presently interpreters, like Paul Ricoeur, turn to heavily theorized accounts of texts and their interpreting subjects and communities. Hermeneutic theory is annexed to the church's reading of Scripture as a kind of prolegomena. The result is that the integrity of explicitly theological language is subordinated to a natural poetic account of texts in their compositional generation and genric diversity and the interpretative subject in terms of imagination and conscience. Moreover, substantive readings of Holy Scripture, proposed by the community for whom these texts function, must be submitted to the scrutiny of the masters of suspicion (Marx, Nietzsche and Freud) to be purged of iconoclastic potential and thus gain critical integrity. Revelation, Holy Scripture and Church, in so far as these terms function to depict the interpretative situation and the nature of the realities implicated in the saving action of God, are muted then by means of a poetic detour (a deferral) and then by a hermeneutic/poetic transposition of their specificity into more general terms, and finally, an interrogation by an outside critique.

Others have noted that the contemporary interpretative climate is conducive to the recovery of the classic mode of biblical interpretation. In the hermeneutic work of Hans Frei, an attempt is made to rehabilitate figural Christocentric reading of the Bible as Scripture, which he believes represents the dominant mode of Bible reading in the history of the Christian church. The Bible is held together as a single story through typology and figuration focused in the ascriptively literal meaning of the stories about Jesus. Through the deployment of literary and social-scientific convention, Frei makes the case that the Bible ought to be read this way: it is required either by the kind of literature that the Bible is (realistic narrative) or, later, by reading conventions embedded in the community for which the Bible functions religiously. Critical reading of Holy Scripture, both in terms of its explicative and applicative sense, is reading in keeping with the conventions most appropriate to the Bible as Scripture of the church. Within such an account, theological language that relates the meaning of the Bible as Holy Scripture of the church to the revelatory action of God almost always remains tacit. The heavy lifting in this proposal is performed by either specification of a literary type, or by means of a construal of the Bible that locates it within a semiotic system, that is, within Christianity as a social construct. Revelation, Holy Scripture and church as this language functions to relate Scripture, its ecclesial setting and reading conventions, meaning and truth, to the action of God, Father, Son and Holy Spirit, is not consistently rendered visible.

It is not the purpose of this essay to divorce itself from the substantive contributions to biblical interpretation made by historical-critical, hermeneutic/poetic or literary and social scientific approaches. Moreover, it is not the intention of this work to argue that the only mode of Bible reading that is licit is theological[3] or that information

---

2 The term is Robert Alter's. *The World of Biblical Literature* (New York, 1992), p. 133.

3 Wayne Meeks notes that more than one kind of interpretative tyranny can be at work in hermeneutics. Many interpretative aims are possible and thus what the Bible means will to

Introduction 3

garnered from other interpretative approaches is irrelevant to theological reading of Scripture for the life of God's people. Meir Sternberg, while he notes that modes of biblical interpretation tend to be oriented toward either sources or discourse, maintains that it is not possible to speak

> as if there were one Bible for the historian, another for the theologian, and another for the linguist, another for the geneticist, and still another for the literary critic . . . There are not enough Bibles to go around, and even Solomon's wisdom cannot divide the only one we do possess among the various claimants. Its discourse remains indivisible for all, and so does its source.[4]

There is no doubt that the multiplicity of modes of biblical interpretation render substantial assistance to the church in its task of Scripture interpretation. The modern concentration on the Bible as a human and historical document has helped the church to avoid the temptation toward a naïve docetism and, what is more, enabled a certain theological clarity about the Bible's character and role as a human witness to the Word of God rather than Word of God *in se*. Moreover, the role of the church, in its various socio-cultural embodiments, in giving shape to the Bible through various stages of its inscripturation, formation and canonization, is important to the ongoing use of the Bible. For example, in so far as precanonical forms of biblical literature have been rendered visible through redaction criticism, interpreters have been able to observe the theological pressures under which the canon was formed and so to follow the trajectories of meaning that shaped the final form of the text in their own exegetical work. So much more could be said on this front: historical-critical investigations so often serve to clarify unfamiliar customs and practices, and poetic attention to semantics and genre have helped to correct the heresy of paraphrase and interpretative anachronism.[5]

However, because the overall thrust of this work is to draw attention to the fallacy of misplaced concreteness, that is, the attempt to offer a partial picture of reality for the whole of it, the positive contributions of the panoply of interpretative approaches is not the primary focus of critical inquiry. In the hermeneutic strategies we investigate, the argument is that the hermeneutic field and the nature and character of critical biblical interpretation are over-determined by their preponderant relation to human actions implicated in the production, interpretation and ecclesial use of the Bible. Such a deflationary account of reality, one that marginalizes (brackets out, defers and transposes or leaves tacit) the origin and nature of the Bible in its relation to

---

a great extent depend upon the interests and purposes of its interpreters. See *The First Urban Christians* (New Haven, 1983), p. 4. See also Jeffrey Stout, "What is the Meaning of a Text?," *New Literary History*, 14 (1982): 1-12.

4 Meir Sternberg, *The Poetics of Biblical Narrative: Ideological Literature and the Drama of Reading* (Bloomington, 1985), pp. 14, 17.

5 James Barr established, for example, that that element of biblical theology, which sought a "Hebrew" mentality and thus assigned theological weight to individual Hebrew words could not bear scrutiny. See *The Semantics of Biblical Language* (Oxford, 1961) and *Biblical Words for Time*, SBT 33 (London, 1962). See also Walter Brueggemann, *Theology of the Old Testament: Testimony, Dispute, Advocacy* (Minneapolis, 1997), p. 96.

God's action and use of Holy Scripture in his work of salvation, is not theologically satisfactory. While it often proves fruitful to restrict the range of interpretative scope and conceptuality for specific hermeneutic interests, for example, to investigate the use of the vocative by Paul, the liability of such approaches is that "thick" theological description can come to be viewed as rhetorical extravagance, as "in others words" description or simply special pleading. The argument here is theologically realist; that is, properly to attend to the nature and function of the Bible and biblical interpretation, is to attend to the agency of God both in terms of the formation and use of "Holy" Scripture. In effect an ontology of Scripture, a true description of the realities implied by the existence of the Bible and the task of Scripture interpretation, requires a substantive doctrinal ordering and account of the church's interpretative task; of the Bible in its relation to the prevenient, generative and sustaining action of God, which elicits and illumines the Bible as Holy Scripture; and of the critical character that accrues to Holy Scripture over and in the life of the church because of God's gracious use of it. The Bible as it is ingredient in and to the revelatory/salvific action of God in Jesus Christ *is* Holy Scripture.

Procedure

The work is divided into three subsequent main chapters: Revelation and Biblical Interpretation; The Bible as Holy Scripture; and The Church and the Bible Critically Read. In each chapter, an exposition of Barr, Ricoeur and Frei is untaken in order to demonstrate how doctrines of revelation, Scripture and church are implicated within the hermeneutic procedure they prescribe. The ordering of the chapters is reflective of a hermeneutic field that is construed in relation to dogmatic thinking about the place of Scripture within the saving purposes of God in Jesus Christ. God's disclosure and salvific initiative is generative of inscripturated witness to the Gospel of Jesus Christ, which by the illuminative work of the Holy Spirit constitutes and sustains the church.

In the first major section, Revelation and Biblical Interpretation, the relation of the Bible to revelation is investigated in the work of Barr, Ricoeur and Frei. In the expository section, classical Christian construals of the doctrine of revelation are first rendered problematic by each author. By means of historical-critical, hermeneutic-poetic and literary/social-scientific analysis, the implication of the doctrine of revelation within a specific construal of the hermeneutic field is offered. Traditional dogmatic notions of revelation within which the Bible evoked human testimony to the saving action of God in Jesus Christ, made effective for faith in the power of the Holy Spirit, are prescinded from (Barr), deferred for the sake of a reconfigured hermeneutic-poetic field only to be admitted in transposed form (Ricoeur), or left tacit in a terminal consideration of mediate realities, genre and semiotic system, implicated in revelation (Frei). The result of these interpretative moves is that Scripture's primary nature in relation to the God by whose action it is evoked and made effective for faith is left out of hermeneutic account. God's action is conflated to human action (Barr), textual dynamics (Ricoeur) or reading conventions required by genre type or communal "thick" description (Frei). The

Introduction 5

basic criticism, in keeping with the work, is that in a theologically realist account of biblical interpretation, interpreters must take into account those features that accrue to Holy Scripture as it is implicated within the revelatory action of God.

In Chapter 2, attention is turned to the Bible as Holy Scripture. The particular features of the Bible as Scripture that receive attention are its unity and authority. Again, we follow the treatment of each author as they render problematic classical construals and offer their rearticulations of the Bible in its unity and authority. While each author presents a positive account of these features of Holy Scripture and articulates them in such a way as to render them serviceable to theological and church use, once again their positive proposals derive their constructive potential in relative independence from a consideration of the use of the Bible vis-à-vis the action of God. Both the unity and authority of the Bible are configured and articulated in relation to the intentional world of text production (Barr), the nature of texts as a world instanced in writing (Ricoeur), or reading conventions appropriate to genre or the community for whom these texts function religiously (Frei). Each account fails to feature a doctrinal account of the Bible as "Holy" Scripture, that is, an account in which the unity and authority of the Bible are derivative from the relationship of the Bible to God or its service to the Gospel, which is the content of the Bible.

Finally, in Chapter 3, a consideration of the church's reading of the Bible as critical reading is undertaken. In each case an exposition of the respective thinker is undertaken with a view to exposing the nature of critical reading as they articulate it, and how such reading modulates the hearing and reading of the Bible for the life of the church. All of the authors considered propose critical reading as essential to the edification of the Christian community—none of them espouse a form of reading which terminates in skepticism or rules out listening to Holy Scripture in a believing mode. However, each author is, in effect, making a case for the ordered reading of Holy Scripture, that is, for how various modes of reading ought to be related for the sake of truthful, authentic or faithful reading within the church. While evidentiary considerations (Barr), iconoclastic insights (Ricoeur) and reading conventions (Frei) are all integral to non-obscurantist Bible reading, the force of the term "critical" is derived apart from a consideration of its meaning in relation to God's communicative action by means of the Bible. What is missing is a thick theological account of the fundamental nature of the term "critical" in relation to God's use of the Bible to create, accost and sustain the people of God.

Persons

The choice of the three interpreters whose hermeneutic proposals are the substantive material for examination within this essay is motivated by two particular considerations. In the first instance each of them proposes an interpretative program that impinges upon the normative interpretative practice of the Christian church in its use of the Bible. Their respective construals of the hermeneutic field and of biblical interpretation and use are offered as preliminary to and normative for the constitutive use of the Bible in the community for which it functions religiously. Indeed, in each case their hermeneutic musings are offered, where they intersect with the ecclesial task of Scripture interpretation, as essential to the integrity of the biblical interpretation. Moreover, while they each construe the interpretative implications of belonging to the church in different terms, their common motivation and interest in biblical interpretation arises on the basis of personal Christian conviction. The importance of their common espousal of a hermeneutic program that is normative for, or preliminary to, church interpretative practice is crucial for this work. For the thrust of the argument is not imperiously to declare without qualification that theological interpretation has hegemony over other interpretative strategies, but rather that when the hermeneutic *aim* is to interpret the Bible for the life of the people of God, the range of interpretative strategies ought to include, indeed, be ordered within and by a theological account of the interpretative field and the nature and character of Bible in its relation to God's revelatory/salvific activity. The argument of the work with the interpretative proposals of Barr, Ricoeur and Frei is thus contentious precisely at the point they wish to maintain—that each respective proposal is normative for or preliminary to the churchly task of Scripture interpretation.

A second reason for the choice of the three interpreters selected is that they stretch across a range and are thus representative of serious hermeneutical options and the preponderant loci of textual meaning in the current interpretative marketplace. Any interpretation of the Bible requires the coordination of at least three loci of meaning— the world "behind" the text, the world "in front of" the text and the world "within" the text.[6] James Barr's interpretative program coordinates these three loci with particular attention to the first of these. The preponderant weight in interpretation is toward the socio-intentional world of text production. The limits of textual meaning are sought primarily, though not exclusively, with respect to circumstances that generate a text. While Barr is by no means inattentive to the Bible's "factual" reality, its applicative sense before the text or in the Bible construed as a whole in its unity, all of these are ordered in terms of their relationship to the world behind the text, that is, to the intentional/productive world of the author. Limits are set on explicative and applicative senses of the Bible by their rootedness and relatedness to the human and historical world that in effect generated a specific text.

The interpretative drive within the hermeneutic program of Paul Ricoeur is oriented to the world "in front of" the text. While Ricoeur is critical of the rush to existential signification that he observes in Bultmann[7] and is attentive to the objectivity of the text in its generic variety, the overall emphasis of his hermeneutic enterprise is on the "possible world" that a text proposes to a reader. Ricoeur is less interested in texts as historical artifacts and more invested in the itineraries of meaning, the possible worlds that propose themselves to the imagination of a reader, through frictive generic interaction, in front of the text. Intentional worlds and original audiences are not so determinative of meaning as the instanciated text that acquires a life of its own through writing. Potential readings arise as imaginative variations brokered by conscience prove themselves, not by being traced to the intentional

---

6 See Sandra Schneiders, *The Revelatory Text: Interpreting the New Testament as Sacred Scripture* (New York, 1991), pp. 95-179.

7 Paul Ricoeur, "Preface to Bultmann," in Lewis S. Mudge (ed.), *Essays on Biblical Interpretation* (Philadelphia, 1980), pp. 49-72.

Introduction 7

world of the author or proved by what the textual ensemble will bear, but in their reception by an audience, in "the transfer from text to life."[8]

Finally, Hans Frei's normative hermeneutic proposal is weighted toward the world "within" the text. The whole of the Bible in its generic diversity is shaped into a coherent story through typology and figuration centered in the ascriptively literal narratives about Jesus Christ, that is, what the Gospels ascribe to Jesus they predicate of him and not everyone in general or no one in particular. The explicative sense of the Bible as Holy Scripture in all its parts is determined by the hermeneutic procedure by which the New Testament appropriates the Old—that is, by a Christocentric logic. Indeed, where the "literal" reading of any part of the Bible is in potential conflict with the ascriptively literal sense of the stories about Jesus, it is read typologically, and even allegorically, such that it conforms with the identity of Jesus narratively rendered. Moreover, the applicative sense of the Bible is rendered by the same means as the scriptural reading of the Bible; through typology and figuration the scriptural story is extended to encompass or "absorb" extratextual reality in relation to the ascriptively literal story of Jesus.

The point here is not to provide a complete overview of the options considered, a more thorough-going exposition is undertaken in the body of the work. This brief description is only to make the point that the range of interpretative proposals under consideration here is representative of options weighted to various hermeneutic loci operative in contemporary biblical/theological hermeneutics.

---

8 Paul Ricoeur, "Naming God," in Mark Wallace (ed.), *Figuring the Sacred: Religion, Narrative and Imagination*, trans. David Pelleur (Minneapolis, 1995) p. 217.

Chapter 1

Revelation and Biblical Interpretation: Divine Disclosure and the Constitution of Faith

In this chapter an exposition and critical examination of James Barr, Paul Ricoeur and Hans Frei on the relation of the Bible to revelation is undertaken. The focus of attention is given to the manner in which the Bible is implicated in the revelatory and saving action of God in Jesus Christ by means of which Scripture is generated and to which it bears witness and is made effective for faith in the power of the Spirit. The manner of procedure will be to provide an overview of each thinker such that the hermeneutic field within which they construe Scripture's implication in a doctrine of revelation is offered. Classic Christian construals of the doctrine of revelation and the implication of Scripture within them are in each case rendered problematic through analysis of a historical-critical (Barr), hermeneutic-poetic (Ricoeur), or literary/social scientific/theological (Frei) variety. While the aim of each primary author is to provide a conceptual overview of the hermeneutic field such that a doctrine of revelation functions in a properly ordered relation to the content of Holy Scripture in the context of the church, the primacy of revelation to the hermeneutic task is bracketed out for the sake of unencumbered historical-critical research (Barr), deferred, because "authoritarian and opaque," for the sake of a preliminary poetic detour (Ricoeur), or left tacit, often hidden from view, through a consideration of the features of mediate realities implicated in revelation (Frei). The net effect of these moves is that Scripture's primary nature in relation to God's revelatory and saving action is conflated to human action (Barr), textual dynamics (Ricoeur), or, at least at the level of textual meaning, reading conventions required by genre type or embedded communal practice (Frei). What each account lacks, to a greater or lesser degree, is a fundamental and thoroughgoing sense of the relation of Scripture—in its generation and use—to God's communicative action in Jesus Christ made luminous and effective in the power of the Spirit.

James Barr: Cumulative Tradition and Its Soteriological Function

For James Barr, critical biblical exegesis must be free from controlling theological belief or its character as both "free" and "critical" is threatened. Doctrines of revelation, when they function as dogmatic prolegomena, ought therefore to be resisted since they determine the rules of engagement prior to the empirical examination of biblical texts in their socio-historical circumstances of origin. Barr rejects theological

10   *Revelation, Holy Scripture and Church*

construals of the hermeneutic field, such as Karl Barth's and Brevard Childs', since they function to contain critical inquiry with their monolithic and Christological dogmatic depictions of revelation. Barr reconceptualizes revelation and expands the scope of its occurrence through a consideration of the longer and broader tradition (pre-text, inscripturation, canonization and post-crystallization effects) in which knowledge of God cumulates and of which "fixed" Scripture is an objectified instance. The formulation and growth of this cumulative tradition provides, on Barr's view, the matrix for "the coming of divine acts and the impulse for their occurrence."[1] However, the basic genre for the formation of Israelite and Christian tradition together with that of inscripturation, canonization and post-biblical effects is human and historical. Barr regards attempts to appeal to an antecedent act of God, which generated the tradition about God, as special pleading since we have no access to such an act apart from the human tradition about God. Thus Barr is resolute both in his account of revelation and inspiration to avoid double-descriptive accounts. While the Spirit accompanies human thoughts and actions, these thoughts and actions are depicted without resort to divine "intervention." The soteriological function of the Bible as "a God given meeting place" is the means by which there is growth in the cumulative tradition.

In the material that follows, the exposition of Barr's position on revelation a critique of his construal of the hermeneutic field is offered. The fundamental point in this section is that, while he introduces theological language into his discussion of revelation, Barr tends to conflate divine action to human action such that the dynamics of inscripturation, canonization and post-biblical effects are all depicted as human historical acts without recourse to theological description. Indeed, in so far as Barr articulates a sense of divine involvement with the Bible, he assumes either, on the one hand, an independent causal nexus within which God works only by way of "intervention," or, on the other hand, one in which divine agency is descriptively confluent with human action virtually without remainder. In the critique of Barr's contrastive understanding of divine action, a theological case is made for the antecedent, generative acts of God to human historical accounts, understood as witnesses to revelation, and an attempt is made to relate human and divine action in a more subtle fashion under the rubric of inspiration.

The Problem of Revelation

Samuel Balentine, in his essay "James Barr's Quest for Sound and Adequate Biblical Interpretation,"[2] notes that in his first book[3] Barr set out the objective that has guided his work in biblical scholarship for three decades. "It is," wrote Barr, "a main concern of both scholarship and theology that the Bible should be soundly

---

1 James Barr, *Old and New in Interpretation: A Study of the Two Testaments* (New York, 1966), p. 156.

2 Samuel Balentine, "James Barr's Quest for Sound and Adequate Biblical Interpretation," in Samuel E. Balentine and John Barton (eds), *Language, Theology and the Bible: Essays in Honour of James Barr* (New York, 1993), pp. 5-15.

3 James Barr, *The Semantics of Biblical Language* (London, 1961).

Revelation and Biblical Interpretation

and adequately interpreted."[4] An axiomatic implication of this guiding concern is, for Barr, that biblical interpretation must be allowed freedom from controlling theological belief.[5] Nowhere is this more evident than with respect to the doctrine of revelation. Throughout his entire corpus of writings, Barr is critical of doctrines of revelation where they are used to privilege the Bible in such a way as to stifle "free" historical-critical investigation. Barr opposes concepts of revelation that "control the methods by which exegesis will be permitted to work."[6]

He notes that in Barth's theology, for example, it is the concept of revelation which, because it forms "part of the dogmatic prolegomena, . . . lays down the conditions on which exegesis will be possible."[7] This pre-determinative character of revelational theologies creates, for Barr, a number of problems in exegesis. The first is its implicit prohibition against the historical-critical interest as to "what really happened" in the world behind the text. While critical investigation can serve to garner insights for biblical exposition, it must not "serve the foolish end of mediating an historical truth lying behind the texts."[8] Theological exposition that is in the service of the God to whom the Scriptures testify makes God the subject of exegesis, not the pre-history of the biblical writings. In this way a revelational theology, which is committed to an object-centered exegetical principle, tends to hold historical-critical investigation, with its non-theological and diachronic interests, in harness.

Barr also notes that revelational theologies, like Barth's, tend to make a radical distinction between revelation and religion such that dogmatic and exegesis are alienated from taking into themselves the pre-canonical development and comparative study of religion. The religious world of Israel and the church are typically given short shrift and "a virtual theological exception" is made "in favour of biblical religion against extra-biblical Christianity and other religions."[9] Religion, in dialectical theology, is viewed as a human, cultural phenomenon or, even more negatively, as human hubris, an attempt to avoid the true God with idolatry. Therefore exegesis must not, on this view, serve the ends of religion, for the Bible is not about religion: "it is about God and his action, his revelation and so on."[10] In this way, revelational theologies, like Barth's, seem to use the idea of revelation to insulate the Bible against its origins as a human, culturally situated product. The result, argues Barr, is that such theologies are in a position of alienation from "scholarship", wherein results must be proven empirically, and left in utter dependence on the concept of

---

4 Ibid., p. vii.

5 See Balentine, "James Barr's Quest," p. 9 and John Barton, "James Barr as Critic and Theologian" in Balentine and Barton, *Language, Theology and the Bible: Essays in Honour of James Barr*, pp. 19-20.

6 *Old and New in Interpretation*, p. 87.

7 Ibid., p. 91. See also James Barr, "Revelation through History in the Old Testament and in Modern Theology," *Interpretation*, 17 (1963): 193-205.

8 *Old and New in Interpretation*, p. 93.

9 Ibid., p. 95. See also James Barr, *The Concept of Biblical Theology: An Old Testament Perspective* (London, 1999), pp. 9, 11, 22, 106ff., 171; James Barr, *The Bible in the Modern World* (London, 1973), pp. 5-6; and John Levenson, "Negative Theology," review of *The Concept of Biblical Theology* by James Barr, *First Things*, 100 (February, 2000): 60.

10 *Old and New in Interpretation*, p. 107.

12   *Revelation, Holy Scripture and Church*

revelation.[11] In contrast to this approach, which privileges piety,[12] Barr maintains that the formulation of tradition, its inscripturation in writing and the decision to gather a group of books together, are all human decisions that can be historically investigated. Where they cannot, it is not because of transhistorical elements or divine intervention, but because we do not yet have the necessary information.[13]

An implicit criticism of theologies which inhibit the use of historical-critical research in deference to a concept of revelation, which occurs consistently in Barr's hermeneutic reflections, is that they are inconsistent with the biblical use of the term. In his study of the use of the term "revelation,"[14] Barr concludes, "it is doubtful whether the common theological use of 'revelation' for the Divine self-communication is appropriate in the light of the Biblical usage."[15] In the Bible "revelation" is used in a variety of ways: sometimes it refers to human acts of unveiling, at other times, in the New Testament, it refers to a message a member of the church might offer, and most often it is used eschatologically—to refer to what is now hidden but will at the end be revealed. What is more, where one would ordinarily expect the use of the term, that is, in the biblical account of the mighty acts of God in the exodus,[16] it is not found at all. The problematic feature of these usages and omissions is that they do not comport to the blanket character of the term "revelation" as it functions in modern theological use. Apart from a minimalist notion of uncovering, there is no overarching biblical

---

11 Barr notes Barth's "painful" consistency on this point. He draws attention to Barth's own comment about his alienation from his colleagues in Old and New Testament. "The time has not yet come when the dogmatician will be able to relate himself with good conscience and confidence to the results of his colleagues in Old and New Testament." *Old and New in Interpretation*, p. 96, n.1. The citation is from Karl Barth, *Church Dogmatics*, 13 vols, ed. and trans. G.W. Bromiley and T.F. Torrance (Edinburgh, 1936-1969), III/2: ix. Barr maintains that Bonhoeffer "wisely blamed Barth for a positivism of revelation." *The Concept of Biblical Theology*, p. 434.

12 Barr is here comparing Barth and Childs, maintaining they are both conservative "positivists" who avoid history and rationality in favor of piety. See *The Concept of Biblical Theology*, pp. 434-435.

13 *The Bible in the Modern World*, pp. 118-119. At least part of what Barr is aiming to avoid in scoring this point is the bifurcation of knowledge into "reason and revelation" and history into "ordinary" and "revelatory" that is a consequence of revelatory theologies such as Barth's. See *The Concept of Biblical Theology*, p. 486; *Old and New in Interpretation*, p. 87; and "Revelation through History in the Old Testament and in Modern Theology," p. 199.

14 James Barr, "Revelation," in James Hastings, Fredrick C. Grant and H.H. Rowley (eds), rev. edn, *Hastings Dictionary of the Bible* (New York, 1963), pp. 847-849. See also "Revelation," *Interpreter's Dictionary of the Bible, Supplementary Volume* (New York/ Nashville, 1962), pp. 748f.

15 Barr, "Revelation," *Hastings Dictionary of the Bible*, p. 849. Barr rejects theological and philosophical definitions of "revelation" that are formed apart from close examination of "how the term works in the Bible." See James Barr, Review of *Divine Revelation and the Limits of Historical Criticism* by W.J. Abraham (Oxford, 1982), *Scottish Journal of Theology*, 36 (1983): 247-250, quote from p. 249. See also *The Concept of Biblical Theology*, p. 484.

16 See *Old and New in Interpretation*, p. 88 and *The Concept of Biblical Theology*, p. 484.

concept of revelation. What is more, argues Barr, its continued use as a monolithic term "may only obscure the sense of its particular occurrences."[17]

Barr's final objection to revelational theologies, offered in *Old and New in Interpretation*, has to do with their effect on the interpretation of the Old Testament. Christian dogmatics, which employ a revelation model for the interpretation of the Bible, are typically Christocentric. This feature, says Barr, is "a ceaseless source of embarrassment for the Christian interpreter of the Old Testament."[18] The expectation of the biblical exegete is that the Old Testament will be understood always with a view to revelation, and that revelation is almost synonymous with Christ. The biblical interpreter must then find some strategy for relating the Testaments. Barr enumerates four possible schemes: (1) the Old Testament is not revelatory, but preparatory, because it does not contain Christ; (2) the prefiguration of the New Testament can be read back into the Old, against obvious historical argument; (3) a general Christocentric theology can be used as a basic framework to guide the exegesis of passages; or (4) a typological connection between the acts of God in history can be proposed which circumvents the historical problems with allegorical interpretation.[19] Barr considers it almost self-evident that all of these possibilities are "hopeless" and "unsatisfactory" alternatives.

His fundamental criticism for refusing them, however, harkens back to the Christocentric character of revelational theologies. The straightforward identification of Jesus Christ with revelation defies, on Barr's view, "the variety of things which have formed the concept of revelation."[20] The plain sense of the term "revelation" would have to allow for some sense of unveiling in the future,[21] something other than what is known presently.[22] And yet, contends Barr, the incarnation is not the unveiling of someone previously unknown but the "new deed of one known, known because the God of Israel was known."[23] What is more, theological attempts to hold Christ and Bible and preaching together in the "three-fold word of God" revelation schema are not feasible.[24] Jesus Christ is not a revelation in the same way in which the Bible is revelation: these terms are incommensurate to a point where the umbrella term "revelation" is misleading.[25]

---

17 "Revelation," *Hastings Dictionary*, p. 847. See also James Barr, *The Scope and Authority of the Bible* (Philadelphia, 1980), p. 121.

18 *Old and New in Interpretation*, p. 99.

19 Ibid., p. 100.

20 Ibid. pp., 100-101. Following Westermann, Barr notes also that the term "revelation" comes out of the dogmatic tradition in its controversy with the Enlightenment. *The Concept of Biblical Theology*, p. 484.

21 It is, as we have noted, Barr's view that the term "revelation," as it is used in the Bible, is more about what is yet to be known (i.e., more eschatological) than it is a "common general term for the source of man's knowledge of God." See *Old and New in Interpretation*, pp. 88, 101 and *The Bible in the Modern World*, p. 121.

22 See *The Concept of Biblical Theology*, p. 485 and "Revelation through History in the Old Testament and Modern Theology."

23 *Old and New in Interpretation*, p. 101.

24 Ibid., p. 101 and *The Bible in the Modern World*, pp. 19-21.

25 *The Bible in the Modern World*, p. 121.

14 *Revelation, Holy Scripture and Church*

Barr does not want to fully extinguish the use of the term "revelation" for biblical theology. He retains it "as an inexact term for all and any of the ways in which God speaks, does anything, communicates, inspires and so on."[26] The point at which is it unhelpful and "positively harmful,"[27] however, is when it becomes a technical criteria to discriminate between the various acts, speeches, words and books that make up the complex of Bible and tradition for what is and is not "revelation." Any attempt to seize on one element within the biblical corpus (its speeches, acts and even appearances of God) as "revelation," including Jesus of Nazareth, will inevitably privilege some part of Scripture and fail to include others.[28] What is more, this problematic cannot be solved by the simple identification of the contents of the Bible with revelation; for much of the Bible records common knowledge put there by humans that cannot be construed as disclosed by God. It is incumbent upon Biblical Theology to avoid such confusing technical use of the term "revelation" or be "lost, or else forced back on uncritical reiterations of older dogmatic assertions."[29] Thus while Barr does not mean to deny revelation, the elements of the Bible usually held together under the rubric of the word are best treated "within a different general approach."[30]

A Historical-Critical Reconceptualization of Revelation

Barr maintains that doctrines of revelation have been used to isolate and immunize the Bible from the rest of tradition "as a totally unique block of divine revelation"[31] or "the closed area of original revelation."[32] Where this isolation takes place the horizon within which we look for the revelation of God is unnecessarily confined to the limits of the Christian canon. On Barr's view, however, "texts are related not only to a revelation of God which preceded them but also to the shape which his work would take thereafter . . ."[33] Today, biblical scholars work under the almost universal conviction that the Bible itself is a product of tradition, and thus they can no longer suppose that "the theological tradition within the Bible is wholly different in nature from the theological tradition after (and indeed, before, and in the midst) of the Bible."[34] Biblical theologians ought, therefore, not only to pay close attention

---

26 *The Concept of Biblical Theology*, p. 485. Barr considers giving up the term altogether throughout his writings. See *The Bible in the Modern World*, p. 120 and *Biblical Faith and Natural Theology*, p. 195. For a devastating critique of Barr's reading of Barth see Anthony Thiselton, "Barr on Barth and Natural Theology: A Plea for Hermeneutics in Historical Theology," *Scottish Journal of Theology*, 47 (1994): 519-528.

27 *The Concept of Biblical Theology*, p. 485.

28 *Old and New in Interpretation*, p. 101.

29 *The Concept of Biblical Theology*, p. 485.

30 *Old and New in Interpretation*, p. 101. Barr summarizes, "My argument is not against the word 'revelation', but against the way in which this word has grouped together a number of different things in a way that does not suit them and so distorts them." Ibid., p. 92.

31 *The Concept of Biblical Theology*, p. 214.

32 Ibid. p. 584.

33 Ibid., p. 283.

34 Ibid., p. 214.

to the pre-canonical biblical traditions, but especially, claims Barr, to the growth of tradition "the existence of which provides the matrix for the coming divine acts and the impulse for their very occurrence."[35] In other words, the biblical materials must be understood within the larger, forward leaning "cumulative tradition"[36] of which they are a part.

Barr maintains that this reconceptualization of the scope of revelation is in congruence with his investigation of the term "revelation" as it is used in the Bible; it is future oriented. Revelation on this model is related to the Bible not so much as antecedent disclosure from God to the people of God, which in turn generates the scriptural witness, "but that of a revelation which *follows upon* the existent tradition, or once it has reached the fixed and written stage, the existent Scripture."[37] Revelation occurs within a human matrix where God is always already known and within which new events have intelligibility.[38] For example, when God speaks with Moses, what God says and does has intelligibility in the light of what is already known about God. The reader may receive additional information about the God who acts or speaks in the narrative, such as when God is identified under another name (Exodus 6:3), but this is not the unveiling of a previously unknown God, "but part of the cumulative effect of a story in temporal sequence."[39]

This example is unremarkable given the thrust of Barr's larger claim. For Barr, while he is interested in the cumulation of information about God *within* the biblical story, has something larger in view. It is his contention that the tradition, "the matrix for the coming of divine acts and the impulse for their very occurrence,"[40] cumulates beyond the boundaries of canonical Scripture such that the horizon of revelation cannot be confined to the Bible. The example of Moses would thus also be appropriate to the present day church. God's people, like Moses, do receive from God additional understanding about God not found in the Bible, although the Bible does provide the frame of reference to which, and because of which, this understanding cumulates. The Bible is itself a locus of revelation, "for it is the expression which the Israelite tradition has in fact formed, the way in which it wants to speak on the basis of that which it has heard."[41] Since the Bible is but an expression of tradition, albeit a "classic" or "paradigmatic expression," it may well be that it is "the growth of the tradition rather than the story itself" where "the dynamics of revelation are to be

---

35 *Old and New in Interpretation*, p. 156.

36 Ibid., pp. 82ff. and pp. 156ff. and *The Concept of Biblical Theology*, p. 486. In this later work, Barr returns to this model he developed 33 years earlier in *Old and New in Interpretation*.

37 *The Bible in the Modern World*, p. 122. The emphasis is Barr's.

38 Barr maintains that the basic revelation of God, God's initial communication with humanity, is not to be found in the Bible, but in the history it presupposes. The tradition flows out of a pre-history where God was recognized and accepted in Israel. See *The Scope and Authority of the Bible*, p. 16 and *Old and New in Interpretation*, p. 89.

39 *Old and New in Interpretation*, p. 82, see also p. 21 and *The Bible in the Modern World*, pp. 122, 146.

40 *The Bible in the Modern World*, p. 156.

41 *The Scope and Authority of the Bible*, p. 16.

16 *Revelation, Holy Scripture and Church*

seen."[42] It is in the broader life of Israel or the people of God set against particular times and places where one finds, in the broadest sense, the locus of revelation.

Barr identifies at least one consequence that this understanding of cumulative tradition has for exegetical method. It has been the case, he maintains, that exegetical research has been too focused on the dynamics of composition—the "coming-to-be" of the text of the Bible. Modern exegetical commentary thus expounds the text of the Bible with a view to its circumstances of production and the context in which it was generated. In this way it gives an impression of the text in its unity. Barr suggests however that, on his model of cumulative tradition, exegetes ought to pay more attention "to the *effect* that text had afterward."[43] This would include following the effect of texts and the way they become built into the structure of a religion. It is Barr's view that, in so far as it can be done, it will take place "through an historical account of the rise of a tradition in conjunction with the newer forms of religion which accompany it."[44] In Barr's transposition of the circumference of the field of revelation, something very much like historical-critical method is extended beyond the bounds of the composition of the Bible to investigate the cumulative tradition engendered by the Bible. It should also be noted that while emphasis on the future direction or effects of a text expands the purview of the field within which the "dynamics of revelation" are operative, Barr's interest in the tradition that cumulates is monitored for authenticity by "a fully historical understanding of Scripture."[45] In this way the future direction of Scripture is only ever licitly realized when it is responsible to references rooted in historically specific texts.

When we turn to an account of the approach by which the "dynamics of revelation" within the growth of tradition are to be sought, the description offered by Barr is, for the most part, non-theological. For apart for the initial communication of God with human beings, presupposed in a mythological prehistory by the Bible but not specifically narrated in the Bible,[46] God does not "reveal" in any immediate or direct fashion. Paul Wells describes Barr's view on the matter:

---

42 Ibid.

43 *The Concept of Biblical Theology*, p. 283 (The emphasis is Barr's). "As we see it today, historical reading should move more towards an understanding of *effects* rather than an emphasis on *origins*." *The Scope and Authority of the Bible*, p. 46. Barr is not here playing one approach to biblical texts against another. He is arguing for the enlargement of historical-critical method to include an historical investigation of the effects of texts. He notes that redaction criticism has already begun to move historical reading in the direction of an investigation of the effects of a text. See ibid., pp. 46-47. One of the factors that has militated against following a text's post compositional effects has been the view that post-biblical developments are deteriorations from New Testament times. This view, says Barr is encouraged by a privileged view of canon. See *The Concept of Biblical Theology*, p. 283.

44 *The Concept of Biblical Theology*, p. 284.

45 *The Scope and Authority of the Bible*, p. 128. Kevin Vanhoozer writes: "For James Barr, the virtue of historical-critical exegesis is precisely that it acts as a check on the subsequent history of a text's interpretation by going back to the original sense." *Is there a Meaning in This Text: The Bible, The Reader, and Morality of Literary Knowledge* (Grand Rapids, 1998), p. 48.

46 *The Scope and Authority of the Bible*, p. 128.

Revelation and Biblical Interpretation

Revelation in the tradition of the people of God takes place in the consciousness which men have of God through communion with him. Whether this is viewed from the angle of the dynamics of the growth of tradition or as located in the stories which the tradition crystallizes, the knowledge of God originates in quite a human way.[47]

When Barr depicts the formation of Israelite and early church tradition, the inscripturation of this tradition in holy writ, the decision to gather a specific set of texts he does so without "special pleading." None of these decisions is ascribed to the action of God, for there is no access to the revelatory initiative of God apart from the human tradition about God.[48] And thus all of the moves within the tradition, Barr maintains, are human decisions, "made by men of faith but are still human decisions and describable as such."[49] It would seem to be logical to claim that his depiction of the post-biblical effects of Scripture would proceed under the same terms. Biblical, patristic and historical scholars in ordinary historical language can describe what takes place in the tradition and where they cannot, it is not due to "elements transcending historical investigation"[50] but to a lack of historical information. It is, writes Barr, "man who developed the biblical tradition and man who decided when it might be suitably fixed and made canonical."[51] The depiction of the cumulative tradition within which the dynamics of revelation are at work is, in this way, accomplished without recourse to theological description.

The Soteriological Function of Scripture

It should be noted, however, that Barr is not bereft of some account of how the human tradition about God is related to God. On his account Barr prefers, with expressed reservations,[52] the term "inspiration."[53] In so far as Barr considers this term to be useful in articulating the way in which the human tradition about God (including the crystallization of this tradition in Scripture) is related to God, it must abandon traditional models. There is no implication of special direct communication from God to persons or a restriction of the term to the biblical period. Moreover, Barr denies that, for him, the term implies any sense of infallibility for the Bible

---

47 Paul Wells, *James Barr and the Bible: Critique of a New Liberalism* (Phillipsburg, NJ, 1980), pp. 221-222.

48 *The Bible in the Modern World*, p. 121.

49 Ibid., p. 118.

50 Ibid., p. 119.

51 Ibid., p. 120. See also Wells, *James Barr and the Bible*, pp. 222ff. He entitles this section (pp. 220-226) of his analysis of Barr on the Bible, "James Barr's Rational View."

52 See *The Bible in the Modern World*, p. 17 and James Barr, *Holy Scripture: Canon, Authority, Criticism* (Philadelphia, 1983), p. 27. Barr considers himself "a spare-time theologian" whose primary competence is as a linguistic and biblical scholar. See *The Bible in the Modern World*, p. xi.

53 Barr claims to have built up his understanding of inspiration partly from the biblical materials but even more "by way of extensions and extrapolations from other more richly witnessed aspects of Christian doctrine." Review of *The Divine Inspiration of Scripture* by W.J. Abraham, p. 373.

18   *Revelation, Holy Scripture and Church*

(contra fundamentalism)[54] or the church (contra Roman Catholicism) or that he is resorting to a merely literary use of the term. For Barr:

> Inspiration would mean then that the God whom we worship was also in contact with his people in ancient times, and that in their particular circumstances, in the stage in which they existed, he was present in the formation of their tradition and in the crystallization of that tradition as a Scripture; but that the mode of this contact was not different from the mode in which God has continued to make himself know to men.[55]

Where it comes to specifying in greater detail the sense of God's mode of contact with his people, Barr comments that, traditionally, language about the Holy Spirit has been introduced at this point. God is "with" his people "in the Spirit." Barr confesses that the sense of this traditional formula is not entirely clear to him, but he does draw out a couple of consequences for his readers. First of all, "in the Spirit", implies a connection between meaning and presence. When human words about God are uttered they must be received "in the Spirit" in order correctly to be apprehended. Barr does not mean to imply that the Spirit somehow supplies additional noetic content; but that when words about God are spoken they are joined with the presence of the one who is the subject of the utterance. For Barr this applies both to the present understanding of Scripture, the tradition which preceded Scripture in Israel and the church, the formation of Scripture and the delimitation of the canon. "The relation of the biblical writers and traditionists to God through the Spirit is thus not basically other than that of the church today in its listening to God."[56] "Inspiration" is thus characteristic of the mode of God's presence with his people through the whole of the cumulative tradition.

It would thus be entirely appropriate, on Barr's view, to preface the reading of Scripture in the church with the phrase, "Hear the Word of God." For this phrase, divorced of its Barthian associations with the implied three-fold Word of God schema, follows on his understanding of inspiration. "Word of God" implies that the reading of Scripture may be heard as such when God appropriates human words to speak to his people.[57] He writes: "Under the terms of the discussion of this book, it

---

54 See James Barr, *Fundamentalism* (London, 1977), pp. 288-299 and *Escaping from Fundamentalism* (London, 1984), pp. 124-130.

55 *The Bible in the Modern World*, p. 18. See also *The Scope and Authority of the Bible*, p. 63.

56 Ibid., p. 132. In *Holy Scripture*, p. 27, Barr writes, "Inspiration is not attached to a small number of exceptional persons like St. Matthew or St. Paul; it must extend over a large number of anonymous persons, so much so that it must be considered to belong more to the community as a whole . . ." In *Fundamentalism*, p. 288, Barr maintains that in a plausible articulation of this doctrine, "inspiration would have its main focus not in the writing down of the sacred books but in the formation of tradition in Israel and the Church . . . The real lively center of the process is the fact that God was with his people in ancient Israel and the early church." The same point is made in *Escaping Fundamentalism*, pp. 127-128, and again in *Biblical Faith and Natural Theology*, p. 198.

57 Barr's emphasis on divine speaking comes out of his critique of the so-called Biblical Theology Movement, particularly the work of G.E. Wright (*God Who Acts: Biblical Theology as Recital* [London, 1952]) as well as von Rad, Vos and Cullmann, in which God's *acts* in

Revelation and Biblical Interpretation 19

would mean that the Bible, a crystallization of the tradition of God's people, is made by him into a vehicle of his own speech to succeeding generations of that people."[58] However, Barr almost immediately takes back this theological depiction of divine agency in relation to Scripture reading as "vague," or prone to misunderstanding along the lines of "verbal inspiration," or liable to "the rather complicated structures of the Barthian type."[59]

The second thought that Barr includes in his reflection on inspiration is this: he wants to avoid a "God-of-the-gaps strategy."[60] Barr's account of the mode of God's presence given above in no way precludes critical human historical description of the traditions of Israel and the church. Barr does not want to introduce a double-description of the human historical life of the people of God, especially of its crystallization in the Bible, by raising divine agency wherever scientific and historical explanation are inadequate or incomplete. The Spirit *accompanies* human thought and action to be sure, but "the human thought and action . . . can be given human and historical description, without resort to supernatural interventions at any points of difficulty."[61] Thus while God *uses* the Bible to speak to his people, the *nature* of the Bible is human and historical. Gaps in our understanding of the Bible are thus best sought in terms of the circumstances of the text's origin in its original setting and not by resort to "supernatural" special pleading.

Barr is not, of course, at this point reducing his account of inspiration or the "Word of God" to what can be accounted for on human, historical terms. Rather, he is pressing a distinction between the Bible as a God-given "meeting ground for our encounter with God"[62] and the source and foundation of Christian faith. Christians do not believe in the Bible *per se*, but in the God who is met in faith by the church in its reading of the Scripture. "It is," writes Barr, "the message of good news, the

---

history is the rubric under which revelation in the Old Testament was construed. See Barr, "Revelation through History in the Old Testament and Modern Theology," and *Old and New in Interpretation*, pp. 65-102. His emphasis on divine speech continues in a more recent essay: James Barr, "Divine Action and Hebrew Wisdom," in Sarah Coakley and David A. Pailin (eds), *The Making and Remaking of Christian Doctrine: Essays in Honor of Maurice Wiles* (New York, 1993), pp. 1-12.

58 *The Bible in the Modern World*, pp. 179-180. Barr makes the point in a later work (*Biblical Faith and Natural Theology*, p. 198) that "Word of God" is used analogically of the operation of Scripture within the community . . . the material of the Bible operates in a mode which deserves to be described as "Word of God."

59 Ibid. Barr is often uncomfortable with theological terms used to specify how God is related to Scripture. While he uses "inspiration" and "Word of God" language, he emphasizes strongly the liability of such language. This is particularly the case in *The Bible and the Modern World*, pp. 13-18, 18-22, 179-181. In more recent monographs, Barr gives a much lower profile to the use of the term "inspiration." In *Holy Scripture*, p. 27, he is consistent with his earlier articulation of inspiration, but his hesitancy is obvious. He writes, "*If there is inspiration at all* then it must extend over the entire process of production that has led to the texts in their final form." Emphasis mine. In a more recent book, *The Concept of Biblical Theology* (1999), a positive exposition of the concept of inspiration is absent.

60 *The Bible in the Modern World*, p. 132.

61 Ibid.

62 *The Scope and Authority of the Bible*, p. 55.

20 *Revelation, Holy Scripture and Church*

Gospel of grace, that is the source and the foundation of faith."[63] The text of the Bible, which can certainly be probed reverently but critically for its scientific, historical and even theological accuracy is nevertheless soteriologically functional (an essential and God-given meeting ground for our encounter with God[64]) in the cumulative tradition of the people of God. Scripture is implicated, writes Barr, "in the process of salvation, in the life of the church, and in the faith of the Christian."[65]

The whole of the inspired, cumulative tradition of the people of God has, for Barr, a soteriological function.[66] He assigns a "positive soteriological place" to the growth of the Old Testament and its embodiment in Intertestamental Judaism, for all of this provides a matrix for divine action, even the impulse for its occurrence. The life, mission and message of Jesus are simply not comprehensible without the existence of a Scripture, already received, "that provided the intellectual basis upon which salvation was achieved."[67] Scripture thus provides a frame of intelligibility for the coming of Jesus to the world.

But more than this, Scripture continues to have an instrumental function in the growth of tradition in life of the church. "Christian faith is," writes Barr, "faith in Christ as the one through whom one comes to God, and faith that through the Bible we meet him, he communicates with us."[68] Through the reading of Scripture, the church (and the world) listens for, is gripped by and made ready to reach out for, the Gospel of salvation.[69] This would seem to cohere with Barr's sense that the Bible speaks of and for the future. That is to say, Scripture anticipates a future fulfillment of God's promise [of salvation] to humankind. For the Gospels themselves are composed in such a way as to function, not only descriptively and historically, but paradigmatically for future Christians in their attempts to understand Jesus Christ in their time.[70]

To sum up: throughout the hermeneutic writings of James Barr a consistent polemic against doctrines of revelation that "control the methods by which exegesis will be permitted to work"[71] is articulated. Barr eschews all attempts to inhibit the

---

63 Ibid., pp. 55-56.

64 Ibid., p. 55.

65 Ibid.

66 *Old and New in Interpretation*, p. 156 and *The Scope and Authority of the Bible*, pp. 53-64.

67 Ibid., p. 52.

68 Ibid., p. 55. Barr writes, "the basis of that authority [of Scripture] lies in its efficacy in the faith-relation between man and God. Ibid., p. 54.

69 See *Escaping from Fundamentalism*, p. 157. "Salvation does not come automatically," writes Barr, "through belonging to a system or institution, but only as a person is gripped in the inner heart, convinced of his need for salvation, and made ready to reach out and receive it. The Gospel, in this evangelical sense, is fully scriptural, in the sense that it is embedded in Scripture, and Scripture supports and witnesses to that Gospel of free grace. But it is not identical with Scripture."

70 *The Scope and Authority of the Bible*, p. 54. See also *Old and New in Interpretation*, pp. 19ff., 82; *The Concept of Biblical Theology*, pp. 283-284 and *The Bible in the Modern World*, pp. 122, 141-146.

71 *Old and New in Interpretation*, p. 87.

"freedom" of critical biblical research by means of dogmatic prolegomena, which "predetermine" the nature of the Bible in its relation to revelation such that critical and comparative investigations into the human origins of the Bible are circumscribed or refused. The exemption of the Bible from critical analysis based on an appeal to revelation (Barth) or canon (Childs), Barr regards as a form of special pleading, that is, privileging piety. It is his positive contention that the inscription of biblical books and their collection together can all be accounted for without recourse to "transhistorical events or divine intervention"[72] and that where this is not yet possible it is only because we lack the relevant historical information to this point. Barr articulates his own understanding of revelation and its dynamics in relation to a cumulative tradition, within which God is always already known. The Bible as a paradigmatic instanciation of the cumulative tradition (of the faith of the people of God) is soteriologically functional; that is, it is the means whereby the tradition is extended. The mode of the Spirit's presence (inspiration) to the composition, collection and use of the Bible is that of accompanying human thought and action such that additional theological description is rendered almost superfluous.

Critique

In the material that follows, a critique of Barr's rejection and reconceptualization of doctrines of revelation in the overall construal of the hermeneutic field is offered. The fundamental point is that Barr, while he introduces theological language into his discussion of revelation, tends to conflate divine action to human action such that the dynamics of inscripturation, canonization and post-biblical effects are all depicted as human-historical acts without recourse to theological description. Barr's critique of doctrines of revelation which inhibit "free" critical inquiry into the origin, nature and assembly of the Bible, while motivated by the desire to offer a human account of the composition and collection of biblical texts, fails in its lack of attention to the overall interpretative program within which such doctrines operate.

In the theological hermeneutics of both Brevard Childs and Karl Barth, critical methods are employed, but their work is penultimate to the "critical freedom" of that toward which the texts of the Bible, as witnesses to revelation, point. Moreover, Barr's whole conception of divine agency assumes either, on the one hand, a sort of independent, causal nexus within which God works only by way of "intervention," or, on the other hand, one in which divine agency is simply descriptively confluent with human action virtually without remainder. In the critique of Barr's contrastive understanding of divine involvement in creaturely reality, a theological case is made for the generative antecedence of God to human historical accounts, understood as witnesses to revelation, and an attempt to relate human and divine action in a more subtle fashion, is implicit in the critique of Barr's position on inspiration.

Critical freedom and the object of the text   In his critical evaluation of the interpretative programs of both Karl Barth and Brevard Childs, Barr fails to grasp that critical, historical inquiry plays a necessary, although preliminary, part in their

---

72 *The Bible in the Modern World*, pp. 118-119.

respective approaches to biblical interpretation. Doctrines of revelation and object-centered exegesis do not cancel out the appropriate use of critical tools but instead locate them within an overall construal of the interpretative task for the life of the church in which the Bible is read as a witness to the reality of which it speaks. Brevard Childs, while insisting that interpreters do justice to the discrete voices of Old and New Testament[73] and that they distinguish between various sources and layers in the compositional growth of the Bible,[74] also maintains that interpreters must press on to a consideration of how these historical considerations can be used "to enrich the book as a whole"[75] and contribute to an understanding of the subject matter of which the Bible speaks. Childs writes, "The goal of the interpretation of Christian Scriptures is to understand both Testaments as witness to the self-same divine reality who is the God and Father of Jesus Christ."[76] Barr's inflated rhetorical response to Childs overall hermeneutic program in which he declares Childs "a theological fundamentalist,"[77] who along with Barth, "favours piety"[78] exposes a fundamental disagreement between Childs/Barth and Barr concerning the realities in relation to which the Bible is best understood. Barr in his interpretative program is most interested in the texts of the Bible as *human* documents in their own right, and thus wants to explore the nature of those documents as artifacts located in a religious history. Childs, on the other hand, while he is appreciative of the complexity of the reception and shaping of the biblical witness, also "wants to see the Bible from a different and unified perspective: that of the community of faith who bore witness by its transmission to the continuing redemptive intervention of the one divine reality, whom the Church confesses to be the God and Father of Jesus Christ."[79]

Barth likewise maintained the value of historical-critical inquiry within an overall interpretative program that terminates, not at the level of establishing a text's historical sense, but at the level of its revelatory significance. In his commentary on Romans, for example, Barth maintained historical science must be able to pass over from establishing the linguistic parameters of the text to what it is about. For interpreters to consider a matter explained by simply tracing it to the "religious

---

73 Brevard Childs, "On Reclaiming the Bible for Christian Theology," in Carl E. Braaten and Robert W. Jenson (eds), *Reclaiming the Bible for the Church* (Grand Rapids, 1995), p. 14.

74 See Brevard Childs, *Introduction to the Old Testament as Scripture* (Philadelphia, 1979), pp. 76-79 and *Isaiah: A Commentary* (Louisville, 2001), pp. 1-5.

75 Childs, *Isaiah*, p. 4. James Sanders, *From Sacred Story to Sacred Text* (Philadelphia, 1987), pp. 160-163 notes that Childs, while he employs traditional literary criticism, objects to "leaving the question of authentic meaning of the text at that point of work on it." Interpreters must move beyond this level "to discern the further meanings of those fragments or pericopes when they were put together in the received manner." Ibid., p. 161.

76 Childs, "On Reclaiming the Bible for Christian Theology," p. 15.

77 Barr, *The Concept of Biblical Theology*, p. 437.

78 Ibid., p. 435. Here Barr refers to a review of Childs', *Old Testament Theology in a Canonical Context* (Philadelphia, 1985) by Margaret Davies in *Journal of Theological Studies*, 37 (1986): 445. Barr includes Davies words to the effect that Childs "ignores both history and rationality . . . and finds solace in a religion of the heart."

79 Childs, "On Reclaiming the Bible for Christian Theology," p. 9.

thought, feeling, experience, conscience, or conviction, of Paul"[80] is for them to miss the "Someone" to whom Paul's attention was given.[81] Barth maintained that "freedom" within biblical interpretation belongs to the object of the text so as to "assert and affirm itself" against the presuppositions of interpreters, who are under obligation to "adopt new presuppositions"[82] in the light of their encounter with it. Barth was convinced that historical study, if it were attentive to the text, ought to be able to make clear the nature of Paul's writing in Romans as witness. Were historical method unable to do that, the problem lies not with the method itself but with the unyielding naturalist presuppositions of its practitioners. That is, where interpreters are unable to read the Bible as witness to revelation, a certain ontological prejudice was at work. Bruce McCormack writes, "The difference between Barth's view of Paul and that of the [historical] critics was fundamental. The reigning biblical science saw him as an object of interest in his own right; Barth saw him as a witness."[83] Real understanding of the Bible, for Barth, thus proceeds from establishing what stands in the text[84] to a second stage in which interpreters must "think along with and after Paul, wrestling with the subject matter until they too are confronted by the same object (or Subject!) which once confronted Paul."[85] On Barth's view, truly scientific exegesis in its confrontation with biblical texts as witness, proclamation, will work with strategies and methods that are in accord with the object of the text. The work of the interpreter is to move to the stage where preliminary historical-

---

80 Karl Barth, *The Epistle to the Romans*, 2nd edn, trans. Edwyn C. Hoskyns (London, 1933), p. 7.

81 Barth is responding here in the preface to the second edition of his commentary on Romans to the criticism of Adolf Jülicher, "A Modern Interpreter of Paul," in James M. Robinson (ed.), *The Beginnings of Dialectical Theology* (Richmond, VA, 1968). Jülicher understood Barth's exegesis as pneumatic or practical and not scientific exegesis, due to its dogmatic presuppositions. Barth's response was that Jülicher too began with dogmatic assumptions, which were historicist in character, and that surely the methods and assumptions of scientific exegesis ought to be appropriate to the reality of which the text spoke. In other words, Barth was not aiming to establish nonscientific exegesis alongside historical-critical inquiry but to incorporate historical-critical inquiry in a form of scientific exegesis ruled by the subject matter of the Bible. See Bruce McCormack, "Historical Criticism and Dogmatic Interest in Karl Barth's Theological Exegesis of the New Testament," in Mark S. Burrows and Paul Rorem (eds), *Biblical Hermeneutics in Historical Perspective* (Grand Rapids, 1991), pp. 322-331 and Bruce McCormack, "The Significance of Karl Barth's Theological Exegesis of Philippians," in Karl Barth, *The Epistle to the Philippians: 40th Anniversary Edition*, trans. James W. Leitch (Louisville, 2002), pp. v-xxii.

82 Barth, *Church Dogmatics*, 1/2: 726.

83 McCormack, "Historical Criticism and Dogmatic Interest in Karl Barth's Theological Exegesis of the New Testament," p. 327.

84 Here Barth includes investigations into those dimensions of the text that have been the purview of historical critics. Barth wrote, "I use the methods of source-criticism, lexicography, grammar, syntax and appreciation of style." *Church Dogmatics*, 1/2: 723.

85 McCormack, "Historical Criticism and Dogmatic Interest in Karl Barth's Theological Exegesis of the New Testament," pp. 327-328.

24   *Revelation, Holy Scripture and Church*

literary considerations fade into the background to encounter "the Word in the words
. . ."[86]

James Barr fails to locate his criticisms of Childs and Barth within an overall
account of their interpretative proposals when he asserts that they privilege piety,
which is to say that the exegesis they propose is unscientific, uncritical, theologically
fundamentalist or rooted in "a religion of the heart." What Childs and Barth privilege
is that to which the authors, redactors and traditionists of the Bible point. For both
Childs and Barth, historical-critical tools are crucial for the *explicatio* of the text as a
preliminary stage in the interpretation of the Bible. However, both of them propose
that in order properly to interpret the Bible, exegetes must press on to the subject
matter to which the Bible as witness points. The character of the Bible as a witness
to revelation entails that critical freedom belongs neither to the historical critic nor
the theologian *per se*, both of whom bring a certain orientation to the text which
will always be more or less adequate, but to the object of the biblical witness which
exerts hermeneutical pressure on the conceptual predilections of the interpreter. G.C.
Berkouwer offers a construal of the critical role of Scripture and the freedom of
exegesis, which is a lucid summary of this discussion:

> The freedom of exegesis is a freedom that has nothing to do with a neutral
> "presuppositionlessness," which is only theoretically interested in the results of biblical
> research, whatever they may be. Anyone who in this way, outside of the implications of
> ecclesiastical confession, seeks to exult in such freedom would forget one thing. In its
> confession the church did not seek to exhibit all the intellectual knowledge of Scripture
> that it had attained, with the inherent note that it was prepared to correct incorrect exegesis.
> Rather, the church sough to confess its faith.[87]

God's intrinsic agency   However, while Barr's contention that doctrines of
revelation privilege the object of the Bible to the point of inhibiting the freedom of
historical investigation can be answered by locating the function of critical method
within an overarching interpretative project, there is a more profound objection to
"controlling doctrines of revelation." For Barr, where the Bible is privileged in terms
of its revelatory content and origin it is usually accomplished by means of appeal to
antecedent revelation to which the Bible is a response.[88] Barr contends that the appeal
to "antecedent" revelation is itself problematic. For interpreters have no access to
God's revelatory initiative apart from the human tradition about God which the Bible
records and there is no way of sorting out revelatory initiative from the human faith
response. Barr maintains that since no access to the revelatory initiative of God is
available apart from human traditions about God, all the moves within the tradition
are human moves, "made by men of faith but still human decisions and describable

---

86 Barth, *Epistle to the Romans*, p. 9.

87 G.C. Berkouwer, *Studies in Dogmatics: Holy Scripture*, trans. Jack Rodgers (Grand
Rapids, 1975), pp. 131, 132-133. Berkhouwer's emphasis. The citation from Abraham Kuyper
is taken from *Principles of Sacred Theology*, pp. 596-597.

88 Barth writes, "The biblical writers testify that the revelation came to them with a
supreme authoritativeness of its own. They answered something that came to them, not from
them." Karl Barth, *Against the Stream* (London, 1954), p. 224.

Revelation and Biblical Interpretation 25

as such."[89] What takes place in both the scriptural and post-scriptural tradition of effects is thus best accounted for in human terms (by patristic, biblical and historical scholars in ordinary historical language) without recourse to "transhistorical events or divine intervention."[90]

Barr's construal of the problematic of revelation in relation to the humanness of the Bible and the whole of the cumulative tradition about God presupposes an understanding of divine agency that is problematic.[91] Barr operates throughout his critical analysis of doctrines of revelation (and inspiration) with an *extrinsic* understanding of God in relation to creation and the human tradition about God.[92] In his attempts to resist what he views as the docetic effect that theologies of revelation can have on accounts of Scripture, Barr moves to an extreme position in which inscripturation, canonization and the subsequent effects of the biblical witness are depicted in "purely human terms." This move seems to presuppose an independent causal nexus to which divine action can only be construed as an intervention in the ordinary course of events. William Placher suggests that this view of divine agency creates its own difficulties by abstracting God from the "normal course of things" in the first place. For theologians such as Aquinas and Calvin, "The only causal continuum is one whose every event God sustains. Divine action is not an interruption in or a violation of the normal course of things, but precisely *is* the normal course of things."[93]

However, even if it is possible to describe inscripturation and canonization, in, say, political or sociological terms, without recourse to prior generative events, does this imply that one has thereby accounted for them in terms most adequate to their reality? Surely central Christian convictions concerning the nature of God and the Gospel, while derived from the human witness about God, would require a properly theological account of God's action in relation to the generation of Holy Scripture. David Demson, following Barth, proposes, that "the Gospels are exponents of Jesus' appointment, calling and commissioning of the apostles" and that their place in the canon with other books be "understood in terms of their inclusion by way of expectation or recollection in the event or movement of Jesus' appointment, calling and commissioning of the apostles."[94] This account is quite able to distinguish the human tradition about God (apostolic witness) from the prior generative action of God (Jesus' appointment, calling and commissioning of the apostles) and yet to relate the two without collapsing them. Moreover, Ronald Thiemann makes the

---

89 Barr, *The Bible in the Modern World*, p. 118.

90 Ibid., pp. 118-119.

91 Kevin Vanhoozer, *First Theology: God, Scripture and Hermeneutics* (Downers Grove, 2002), p. 144.

92 See Ronald F. Thiemann, *Revelation and Theology: The Gospel as Narrated Promise* (Notre Dame, 1985), pp. 80-82.

93 William Placher, *The Domestication of Transcendence: How Modern Thinking about God Went Wrong* (Louisville, 1996), p. 190. The emphasis is Placher's. See also Kathryn Tanner, *God and Creation in Christian Theology: Tyranny or Empowerment?* (Oxford, 1988), p. 89.

94 David Demson, *Hans Frei and Karl Barth: Different Ways of Reading Scripture* (Grand Rapids, 1997), p. 47.

26 *Revelation, Holy Scripture and Church*

point that when Christians use the "the logically odd category of Gospel" they are at one and the same time referring to a "human communication and a divine actor." The very sense of the Gospel (in Christian belief and practice) implies that God is intrinsically related to human communication about God. "The report about God's reconciliation cannot be separated from the good news itself . . ."[95] Thus to treat inscripturation and the collection of texts into a canon, which are acts implicated in the good news, in abstraction from God's intrinsic and generative relation to them is a form of theological reductionism. A thicker account of inscripturation and canonization would construe these acts in terms of fulfillment of a commission in which God is the one who generates, commissions and authorizes these human acts (revelation and sanctification) and by whose agency the commission is sufficiently performed (inspiration).[96]

Cumulative tradition and the dynamics of revelation   Kevin Vanhoozer writes, "The doctrine of God is somewhat underdeveloped in the thought of James Barr."[97] In this remark Vanhoozer points to a matter that is something of a puzzle. Although Barr is not a theologian, he nevertheless ventures into theological territory with what appears, at first, to be a fruitful proposal for speaking of God's ongoing and active presence among his people, and even of God's generative priority to the human tradition about God, only to withdraw from theological description altogether. Perhaps Barr supposes that human actions exhibit the dynamics of revelation such that God's actions can be taken to be immanent within or behind human action. The historical description of human action in the formation of Scripture and tradition would thus, in some sense, also exhibit the dynamics of divine intentionality. Paul Wells suggests as much in his description of Barr's view of revelation: "Revelation in the tradition of the people of God takes place within the consciousness which men (*sic*) have of God through communion with him . . . Barr does not consider revelation in terms of verticality, but as a result of a disclosure on the level of a horizontal witness from man to man."[98] Human acts, like canonization and the growth of tradition, could thereby be said to be indicative of God consciousness. Vanhoozer concurs with this view: "God" for Barr, "can only be known through his effects— through his contact with the believing community" and "the liberal view we are now considering affirms an immanent God who is known through reflection on human experience."[99] However, Barr contends that what takes place in the tradition can be described without recourse to "elements transcending historical investigation"[100] and that where they cannot, it is due not to the inadequacy of the method, but to

---

95 Thiemann, *Revelation and Theology*, p. 81.

96 See Nicholas Wolterstorff, *Divine Discourse: Philosophical Reflections on the Claim that God Speaks* (New York, 1995), p. 295; Richard Swinburne, *Revelation: From Metaphor to Analogy* (Oxford, 1992), pp. 174-180; and John Webster, *Holy Scripture: A Dogmatic Sketch* (Cambridge, 2003), pp. 11-39.

97 Vanhoozer, *First Theology*, p. 144.

98 Wells, *James Barr and the Bible*, pp. 221-222.

99 Vanhoozer, *First Theology*, p. 144. Vanhoozer maintains that the view of God operative in Barr's work is analogous to that found in process theology.

100 Barr, *The Bible in the Modern World*, p. 119.

Revelation and Biblical Interpretation

a lack of historical information. However, one might ask: is a depiction of divine agency with and in human decisions with respect to the Bible and subsequent church tradition a factor that, because it eludes historical description, can be left to one side? Moreover, without some account of what is generative of the Bible and the tradition it engenders, Barr is left with an account of the effects of revelation apart from an account of who effects revelation. Rowan Williams writes: "Any theology of revelation is committed to attending to event and interpretation together, to the generative point and to the debate generated."[101]

A second difficulty with the idea of "cumulative tradition" as Barr employs the concept is that it tends to run pre- and post-scriptural tradition and fixed Scripture together within a singular category, cumulative tradition. This move pushes in the direction of leveling the uniqueness of Scripture in its relation to revelation, and thereby threatens to deprive him of the luminous and normative means by which to discriminate between positive developments and distortions in the post-biblical accumulated tradition. In *The Concept of Biblical Theology*,[102] Barr returns to the cumulative tradition proposal he developed 33 years earlier in *Old and New in Interpretation*.[103] Interestingly in *The Concept of Biblical Theology*, Barr cites Hendrikus Berkhof[104] as endorsing the view of cumulative tradition he espoused. Berkhof had used Barr's articulation of cumulative tradition and worked it into his dogmatic account of revelation: "revelation consists of a cumulative process of events and their interpretations" (1979 edn, p. 62; 1986 edn, p. 69). However, at the time of the publication of Barr's *The Concept of Biblical Theology* (1999), Berkhof's *The Christian Faith* was available in a revised edition (1986). In this new edition, Berkhof qualifies his use of cumulative process from Barr's *Old and New in Interpretation*. He writes, "I differ from Barr in that for me this [cumulative tradition] does not imply a rejection of the 'revelational model.'"[105] Instead, Berkhof offers an account of the "indirect" and yet "very intimate and positive" relationship between revelation and Scripture. "Nowhere else but in the Bible," he writes, "does the word of the primary witnesses to revelation come to us. Their authority, that is, the authority of revelation that came to them, comes to us in the words of Scripture."[106] Moreover, in a subsequent footnote in which Berkhof takes up a critical review of recent reformulations of the authority of Scripture (which includes Barr's *The Bible in the Modern World*); he notes how "more and more the doctrine of Scripture is connected with that of tradition and the church. The result is that the boundary with the interpretative transmission is blurred."[107] He maintains:

---

101 Rowan Williams, "Trinity and Revelation," in *On Christian Theology* (Oxford, 2000), p. 135.

102 See *The Concept of Biblical Theology*, p. 486.

103 *Old and New in Interpretation*, p. 156.

104 Hendrikus Berkhof, *The Christian Faith: An Introduction to the Study of the Faith*, rev. edn trans. Sierd Woudstra (Grand Rapids, 1986), pp. 64-65.

105 Ibid., p. 71.

106 Ibid., pp. 94-95.

107 Ibid., p. 97.

28   *Revelation, Holy Scripture and Church*

[T]hat would be alright if the origin of Scripture was perceived as an aspect of the way the Spirit goes through history in his coming to man. But in modern hermeneutics the danger is real that the character of Scripture as the element of "fixation" no longer functions, and that Scripture is used to justify one's own ideas. Scripture criticism should first of all be Scripture's criticism of us![108]

The other way in which Berkhof's account of cumulative tradition differs from Barr's is that Berkhof, unlike Barr, does not observe a difficulty in making Christ the center of the cumulative process. Like Barr, he affirms, "it is certainly the case" that the cumulative process "history of salvation" continues after "the decisive crisis and freedom that have come in Christ."[109] However, Berkhof goes on to affirm: "What has happened in him [Christ] is and remains the basis, the limit and the norm for all revelational events after him. Faith, believing in him as the central revelation, can only accept as revelation whatever can be discerned as a disclosure of God's heart in human history."[110] Barr argues that this theological move monopolizes the term "revelation," in its singular application to Christ, that is, it defies "the variety of things which have formed the concept of revelation,"[111] and that it is inevitably supersessionist.[112]

One way of answering Barr is by means of a proposal made by H. Richard Niebuhr. Niebuhr wrote:

Sometimes when we read a difficult book, seeking to follow a complicated argument, we come across a luminous sentence from which we can go forward and backward and so attain some understanding of the whole. Revelation is like that . . . The special occasion to which we appeal in the Christian church is called Jesus Christ.[113]

While, as was suggested above, God is never extrinsic to the course of events and their interpretation in the Bible, there are some events borne witness to in the Bible that are luminous centers from which the meaning of the whole of the Bible and extratextual reality can be discerned. Moreover, such events are not exceptions to the "normal operations" of the universe; rather such a revelatory "mighty act" of God "might be simply that event which enables us to see with particular clarity how we had daily been surrounded by God's mighty acts, the 'wonder' of the event wherein we recognized the work of a divine agent we could in principle have seen in all things."[114] What if the life, death and resurrection of Jesus Christ is the luminous sentence by means of which the modes of God's agency in the whole of the Bible

---

108 Ibid.

109 Ibid., p. 70.

110 Ibid., p. 71.

111 *Old and New in Interpretation*, pp. 100-101.

112 Barr's arguments against construing the canon in Christocentric unity are taken up in the next chapter on Scripture.

113 H. Richard Niebuhr, *The Meaning of Revelation* (New York, 1941), pp. 68-69 cited in Placher, *The Domestication of Transcendence*, p. 191. Placher makes the important point that Niebuhr's luminous line metaphor is too subjective as it stands. "The Bible seems more firmly to say that some particular events *are* clues to the meaning of the whole." My emphasis.

114 Placher, *The Domestication of Transcendence*, p. 191.

Revelation and Biblical Interpretation 29

and subsequent cumulative tradition are uncovered?[115] The Christ event as the self-revelation of God does not thereby downgrade or overwhelm other penultimate revelatory occasions, events or persons; it is the rather the opposite: the Christ event is the means whereby occasions, persons, or events acquire revelatory density within the scriptural story or their critically sifted (typological) place within the extra-biblical cumulative tradition. Niebuhr writes, "Revelation means this intelligible event which makes all other events intelligible."[116]

God's relation to the human tradition about God   John Webster maintains there are three important features of a doctrine of inspiration which make it dogmatically fruitful: (1) it needs to be located in a place subordinate to and dependent upon an account of revelation; (2) it needs to avoid objectifying or spiritualizing this divine activity; and (3) it needs to be articulated in relation to the end for which it functions, "which is service to God's self-manifestation."[117]

Barr is most attentive to the third feature of a dogmatically fruitful account of inspiration. Against fundamentalist notions of inspiration, which want to establish the Bible as an inerrant source of knowledge about God, Barr is careful to articulate inspiration in terms of the use of the Bible for soteriological ends within the community of faith. The use of the Bible in the context of the church, where it is heard in faith, is effective for faith, and thus the extension of the cumulative tradition of the people of God. This is consistent with Barr's emphasis on how biblical interpreters ought to pay more attention to the forward motion, the effects, of the Bible in its paradigmatic function in the life of community for which it functions. What remains unsolved by this account, however, is whether the efficacy of the Bible in the growth of the cumulative tradition is the result of the church's use of the Bible or God's (the Spirit's) use of the church's use of the Bible.[118] For while Barr goes so far as to indicate that "Word of God" may be used as a licit description of the *mode* in which the church uses the Bible, he is not specific as to *whose* use this term describes.[119]

However, at the level of the second feature of doctrinally fruitful notions of revelation—the need to avoid objectifying or spiritualizing divine activity—Barr is less successful. For while he is most attentive to the objectifying extreme in accounts of inspiration in which the Bible is portrayed as the Word become text, in his desire

---

115 The disclosure of architectonic structure from the perspective of the end of the story is not a subversion of the plot but "a compelling and persuasive disclosure of what the story was about all along." See David C. Steinmetz, "Uncovering a Second Narrative: Detective Fiction and the Construction of Historical Method," in Ellen F. Davis and Richard B. Hays (eds), *The Art of Reading Scripture* (Grand Rapids, 2003), pp. 54-55.

116 H. Richard Niebuhr, *The Meaning of Revelation*, p. 69. See also Barth, *Church Dogmatics*, 1/2: 683.

117 Webster, *Holy Scripture*, p. 35.

118 David Kelsey, "The Bible and Christian Theology," *Journal of the American Academy of Religion*,48/3 (1980): 396.

119 See *Biblical Faith and Natural Theology*, p. 198. In preference to William Abraham's notion of the Bible as the inspired teacher, Barr takes up what he calls "the more realistic and germane pattern of the inspired and inspiring church." See Barr, ibid., pp. 197-198 and William Abraham, *The Divine Inspiration of Scripture* (Oxford, 1981).

30 *Revelation, Holy Scripture and Church*

to avoid a "God-of-the gaps" strategy and the double description of the process of scriptural formation and use it engenders, he almost completely collapses theological description into human historical description. The Holy Spirit accompanies human thought and action to the point that theological description dissolves into human thought and action. Paul Wells identifies the liability of this account:

> The problem remains in this vague formulation that the Spirit's presence is so imperceptible that it may be impossible to say anything concrete about it at all. If nothing tangible can be said about this being "in the Spirit" does the Spirit's presence make any difference to human situations? Would its absence amount to the same thing?[120]

Presumably any doctrine of inspiration is an attempt to hold together in a single account a description of human *and* divine agency with respect to the formation, use and efficacy of Holy Scripture.[121] While there are stronger and weaker accounts of inspiration, it would seem that the introduction of the notion itself requires some accounting of divine activity in which it is related to human writing, fallibility, personality and style without reducing one to the other. Richard Swinburne, in his exploration of the theological concept of inspiration, examines strong versions, in which God is the author of the Bible who "moved human authors and compilers to record his message,"[122] and weaker versions in which human writers were "less than fully pliable."[123] Across the whole spectrum of inspirational options, however, Swinburne maintains a lively sense of divine authorship of the Bible and divine action by means of the Bible, not as a God-of-the-gaps strategy, but as part of a theologically realist account of Scripture. Barr, however, seems to propose that one cannot keep a double description going without special pleading. Either one tacitly assumes immanent divine activity in such a manner that it is portrayed under human, historical description or asserts a form of "supernatural intervention" at difficult points, which seems to threaten a human account. However, such an either/or account, as Kathryn Tanner has demonstrated, is rooted in a contrastive understanding of divine agency—in which God is either here (immanent) or there (transcendent)—that does not bear theological scrutiny. Tanner writes:

---

120 Wells, *James Barr and the Bible*, p. 226.

121 See Schneiders, *The Revelatory Text*, p. 48. Schneiders notes that theologically satisfactory accounts of inspiration will involve an account of divine–human cooperation or interaction. However, Schneiders moves to a subjectivist account of inspiration on the very next pages where she speaks of inspiration *solely* in terms of the experience engendered in the reader by the text. Ibid., p. 50.

122 Swinburne, *Revelation*, p. 196. In the strong version of inspiration, human writers are fully open to divine truth and, while they have their own style and presuppositions, often understood divine purposes in their writing, and where they did not, they wrote down sufficient truth that in a later context it came to have a sense which was altogether true. See ibid., pp. 196-197.

123 Ibid., p. 198. The weaker view of inspiration supposes that human writers and canonizers were "not fully open to divine truth and allowed some small amount of falsity on important matters to infect Scripture." In an analogy Swinburne likens this picture of inspiration to "a symphony written and conducted by a genius, but played by an orchestra of willful amateurs." Ibid.

Revelation and Biblical Interpretation   31

[R]adical transcendence does not exclude God's positive fellowship with the world or presence within it. Only created beings, which remain themselves over and against others, risk the distinctiveness of their own natures by entering into intimate relations with another. God's transcendence alone is one that may be properly exercised in the radical immanence by which God is said to be nearer to us than we are to ourselves.[124]

Finally, to be theologically fruitful doctrines of inspiration need to be dependent on and subordinate to a larger concept of revelation. In one sense, Barr's articulation of inspiration is consistent with a larger concept of revelation articulated in terms of cumulative tradition. However, the sense of "dependent and subordinate" implies a greater interrogation of the concept of inspiration than that of its coherence with revelation as Barr depicts it. In both his articulation of revelation and inspiration, Barr construes God's involvement solely in terms of mediate human acts and decisions. The fundamental rationale for this preference is that Barr resists notions of divine antecedence; interpreters and theologians have no access to divine action apart from the human tradition about God. What this means for inspiration is that it is not so much about what God did, does and says by means of Holy Scripture, as it is an articulation of the paradigmatic effect that the objectification of the people of God's faith, expressed in a human, historical way, has on subsequent generations. However, as Ronald Thiemann has argued there is more than one way to render an account of God's prevenience. On Thiemann's descriptive theology, "God's reality (and thus his 'ontological' priority) is implied by a set of concrete Christian beliefs concerning God's identity. Revelation in this view is not simply a temporally prior event to which faith is a response. Revelation is the continuing reality of God's active presence among his people."[125] It is God's presence that generates written human witnesses and renders them bearers of the Word of the Gospel. Moreover, by virtue of the resurrection of Jesus Christ from the dead and his ascension to the right hand of God, Christ is present to testimony about him. Karl Barth remarks: "There is the indispensability of an indirect and historical connection with Him in the service or as a garment of the true and direct connection which He Himself institutes and continues between Himself and us from the right hand of the Father."[126]

Paul Ricoeur: Manifestation and the Hermeneutic Constitution of Faith

In one of Paul Ricoeur's more recent books, *Critique and Conviction*,[127] he returns to the theme of revelation, which he had taken up in a direct way some twenty years earlier.[128] The term "revelation", where it is articulated in relation to "the

---

124 Tanner, *God and Creation in Christian Theology*, p. 79.

125 Thiemann, *Revelation and Theology*, p. 80.

126 Barth, *Church Dogmatics*, IV/1: 325.

127 Paul Ricoeur, *Critique and Conviction: Conversations with Francois Azouvi and Marc de Launay*, trans. Kathleen Blamey (New York, 1998), pp. 148-149.

128 Paul Ricoeur, "Toward a Hermeneutic of the Idea of Revelation," in Lewis S. Mudge (ed.), *Essays on Biblical Interpretation* (Philadelphia, 1980), pp. 73-118.

texts of faith"[129] is, for Ricoeur, "too often reduced to inspiration, which I showed earlier is appropriate only for a certain category of text, and because, extended to the entire Biblical corpus, it introduces a psychologizing interpretation of canonical authority."[130] Ricoeur continues to insist that where prophetic discourse becomes the paradigm for all forms of biblical discourse, a single form threatens the genric variety of the biblical corpus. The paradigm of prophetic speech, in which the prophet speaks for God, imprisons "the idea of revelation in too narrow a concept."[131] The psychologized concept of "insufflation"[132] is not sufficiently rich to typify the whole of the biblical corpus. The texts of faith, when encountered in the variety of their biblical forms (narrative, legislative, hymnic and sapiential), yield a concept of revelation that is more pluralistic and polysemic.

Narrative discourse, for example, which focuses on tracing the activity of God in the founding event(s) of the community of faith, does not easily comport to a notion of revelation derived from prophetic discourse. Although Ricoeur does indicate the mutual relations between prophetic and narrative discourse (as well as the rich interplay between others forms of discourse), in narrative the author very often disappears from view and Yahweh is designated in the third or second person. "Confession takes place through narration and the problematic of inspiration is in no way the primary consideration. God's mark is in history before being in speech."[133] The notion of revelation herein contained moves away from psychologized accounts of the Holy Spirit—the double voice of the prophet—to the luminosity of the generative founding events recounted. "In this way, a less subjective concept of inspiration is roughed out."[134]

In this same discussion, a different mode for the authority of revelation is also envisaged. For once the reduction of revelation to inspiration along the lines of prophetic discourse is overcome, through a consideration of other forms of discourse, the mode of the Bible's revelatory appeal is freed up for transposition through a consideration of poetics. It is Ricoeur's contention that the poetic function of all the modes of discourse (prophetic, narrative, legislative, hymnic, sapiential) is revelatory, in the sense that in the rich interplay between modes of discourse,

---

129 Ricoeur moves quickly through what he calls "opaque and authoritarian" understandings of the concept of revelation, by which he means (1) an authoritative body of doctrines imposed on the faithful by the magisterium and, to a lesser degree, (2) the level of dogma where "a historic community interprets for itself and for others the understanding of faith specific to its tradition." "Toward a Hermeneutic of the Idea of Revelation," pp. 73-75.

130 *Critique and Conviction*, p. 148.

131 "Toward a Hermeneutic of the Idea of Revelation," p. 76.

132 See "Philosophy and Religious Language," in Mark I. Wallace (ed.), *Figuring the Sacred: Religion, Narrative, and Imagination*, trans. David Pellaur (Minneapolis: Fortress Press, 1995), p. 44; "Toward a Hermeneutic of the Idea of Revelation," pp. 76, 93, 98, 104; "Philosophical Hermeneutics and Biblical Hermeneutics," in Kathleen Balmey and John B. Thompson (eds and trans.), *From Text to Action: Essays in Hermeneutics, II* (Evanston, 1991), p. 96; *Critique and Conviction*, pp. 143-144, 148-149; and "Naming God," in *Figuring the Sacred*, p. 221.

133 "Toward a Hermeneutic of the Idea of Revelation," p. 79.

134 Ibid., p. 93.

Revelation and Biblical Interpretation   33

possible worlds (itineraries of meaning) are proposed. Through the suspension of the ordinary referential function of language, poetic language re-describes reality; it proposes a possible world. It is this world, the "issue," the "thing", the "new being", opened up by text that takes us beyond psychologized interpretations of canonical authority. Ricoeur rejects attempts to read biblical texts primarily in terms of their appeal to the will for obedience or submission.[135] For the mode of appeal to the reader made by the manifestation of a possible world, unfolded before the text, is that of a non-violent appeal addressed to the imagination.[136] The reader is not commanded to submission, but invited to adopt a mode of being-in-the-world, which follows the itinerary of meaning proposed by the "thing" of the text. Where readers will disappropriate themselves (renounce the sovereignty of the self) to receive this new mode of being from the Bible, Ricoeur speaks of the hermeneutic constitution of faith.

Faith is, however, a wager on the symbolic network of the Bible and the itineraries of meaning projected imaginatively in front of the text. Ricoeur simply finds that the Bible is worth listening to and that he is in the "unravelable" situation of listening to it. One might say, the Bible has captured his imagination. In his most recent writings, Ricoeur has introduced conscience alongside of imagination, which adds a moral dimension to the deliberations of the self as it receives into its inner dialogue possible worlds mediated to it by a structural examination of the Bible. Together conscience and imagination function as the point of contact between the reading self and the Word of God.

Following the exposition of Ricoeur's reconceptualization of revelation and faith by means of poetics, we engage in a critical review of Ricoeur's proposal. This critical reflection will examine the degree to which Ricoeur is successful in (1) his modulation of the doctrine of revelation, (2) his articulation of the corresponding imaginative appeal, which such a modulation entails, and (3) his understanding of text appropriation by creative imagination brokered by conscience. The argument will be made that Ricoeur's modulation of revelation, away from understandings of it that rely too heavily on inspiration, is rendered problematic by casting the doctrine in poetic terms that are unfriendly to the agency of God by means of Holy Scripture. Moreover, because of his pre-emptive poetic and hermeneutic construal of the interpretative field, the rich doctrinal heritage of the Christian church is effectively supplanted as a substantial resource in the articulation of an appropriate understanding of revelation and faith. While Ricoeur resists the notion that he engages in apologetics in his articulation of an understanding of revelation as non-violent appeal, the case will be made that he is trying to engender an understanding of revelation that is consistent with the ethics of autonomy. The primacy of poetics

---

135 Ibid., p. 117 and *Critique and Conviction*, p. 149.

136 See "Toward a Hermeneutic of the Idea of Revelation," pp. 73, 95-117; *Critique and Conviction*, pp. 143-144; "Theonomy and/or Autonomy," in Miraslov Wolf, Carmen Craig and Thomas Kucharz (eds), *The Future of Theology: Essays in Honor of Jürgen Moltmann* (Grand Rapids, 1996), pp. 284-298; and "Thou Shalt Not Kill: A Loving Obedience," in André LaCocque and Paul Ricoeur (eds), *Thinking Biblically: Exegetical and Hermeneutical Studies*, trans. David Pellauer (Chicago, 1998), pp. 124ff.

34   *Revelation, Holy Scripture and Church*

and the apologetic interest to render revelation amenable to Kantian notions of autonomy eclipse God's relation to and use of the Bible. In contrast to Ricoeur's account, a theological rendering of divine communicative action by means of Holy Scripture and a corresponding account of the appeal of revelation and the capacities of human response are offered.

A Poetic Reconceptualization of the Idea of Revelation

Ricoeur introduces "poetics" as a site most promising for the development of an idea of revelation as nonviolent appeal. Rather than set out an idea of revelation that begins with a phenomenology of perception or care/preoccupation, Ricoeur proposes to begin "directly from the manifestation of the world by the text and by Scripture."[137] Ricoeur does not, however, move directly to a consideration of the revelatory function of poetic discourse, he takes a detour via the consideration of the hermeneutic of a written work.

Drawing on his writings in interpretation theory,[138] Ricoeur introduces three preparatory concepts which lay the groundwork for his recovery of the idea of revelation as nonviolent appeal. The first is the concept of writing itself. Through the fixation of speech in writing, discourse is set loose from its originating context. A text, on Ricoeur's view, is autonomous with respect to the world of its production through its fixation in writing. It "bursts" the world of the author and "emancipates" readers from the limited scope of its "original audience."[139] In other writings, Ricoeur calls the dynamic by which discourse is liberated through writing from authorial intention, the world of its production and its original recipient(s), "distanciation."[140]

The second preparatory hermeneutic concept that Ricoeur uses to introduce the idea of a "revelatory function of poetic discourse"[141] is that of "the work." A text, as a work, is for Ricoeur, a sequence longer than the sentence, a structured reality—a composition, shaped through literary genre—and finally, a unique configuration; it has a style. "To say that a text is a work is to say that it is a structured totality which cannot be reduced to the sentences whereof it is composed."[142] The inscription of discourse in writing involves submitting language to rules of composition and formation (codification) such that it is transformed through labor into a story, poem, essay, and the like. "This codification is known as a literary genre; a work, in other words, is characteristically subsumed to a literary genre."[143] The unique configuration of discourse, which gives it particularity or individuality, Ricoeur calls

---

137 Ibid., p. 98.

138 Paul Ricoeur, *Interpretation Theory: Discourse and the Surplus of Meaning* (Fort Worth, 1976).

139 "Toward A Hermeneutic of the Idea of Revelation," p. 99.

140 See, for example, John B. Thompson (ed.), *Hermeneutics and the Human Sciences*, ed. (Cambridge, 1981), pp. 91-92, 131-144, 147-149.

141 "Toward a Hermeneutic of the Idea of Revelation," p. 99.

142 Thompson, "Editor's Introduction," in *Hermeneutics and the Human Sciences*, p. 13. See also Paul Ricoeur, "The Hermeneutical Function of Distanciation," in *Hermeneutics and the Human Sciences*, pp. 136-138.

143 Ibid., p. 136.

"style." At the confluence of the indeterminacies and possibilities of an event and the promotion of a particular standpoint, through inscription of discourse in language, lies the "style" of a work. "This shaping of the work concurs with the phenomenon of writing in externalizing and objectifying the text into what one literary critic has called 'a verbal icon.'"[144]

The third introductory concept carries Ricoeur a bit further. "It is what I call the world of the text."[145] Hermeneutics is neither, on Ricoeur's account, an attempt to search out the psychological intentions of the author behind the text, nor a dismantling of the structures immanent within the text. Ricoeur distances himself from both Romantic hermeneutics and structuralism. Detached from their original intentions and circumstances through inscription, texts project or unfold a possible world in front of themselves. What is finally to be understood in a text, the object of interpretation, the "issue" of the text, is the world toward which the text points, the possible world to which it refers.[146] "[W]hat must be interpreted in a text is a proposed world which I could inhabit and wherein I could project my ownmost possibilities. That is what I call the world of the text, the world proper to this unique text."[147] Through the use of these three concepts—autonomy through writing, externalization by means of the work, and the reference to a world—Ricoeur takes up a poetic re-conceptualization of revelation.

All of the genres of biblical literature have a poetic function. Ricoeur defines this function negatively: "they exercise a referential function that differs from the descriptive referential function of ordinary language and above all scientific discourse."[148] Biblical texts, in all their genric variety refer to a world then, but they refer, in their poetic mode, non-ostensively.[149] Poetic discourse is about the world, but not about the ordinary objects of our everyday world. Instead the poetic dimension refers to "the many ways of belonging to the world before we oppose ourselves to things understood as 'objects' that stand before a 'subject.'"[150] Poetic discourse is thus more primitive or fundamental in the sense that it conveys to us an order of things in which we (may) participate prior to our parsing up the world. Through a suspension of first-order (ostensive) reference, poetic discourse projects

---

144 "Toward a Hermeneutic of the Idea of Revelation," p. 100. W.K. Wimsatt, *The Verbal Icon: Studies in the Meaning of Poetry* (Kentucky, 1954) is the literary critic in view here. See "The Hermeneutic Function of Distanciation," p. 137.

145 "Toward a Hermeneutic of the Idea of Revelation," p. 100.

146 Ibid., p. 100. See also "Naming God," pp. 220-221.

147 "The Hermeneutical Function of Distanciation," p. 142.

148 "Toward a Hermeneutic of the Idea of Revelation," p. 100.

149 See "Naming God," p. 222 and "Toward a Hermeneutic of the Idea of Revelation," pp. 100-101. In this latter discussion Ricoeur calls attention in a footnote (n. 7) to *The Rule of Metaphor: Multi-Disciplinary Studies of the Creation of Meaning in Language*, trans. Robert Czerny with Kathleen McLaughlin and John Costello, SJ (Toronto, 1977). See also Paul Ricoeur, "Biblical Hermeneutics," *Semeia*, 4 (1975): 99.

150 "Naming God," p. 222.

36 *Revelation, Holy Scripture and Church*

a possible world, through fictive re-description,[151] to which we (may) belong. James Fodor nicely summarizes Ricoeur's discussion of poetic discourse:

> Poetic discourse suspends the direct descriptive use of language, thereby making possible an alternative use of language in which the referential function is redirected and reshaped in such a way that it intends reality in a different mode and at a different level. Moreover, the abolition of a first-order reference to the world as experienced in discourse constitutes the necessary condition which makes possible the institution of a second-order or non-ostensive reference to that more fundamental level of reality previously identified as our rootedness in the world . . .[152]

Drawing together his considerations on the dynamics of writing and poetic discourse, Ricoeur offers his areligious idea of revelation. Through the instantiation of speech in writing, a world of discourse is distanciated from its author's intentions and its original audience and an order of things, a world, is revealed. The specific plus of the poetic function of discourse is that the order of things revealed is liberated from ostensive reference such that a possible world (a secondary or split referent) and a corresponding way of being is manifest before the text. A world shows itself, a world that may be inhabited by the reader. "It is in this sense of manifestation that language in its poetic function is a vehicle of revelation."[153] Revelation as inspiration or insufflation is thus transposed to revelation as manifestation.

A positive feature of this move is that a greater emphasis falls on the "issue" of biblical texts and the interruptive potential of possible world(s) projected by the text. Instead of a preoccupation with the voice of God behind the writers of Scripture, more attention is given to the issue the texts tell about. Ricoeur maintains that by laying emphasis on the realities that unfold before the text, greater objectivity is accorded to revelation. "Revelation, if the expression is to have a meaning, is a feature of the biblical *world*."[154] And for Ricoeur the proposed world that unfolds in front of the biblical text, through the genric friction of its component parts, is variously designated: "a new creation, a new covenant, the Kingdom of God."[155] It is these realities that cut through the ordinary world of our experience to open readers to new possibilities. Through a power Ricoeur calls "projection," texts—including biblical texts—uncover the modalities of our prevenient belonging to the world, which offer a break and a new beginning to us. To cite a Ricoeurian example: in the case of naming God, before it is an act of which a person is capable, it is something

---

151 See Kevin Vanhoozer, "Philosophical Antecedents to Ricoeur's Time and Narrative," in David Wood (ed.), *On Paul Ricoeur: Narrative and Interpretation* (New York, 1991), p. 48.

152 James Fodor, *Christian Hermeneutics: Paul Ricoeur and the Refiguring of Theology* (Oxford and New York, 1995), p. 134.

153 "Toward a Hermeneutic of the Idea of Revelation," p. 102.

154 "Philosophical Hermeneutics and Biblical Hermeneutics," p. 96. Ricoeur's emphasis. And elsewhere: "If the Bible may be said to be revealed this must refer to what it says, to the new being it unfolds before us." "Toward a Hermeneutic of the Idea of Revelation," p. 104.

155 "Toward a Hermeneutic of the Idea of Revelation," p. 103.

Revelation and Biblical Interpretation

that "the texts of my predilection do . . . when they deploy their world, when they poetically manifest and thereby reveal a world we might inhabit."[156]

The Hermeneutic Constitution of Faith

For Ricoeur, the world in front of the text is a possible world to which a text, including the Bible, productively refers through the use of metaphor and narrative (i.e., through non-ostensive reference). The mode of being which readers can project is mediated by a structural study of the text. Ricoeur, unlike Bultmann who rushes to inauthentic existential signification,[157] wants to maintain the clear priority of the "thing" of the text in the poetic opening up of a possible world. Ricoeur writes, "The ideality of the text remains the mediator in this process of the fusion of horizons."[158] The possible world a text discloses in front of itself, ought therefore to have a logical, although not temporal, priority over the appropriative possibilities which readers see for themselves in the light of it, even though they may be simultaneously disclosed. Thus the world a text reveals in front of itself has its own reality, albeit an ideal reality, even though the possibilities it discloses are always reader-oriented and reader-relative. Ricoeur writes, "If the reference of the text is the projection of a world, then it is not in the first instance the reader who projects himself. The reader is rather broadened in his capacity to project himself by receiving a new mode of being from the text itself."[159] While the scope of meaning in front of the text includes the reader, Ricoeur is clear about the logical priority of the disclosed possible world over the possibilities (modes of being) which readers may project in the light of it.

Access to the meaning world which texts, biblical texts included, disclose in front of themselves, along with the corresponding mode(s) of being they enable their readers to project, is mediated by a structural analysis (explanation) of the text and enabled by the reader's disappropriation of the sovereign self. In order to gain access to the meaning world in front of the text, the reader must consider the text's inner organization, architecture, or immanent sense. This involves, as was observed, a rich appreciation genre, intra-generic friction as well as the style of the piece as a "work." This task can be accomplished with a minimum of existential involvement on behalf of the reader, because it can be accomplished at a critical distance from the

---

156 "Naming God," p. 223. Mark Wallace describes the disruptive potential of Ricoeur's rhetoric of revelation: "Classic texts like the Bible . . . are revelatory because they place one's everyday perceptions of reality in abeyance by opening up new ways of being human, novel redescriptions of self and world, that are fertile and transformative." See Mark I. Wallace, "Ricoeur, Rorty and the Question of Revelation," in David E. Klemm and William Schweiker (eds), *Meanings and Texts and Actions: Questioning Paul Ricoeur* (Charlottesville, 1993), p. 235.

157 See Ricoeur, "Preface to Bultmann."

158 Paul Ricoeur, "Appropriation," in *Hermeneutics and the Human Sciences*, p. 192. Thus although Ricoeur takes issue with Frege on the issue of whether poetic language may refer he does acquiesce on the issue of the necessity of reference to a possible world, as necessary to meaning properly speaking. See "The Hermeneutical Function of Distanciation," pp. 140-141.

159 "Appropriation," p. 192.

38   *Revelation, Holy Scripture and Church*

text. However, it is a necessary stage in access to the meaning world in front of the text since it mediates an informed or critical understanding of the text to the reader's imagination, thus enabling the reader to consider more adequately its appropriative possibilities.[160] Vanhoozer writes, "The reader by following the semantic itineraries sketched out in the text, eventually comes to see the text's world, and himself, in the light of that world."[161] However, in order for readers to be granted full access to the world disclosed in front of the text, and to the appropriate possibilities it presents for them, they must disappropriate themselves. In other words, in order to receive alien meaning readers must renounce the sovereign self in front of the text. Ricoeur writes, "the matter of the text becomes my own only if I disappropriate myself, in order to let the matter of the text be. So I exchange *me, master* of itself, for the *self, disciple* of the text."[162]

In his essay, "Philosophical Hermeneutics and Biblical Hermeneutics,"[163] Ricoeur undertakes an exploration of the contribution his general philosophic hermeneutic for the interpretation of texts can make to biblical interpretation. While he begins with a general philosophic hermeneutic, he does so under the conviction that "theological hermeneutics presents features that are so original that the relation is gradually inverted, and theological hermeneutics finally subordinates philosophical hermeneutics to itself as its own organon."[164] In the fourth section of this essay, "The Hermeneutical Constitution of Biblical Faith," Ricoeur introduces the general hermeneutic category of "appropriation" with a view to underscoring "three consequences for biblical hermeneutics of the relation that we have posited between the world of the work and the understanding the reader has of himself or herself vis-à-vis the text."[165]

Because appropriation is preceded in Ricoeur's hermeneutic by textual explanation it serves biblical hermeneutics very well. The priority of the "thing" of the text leads to the recognition that faith is constituted, "in the strongest sense of the term,"[166] by the "thing" of the Bible. In theological terms, the priority of the Word over human response is maintained[167] and the psychologizing reduction of faith is resisted. Faith is, however, an act which is irreducible to linguistic treatment; it has a prelinguistic

---

160 See Paul Ricoeur, "What is a Text?: Explanation and Understanding," in *Hermeneutics and the Human Sciences*, p. 161.

161 Kevin Vanhoozer, *Biblical Narrative in the Philosophy of Paul Ricoeur: A Study in Hermeneutics and Theology* (Cambridge, 1990), p. 89.

162 Paul Ricoeur, "Phenomenology and Hermeneutics," in *Hermeneutics and the Human Sciences*, p. 11. Ricoeur's emphasis.

163 In Blamey and Thomson, *From Text to Action: Essays in Hermeneutics, II*, pp. 89-101.

164 Ibid., p. 90.

165 Ibid., p. 99.

166 Ibid.

167 Mark Wallace argues that at this level the theological approaches of Ricoeur and Karl Barth converge. See his "The World of the Text: Theological Hermeneutics in the Thought of Karl Barth and Paul Ricoeur," *Union Seminary Quarterly Review* 41/1 (1986): 2-7. See also Paul Ricoeur, "Myth as the Bearer of Possible Worlds," in Richard Kearney (ed.), *Dialogues with Contemporary Continental Thinkers* (Manchester, 1984), p. 4.

Revelation and Biblical Interpretation   39

or hyperlinguistic character, and thus is an elusive topic for hermeneutic treatment. It is an endlessly mobile movement responding to a prior word, which engenders hope "that turns reasons to despair into reasons for hope, following the paradoxical laws of overabundance."[168] All of these dynamics render hermeneutic reflection on faith precarious and partial. And yet, the character of faith as receptive and responsive to the biblical world of signs and symbols by which it is formed and engendered raises it to the "level of language." Ricoeur comments; "Unconditional trust would be empty if it were not based upon the continually renewing interpretation of the sign-events reported by Scripture, such as the Exodus in the Old Testament and the Resurrection in the New."[169] In these events of deliverance, which become the word of God for the reader, one can properly speak of the hermeneutic constitution of faith.

Ricoeur offers an example of how in the diverse genres of Scripture a possible world is disclosed (revealed) and a corresponding mode-of-being in the world (faith) is engendered. In the context of the example, Ricoeur is making a case for an idea of origin that does not coincide with a beginning in time. He turns to narrativized sapiential writings, which he considers able to offer such an alternative. The sage tells a story of a man, who although originally good, has become bad. He presents in narrative form the fact that original goodness is more profound than radical evil: it never entirely erases the fundamental disposition. Ricoeur then turns to the lives of the prophets, who stand up to threatening circumstances mourning but hopeful, and this rhythm of destruction and reconstruction is repeated. He finds this same rhythm in the great prophetic tradition: destruction—exile—promise of restoration. And again in the grand model of the passion and resurrection of Christ: cross—death—resurrection. "This type of rhythm" writes Ricoeur, "can be put in the category of "revelation" in the sense that, when I read this, I myself am constituted in accordance with this assertion—destruction—restitution rhythm; I do not draw it out of myself, I find it already inscribed prior to me."[170] What is revealed in this inter-genric reading of the Bible is a rhythm of death and resurrection, which, I would gather, could be appropriated by being-in-the-world in a hopeful mode despite the "denials of experience."[171]

Returning to the interplay between general and special hermeneutics, Ricoeur draws a second consequence for the interpretation of faith. This consequence is the result of the divestment (distanciation) of the self before the world of the text. In the hermeneutic writings of Ricoeur, "self understanding in front of the text" is a critical moment in which the selfhood of the reader stands exposed to the text "receiving from it an enlarged self, which would be the proposed existence corresponding in the most suitable way to the world proposed."[172] Here Ricoeur draws attention to the

---

168 "Philosophical Hermeneutics and Biblical Hermeneutics," p. 99.

169 Ibid.

170 *Critique and Conviction*, p. 148. Ricoeur continues:

I return again to Kant—he is always my preferred author for the philosophy of religion—who speaking of the Christ figure as being the man pleasing to God, giving his life for his friends, declares that he could not have drawn that figure out of himself, and that he found it inscribed in a sort of imaginary or a schematism constitutive of the religious.

171 "Philosophical Hermeneutics and Biblical Hermeneutics," p. 99.

172 "The Hermeneutic Function of Distanciation," p. 143.

40 *Revelation, Holy Scripture and Church*

critical potential of his general hermeneutic in the appropriation of biblical texts. In the reading of the Bible the reading subject submits him or herself to the thing of the text to deconstruct prejudice and illusion, such that self-critique is an integral part of the reading by which faith is engendered. Moreover, a hermeneutics of suspicion is incorporated into an internal critique, which allows the world of the text to be, without assimilating or baptizing by force the external critique of religion by Marx, Nietzsche, or Freud.

The third and final consequence drawn from the hermeneutics of appropriation for biblical hermeneutics has to do with the formation of new being in the reader. It is, in a sense, the positive or creative side of the de-construction of prejudice and illusion; it is "the creative aspect of distanciation."[173] In following the "productive imagination"[174] at work in the text of the Bible, figures are proposed to the "creative imagination"[175] of the reader, figures which may be decontextualized and recontextualized in today's *Sitz im Leben* such that they enable a re-description of reality[176] and become "the figures of my liberation."[177] Imagination is thus the dimension of subjectivity where these playful possibilities for the ego are envisaged in the light of the "thing" of the text. Faith is "the fullness of the act of appropriation"[178] in the sense that it responds to imaginative solicitation in a transfer from text to life. Although this solicitation occurs through the whole of Scripture, biblical narrative is the place where this intersection between text and life is, on Ricoeur's view, best apprehended. It is where the imagination of the reader is most conspicuously engendered according to the Bible.[179]

Before this section is concluded, three considerations with respect to the role of "imagination" in Ricoeur's biblical hermeneutic should be offered. First, Ricoeur articulates the place of "imagination" in appropriation over against what has traditionally been the place of the will. The imaginative appeal of the Bible, the wooing of the reader by new possibilities, at the very least precedes the appeal of the text to the will,[180] and in other cases replaces or qualifies the heteronomous command to obey. Ricoeur uses the German terms, *Anspruch* ("a claim which does not force

---

173 "Philosophical Hermeneutics and Biblical Hermeneutics," p. 100.

174 By "productive imagination" Ricoeur points to imagination "as a rule-governed form of invention, or in other terms, a norm-governed productivity." Paul Ricoeur, "The Bible and the Imagination," in Hans Dieter Betz (ed.), *The Bible as a Document of the University* (Chico, 1981), p. 49.

175 By "creative imagination" Ricoeur means the dynamic activity in which readers do not simply repeat forever fixed significations of a text, but prolong the itineraries of meaning opened up by the work of interpretation. "Reading," writes Ricoeur, "should be seen as the meeting point of the itineraries of meaning offer by the text as a production of fiction (in the sense given above) and the free course (*parcours*) of meaning brought about by the reader seeking 'to apply' the text to life." "The Bible and the Imagination," p. 50.

176 Ibid., p 50.

177 "Philosophical Hermeneutics and Biblical Hermeneutics," p. 101.

178 Fodor, *Christian Hermeneutics*, p. 246.

179 "The Bible and the Imagination," p. 51.

180 Ricoeur writes, "I am indeed speaking here of imagination and not of will. For the power of allowing oneself to be struck by new possibilities *precedes* the power of making

Revelation and Biblical Interpretation

one to accept its message")[181] and *Andenken*[182] ("a call to reflection, meditation") across the entire corpus of his writings on the topic of appropriation. Encountering biblical discourse in its function poetic, one responds with the imagination, that part of ourselves, "that can encounter revelation no longer as an unacceptable pretension, but a nonviolent appeal."[183]

Working as a philosopher in this modulation of the nature of revelation's appeal, Ricoeur is very much in conversation with "an ethics of autonomy,"[184] which resists the heteronomy of obedience to command. Although he recognizes that this conversation is "perilous," he claims that he works to avoid two pitfalls, apologetics and refutation.[185] Early on, Ricoeur tempered the notion of autonomous consciousness through a consideration of testimony, signs and institutions which mediate the self.[186] The tack that Ricoeur took in his subsequent writings was to employ the term "theonomy," "which can confront autonomy without mutual exclusion, and occupy a place different from that of heteronomy."[187] On Ricoeur's view, theonomy consists in the obligation to love because we have been loved.[188] Concern for another, even to the point of substitution, does not threaten autonomy, understood as the summons to responsibility, but rather engenders it.[189]

Second, there is for Ricoeur an element of risk in the hermeneutic constitution of faith. The imaginative variations that the reader is invited to play out in conversation with the "thing" of the Bible constitute a wager on the part of the reader. "The reference of biblical faith to a culturally contingent symbolic network requires that this faith assume its own insecurity, which makes it a chance happening transformed into a destiny by means of a choice constantly renewed, in the scrupulous respect of different choices."[190] There is simply no way to guarantee from the outset that the contingent "texts of my predilection"[191] are the right texts, that they contain the

---

up one's mind." "Philosophical Hermeneutics and Biblical Hermeneutics," p. 101 (emphasis mine).

181 "Toward a Hermeneutic of the Idea of Revelation," p. 95.

182 *Critique and Conviction*, p. 149.

183 "Toward a Hermeneutic of the Idea of Revelation," p. 117.

184 Ricoeur has the Kantian notion of moral autonomy in view. See "Thou Shalt Not Kill: A Loving Obedience," p. 124, n. 24 and "Theonomy and/or Autonomy," p. 284.

185 "Thou Shalt Not Kill: A Loving Obedience," p. 124.

186 "Toward a Hermeneutic of the Idea of Revelation," pp. 105ff.

187 "Theonomy and/or Autonomy," p. 289.

188 Ricoeur writes concerning the relation between the text of Scripture and the community that reads it. He speaks of this relationship surpassing "that between authority and obedience to become one of love . . ." Lacocque and Ricoeur, "Preface," in *Thinking Biblically*, p. xvii.

189 Ricoeur recognizes that the concept of autonomy must be also be massaged in order to permit the sense of theonomy he wants to admit. See his discussion of the two points at which moral autonomy seems to be incompatible with theonomy. "Thou Shalt Not Kill: A Loving Obedience," pp. 134ff. This discussion throws some doubt on whether Ricoeur has successfully avoided the "apologetic" pitfall he sought to evade. See ibid., p. 124.

190 Paul Ricoeur, *Oneself as Another*, trans. Kathleen Blamey (Chicago, 1992), p. 25.

191 "Naming God," p. 223.

42 *Revelation, Holy Scripture and Church*

"figures of my liberation."[192] One begins with the unaccounted for presupposition that the Bible is worth listening to and in the "unravelable" situation in which one desires to hear.[193] Ricoeur realizes there is a certain circularity to this position. And yet, "I boldly stay within this circle of hope that, through the transfer from text to life, what I have risked will be returned a hundredfold as an increase in comprehension, valor, and joy."[194]

Finally, an account of the relationship of conscience and imagination in *Oneself as Another* and "The Summoned Subject in the School of the Narratives of the Prophetic Vocation"[195] ought to be given. In the final chapter of *Oneself as Another*, Ricoeur introduces conscience as the place where human selfhood is constituted. Conscience is that formal feature of human interiority through which the self attests its "ownmost power of being before measuring the inadequation of its action to its most profound being."[196] Only by presupposing the intimacy of the self with conscience, a self already in relation in internal dialogue, does it make sense to solicit or summon the self. For otherwise there is no "I" in the position of respondent. An external voice, a summons to the self then, must suppose this conversation into which it should be able to be received.[197] Ricoeur maintains that St. Paul first caught sight of the connection between self-knowledge (*suneidesis*) and the Christian kerygma—which he understood as justification by faith. It is crucial that this justification, which is alien to us, be appropriated into the intimacy of the conscience which already contains a dialogical structure of testimony (calling) and judgment (response). "Conscience," writes Ricoeur, "is thus the anthropological presupposition without which 'justification by faith' would remain an event marked by a radical extrinsicness. In this sense, conscience becomes the organ of the reception of the kerygma . . ."[198]

While neither the "productive" nor "creative" imagination is specifically mentioned in Ricoeur's discussion of conscience, this account does not supplant the function Ricoeur has given to imagination in his other writings. Where in his earlier writings, suggests Wallace, "the imagination played the role of a sort of *praeparatio*

---

192 "Philosophical Hermeneutics and Biblical Hermeneutics," p. 101.

193 "Naming God," p. 217.

194 Ibid. For a discussion of the element of "risk" in Paul Ricoeur's theological hermeneutics see Mark I. Wallace, *The Second Naiveté: Barth, Ricoeur and the New Yale Theology* (Macon, 1990), pp. 27-30.

195 In *Figuring the Sacred*, pp. 262-275.

196 Ibid., p. 271.

197 Conscience is for Ricoeur the most "internalized expression of the responding self, which," he writes, "is internalized to the point of constituting itself as an autonomous instance in the ethical tradition issuing from the Enlightenment." In this essay Ricoeur is not interested in a polemic against conscience so understood, but in deploying its potential for understanding the "dialogic" structure of Christian existence. "The Summoned Subject in the School of the Narratives of the Prophetic Vocation," *Figuring the Sacred*, p. 271. Once again Ricoeur is working between the autonomy of conscience and the symbolics of faith, which is the "modern condition of the summoned self." Ibid, p. 274.

198 Ibid., p. 272.

evangelica for the reception of the divine word,"[199] now conscience is included in this anthropological possibility. In a lengthy footnote on Bultmann's situating of human conscience, Ricoeur notes that it plays a moral role, conscience is "always in relation with some demand marked with the distinction between good and evil."[200] The conscience adds an ethical component to the consideration of imaginative possibilities that are received into the intimacy of a responsive self. "The focus," in Ricoeur's more recent work, says Wallace, "is now on the subject's moral capacity to select which images of the imagination best enable the subject's care and concern for the other."[201]

Critique

In this section a critique is undertaken of Ricoeur's understanding of revelation and faith, both of which he reconceptualizes by means of a detour through poetics, that is, through hermeneutic reflection on the nature of writing and texts and the poetic function of biblical literature in its genric variety. By means of an "areligious sense of revelation," Ricoeur aims at restoring "the concept of biblical revelation to its full dignity."[202]

We undertake this critical reflection in terms of three headings. The first two, *The poetic nature of revelation* and *The mode of its appeal*, constitute an examination of Ricoeur's poetic rearticulation of revelation and the degree to which he is successful in restoring the "concept of biblical revelation to its full dignity."[203] In these sections an examination is undertaken of Ricoeur's proposal of the nature of revelation as the manifestation of a proposed world projected via poetic referencing "in front of the text" and the nature of this appeal, not to the will for obedience, but to the imagination as a possibility for a break and a new beginning. The third heading, *The hermeneutic constitution of faith*, is the one under which a critical examination of the corresponding appropriative dimension of Ricoeur's hermeneutic is taken up. Here the dialectic of disappropriation of the self as master, and appropriation of a new self as disciple of the text, is examined together with the underlying conviction that creative imagination and conscience are the anthropological sites, that is, the means of reception and discrimination, which revelation presupposes if it is not to remain extrinsic.

The central criticism raised against Ricoeur's polemic against revelation as inspiration, and his hermeneutic proposal for the restoration of the idea of revelation as manifestation and faith as hermeneutically constituted, is that it assigns primacy to a poetic description in the hermeneutic field and is over-attentive to an ethics of autonomy. Theological concepts are introduced into his account, but their constructive potential is supplanted, deferred, by means of a prior poetic and hermeneutic detour. This leads, on the one hand, to an under-appreciation of the theological density and

---

199 Ibid.
200 Ibid., p. 272, n. 13.
201 Wallace, "Introduction," in *Figuring the Sacred*, p. 29.
202 "Toward a Hermeneutic of the Idea of Revelation," p. 103.
203 Ibid., p. 104.

44   *Revelation, Holy Scripture and Church*

particularity of the confessional heritage of the Christian church for a constructive account of revelation and faith and, on the other hand, (1) to an account of revelation in which divine communicative action by means of Holy Scripture is made into the text's immanent capacity of projecting a possible world in which God is "implied" but is not the object, and (2) to an account of faith in which revelation is a non-violent appeal received by imagination and brokered by conscience. In contrast to Ricoeur's account, a theological rendering of divine communicative action by means of Holy Scripture and a corresponding account of human response are offered.

The poetic nature of revelation   Ricoeur's critical evaluation of ideas of revelation and attendant notions of inspiration that are derived by means of an exclusive consideration of prophetic discourse is problematic on a number of levels. First, Ricoeur fails to consider that "the attributions of speech to God pervade all the discourse genres of the Bible."[204] While Ricoeur does speak of the revelatory function of genric inter-animation or frictive animation between genres, the attribution of speech to God in the varieties of discourse contained in the Bible is hidden from view in his, at least on this account, hermetic taxonomy, and thus divine speech does not function as a unitive factor in his articulation of an idea of revelation. Ricoeur's rejection of ideas of inspiration as "insufflation," which he claims are psychologized accounts of the Holy Spirit (1) does not account for the diversity of constructive accounts of "inspiration"; and (2) abstracts inspiration out of the dogmatic context within which it is most properly understood. Sandra Schneiders notes, for example, that Aquinas' account of inspiration, while following the church Fathers' prophetic model of inspiration, was not a psychologized account of inspiration. For Aquinas, God was the true author of Scripture as primary efficient cause "without denying the real, though instrumental, secondary causality of the human writer."[205] What is more, through the history of the church, understandings of inspiration, which focused less on the relation between God and the authors of the Bible and more on "the quality of the text" produced, have been operative. Indeed, Schneiders maintains that most contemporary dogmatic depictions of inspiration are historical, communal and interactional accounts.[206] Ricoeur's polemic against revelation as inspiration seems focused on the "orthodox Protestant perversion of the Reformers' insights in terms of

---

204 Wolterstorff, *Divine Discourse*, p. 62.

205 Schneiders, *The Revelatory Text*, p. 47. Wolterstorff notes that Ricoeur operates with a "simplistic understanding of prophetic discourse." He demonstrates that, for example, "the diplomat can speak on behalf of the head of the state without the head of state whispering things in the diplomat's ear; why should it be any different in the case of the prophet? Why must supervision take this form?" *Divine Discourse*, p. 63.

206 Schneiders, *The Revelatory Text*, p. 47. Schneiders has in view the work of Karl Rahner, *Inspiration in the Bible*, 2nd rev. edn vol. 1 of *Quaestiones Disputatate*, trans. C. Henkey (New York, 1964); Paul Achtemeier, *The Inspiration of Scripture: Problems and Proposals* (Philadelphia, 1980); and Robert Gnuse, *The Authority of the Bible: Theories of Inspiration, Revelation and the Canon of Scripture* (New York, 1985). Gnuse explores theories of "social inspiration," pp. 50-62.

Revelation and Biblical Interpretation   45

a Spirit-dictation theory of biblical interpretation."[207] This leads, according to Mark Wallace, to a non-pneumatic hermeneutic in which the talk of the inner witness of the Holy Spirit is absent. However, perhaps the most significant difficulty with Ricoeur's analysis and rejection of inspiration as "insufflation" is the manner in which such an account is an abstraction of doctrines of inspiration from their place within a larger dogmatic field. An account of the Spirit's relation to biblical authors, the collection of biblical materials, their canonization and ongoing use as Holy Scripture within the community of faith in terms of "inspiration" is not reducible to "insufflation" or a psychologized rendering of the Spirit's activity. Theological concepts such as divine election, sanctification, providence and the economy of salvation very often serve as ancillary to and supportive of doctrines of the inspiration of Holy Scripture. Scripture is the Spirit-generated, preserved and sufficient witness to God's salvific movement in the life, death and resurrection of Jesus Christ. Abstracted out of this larger doctrinal constellation, "inspiration," as a consideration of the psychologized mechanics by which divine human intercourse took place in the past and was recorded as a *positum*, no longer functions as a way of speaking about the purpose of Holy Scripture in the ongoing reconciling activity of God.

In his movement toward a poetic reconceptualization of an idea of revelation, that can restore the biblical idea of revelation to its "full dignity," Ricoeur bypasses derivative understandings of revelation, bodies of dogmatic teaching imposed by the church Magisterium and, to a lesser degree, confessional statements, as "opaque" and "authoritarian." This amalgam of church teaching, held together with the originary confessions of faith under the rubric "truths of revelation," obscures from view the historical character of church doctrine, which is secondary and derivative to the discourse of faith. While Ricoeur properly regards the texts of the Bible as primary for any formulation or reformulation of an idea of revelation, and rightly resists the undifferentiated application of the term "revelation" to a variety of materials that are properly held in relations of sub- and super-ordination, he undervalues the constructive and instructive potential of the doctrinal heritage of the church for the present life of the people of God in their listening to Scripture. Ricoeur announces that "a hermeneutic of revelation must give priority to those modalities of discourse that are most originary within the language of a community of faith; consequently those expressions by means of which the members of that community first interpret their experience for themselves and for others."[208] And yet as Nicholas Wolterstorff comments:

> That is not what he does. He does not ask how the concept of revelation functions in the religious lives of Jews and Christians. Instead working *de facto* as a theologian of the Christian community with deep sympathies for Judaism, he looks for that concept of revelation which to his mind, best fits the Hebrew and Christian Bibles.[209]

---

207 Wallace, "The World of the Text," p. 11. Wallace maintains that Ricoeur's hesitation may be related to his desire not to mix genres—philosophical and theological—but, nevertheless, insists that Ricoeur might learn from Barth's hermeneutic at this point.

208 "Toward a Hermeneutic of the Idea of Revelation," p. 90.

209 Wolterstorff, *Divine Discourse*, p. 59.

46   *Revelation, Holy Scripture and Church*

In other words, Ricoeur flanks the doctrinal heritage of the church in order to develop an idea of revelation which is congruent with its operative sense within the church. And yet, where is the operative sense of the term "revelation" for the church to be reflected but in its confessional tradition?

Moreover, Ricoeur's application of the adjectives "authoritarian" and "opaque" function to set the originary confessions of faith in an almost hostile relation to the later doctrinal heritage of the church. This move obscures from view the positive role of creeds and confessions as "hermeneutical touchstones"[210] or "theological benchmarks"[211] for faithful reading of, and attentive listening to, Holy Scripture for the Gospel. David Yeago writes,

> [O]ne only has to look at the sermons, commentaries, and treatises of the Fathers, Aquinas, or Luther to see how seriously they took, for example, the Trinitarian and Christological doctrine as analyses of the logic of the scriptural discourse, formal descriptions of the apprehension of God *in* the texts, which then serve as guides to a faithful and attentive reading *of* the texts.[212]

As theological norms normed by the reading of Scripture, Trinitarian and Christological confessional reflected in the Nicene and Chaledonian Creeds, for example, are articulations of how to read the Bible in all of its variety in a manner that is conducive to what, or better, who the Bible is about. While Ricoeur is correct to imply that the Creeds do not absolve the present church from its primary responsibility to listen to the Gospel through attentive reading of Holy Scripture, he underplays the guidance and direction that creeds and confessions offer in this ongoing task. John Webster writes, "We may think of the creed as an aspect of the church's exegetical fellowship, of learning alongside the saints and doctors and martyrs how to give ear to the Gospel."[213]

Against the backdrop of his rejection of concepts of revelation, which are over-determined by a single genre and too distant from the primary expressions of faith in the Bible, Ricoeur offers a constructive account by means of a detour through the hermeneutics of a written text and a consideration of the poetic function of language. In the passage from speech to writing, texts are liberated from the world of their production, given shape through generic inscription and unfold a possible world in front of themselves, which is the proper object of textual interpretation. Understanding a text does not involve probing authorial intention behind the text, or dismantling structures within it. What is to be understood as the object of interpretation is the world toward which a text points, a possible world "in front of

---

210 Swinburne, *Revelation*, p.178. Swinburne writes; "The idea that the Bible could be interpreted naked, without a tradition of interpretation which clarified its meaning, is not intrinsically plausible and would not have appealed to many before the fifteenth century."

211 David Yeago, "The New Testament and the Nicene Dogma: A Contribution to the Recovery of Theological Exegesis," in Stephen Fowl (ed.), *The Theological Interpretation of Scripture: Classic and Contemporary Readings* (Oxford, 1997), p. 87.

212 Ibid.

213 John Webster, "Confession and Confessions," in Christopher Seitz (ed.), *Nicene Christianity: The Future for a New Ecumenism* (Grand Rapids, 2001), p. 125.

the text." What enables the proposal of a possible world across the whole field of biblical literature is the poetic function of language. Unlike scientific and ordinary discourse, biblical texts not only refer ostensively, but also in a poetic mode, to a possible world. By means of a suspension of first-order reference, biblical texts project a world to which we may belong through fictive re-description. This poetic function of language through which a possible world, and a correlative possible mode of being in the world, is projected is "a vehicle of revelation."[214] By means of poetics and hermeneutic reflection then, Ricoeur has gone behind contaminated concepts of revelation to the originary sources of faith to restore a concept of revelation which avoids the psychologized notion of "inspiration" by focusing on the "issue" of the texts. In the process revelation as "inspiration" is transposed to revelation as "manifestation."

In the next section on Scripture, a critical examination of Ricoeur's detour through the hermeneutics of a written text and a consideration of the poetic function of language is undertaken. In this final part of our critical review of Ricoeur's reconceptualization of the nature of revelation, the question of how his nuanced retrieval of "an areligious idea of revelation" which "restores the concept of biblical revelation to its full dignity" is related to God's communicative activity by means of the Bible is undertaken. Two questions are pertinent: (1) on Ricoeur's poetic reconceptualization of revelation, who or what reveals, that is, who or what is the agent of revelation?; and (2) what or who is revealed by means of the poetic function of language? On a robust account of revelation as inspiration, it is clear that revelation takes place by means of God's use of Scripture. Scripture becomes the Word of God.

> The Scriptures do not speak unless the Triune God through the Spirit's initiative makes the reader a real recipient of revelation. The Bible is not a static Word of God; it only becomes God's Word through our recognition of it as this Word by the inward work of the Spirit in our hearts and minds.[215]

On Ricoeur's modulation of revelation as "manifestation," by whose action does the Bible unfold its world before the reader? Ricoeur seems to ascribe "projective power" to the texts themselves so that by means of intergenric friction and the metamorphic power of religious language, possible worlds are projected which might be inhabited.[216] A recurrent emphasis in Ricoeur's overall corpus of writings, says Wallace, is "the power of religious language to metamorphize the world of the reader by opening new possibilities of being-in-the-world."[217] In this way, what was ascribed to the action of God the Holy Spirit is transposed on Ricoeur's manifestation model into a text or language-immanent feature. The revelatory capacity of the Bible

---

214 "Toward a Hermeneutic of the Idea of Revelation," p. 102.

215 Wallace, "The World of the Text," p. 11. Here Wallace describes the position of Karl Barth.

216 See for example, "Naming God," p. 223.

217 Wallace, "Introduction," in *Figuring the Sacred*, pp. 15-16.

48 *Revelation, Holy Scripture and Church*

is "agentless"[218] on this account; that is, it is granted self-generating independence from the action of God. Mark Wallace argues that Ricoeur's hermeneutic lacks a pneumatic dimension, and in a comparison with Barth's approach to Scripture interpretation maintains: "Barth's Calvinist attempt to correlate theological interpretation and God's Trinitarian life (interpretation is always guided by the Spirit's witness to God's self-disclosure in Christ) appears a more faithful appropriation of the Christian heritage on this theme than Ricoeur's relative inattention to the witness of the Spirit in biblical hermeneutics."[219]

In his discussions concerning what or who the Bible manifests, its poetic referent, the "issue" or the "thing" of the text, Ricoeur offers a variety of possibilities. Sometimes it is "God," as in his essay "Naming God," where God is the coordinating referent of all biblical genres. "God . . . is . . . the ultimate referent of these texts. God is in some manner implied by the issue of these texts, by the world—the biblical world—that these texts unfold."[220] At other times, the referent of the polyphonic ensemble of biblical texts is to "new being," which in the case of the Bible is "a new world, a new covenant, the kingdom of God, a new birth."[221] In other cases, Ricoeur asserts that in Jesus' preaching of the Kingdom of God, "God is named at the same time the kingdom is named."[222] One way of holding all of this discussion together would be to say that while God is the implicated subject of the Bible, what the Bible reveals, refers to, are possible ways of being that are congruent with the world disclosed in the Bible where God is central. God is implicated by the "issue" of the texts, but what is revealed is a "world we might inhabit."[223] Or as Ricoeur writes in his essay on revelation, "If the Bible may be said to be revealed this must refer to what it says, to the new being it unfolds before us."[224]

Here the question to be raised is the extent to which Ricoeur's account makes what is primary secondary, and what is secondary primary. In other words, especially given Ricoeur's interest in narrative,[225] would it not be more accurate to assert that

---

218 Wolterstorff, *Divine Discourse*, p. 62. Wolterstorff writes, "At the end of the discussion, God's speech has entirely disappeared from view, completely absorbed by manifestation; and it is not even clear that the manifestation brought to speech in biblical discourse is God's self-manifestation, as opposed to agentless manifestation." See also Dan Stiver, *Theology After Ricoeur: New Directions in Hermeneutical Theology* (Louisville, 2001), pp. 133-134.

219 Wallace, "The World of the Text," p. 12. See also Fodor, *Christian Hermeneutics*, p. 302. Fodor asks rhetorically: "In what sense does describing the Bible as a poetic, metaphorical text significantly illumine its function as the Word of God?" See also Eberhard Jüngel, *God as the Mystery of the World*, trans. Darrell L. Guder (Grand Rapids, 1983), p. 158. Jüngel writes, "Revelation means only that God is the unconditional subject of himself and as such is accessible only because and to the extent that he makes himself accessible. Apart from the access he himself *affords*, no thinking will ever find its way to God."

220 "Naming God," p. 221.

221 See "Philosophical Hermeneutics and Biblical Hermeneutics," p. 96.

222 "Naming God," p. 228.

223 Ibid., p. 223.

224 "Toward a Hermeneutic of the Idea of Revelation," p. 104.

225 See "The Bible and the Imagination," p. 51 where Ricoeur notes the exceptional role of narratives in the broad sweep of the biblical story. See also *Oneself as Another*, p. 143.

Revelation and Biblical Interpretation 49

the Bible refers to God; that is, it functions primarily to narrate the identity of God and tells us what Christ has done in ordinary descriptive language, and that forms of life congruent with this overarching story are in "some manner implied" by the nature and action of God therein described? While Ricoeur recognizes the overarching narrative of Scripture, his treatment of narrative, as Placher notes, "consistently focuses on the stories of parables."[226] By taking this tack, Ricoeur is able to emphasize the disruptive character of narrative and highlight poetic second-order extravagant referencing as of first order importance; for parable employs depiction of everyday experience which it transforms into a means of inviting readers to think of life in new ways. However, as Hans Frei notes:

> The marvel or miracle of at least some of the parables is not that their ordinary and everyday referential descriptions are subverted by a metaphorical extravagance that provides us and them with a new secondary referent (which is what Professor Ricoeur suggests when that reference becomes transcendence or "a mode-of-being-in-the world") but rather the reverse, namely the reign of the One is who beyond all description, beyond metaphorical thrusts, is depicted fitly by ordinary, realistic, literally referential language: "The Kingdom of heaven is like" . . . It does not say unlike.[227]

This is not to suggest that second-order referencing by means of metaphorical extravagance is absent from parable; rather it is to make the case that it is "subordinate to, and in the service of, literal, ordinary language within the text."[228] Moreover, as Placher shows,[229] Ricoeur's concentration on parables as instances of poetic second-order referencing, apart from their subordinate place in the overarching narrative of Scripture in which God is referent and subject matter, takes Ricoeur in the direction of affirming that the subject matter of the Bible, its referent, is human experience.

> What religious language does is to redescribe; what it redescribes is *human experience*. In this sense we must say that the ultimate referent of the parables, proverbs, and eschatological sayings is not the kingdom of God, but human reality in its wholeness . . . Religious language discloses the religious dimension of *common* human experience.[230]

---

226 William Placher, "Paul Ricoeur and Postliberal Theology: A Conflict of Interpretations?," *Modern Theology*, 4/1 (1987): 42.

227 Hans Frei, "Conflicts in Interpretation: Resolution, Armistice, or Coexistence?," in George Hunsinger and William C. Placher (eds), *Theology and Narrative: Selected Essays*, (New York, 1993), p. 165.

228 Ibid. Placher makes the objection that this account of the parables "seems to me inadequate both to the meaning of the narratives themselves and to the accounts of theological language Ricoeur himself offers elsewhere." Placher's criticism is particularly aimed at the way Ricoeur handles questions of reference with respect to biblical narrative. Placher, "Paul Ricoeur and Postliberal Theology," p. 43.

229 Ibid. Placher notes that for Ricoeur parables are poetic texts, and poetry unlike history "proceeds directly to the universal." However, he asks, "when we turn to other biblical narratives—do the stories of David or Jesus or Paul mean to tell only what a certain type of man would probably or necessarily do?"

230 Ricoeur, "Biblical Hermeneutics," pp. 127-128.

In this citation, Ricoeur seems to lean in the direction of making human wholeness, not naming God, the ultimate reference of biblical language.[231] However, the larger context of parables, within the literary frame of a Gospel's depiction of the identity of Jesus, offers a counterpoint to such a proposal concerning the subject matter or reference of parables. Frei maintains that the parables are held in the Gospels such that they are involved, although not without residue, "in the identification of Jesus, an ordinary man who was the presence of God."[232] Jesus chooses parables as a means of self-identification or concealment. And thus, although one might speak of the second-order reference of a parable, it would be in the service of its first-order literal sense. Frei notes that this implies a certain directionality to interpretation: "My suggestion is that . . . one moves better from the self-identification of Jesus through the Passion and Resurrection stories toward the parables rather than the other way around."[233]

The mode of appeal   While Ricoeur recognizes a "difference in altitude between the word that teaches with authority and the one that responds with acknowledgement"[234] and maintains a sense of human dependence on an eternal word or the prior love of God, his account of the nature of the appeal of revelation seems insufficiently attentive to the theological dynamics of the interpretative field.

In the first instance, Ricoeur misidentifies, at least on a Reformation view, the nature of the appeal of revelation. Revelation is not only an appeal to the human will for obedience, but also, as the vivifying word of the living God speaking through Holy Scripture, the voice that enables obedience. Barth asks, "How does obedience to the Word of God in Holy Scripture arise? The question is analogous to the basic question: how is the revelation of the Triune God effected?" He answers, "objectively by the incarnation of the divine Word in Jesus Christ and subjectively by the outpouring of the Holy Spirit of God."[235] Or in Luther; "knowledge of Christ and of faith is not a human work but utterly a divine gift . . .The sort of doctrine which reveals the Son of God is revealed first by the external Word and then inwardly through the Spirit."[236] And finally in a contemporary Reformed account: "the Bible as text is the *viva vox Dei* addressing the people of God and generating faith and

---

231 Vanhoozer, *Biblical Narrative in the Philosophy of Paul Ricoeur*, p. 122. Vanhoozer writes: "It would be ironic indeed if Ricoeur, who so painstakingly attends to the differences between various forms of biblical discourse, ultimately fails to distinguish between God and man." Ibid.

232 Frei, "Conflicts in Interpretation," p. 165.

233 Ibid., pp. 165-166. Frei also makes the point that it is the literal sense of the Bible that has a "puzzling but firm relationship to a truth" and that in the Christian confession of divine grace "the truth is such that the text is sufficient." Ibid., p. 166.

234 Ricoeur, *Thinking Biblically*, p. xvii.

235 Barth, *Church Dogmatics*, 1/2: 538.

236 Martin Luther, in Jaroslav Pelikan and Helmut Lehmann (gen. eds), *Luther's Works*, vol. 26: *Lectures on Galatians 1535, Chapters 1-4*, trans. Jaroslav Pelikan (St Louis, 1963), p. 72.

obedience."[237] While there is a human subject to which revelation is addressed, the theologically crucial point is that the hearer is enabled in revelation *to receive* from God *what* God has to bestow.[238] Given the gracious character of Divine speaking and acting by means of Holy Scripture, it would be inaccurate to regard revelation as a "heteronomous appeal" that threatens human integrity since it is the act of God by means of which the human subject is constituted as a glad hearer of the Word in the economy of grace.

Ricoeur's attempt to refocus the appeal of revelation in terms of theonomy, "as a summons to loving obedience" which "engenders autonomy, understood as the summons to responsibility,"[239] is likewise theologically inadequate. For while the motivation and ability to take up and enact the summons to loving obedience is rooted in the prior love of God, "a certain founding passivity,"[240] the present possibility of loving obedience is grounded in "active acceptance of responsibility."[241] God's prior love summons to rather than enables human acceptance of moral responsibility. Moreover, Ricoeur's emphasis on the faculty of the imagination which "opens itself" to revelation, tends toward a Pelagian account of human capacity and freedom. If Luther could speak of the "Bondage of the Will" apart from vivifying grace, on Ricoeur's transposition, it would be licit to ask whether the imagination can "open itself" to possible modes of being in the world apart from vivifying grace. Vanhoozer writes, "[A]s the Reformers saw long before, Word and Spirit together are the necessary and sufficient conditions for new life, for the possibility of true freedom. A theological analysis of Ricoeur's biblical hermeneutics will therefore inquire into the role played by the Holy Spirit in effecting Christian transformation . . ."[242]

The hermeneutic constitution of faith

> Theologians cannot just adopt Ricoeur's anthropology as it is, because to this point he omits another dimension of the self as another, the other being God or the spiritual self.[243]

Whereas for James Barr the cumulative human tradition about God always stands antecedent to and is the condition for the possibility of receiving further revelation

---

237 John Webster, "Hermeneutics in Modern Theology: Some Doctrinal Reflections," *Scottish Journal of Theology*, 51/3 (1998): 317.

238 On the character of revelation as gift and its reception as enabled see Placher, *The Domestication of Transcendence*, pp. 185-186; Jüngel, *God as the Mystery of the World*, p. 158; and Kathryn Tanner, *Theories of Culture: A New Agenda for Theology* (Minneapolis, 1997), p. 117. Tanner notes that in Barth the common-sense notion that people only receive what they are capable of receiving is "radically revised." For Barth, "in the case of the reception of divine grace" the principle holds only if "God supplies us with new capacities."

239 Ricoeur, "Thou Shalt Not Kill: A Loving Obedience," p. 133.

240 Ibid.

241 Ibid., pp. 133-134.

242 Vanhoozer, *Biblical Narrative in the Philosophy of Paul Ricoeur*, p. 227. See also p. 233 where Vanhoozer suggests that on Ricoeur's account the problematic of revelation's appeal is transposed from "a will that is bound" to a "forgetful imagination."

243 Stiver, *Theology after Ricoeur*, p. 186.

52   *Revelation, Holy Scripture and Church*

from God, in the writings of Paul Ricoeur, human subjectivity performs the same function. Human imagination and conscience, as native capacities, logically precede the Divine Word and are, as such, the anthropological conditions, "a sort of *praeparatio evangelica*," for the possibility of the reception and appropriation of the *viva vox Dei*. The central theological difficulty with this account is that the derivative and formed or created status of imagination and conscience in encounter with the prevenient Word of God are almost hidden from view. In other words, the achievement of salvation tends toward synergism in which imagination receives, and conscience brokers, the reconciling Word of God spoken in Jesus Christ. Two points are worth making here. The first relates to Ricoeur's appropriation of Barth's point regarding the subject as auditor, not master, of a language larger than itself. Ricoeur's appropriation takes a specific theological point in Barth and renders it generic with respect to the power of texts to invite the self to divestment. For Barth, "the power of the revelation of the salvation accomplished for each and all on Golgotha"[244] is singular, not to be confused with other powers, especially not with human capacity or the human ability to open our hearts to it. "The opening of men for Jesus Christ and their own being in him—is a miraculous work."[245] Moreover, this miraculous work is formative, creative of human capacity.

> Where it is at work, it always means light for the mind too, so that the eyes and ears and understanding are used as they have never been used before. The man at whom it is at work becomes a scholar. He begins to learn and think. He *acquires* a conscience, i.e., he becomes *consciens*, one who knows with God.[246]

Revelation, for Barth, establishes its own beachhead; that is, revelation is miraculously creative of the human faculties that correspond "to the ways and works of Father, Son and Holy Spirit."[247]

The second point worth exploring is Ricoeur's contention that for St Paul any appeal to the self from an external voice engages a self already in internal dialogue with conscience. This conversant "I" must be presupposed in any appropriation of an external word, like justification by faith, as that onto which or into which it is grafted. Conscience is the moral faculty by means of which an external word addressed to the self is evaluated. Three exegetical/theological difficulties arise on this view of the matter.

The first is that, Bultmann's exegesis, on which Ricoeur draws for his understanding of *syneidesis* as a faculty of moral direction, is open to serious question. Paul's use

---

244 Barth, *Church Dogmatics*, 4/2: 314.

245 Ibid. p. 309.

246 Ibid., p. 313. My emphasis. Thiemann articulates a sense of how imagination might function for Barth in the work of theology. He notes that, for Barth, theology is a hermeneutical procedure and that knowledge of God is indirect and thus that imagination is required for constructive theology. However, Thiemann also notes that Barth prefers to speak of theology, always under the control of the biblical narrative, as an act of obedience. Ronald F. Thiemann, "Revelation and Imaginative Construction," *Journal of Religion*, 61/3 (July, 1981): 263.

247 John Webster, "God and Conscience," *Calvin Theological Journal*, 33/1 (April, 1998): 108.

of *syneidesis* from the Greco-Roman world involved the sense of self-awareness in which "one knows one has done something wrong."[248] However, in medieval and modern usage this minimalist understanding of conscience has been inflated to "the whole faculty of moral understanding and self-direction."[249] Oliver O'Donovan writes: "But nowhere in the New Testament (nor indeed in the classical world as a whole until a later period) does *syneidesis* mean a faculty of *moral direction*."[250]

The second, as Melanchthon noted, is that the Word of justification by faith addressed to the human subject can only ever be appropriated by a "shocked conscience."[251] Melanchthon's point is that natural conscience, like natural reason, will only ever find the gift of salvation an offense. The self in conversation with conscience cannot make a judgment that leads to the appropriation of the righteousness of God in Jesus Christ.

And third, in Ricoeur's proposal with respect to conscience, it is abstracted from the history of salvation. He seems to propose that conscience is a region of human subjectivity that has its own integrity outside the story of creation, fall and redemption. However, as Webster notes, "Conscience is an aspect of our fellowship with this God; it is what it is in the history of that fellowship, destroyed by human wickedness and restored by divine mercy."[252] Paul's discussion of conscience must be set within the purview of God's communicative action where conscience is what it is in relation to the new creation (2 Cor. 5:17), the new self in the likeness of God created in righteousness and holiness (Eph. 4:24), wrought in Jesus Christ. Luther's remarks on conscience set it within the context of salvation. He speaks of conscience and sin as "the two devils who plague us. But Christ has conquered these two monsters and trodden them underfoot both in this age and in the age to come." Thus those who receive passive righteousness as a gift by faith have a conscience that is "reigned" over and "preserved" by Christ, "the Son of God, the King of peace and righteousness, the sweet Saviour and Mediator."[253]

Hans Frei: Apologetics, Christology and Anthropology

Hans Frei's does not offer a constructive dogmatic discussion of the doctrine of revelation *per se*. While his doctoral thesis was an engagement with the development of Barth's doctrine of revelation between 1909 and 1922 and most of the corpus of his writings contains historical or critical accounts of the same doctrine, the expression of his own position on revelation is, as in the thesis, usually implicit in

---

248 Oliver O'Donovan, *Resurrection and Moral Order: An Outline for Evangelical Ethics* (Grand Rapids, 1986), p. 114.

249 Ibid.

250 Ibid., p. 115. O'Donovan's treatment of conscience and autonomy can be found in ibid., pp. 114-120. The biblical material in Paul that O'Donovan surveys on conscience closely parallels that brought forward by Ricoeur. Compare Ricoeur, "The Summoned Subject," p. 272, n. 13.

251 See Berkhof, *The Christian Faith*, p. 442.

252 Webster, "God and Conscience," p. 116.

253 *Luther's Works*, vol. 26, *Lectures on Galatians*, pp. 11, 26.

54   *Revelation, Holy Scripture and Church*

a historical-descriptive or polemic context. Moreover, when he raises the doctrine in ways that tend toward a constructive cast, he does so with reticence about the term;[254] a reticence suggestive that, for him, a certain sort of doctrine of revelation may have run its course after "more than two and a half centuries of preeminence."[255] However, while not without its risks,[256] a retrieval of the doctrine of revelation, implied in Frei's historical, analytical and constructive works, can be discerned.

Our exposition proceeds by way of an overview of the shape the doctrine of revelation acquired in the eighteenth and nineteenth centuries, which became definitive for the modern period. Frei maintains that the modern doctrine of revelation become situated within a theological method that was apologetic in aim, anthropological in organizing principle and Christological in content. These three features are related in the following manner. By means of a prior heavily theorized account of the human condition, the meaningfulness or need of revelation in Jesus Christ is demonstrated such that the object of theological depiction is the "faith relationship." Frei argues that such an approach is not congruent with the character of the Gospels' depiction of Jesus Christ. In aesthetic or realistic, history-like, narrative, the mode of depiction is "ascriptive literal." This means that the portrait of Jesus offered is not amenable to Procrustean anthropological schemes, which distort and dissolve Jesus into the scheme by which his significance is achieved. The Jesus depicted in the Gospels is this person, and not everyone in general or no one in particular. He is unsubstitutably rendered through the interaction of character and circumstance in a narrative sequence. Reading the Gospels in the ascriptive literal mode then, Jesus' meaningfulness to the human subject comes not by way of perceived need or receptive anthropological constitution, but by way of who Jesus is, his identity as the Risen Saviour. Later, Frei moves to embedded church practice to achieve the same result. He claims that working on analogy with the social anthropologist, one can observe within the Christian church a consensus on ascriptive literal reading of the Gospels and the rest of the Bible in relation to them. The result of this careful attention to the kind of literature present in the Gospels and the embedded reading practices of the church is Frei's reconfiguration of theological method. On his articulation of the matter, theology is *dogmatic in aim*—it begins from the actuality of revelation and proceeds descriptively, *Anselmian in method*—where it employs

---

254 See Hans Frei, *The Identity of Jesus Christ: The Hermeneutical Bases of Dogmatic Theology* (Philadelphia, 1975), pp. vii-viii: "I agree with the recently emerged consensus among a good many theologians that "revelation" is not a wholly unambiguous or satisfactory central concept for stating what Christianity is all about."

255 Hans Frei, *The Eclipse of Biblical Narrative: A Study in Eighteenth and Nineteenth Century Hermeneutics* (New Haven, 1974), p. 52. See also Hans Frei, "Remarks in Connection with a Theological Proposal," *Theology and Narrative*, pp. 27, 29 and "Karl Barth: Theologian," in *Theology and Narrative*, pp. 174-175.

256 See Mike Higton's negative evaluation of Marguerite Abdul-Masih's attempt to articulate Frei's understanding of revelation by implication in his review of her book: *Edward Schillebeeckx and Hans Frei: A Conversation on Method and Christology, Modern Theology*, 19/4 (October, 2003): 590-592. Higton maintains that Abdul-Masih, especially in her use of the Frei thesis, confuses Frei's own position on revelation with Frei's description of Barth's views. Ibid., p. 591.

Revelation and Biblical Interpretation   55

conceptual schemes it does so on an *ad hoc* basis and in subordination to the logic or grammar of faith, and *Christological in content*—however, unlike liberal theology, it moves from *Christus extra nos* (idenity) to *Christus pro et en nobis* (presence), not the other way around.

In the sympathetic critique that follows, an examination of Frei's understanding of the relationship between the "literal reading" of the Gospels and revelation is undertaken. The structure of the critique follows that of the exposition—the aim, method and content of theology. The central criticism of Frei throughout is that a dogmatic description of the illuminating work of the Holy Spirit in relation to the scriptural witness, especially at the level of its meaning (perspicuity), does not consistently inform his hermeneutic proposal. Whether he warrants his theological approach (and the accompanying mode of Scripture interpretation) by appeal to literary genre or communal practice, he so consistently focuses on creaturely action in construing the interpretative field that the illumination of Scripture and the formation of faith by the Holy Spirit is often hidden from view or simply remains tacit in his hermeneutic. In the argument that follows, a sideways glance at Frei's appropriation of Barth's biblical/theological hermeneutic is undertaken, since this throws into relief Frei's failure to conceive of literal reading as a human act dependent on the illumining grace of the Holy Spirit.

The Birth and Shape of Modern Doctrines of Revelation

Eighteenth-century disputes with Deism, according to Frei, lead to the marshalling of external evidence to establish the empirical and rational credibility of biblical accounts against skeptical challenges. This apologetic enterprise in both England and Germany was centered on a defense of the Gospel narratives and "the claims about unique historical revelation, in particular that Jesus was the Messiah."[257] The feature of this period which Frei finds definitive for the modern liberal doctrine of revelation is the dominant strategy by which the positivity of revelation is maintained. In other words, Frei is chiefly interested in how this period comes to articulate the manner in which salvation depends on the relation between *what* Jesus taught and did and *that* he taught and did it. When the direct ostensive reading of the Gospel narratives is thrown into question by skeptical historical analysis, Christian apologists and mediating theologians increasingly turned to some aspect of Jesus' inwardness (often of a moral sort) or personal character to retain a measure of relational positivity.[258]

In his historical account of the development and shape of modern doctrines of revelation, Frei maintains that while its tenor has been largely apologetic in aim and Christological in doctrinal content, the variable factor, which came into focus in the nineteen century, is deployment of an analysis of human existence. While Frei maintains that the organizing principle of Christian, predominately Protestant, doctrines of revelation has been anthropological for three hundred years, this

---

257 *The Eclipse of Biblical Narrative*, p. 57.
258 Ibid., p. 58.

56   *Revelation, Holy Scripture and Church*

feature acquired its definitive shape in the early nineteenth century.[259] In post-Kantian religious theory, with its strict division of knowledge into its theoretical and practical functions, and more importantly, with the change of the scope of inquiry from *that* which is known to the subjective structures or conditions for knowing, a corresponding shift was undertaken in accounts of revelation. The positivity of revelation is no longer focused on metaphysical definitions of the person of Christ, on the *that* of Jesus as Messiah, for this would be to push in the direction of knowledge of things in themselves and, at least on Schleiermacher's view, lead to "idle speculation."[260] Rather, the focus is deflected toward the work and teachings of Christ and their relation to appropriation, the feeling of absolute dependence, in human consciousness. "Christ *extra nos* must be seen as *Christus pro et in nobis*."[261] This movement toward and in human subjectivity is revelation; post-Kantian theological accounts of its efficacy, which hold together "temporal positivity" and "moral or self-conscious presence" usually result in dogmatic constructions that unite the work of Christ and the Spirit "at the level of immanence."[262] Schleiermacher more than anyone else typifies this early-nineteenth-century turn toward the subject in theology. "[H]e sought to develop" writes Frei, "a principle of mediation in which the epistemic and ontic gulf between the finite and the infinite would be transcended."[263] Schleiermacher accomplishes this feat by means of the category of consciousness, a constant "in which the togetherness of God and man could be posited and assumed."[264] On his view, God-consciousness and self-consciousness in relation to God are given together in immediate relation in human subjectivity.

It will be useful to conclude Frei's exposition of Schleiermacher with an account of how Scripture is implicated in this view. Frei writes: "The New Testament is simply an authoritative or normative expression of the pious Christian self-consciousness of the first Christians, and indirectly the self-communication of the perfect God consciousness of Jesus Christ through that derived communal self-consciousness before, within, and after Scripture."[265]

Three features of this construal are particularly important. Schleiermacher treats Scripture under his doctrine of the church. It is a permanent feature of the church in its existence in the world. "Scripture is part of that larger institutionalized complex which is the Christian church"[266] and it functions in a correlative mode to hold present self-description accountable to the experience, which has been a part of the

---

259 See "Remarks in Connection with a Theological Proposal," pp. 27-28; Hans Frei, *Types of Christian Theology*, George Hunsinger and William Placher (eds) (New Haven, 1992), p. 8; and "Niebuhr's Theological Background," in Paul Ramsey (ed.), *Faith and Ethics: The Theology of H. Richard Niebuhr* (New York, 1957), p. 33.

260 "Niebuhr's Theological Background," p. 38.

261 "Remarks in Connection with a Theological Proposal," p. 29. See also *The Eclipse of Biblical Narrative*, p. 283; "Niebuhr's Theological Background," pp. 32-40; and *Types of Christian Theology*, p. 74.

262 "Remarks in Connection with a Theological Proposal," p. 29.

263 "Niebuhr's Theological Background," p. 36.

264 Ibid., p. 39.

265 *Types of Christian Theology*, p. 65.

266 Ibid.

Revelation and Biblical Interpretation 57

Christian community from the beginning. Second, Schleiermacher's understanding of the role of Scripture in revelation is Christocentric. It is the incarnate Word that is experienced in the church and in Christian consciousness and "the person described in the Gospels [is] taken as a source of historical information."[267] And finally, this Gospel-based understanding of Jesus functions in the corporate life of the church redemptively. "In this corporate life," says Schleiermacher, "which goes back to the influence of Jesus, redemption is effected by him through the communication of his sinless perfection."[268] The change in human consciousness, the engenderment of the feeling of absolute dependence on God, or God-consciousness, is wrought individually or communally through the one who, "had steady, unclouded God-consciousness throughout his life—as we might say, tempted but never turned."[269] While the feeling of absolute dependence is characteristic of all religions and thus provides a kind of unity of religion in a common experience, it is expressed most clearly in Christian faith.[270] Testimony to Jesus of Nazareth, as the expression of earliest Christian experience of the change made in others, demonstrates that he is the "indispensable condition" for turning from sin to grace.

To sum up: on Frei's view, doctrines of revelation from the eighteenth century have been formulated (1) with an apologetic aim, (2) a Christological content, and (3) from the nineteenth century, by means of an anthropological organizing (correlating) principle. "Theology has to validate the possibility and, hence, the meaning of Christian claims concerning the shape of human existence and the divine relation to it."[271] Because post-Kantian Protestant theology is set within these parameters, rather than speaking of God, it tends to focus on the "faith relationship" between human beings and God under a (common ground) depiction of human existence or one sort or another.[272] Frei writes:

> The common heritage of neo-orthodox and liberal theologians—from their Protestant origins, as they saw it . . .—is that it is not God "in himself" but only "God revealed," or rather our relation with God, that is the object of our communion with God. "Faith" not only removes into a special, self-based kind of insight, but gradually, by a kind of merciless Kantian or perhaps Fichtean logic, is deconstructed into a totally originative human construction, in which the moment of divine revelation is no more than a self-

---

267 Ibid., p. 67. Frei writes, "Schleiermacher once declared passionately that he wished to have his whole theology guided by the one text that was most important to him, John 1:14."

268 Friedrich Schleiermacher, *The Christian Faith*, trans. H.R. Mackintosh and J.S. Stewart (Edinburgh, 1928), p. 361. Cited in *Types of Christian Theology*, p. 75.

269 *Types of Christian Theology*, p. 75.

270 Ibid., p. 66. Frei writes that for Schleiermacher, "the essence of Christianity is determined by . . . the sense of absolute dependence as the universal form underlying every positive religion and making all positive religions individually and on a common scale susceptible to systematic analysis." See also Stiver, *Theology after Ricoeur*, pp. 85-86. Compare Frei's own view in *Types of Christian Theology*, p. 12, where he notes that Christianity is first of all a "religion."

271 "Remarks in Connection with a Theological Proposal," p. 30.

272 Ibid. See also *The Eclipse of Biblical Narrative*, p. 129 and *The Identity of Jesus Christ*, p. viii.

58 *Revelation, Holy Scripture and Church*

positing move of the constructive intellectual capacity, in which the mind imagines or sets over against itself a transcendent "other" for its own regulating and constructing purposes.[273]

Critique of Liberalism

In this section, an exposition of the central thrust of Frei's critique of the dominant "liberal" construal of the theological task and its implications for the doctrine of revelation is undertaken. Following this overview, we turn to Frei's constructive proposal for conceiving the work of theology and observe how and to what degree an understanding of revelation is operative on its terms. Frei's critique of hermeneutic and theological liberalism takes place on both a formal literary and substantive doctrinal level. On the formal level, Frei makes the point that through the interposition of heavily theorized accounts of the human condition, interpretations of the Bible become arbitrary. The question of religious significance, and the anthropological Procrustean bed to which it accumulates, demean what the text actually says and what it is about.[274] "The story seems to mean whatever you want . . . depending on what perspective or modern view of man you happen to come from as you read the story and want to find substantiated there."[275] Frei's critique of the strategy of theological liberalism centers, at least in his early work, on a literary consideration; namely, that "aesthetic" or "quasi-aesthetic" texts, what he will call "realistic narratives," bear a constancy of meaning. "The sense of a story . . . is in the final analysis that of reading the story itself."[276] A normative interpretation of such texts, in which the meaning is constant, regardless of interpretative perspective, is possible. The implication for biblical hermeneutics is that one need not come to reading and interpreting the Bible so heavily armed, indeed to do so is to "overwhelm exegesis and subject matter."[277]

The theologically substantive criticism implicated in this formal move is that when an independent account of human existence sets the terms of engagement for his significance, the specificity of Jesus of Nazareth, *Christ extra nos*, is dissolved into anthropology:[278] "Theologically, Christology becomes a function of an independently generated soteriology. That is, an analysis of the human situation shapes the understanding of what salvation can mean, and then Jesus Christ is provided

---

273 Hans Frei, "H. Richard Niebuhr on History, Church and Nation," in *Theology and Narrative*, pp. 223-224.

274 *The Identity of Jesus Christ*, pp. xvi-xvii.

275 "Remarks in Connection with a Theological Proposal," p. 32.

276 *The Identity of Jesus Christ*, p. xv. "In realistic narratives the depiction coincides with what it is about." Ibid., p. xvi.

277 Ibid., p. xvi.

278 Indeed Frei maintains that where the faith relationship (the correlated movement of Christ toward us and we toward Christ under an anthropological salvation scheme) becomes the primary object of theological interest, the result is "the ultimate dissolution of both our own presence and his." Ibid., p. 86. Compare "Remarks in Connection with a Theological Proposal," p. 29.

Revelation and Biblical Interpretation 59

as the answer to the soteriological question."[279] In this way, the specificity, or as Frei says, the identity of Jesus becomes a mere vessel filled with anthropological content. When Frei draws his formal literary observation about aesthetic texts and realistic narrative into this doctrinal sphere, he makes the point that the Gospels, when read in keeping with their genric nature as "realistic narrative" resist this reading strategy. Frei maintains (1) that realistic narratives, by means of a capacity particular to them—their history-likeness—render their own world through the interaction of character and circumstance,[280] such that extraneous independent construals of the hermeneutic situation are not required to garner—indeed they disrupt—textual meaning; and (2) that realistic narrative does so in the "ascriptive" rather than "descriptive" mode.

It is this last point that is crucial to Frei's polemic against liberal anthropocentricism. "Ascriptive" reading, which is the convention most appropriate to the non-symbolic, "literal" character of realistic narrative, will not allow that the Gospel rendering of Jesus' life, death and resurrection should be read as a cipher for human experience. Frei maintains that ascriptive reading entails: "That 'Jesus'—not someone else or nobody in particular—is the subject, the agent and patient of these stories . . . and the descriptions of events, sayings, personal qualities, and so forth, become literal by being firmly predicated of him."[281] This firm sense of the "ascriptive literalism" of the Gospels by which the "unsubstitutable identity"[282] of Jesus is rendered is a sort of Occam's razor in Frei's evaluation of mythic and literary Christ figures in *The Identity of Jesus Christ*. Unlike the mythical Savior figure, who bears striking resemblance to the liberal Christ,[283] Jesus is not a generalized figure who can be represented by any number of stories. He and the story that depicts him are singular and non-transferable. Moreover, unlike literary "Christ figures," Jesus' identity, as depicted in the Gospels, is not a member of a class of instances found across a species of novel-like stories. Frei concludes, "The identity of the Christian Saviour is revealed completely by the story of Jesus in the Gospels and by none other."[284]

---

279 Charles Campbell, *Preaching Jesus: New Directions for Homiletics in Hans Frei's Postliberal Theology* (Grand Rapids, 1997), p. 39.

280 See *The Eclipse of Biblical Narrative*, pp. 13-14. "In all these respects—inseparability of subject matter from its depiction or cumulative rendering, literal rather than symbolic quality of the human subject and his social context, mutual rendering of character, circumstance, and their interaction—a realistic narrative is like a historical account." Ibid., p. 14.

281 Hans Frei, "The 'Literal' Reading of Biblical Narrative," in *Theology and Narrative*, pp. 122-123. See also *Types of Christian Theology*, pp. 5, 84-91, 125, 140-143. Frei makes the point that Jesus' identity is not illustrated by his story but constituted by it. Ibid., p. 142.

282 By unsubstitutable identity Frei points to the exclusiveness with which the Gospels refer certain words, sufferings and accomplishments to Jesus. The Gospel writers allow no human substitute for Jesus, he is primary and he bestows identity on the saviour figure. *The Identity of Jesus Christ*, p. 60.

283 George Hunsinger makes the point that Frei's rejection of the mythic Christ is correlated with his rejection of the Liberal Christ. "Afterword: Hans Frei as Theologian," in *Theology and Narrative*, p. 239. See *The Identity of Jesus Christ*, pp. xi-xii, 86-87, 89-90, and explicitly on pp. 98-101. Hunsinger might have drawn on Frei's treatment of myth in *The Eclipse of Biblical Narrative*, pp. 233-244 to provide further evidence of this connection.

284 *The Identity of Jesus Christ*, p. 88.

60 *Revelation, Holy Scripture and Church*

Constructive Proposal

Frei's polemic against liberal symbolic, or at least non-literal readings of the Bible, proceeds initially from his formal observation regarding the ascriptive literalism of realistic narrative. The grounds by which ascriptively literal reading is warranted will shift beginning with "Theology and the Interpretation of Narrative" and "The 'Literal' Reading of Biblical Narrative" in which he maintains that such reading is grounded in the preponderance of church practice. Whether or not this background shift affects his positive theological proposal regarding revelation and its relation to Holy Scripture will be a subject of the critique that follows this exposition. Within this section, an attempt is made to offer a sympathetic account of his constructive alternative to liberal anthropocentrism and its implications for the relationship between a doctrine of revelation and Holy Scripture.

Charles Campbell writes, "In terms of the earlier categories—aim, method and content—Frei's theology may be described in contrast to liberal theology, as having a dogmatic aim, an Anselmian method, and a Christological content."[285] Following Barth,[286] and Christological instincts *formally* expressed, Frei proposes (1) that theologians work from the actuality of revelation, not toward the possibility of its meaningfulness to the human condition; and, therefore (2) that theologians work descriptively in keeping with the ascriptively literal narratives of the Gospels. On Frei's account it is not the business of Christian theology to make an apologetic case for the meaningfulness of divine grace to "one's own autonomous life quest."[287] Indeed, when understanding Christianity is construed as providing an account of the how one comes to believe, that is, of the conjunction of divine grace and its meaningfulness to one's life under some general depiction of the human condition, the content of faith is subverted to an account of religious significance.[288] Reading the Gospel narratives of the life, death and resurrection of Jesus, with as little conceptual baggage as possible, is however "religiously significant." Frei writes; "Dogmatically, belief that Jesus is Lord, grounded in believing Jesus' death and resurrection, is itself the explanation for the enablement of (and so mirrored in) a life of faith, hope and love."[289] In this statement Frei's overall procedure in *The Identity of Jesus Christ* is reflected; the movement is not from the question "how is Christ present?" to "who is Jesus Christ?" Interpreting in this fashion leads to the dissolution of both the identity of Jesus and the human subject in a "faith relationship." If however, maintains Frei, one proceeds descriptively, that is, from identity to presence, respective identities are held intact without evaporating the revelatory and salvific significance for the human subject of the one identified as Savior in the ascriptively literal Gospel depiction of him.

---

285 Campbell, *Preaching Jesus*, p. 44.

286 See Frei, "Karl Barth: Theologian," pp. 170, 171.

287 *The Identity of Jesus Christ*, p. xi. See also "Remarks in Connection with a Theological Proposal," p. 30.

288 *The Identity of Jesus Christ*, p. xiii.

289 Ibid.

Revelation and Biblical Interpretation 61

This dogmatic theological procedure, descriptive and from actuality, Frei finds exemplified in Barth,[290] and warranted by the kind of literature that the Gospels are. In a curious move,[291] Frei proposes to break with the liberal tradition and to discover the "essence of" or "continuity within" Christianity by starting with the Synoptic Gospels. He does not immediately identify why he makes this particular move, other than to say that in terms of understanding Christianity it keeps conceptual-theoretical commitments to a minimum and is relatively non-perspectival.[292] Here he seems to be implying that liberal apologetic efforts are burdened with overly theorized accounts of the human condition. Moreover, he chooses to begin with the Gospels "because their nature as narratives, or at least partial narratives, makes some hermeneutic moves possible that we don't have available elsewhere in the New Testament."[293] The hermeneutic moves made possible by beginning with the Gospels revolve around, as we have noted, their ascriptive literalism, which in this case implies at least two things. First, as noted, there is within narrative a mutual dependence between person and circumstance such that they are not separable. Identity is rendered through the interaction of character and circumstance in a sequence through narrative. Second, there is cohesion of "inner" and "outer" dimensions of human being in narrative. In narrative we are presented with a subject whose intentions are known in their actions, that is, actions are objectifications of intentions. These two points are, on Frei's account, the kind of understanding "called for at the level of anthropology"[294] by the type of narrative that he finds in the Gospels. Moreover, they warrant dogmatic theology that (1) begins from the actuality of revelation, under a narrative depiction to be sure but a depiction normatively rendered apart from interpretative self-positioning; and (2) that proceeds descriptively, since the interactive unity of character and circumstance and "inner" and "outer" human being in narrative cannot be explained only described, most often by way of narration.

Frei maintains the priority of the dogmatic aim of theology throughout his work. What shifts is the background knowledge against which theology is asserted to begin from the actuality of Christian truth (revelation) and to proceed descriptively. While Frei initially maintained that realistic narrative warrants and enables such a

---

290 "Remarks in Connection with a Theological Proposal," pp. 30, 35. See also Hans Frei, "An Afterword: Eberhard Busch's Biography of Karl Barth," in Martin Rumscheidt (ed.), *Karl Barth in Review: Posthumous Works Reviewed and Assessed*, Pittsburgh Theological Monograph Series 30 (Pittsburgh, 1981), pp. 113, 115.

291 The move is curious in the sense that Frei does not offer a theological warrant for this move. The Gospels, because they are realistic narratives, hold a certain hermeneutic promise for Frei, and thus his choice of them as the starting point appears more the result of form than substance. See Hunsinger, "Afterword: Hans Frei as Theologian," p. 246. Hunsinger remarks that Frei makes "very large claims" for his interpretative method.

292 "Remarks in Connection with a Theological Proposal," pp. 30-31.

293 Ibid., p. 32.

294 Ibid., p. 34. Frei's appropriation of this sort of low-level anthropology from Gilbert Ryle, on the unity of intention and action as constitutive of identity, is justified by its serviceability to narrative of the sort found in the Gospels. The critical principle of appropriation seems to be a concept's amenability to realistic narrative. See *The Identity of Jesus Christ*, p. 92.

62   *Revelation, Holy Scripture and Church*

theological program, he came to articulate this same aim less in terms of literary categories and more in social-scientific categories. Charles Campbell writes:

> The goal of theology is the second-order description of the logic and content of Christian belief, as they are embodied in the first-order language and practices of the Christian community, particularly, but not exclusively, in the Scripture that functions authoritatively within the church . . . The aim of theology, in distinction from apologetics, is Christian self-description; theology is religion "specific," internal to the Christian community, and not subsumed under general theories of meaning or meaningfulness.[295]

Several features of this summary of Frei's work, in *Types of Christian Theology*,[296] are important to his understanding of the background knowledge by which the dogmatic aim of theology (as an enterprise which proceeds descriptively from the actuality of Christian truth) is warranted. First, the material context within which the dogmatic aim of Christian theology is realized exhibits a broader range. The first-order embodied logic and use of Christian language including, but exceeding, Holy Scripture form the purview of the dogmatic enterprise. The raw material or given (what was Christian truth or revelation) from which theology proceeds as second-order re-description, is now the entirety of embodied Christian practice; that is, Christianity as a religion. "Christianity, on which theology reflects, is first of all a religion. . . . It is first of all a complex, various, loosely held, and yet really discernible community with varying features—a religious community of which, for example, a sacred text is one feature that is typical of a religion."[297] Second, the descriptive method of theology is analogous to that of the social scientist's "thick description." The theologian, like the social anthropologist, works not at explaining a religion by means of a high power explanatory hypothesis, but at offering a sympathetic and specific self-interpretation of how language functions within the semiotic system that is the Christian religion. In the case of Scripture, this means that how one reads Scripture Christianly, that is, for revelation,[298] is determined not so much by the genre, realistic narrative, as it is by rules embedded in consensual community practice through time. Frei discovers by means of theological "thick description" that a consensus on how to read the Bible emerges in which the ascriptively literal sense of the stories about Jesus provides the terms by which the whole of Scripture is read.[299] Whereas in his early work Frei's biblical hermeneutic was conceived in terms of how aesthetic/realistic texts *qua* texts constrained and directed interpreters, his later work is conceived of as how embedded church practice constrains and directs

---

295 Campbell, *Preaching Jesus*, p. 45.

296 See *Types of Christian Theology*, pp. 2, 11-14, 19-27, 124.

297 Ibid., p. 12. See also "Theology and the Interpretation of Narrative," p. 100. In this essay Frei appropriates Geertz's "thick description" model to depict the Christian church as a language-forming community within which this language is imbedded in "religion specific ways" in practices, doctrines and so on. This is, writes Frei, "a distinctive and irreducible social fact."

298 Compare Swinburne, *Revelation*, p. 177.

299 See "The 'Literal' Reading of Biblical Narrative," pp. 144-148.

Revelation and Biblical Interpretation

Christian Scripture reading.[300] On a more doctrinally substantive level, the high Christology which Frei believed he could achieve by means of aesthetic/realistic texts, which enable normative readings and hold heavily theorized accounts of the human subject at bay, he now achieves by means of appeal to embedded "catholic" church practice.[301]

The two other features of Frei's theological program, Anselmian method and Christological content, are already implicit in the material we have reviewed. In terms of his method, Frei resists not only the liberal apologetic aim of theology, but the method of correlation by which the meaningfulness of Christian claims is defended in terms of a general account of human existence. Faith seeking understanding begins not from a general epistemological and foundational account of revelation, but rather with reflection on those texts, which are formative and authoritative for the Christian church, as they are understood in their embedded context within the church. Frei, as we have noted, resists accounts of faith that force theological reflection in the direction of inwardness such that the "faith relation" becomes the object of theological reflection. The faith that seeks understanding, on Frei's account, is, as Campbell notes, "the faith 'which is believed' as well as the faith 'which believes;' it is faith with an inescapably cognitive dimension, which is first given to the believer in the language of the church's Credo."[302]

This does not mean that the language of hermeneutics and theology is exclusively biblical or theological; rather it implies that other language—such as that of a literary, social-scientific or philosophical nature—is appropriated in such a manner that it serves the grammar or logic of Christian faith. Jeffery Stout sums up:

> Frei is an Anselmian theologian whose theological metalanguage includes the term "narrative," as well as such other expressions as "the literal sense," "meaning" and "reference" ["*thick description*" *might be added here*]. At his best, Frei uses these expressions without relying upon or committing himself to any particular philosophical theory in which they play a part. He abandoned the term "presence" when he sensed he could not go on using it without implicitly buying into such a theory.[303]

---

300 One way of getting at this changing emphasis in Frei is by way of a distinction made in the work of Kendall W. Folkert. Folkert notes that there are two different, although related ways, in which Scripture may function within a religion. It can either be carried by (Canon 1) communal religious activity or the whole or part of Scripture (the Gospel depictions of the identity of Jesus) can be a carrier of religious activity, authority and piety (Canon 2). The weight of Frei's position moves from Canon 2 to Canon 1 over the course of his work. See Folkert, "The 'Canons' of Scripture," in Miriam Levering (ed.), *Rethinking Scripture* (New York, 1989), pp. 170-179.

301 Compare "Remarks in Connection with a Theological Proposal," p. 32 with *Types of Christian Theology*, pp. 12, 15.

302 Campbell, *Preaching Jesus*, p. 52. See Frei, *Types of Christian Theology*, pp. 25-26. Frei, tracing Barth's appropriation of Anselm, remarks, "that God is present as the object of the intellect only in the concept or the use of the word God, is the meaning of the concept 'faith' or 'Christian faith' when used in the context of reflection on the grammar of the word God as it is used in the Christian Church." Ibid., p. 79.

303 Jeffery Stout, "Hans Frei and Anselmian Theology," in Giorgy Olegovich (ed.), *Ten Year Commemoration to the Life of Hans Frei 1922–1988* (New York, 1999), p. 34. The

64 *Revelation, Holy Scripture and Church*

While Frei, following Barth, asserts that borrowed language is inevitably appropriated to Christian hermeneutic and theological description,[304] he can also frustrate his interpreters when his Anselmian orientation leads to the carefully qualified use of categories like "reference," "historical fact" and "objective truth." Take, for example, his exchange with Carl F.H. Henry in which Henry displays no small degree of frustration with Frei's reluctance to give a clear account of (1) the mode of reference implicated in biblical and theological language with respect to God, and (2) the resurrection of Jesus as an historically factual objective event that can be truth tested by means of evidence.[305] Frei, while he asserts that biblical language about God refers, defers on the question of *how* it refers since that would commit him to a theory of reference and, in another place, asserts that there is not ecclesiastical unanimity on the question.[306] Frei prefers to modulate or, as he puts it elsewhere to "re-shape extravagantly" the notion of truth and reference to suit "the condescension of truth to the depiction of the text, and not vice versa."[307] And what is more, in a rare theologically dense comment, Frei notes that the text is made a "sufficient" witness to the Word of God by means of the "Spirit's grace";[308] not by the evidence that an apologist can amass. On the matter of the resurrection as an "historical fact," Frei responds, "of course, I believe in the 'historical reality' of Christ's death and resurrection"; but he continues, "if those are the categories

---

reference to Frei's reticence regarding the term "presence" comes from *The Identity of Jesus Christ*, pp. viii-ix.

304 In his description of Barth's position, Frei notes that "we cannot read the text [of the Bible] without the use of philosophy. But obviously this use of philosophy must be a ruled use." *Types of Christian Theology*, p. 81. The editors of this volume note that Frei left a space in the manuscript here—suggestive of the enumeration of the five rules for the *ad hoc* usage of philosophical language that Barth enumerated in the *Church Dogmatics*, 1/2: 729-736. See *Types of Christian Theology*, p. 167, n. 14. Anselmian method implies the *ad hoc* usage of concepts and language borrowed from philosophy, to deny this is "to dispute the grace and finally the incarnation of the Word of God," writes Barth. *Church Dogmatics*, 1/2: 729. However, for Barth, the use of such concepts and language is strictly subordinate to "the object mirrored in the text" (ibid., p. 734), which is "God's revelation in Jesus Christ." Scriptural testimony to this revelation "inspired by the Holy Ghost" can become "luminous for us only through the same Holy Ghost" (ibid., p. 730). Frei refers to this very passage, and Barth's appropriative rules, in his description of Barth's "ad hoc" correlation method in theology. Frei considers the first of Barth's appropriative rules the most important. See *Types of Christian Theology*, pp. 85-86.

305 Carl F.H. Henry, "Narrative Theology: An Evangelical Appraisal," *Trinity Journal*, 8 NS (Spring, 1987): 12-15.

306 *Types of Christian Theology*, pp. 5, 84, 140-141.

307 See "Conflicts in Interpretation," p. 164 and "The Doctrine of Revelation in the Thought of Karl Barth, 1909–1922: The Nature of Barth's Break with Liberalism," New Haven: Yale University, 1956, Doctoral dissertation, p. 447.

308 "Conflicts in Interpretation," p. 164. Frei also writes, "The *modus significandi* will never allow us to say what the *res significata* is. Nonetheless, we can affirm that in the Christian confession of divine grace, the truth is such that the text is sufficient. There is a due fit to the mystery of grace between truth and text." Ibid., p. 166.

Revelation and Biblical Interpretation 65

which we employ."[309] Frei continues, in Anselmian fashion, to make the point that "fact" language is not theory neutral, and asks whether Jesus Christ, his death and resurrection, is a "fact" "like other historical facts?"[310] In doing so, he is looking for a way out of construals of the doctrine of revelation which function as an epistemological foundation to secure knowledge of God; that is, "a view of certainty and knowledge which liberals and evangelicals hold in common."[311] Once again, he prefers to say yes, the name Jesus refers; but the name Jesus Christ does not refer in a self-enabled, ostensive and univocal fashion. It refers, in a manner, "I do not know . . . only by the miracle of grace."[312]

Finally, Frei's theological and hermeneutic approach is Christological in content. It is important when examining this feature of Frei's work to put a distance between his account of Christological content and the liberal theology of the nineteenth century, which was also Christological. Frei's critique of liberal theology was that it was not Christological but anthropological. In the correlation of some generalized account of human experience or consciousness with the content of the Gospels, the identity of Jesus was so molded to the account by which its meaningfulness was demonstrated (shown to be possible) that it took on its shape. Jesus' identity conformed to an independently derived anthropological given. Frei, like Barth, rejects the synergism of liberal "relationalism,"[313] inherent in this view, and thus articulates his Christology, not in correlation with a generalized account of human experience (the amalgam of which is the faith relationship), but by means of the narratively rendered, unsubstitutable identity, of Jesus in the Gospels. The Gospel of Jesus Christ is meaningful, then, not because it answers or satisfies or correlates to a particular human question or need determined by a prior depiction of humanity. The Gospel is meaningful, salvific, because of the identity of Jesus; that is, because of who Jesus is (and who he is is what he does). "Dogmatically, belief that Jesus is Lord, grounded in believing Jesus' death and resurrection, is itself the explanation for the enablement of (and so mirrored in) a life of faith, hope and love."[314] In this way, Frei resists the liberal tendency to make Christology an implication of soteriology and instead supplants it by making soteriology a function of Christology.

---

309 Hans Frei, "Response to 'Narrative' Theology: An Evangelical Appraisal," *Trinity Journal*, 8 NS (Spring, 1987): 23, reprinted in *Theology and Narrative*, pp. 207-212. I follow the pagination of the original publication since Henry's evaluation of narrative theologies and Frei's response to him are there printed together.

310 Ibid., p. 24.

311 Ibid.

312 Ibid. See also "Of the Resurrection of Christ," in *Theology and Narrative*, p. 203.

313 See "The Doctrine of Revelation in the Thought of Karl Barth," pp. 551-555. Frei writes (p. ii):

To liberalism faith is a given state in which revelation and history are included as direct or internal relations or contents, a position we have called "relationalism." . . . Barth breaks with this outlook in the conviction that the sole basis and intention of theology must be God's sovereignty and freedom in his grace and revelation, including his freedom over faith, the recipient mode of revelation.

314 Ibid., p. ii.

66 *Revelation, Holy Scripture and Church*

However, if the difficulty inherent in liberal Christology is that Jesus Christ and humanity are so closely linked under the guise of *Christus pro et in nobis* that they dissolve into each other, does Frei maintain such a hermetic distinction between Jesus Christ *extra nos* and the human creature that they are impossible to relate? Interpreters of Frei have noted that his is an "objectivist soteriology"[315] and that he tends to "overprotect the Gospel"[316] with the categories of uniqueness and singularity such that bringing the human into relation with Jesus as redeemer is rendered problematic.[317] At least two comments can be offered. The first is that in Frei's conceptual analysis of *The Identity of Jesus Christ* he makes the case that one *can* move from identity to presence. Indeed his essay is an experiment written to test out "a unique affirmation about Jesus Christ, viz., not only that he is the presence of God but also that knowing his identity is identical with having him present or being in his presence."[318] By means of what numerous authors have noted as "Anselmian logic,"[319] Frei maintains that to grasp the unsubstitutable identity of Jesus as it is rendered in the ascriptively literal accounts of the Gospels, is to know him as the one who is present. William Placher writes:

> For Anselm, the logic of talk about God implies that God exists; God cannot be conceived as not existing . . . For Frei, the Bible, as Auerbach had said, 'seeks to overcome our reality: we are to fit our own life into its world' and its world is one in which Jesus has been resurrected. The logic of Christian faith implies that a Christian cannot, as a Christian, imagine a coherent world in which Jesus is not the resurrected one.[320]

The strength to hold together Jesus as he is unsubstitutably depicted as the risen one in the Gospels, and his presence as that one, does not, for Frei, belong to human imaginative capacity and effort. For while Christians cannot even "think of him without his being present," it is "not the power of our thinking that makes him present; it is he who presents himself to us."[321] Here Frei guards the sovereign freedom of

---

315 See Hunsinger, "Afterword: Hans Frei as Theologian," p. 252.

316 Daniel D. Williams, "Comment," *The Christian Scholar*, 49 (1966): 311-312. Williams' comments are offered by way of a response to Frei's essay, "Theological Reflections on the Accounts of Jesus' Death and Resurrection," *The Christian Scholar*, 49 (1966): 263-306. This essay is a precursor to *The Identity of Jesus Christ* and is reprinted in *Theology and Narrative*, pp. 45-93.

317 Frei has a similar anxiety about the tendency toward "Christomonism" in Barth's early work, although he does note that Barth mitigates this tendency in the *Church Dogmatics* with the introduction of the "doctrine of analogy." See "The Doctrine of Revelation in the Thought of Karl Barth," pp. 575-576.

318 *The Identity of Jesus Christ*, p. vii.

319 See Campbell, *Preaching Jesus*, p. 14; Placher, "Introduction," in *Theology and Narrative*, p. 14; and Hunsinger, "Afterword: Hans Frei as Theologian," pp. 253-254.

320 Placher, "Introduction," p. 14. The citation from Eric Auerbach is taken from *Mimesis: The Representation of Reality in Western Literature*, trans. William R. Trask (Princeton, 1953), p. 15.

321 *The Identity of Jesus Christ*, p. 14.

Revelation and Biblical Interpretation 67

God while at the same time making the point that in his sovereign freedom the risen Lord Jesus Christ is, for us, present to us "due to his powerful goodness."[322]

Frei also makes the point, however, that the mode of Christ's presence with us is not "having been raised from dead," although this is the basis for his ongoing presence with us now. Frei speaks of the presence of Jesus to the church as "indirect." The term "indirect" implies that Jesus is not present in the same manner in which he was present in his earthly life, or will be in his and our future. Here Frei introduces a doctrine of the Holy Spirit to speak of the self-focused "presence" of Christ now, which is a term used in analogy with "physical presence and verbal communication."[323] While not confined to or identical with certain spatial (sacraments) and temporal-verbal (written Scripture) bases for his self-focused presence, these are the current mode of Christ's presence, which are effective for the believer. Christ's indirect presence to the church in Word and Sacrament engenders worship, and forms of discipleship which, while not imitations of the unsubstitutable identity of Jesus and his once for all enactment of salvation for all, replicate the pattern of exchange embodied in the life of Jesus "at a distance."[324] "The church," writes Frei," is both the witness to that presence [of Jesus] and the public and communal form the indirect presence of Christ now takes, in contrast to his direct presence in his earthly days."[325]

Critique

In the sympathetic critique that follows, an examination of Frei's understanding of the relationship between "realistic" and "literal reading" of the Gospels and revelation is undertaken. The structure of the critique follows that of the exposition—the aim, method and content of theology. The central criticism throughout is that a dogmatic description of the illuminating work of the Holy Spirit in relation to the scriptural witness, especially at the level of its meaning (perspicuity), does not consistently inform his hermeneutic proposal. Whether he warrants his theological approach (and the accompanying mode of Scripture interpretation) by appeal to literary genre or communal practice, he so consistently focuses on creaturely action in construing the interpretative field that the illumination of Scripture and the formation of faith by the Holy Spirit are often hidden from view or simply remains tacit in his hermeneutic. In the argument that follows, a sideways glance at Frei's appropriation of Barth's biblical/theological hermeneutic is undertaken since this throws into relief Frei's failure to conceive of literal reading as a human act dependent on the illumining grace of the Holy Spirit.

---

322 Ibid. See also "The Doctrine of Revelation in the Thought of Karl Barth," p. 447; and "Niebuhr's Theological Background," pp. 40-53. Frei, in describing Barth's position, describes his own: "Thus, revelation and grace are always God's sovereign acts, miraculous acts and not constants of a relational datum." Ibid., pp. 40, 42.

323 *The Identity of Jesus Christ*, p. 155.

324 Ibid., p. 160. See also Gene Outka, "Following at a Distance: Ethics and the Identity of Jesus," in Garrett Green (ed.), *Scriptural Authority and Narrative Interpretation* (Philadelphia, 1987), pp. 144-160.

325 *The Identity of Jesus Christ*, p. 157.

Aim: following Barth? In order to prevent the arbitrary interpretation of the Bible endemic to liberal theological method, which bends the particularity and specificity of revelation in Jesus Christ to serve a prior independently determined human need, Frei proposes that theology pursue a dogmatic course. It is not the primary aim of theology to engage in apologetic efforts, which seek a demonstration of the meaningfulness of Jesus Christ to the human condition, or to describe the process by which one comes to believe. Theology ought to work "descriptively" from the "actuality" of revelation. In this move Frei takes Barth as his exemplar. "Barth's theology proceeds by narrative and conceptually descriptive statement rather than by argument or by way of an explanatory theory undergirding the description's real or logical possibility." Frei continues, drawing together his interest in New Criticism and Barth's theological approach:

> In much the same way as the now old fashion "newer" literary critics, he set forth a textual world which he refused to understand by paraphrase, or by transposition or translation into some other context but interpreted in second order reflection with the aid of an array of formal technical tools.[326]

What this theological aim and example imply for Frei's hermeneutic endeavor is that beginning with the Gospels, he will precede descriptively to offer an identity description of Jesus Christ.

Frei's own observation that he may have been over-invested in a theory of aesthetic or realistic texts in the realization of his aim—to do theology descriptively from the actuality of revelation—seems largely correct.[327] In the phase of his work in which he deploys the category "realistic" narrative in a preliminary fashion, almost as a prolegomena to secure the ground for dogmatic re-description, he tends to ascribe to a species of texts and an interpretative method "very large claims"[328] and even to ascribe to texts features that Barth ascribed to God. Lynn Poland writes, "For Barth, *homo peccator non capax verbi Domini*; one cannot obtain valid knowledge of God on one's own. Rather, God is known through his Word, Jesus Christ, and the Word provides the conditions under which it may be understood." Poland concludes, "For Barth's sovereign Word, Frei seems to substitute the autonomous biblical text."[329]

Poland's and Hunsinger's comments however, do not necessarily entail a wholesale rejection of the categories of "aesthetic" or "realistic narrative" texts. Frei might have redeployed the category in a manner *internal* to dogmatics; that is, in subordination to the Word, who generates his own witnesses and provides the conditions under which those witnesses may be understood.[330] In this way, Frei might

---

326 "An Afterword: Eberhard Busch's Biography of Karl Barth," pp. 113, 115.

327 See "The 'Literal' Reading of Biblical Narrative," pp. 139-144. See also Placher, "Introduction," in *Theology and Narrative*, pp. 16-17, 24 n. 54. Placher prefers Frei emphasis on "normative" interpretation under the constraints of realistic narrative in his earlier work.

328 Hunsinger, "Afterword: Hans Frei as Theologian," p. 246.

329 Lynn Poland, "The New Criticism, Neoorthodoxy, and the New Testament," *Journal of Religion*, 65/4 (October, 1985): 469.

330 "It is basic to Christian theology," writes Brevard Childs, "to reckon with an extrabiblical reality, namely with the resurrected Christ who evoked the New Testament

Revelation and Biblical Interpretation

have retained the critical potential of realistic narrative, which is generated and made luminous by that to which it bears witness, against the institutional calcification of Bible reading. William Placher articulates a virtue resident in Frei's sense of textual rigidity by means of Auerbach and New Criticism:

> I would like to free the text from how it has, through so much of history, become a defense of power structures in ways that seem to me at odds with something one might naively want to call its real meaning, as the Gospel of Jesus crucified in solidarity with the oppressed.[331]

Frei might have accomplished what Placher suggests by introducing his account of realistic narrative, which was preliminary to and independent from the dogmatic task, within the context of the sort of theological description that comes at the end of *The Identity of Jesus Christ*. Here, in what amounts to a case for the *sufficiency* and *efficacy* of Scripture, Frei maintains that the Holy Spirit renders the verbal-temporal witness to revelation an indirect basis for the presence of the One therein depicted. Frei might have invoked this theologically thick description at the level of the *perspicuity* of the Gospels as realistic narrative; or he might have appropriated the material he finds in Calvin[332] in which the Spirit illumines the reader so that he or she faithfully follows the story engendered by revelation, which is perspicuous in its own right; but he does not. What Frei does instead is to move from what "the text forces" to what "the church fosters" as the basis for the ascriptively literal reading of the Gospels that yields a Christology consistent with his dogmatic aim. "Instead of a literary theory providing the warrant for his christological claims, therefore, Frei's later work focuses on the contingent, contestable practices of a certain set of communities."[333]

However, does Frei's theoretical shift from a hermeneutic that first establishes the literal sense of the text by appeal to literary theory to one in which social-scientific "thick description" establishes the plain sense by second-order reflection on communal use, solve the difficulty it seeks to avoid? Remember Frei's dogmatic aim, following Barth, is "to proceed by narrative and conceptually descriptive statement rather than by argument or by way of an explanatory theory undergirding the description's real or logical possibility." One has to raise the question of whether construing the hermeneutic field in social-scientific terms, where the embedded practices of a community (any religion) is the means by which the plain sense of

---

witness." See *Biblical Theology of the Old and New Testaments: Theological Reflection in the Christian Bible* (Minneapolis, 1993), p. 20.

331 Personal correspondence, 8 August 1993. See also Mike Higton, "Hans Frei and David Tracy on the Ordinary and the Extraordinary in Christianity," *Journal of Religion*, 79/4 (October, 1999): 572.

332 *The Eclipse of Biblical Narrative*, pp. 21-22.

333 Higton, "Hans Frei and David Tracy on the Ordinary and the Extraordinary in Christianity," p. 572. See also Vanhoozer, *First Theology*, p. 219. Vanhoozer remarks, "No conflict between letter and spirit here; it is spirit, *or community reading conventions*, all the way down . . . It is the community, ultimately, that enjoys interpretative authority." My emphasis.

a sacred text (any sacred text) is established escapes the impasse it was developed to overcome. Does not this move also veer toward a depiction of the hermeneutic field in which "an explanatory theory undergirds the real or logical possibility" of dogmatic depiction?[334]

However, the greater difficulty is that whether Frei construes the hermeneutic field in terms of New Critical literary or social-scientific categories, both of these options both tend to feature human realities. Either the Bible, particularly the Gospels as realistic texts, or Christianity, as a cultural-linguistic semiotic system, is the construct in terms of which "literal meaning" is established, specified and garnered. The result is that texts in their relation to genre type or reading community bear too much interpretative/theological weight at the level of preliminary orientation to and construal of the hermeneutic field. This altogether immanent construal threatens to render Christian Bible reading solely dependent on the *mediate* realities of "aesthetic" or "realistic" texts or on the "plain sense" reading rules imbedded in the Christian semiotic system.[335] Frei, as noted, does invoke pnematological language, in terms of the Spirit's role in rendering Scripture a temporal-literary basis of the indirect presence of Christ[336] or a sufficient witness to the Word of God,[337] that is, in making Scripture refer, sufficiently and effectively, by grace. However these claims are rendered theologically vulnerable since they are logically dependent upon a hermeneutic in which either (1) narrative texts, of which the Gospels are an instance, are capable of rendering "normative"—perspectivally independent—meaning through a capacity all their own;[338] or, in Frei's later work (2) "religions," of which Christianity is an instance, are capable of socializing their adherents into communal plain sense reading rules of its sacred texts and its central story. A greater, more explicit, sense of the dependence of the human realities of biblical text and Christian church on the illumining grace of God the Holy Spirit, at the level of the meaning or the reading of Holy Scripture as a witness to Jesus Christ, would give dogmatic integrity and critical potential to Frei's proposal, particularly in its later form.

It might also be noted that Frei's hermeneutic proposal, particularly in its appeal to communal reading practice, steers close to the eighteenth-century conjunction of Protestant biblicism and rationalist philosophy where the influence of the Holy

---

334 Vanhoozer asks, "Has Frei exchanged his hermeneutical birthright for a mess of pottage, or rather Fish-stew? It was Fish . . . who first suggested that meaning is a product of the way it is read." *First Theology*, p. 219.

335 Webster writes, "[B]y treating Scripture as a semiotic *positum* in the culture of the church as visible social entity, it risks severing the transcendent reference of both Church and Scripture. Scripture's externality is its reference to revelation, not its visible textuality; that textuality serves the *viva vox Dei*." *Holy Scripture*, pp. 49-50.

336 *The Identity of Jesus Christ*, pp. 164-165.

337 See "Conflicts in Interpretation," pp. 163-164 and "Response to 'Narrative' Theology: An Evangelical Appraisal," pp. 23-24.

338 Frei, while he acknowledges that he once held this position, comes to reject it since "Christian claims" regarding the necessity and sufficiency of this text "for our orientation within the real world" is "hardly the sort of claim which one would want to turn into the instance of a general class [i.e., realistic narrative]. "The 'Literal' Reading of Biblical Narrative," p. 143.

Spirit is expunged from Bible reading since textual perspicuity, in this precursor to "general hermeneutics," does not rest on "the direct influence of the Holy Spirit" [339] but is a matter of following generalized "rules of interpretation." The fundamental difference between Frei and Protestant biblicism in its joint venture with rationalist philosophy is that for the former the rules to be followed are local and derived from communal practice, whereas for the latter the rules are general and apply across all texts. However, for both, no dogmatic account of the illumination of the Holy Spirit is necessary to garner the plain sense, which is the literal meaning of Scripture.

Method: appropriative rules   Borrowed language for the expression of theological re-description is inevitable if theology is going to be something more than reiteration of the Bible. On Frei's account, this means appropriating non-biblical schemes of thought to express the material of dogmatic construction garnered by means of the attentive literal reading of Gospels and the rest of Holy Scripture in relation to them. The liability of the deployment of extra-biblical categories and idioms for the expression of the content of Scripture is that they can, as in liberal correlationist theology, subvert the logic of faith to their own alien logic. Frei, following Barth, maintains therefore that the grammar of appropriation ought to—as in Anselm— subordinate what is borrowed to the integrity of faith. Put another way, there can be no systematic correlation between the content of faith and extra-biblical categories or idioms, they can only be drawn into the service of Gospel explication on an ad hoc basis in which the integrity of Christian faith rules the manner of appropriation. By extension, Anselm's "faith seeking understanding" or Barth's ruled appropriation would resist construals of the whole of the Christian church and its interpretative practices in terms of an idiom that constricts a properly Christian understanding of the hermeneutic situation. In this section, working by a specific case study in a way which fills out and extends the previous section, an argument is made that the idiom by which Frei construes the Christian community and its interpretative practices hides from view biblical interpretation as a human act dependent on the illumining work of the Holy Spirit. Moreover, where Frei might have avoided this constriction through the guidance offered by Barth's rules for appropriation of extra-biblical schemes of thought, Frei instead gives an immanentist cast to his reading of Barth's appropriative rules.

The place in Frei's later writings where his construal of the hermeneutic field tends to minimize the ongoing dependence of the Bible and the church on the illumining and guiding work of the Spirit, that is, where he fails to relate textual constraints and communally embedded reading conventions to the action of God by which they are rendered transparent to the subject matter of the Bible, occurs in *Types of Christian Theology*. In this posthumous publication, Frei made explicit his intention to employ low-level social-scientific categories by which to construe Christianity as a religion, which like other religions has a sacred text and a central story. "There is a sacred text—a typical element in a religious system—and there are informal rules and

---

339 See *The Eclipse of Biblical Narrative*, pp. 55-56.

72   *Revelation, Holy Scripture and Church*

conventions governing how the sign system works in regard to sacred Scripture."[340] On this construal of Christianity and the Bible, the "literal sense" of the Bible is "precisely that meaning which finds the greatest agreement with the use of the text in the religious community." Frei continues, "If there is agreement in that use, then take that to be the literal sense."[341] This view must, in all fairness, be held together with a minimal sense of textual autonomy which, while it was stronger in Frei's early emphasis on "realistic narrative," nevertheless abides throughout his work.[342] Thus while the literal sense of the Bible is that meaning which best corresponds to consensual communal interpretation and use, communal use never exhausts the meaning of the Bible without remainder, it continues to "exerts a pressure of its own on the inquiring reader."[343]

However, while Frei's emphasis on "literal sense" as the communally authoritative meaning of the Bible does not extinguish a minimal notion of textual resilience, he confines the constraints under which biblical interpretation takes place to the immanent features of embedded Christian practice and textual resilience. What is theologically required here is a better sense of the ongoing dependence of church practice and textual lucidity on the sustaining and enlightening grace of God the Holy Spirit. In Barth's discussion of the interpretation of Scripture, for example, while interpretation of the Bible is certainly a human work, interpretation always takes place in dependence on God. This dependence is reflected in the church's prayers for the Holy Spirit which acknowledge that interpreting Scripture in a way which illumines our own circumstances is always beyond the church's resources. It is, nevertheless, a task that can be carried out in obedience to and in freedom under the Word, which sustains the church in this task. When Barth speaks of prayer he is pointing to the only posture possible for the church as it seeks to interpret Scripture for its own life. The church is, for Barth, completely dependent upon the continuing

---

340 *Types of Christian Theology*, pp. 11-12. This work extends a trajectory begun at the close of Frei's essay, "The 'Literal' Reading of Biblical Narrative." In both of these works, the influence of George's Lindbeck's "cultural-linguistic" theory of religion is formative. Moreover, methodologically speaking, Frei's movement from a general description of Christianity as a religion with a sacred text to the specifics of Christian faith and Holy Scripture bears a striking resemblance to Schleiermacher's hermeneutic as Frei has described it. See *Types of Christian Theology*, pp. 112-115. The fact that Frei places Schleiermacher and Barth together as *ad hoc* correlationalists in *Types of Christian Theology* represents a movement toward Schleiermacher by Frei in this book.

341 *Types of Christian Theology*, p. 15. See also "The 'Literal' Reading of Biblical Narrative," pp. 144-145.

342 See *Types of Christian Theology*, pp. 86-87. In this passage Frei notes that the relation between text and reader is asymptotic in the case of a complex and rich text.

343 Ibid., p. 86. David Lee notes that in Frei's later work there is an "eclectic mix of literary interests in the service of the sociolinguistic reading of Christian Scripture . . .". *Luke's Stories of Jesus: Theological Reading of Gospel Narrative and the Legacy of Hans Frei*, Journal for the Study of the New Testament Supplement Series 185 (Sheffield, 1999), p. 88. Frei's interest in new criticism wanes and in its place there is an increasing interest in Frank Kermode. See *Types of Christian Theology*, p. 87 and "Conflicts in Interpretation," pp. 158-162.

Revelation and Biblical Interpretation 73

gift of divine mercy in scriptural exegesis to carry out a task which, while "serious and hard work," is accepted in prayer for the free grace of God, apart from which exegesis is hubris.[344]

Frei minimizes this element in Barth's theological hermeneutic, even when it is right on the surface of his exposition of Barth's theology. He seems to overlook it because theological discussion of the action of the Holy Spirit in Scripture interpretation does not easily accord with a prior construal of the interpretative field in social-scientific terms. "Thick description"—with its emphasis on "meaning as use"—is confined to a description of the community's deployment of the Bible in which the church is the only significant actor. This methodological orientation appears to force Frei into an immanentist ecclesiological interpretation of Barth. The most obvious example of this interpretation appears in Frei's discussion of Barth's "rules" for the appropriation of schemes of thought in the reading of Scripture. Frei correctly notes that for Barth, the use of some scheme is necessary for reading the Bible or it becomes "a mechanical exercise, no more than the reiteration of words."[345] However, he presents a partial picture when he declares that for Barth the use of extra-biblical schemes are strictly subordinate to "the text in the context of the self-description of the Christian community."[346] The inadequacy of this description of Barth's biblical hermeneutic can be observed in the first and most important of Barth's appropriative rules, which Frei cites:

> When the interpreter uses the scheme of thought he brings with him for the apprehension and explanation of what is said to us in Scripture, he must have a fundamental awareness of what he is doing. We must be clear that every scheme of thought which we bring with us is different from that of the scriptural word which we have to interpret, for the object of the latter is God's revelation in Jesus Christ, *it is the testimony of this revelation inspired by the Holy Spirit, and it can become luminous for us only through the same Holy Spirit.*[347]

In Frei's discussion, which follows this passage from Barth, he emphasizes that for Barth (1) the subordination of borrowed concepts and language is worked out at the level of application and exegesis, that is, in the church's use of Scripture; and (2) that the text of the Bible is able to resist conformity to the pre-understandings of readers and appropriated concepts because of the resilience of the text. However, Frei minimizes Barth's theological realism in his assertion that, "the function of Scripture as a concept" is "to shape and constrain the reader, so that he or she discovers the very capacity to subordinate him or herself."[348] This is just what Barth does not ascribe to Scripture as a concept. Barth maintains: "The testimony of this

---

344 Barth, *Church Dogmatics*, I/2: 755. See also ibid., pp. 687, 755, 768. He writes (p. 695): "Because it is the decisive activity prayer must take precedence even of exegesis, and in no circumstances must it be suspended."

345 *Types of Christian Theology*, p. 85.

346 Ibid.

347 Barth, *Church Dogmatics*, 1/2: 713, cited in *Types of Christian Theology*, p. 86. My emphasis.

348 Ibid.

74   *Revelation, Holy Scripture and Church*

revelation . . . can become luminous for us only through the same Holy Spirit." What Barth ascribes to the action of God, Frei ascribes to a "good enough"[349] text; that is, one that is rich and complex enough to resist readers, to act on them. David Dawson makes a pertinent criticism of Frei's interpretative project:

> If Jesus the Messiah is really unsubstitutable, should not normative intratextualists [Frei and Lindbeck] be more suspicious of all substitutions—the church as well as the text? A spirit that escapes all textual particularity is but a tremulation in the ether, but a spirit no longer free in the letter (or the institution) is but old works righteousness writ large.[350]

Frei's interpretation of Barth on this point bears a striking resemblance to that of his former Yale colleague, George Lindbeck.[351] In his article, "Barth and Textuality,"[352] Lindbeck invokes the theology of Karl Barth as exemplary of "intratextual theology." In a manner analogous to Frei's argument for the subordination of extra-biblical schemes of thought to the resilience of the "good enough" text of Scripture, Lindbeck maintains that the church is more likely to achieve long-term relevance by deliberately misreading present realities and issues by means of the framework of the Bible. This can be accomplished argues Lindbeck, only as the church initiates its members in the language of Zion such that they imaginatively live in a Christ-centered world. For the Bible permits us to dwell within its world linguistically and imaginatively through its internal dynamic of self-referencing, which textualizes everything such that the character description of God supremely given in the story of Jesus becomes "the basic text"[353] in relation to which all else has meaning.

Perhaps the most striking aspect of Lindbeck's citation of Barth at this point is that, like Frei, Lindbeck almost completely transposes Barth's sense of divine agency into a textual-communal dynamic.[354] Although Lindbeck seems to be aware that "something more" than linguistic and imaginative familiarity with the world of the

---

349 Frei borrows the phrase "good enough" as a description of the Bible's capacity to resist readerly imposition from Frank Kermode. See *Types of Christian Theology*, p. 87.

350 David Dawson, "Allegorical Intratextuality in Bunyan and Winstanley," *Journal of Religion*, 70/2 (April, 1990): 212. See also Stephen L. Stell, "Hermeneutics in Theology and the Theology of Hermeneutics," *Journal of the American Academy of Religion*, 61 (1993): 691-697 and Timothy Ward, *Word and Supplement: Speech Acts, Biblical Texts, and the Sufficiency of Scripture* (Oxford, 2002), p. 201. Ward maintains: "The classic Christian understanding of Scripture is that the biblical texts are the medium of the address of Another."

351 Vanhoozer maintains that the context within which one determines the literal sense went from literary to social-linguistic in the work of Hans Frei under the influence of David Kelsey and George Lindbeck. See *First Theology*, p. 218, n. 47. See also David J. Lose, *Confessing Jesus Christ: Preaching in a Postmodern World* (Grand Rapids, 2003), p. 117.

352 George Lindbeck, "Barth and Textuality," *Theology Today*, 43 (1986): 361-382.

353 Ibid., p. 374. The citation is from Barth, *Church Dogmatics*, IV/2: 122. Lindbeck takes Barth to exemplify the strong misreading model of biblical interpretation he proposes.

354 The longer citation of Barth from *Church Dogmatics*, IV/2: 673-675 in the "Barth and Textuality" essay excludes the following: "It is the Spirit who upholds the community . . . but according to the defiant saying in Eph. 6:17, that 'sword of the Spirit' which protects and defends [the community] is the Word of God . . .".

Revelation and Biblical Interpretation 75

Bible is necessary to dwelling within its world, and even that this "something more" has to do with hearing Scripture in "the power of the Spirit," he almost immediately transposes the Barth material on Spirit into a discussion of textual dynamics. He writes, "Barth has a way of speaking about this more, which, if I understand it rightly, is remarkably prosaic. As far as I can make out, it is self-reference which turns the biblical world into the strange new world."[355] It would seem that Lindbeck has effectively replaced divine agency with the capacity of Scripture, or the church in its interpretation and use of Scripture, to textualize everything. As Ronald Thiemann observes, in a point applicable to both Frei and Lindbeck, "There is, indeed, the very real danger that in much of Lindbeck's essay talk about text stands in the place of talk about God."[356]

Christological content and faith   Frei's reticence toward liberal Christology which collapses the presence of Jesus into the human subject such that *Christus extra nos* dissolves into *Christus pro et en nobis* leads him to focus his constructive efforts in *The Identity* on the realistically depicted identity of Jesus in the Gospels. The potential difficulty with this focus on *Christus extra nos* is that, as noted, it implies an objectivist soteriology. In other words, the potential difficulty with Frei's program is the opposite of that of liberal theology. How is Jesus related, as the one whose textual identity is depicted as Savior in the Gospels, to the human subject? Frei makes the case that Christians cannot think of Jesus, as the one whose identity is depicted in the Gospels—the Savior who is risen—without his being present. "Due to his powerful goodness," Christians cannot think his identity and presence apart. "Our argument is that to grasp this identity, Jesus of Nazareth, is to believe that, in fact, he has been raised from the dead."[357] It would be fair to say that faith in Jesus the Savior as he is textually identified is engendered by the presence of Jesus to that description. Moreover, Frei makes the case that Word and Sacrament are the temporal-verbal and spatial means of the indirect presence of Christ in the Spirit. Once again faith is engendered and supported by the indirect presence of Jesus to his depicted identity as the Risen Savior. Charles Campbell writes, "For Frei the salvific meaning of Jesus Christ becomes a contemporary reality not by being correlated

---

355 Lindbeck, "Barth and Textuality," p. 374.

356 Ronald Thiemann, "Response to George Lindbeck," *Theology Today*, 43 (1986): 378. In fairness to Lindbeck, he does respond to Thiemann's criticism. He seems to recognize that the self-enclosed nature of biblical interpretation in his thick description (social-scientific) model needs to be complemented by interpreting for witness (like Barth and Childs) and interpreting for authorial discourse (Wolterstorff). Moreover, he concedes Childs' point that "theologically fruitful interpretation does not happen apart from the guidance of the Holy Spirit." See George Lindbeck, "Postcritical Canonical Interpretation: Three Modes of Retrieval," in Christopher Seitz and Kathryn Green-McCreight (eds), *Theological Exegesis: Essays in Honor of Brevard S. Childs* (Grand Rapids, 1999), pp. 43 and 51. However, this acknowledgement comes in the final short paragraph his essay; which is to say that a doctrine of the Spirit does not seem integral to Lindbeck's interpretative proposals. For a contrary view see C.C. Pecknold, *Transforming Postliberal Theology: George Lindbeck, Pragmatism and Scripture* (London, 2005), pp. 114-116.

357 "Theological Reflections on the Accounts of Jesus' Death and Resurrection," p. 83.

76 *Revelation, Holy Scripture and Church*

with human experience, but through the mysterious, eschatological work of the Holy Spirit in the church."[358] By this work of the Spirit, faith and faithfulness are formed in the life of the Christian community as the shape of its life is patterned according to the life of Jesus Christ.

However, this lively Trinitarian sense of divine agency with respect to the appropriation of the saving work of Christ (or perhaps this appropriation of the human subject by the saving Work of Christ) and Christ's indirect presence in Word and Sacrament is altered when the background idiom against which it is articulated becomes less Christological and pneumatological and more ecclesiological or, at least, inverts their relationship. Following Lindbeck's notion that "to become religious—no less than to become culturally or linguistically competent—is to interiorize a set of skills by practice and training,"[359] Frei moves toward the position that coming to be a Christian is less about "religious experience" and more about socialization in a skill set (including language use and behavior) embodied in the ecclesia, that is, being Christian is primarily acquired fluency in ecclesial practice.[360] By this move Frei continues to resist liberal correlation in which Christology is collapsed into human inwardness through the social objectivity of the church. However, this move implies not the dissolution of Christology into anthropology, but into a functionalist ecclesiology. Frei had made the point in *The Identity of Jesus Christ* that the church is both "the witness to and the form that the indirect presence of Christ now takes." However, in this context ecclesiology was strictly subordinate to the Christology he had articulated in the previous pages. Jesus Christ owns his presence and in an act of "powerful goodness" turns toward us. "[I]t is he who presents himself to us."[361] In this context, as Barth puts it, the church is a creature of the Word "built afresh each time"[362] it hears the word in the power of the Spirit who creates faith. However, by moving toward a functionalist ecclesiology, Frei renders the Spirit's work of miraculously making Word and Sacrament the indirect bases of the spatial and temporal presence of God in Jesus Christ, immanent to, not sovereign over, church practice and thereby mutes the critical power of Bible reading by which the Holy Spirit illumines the identity of Jesus Christ over against church practice. Brevard Childs summarizes:

My reaction to this ecclesiastically functional view of theology is to question whether one can speak meaningfully about faithful forms of life within the Christian community before first establishing the identity and will of God who in Jesus Christ calls the church in being, and whose purpose encompasses the entire creation. In

---

358 Campbell, *Preaching Jesus*, pp. 60-61.

359 George Lindbeck, *The Nature of Doctrine: Religion and Theology in a Postliberal Age* (Philadelphia, 1984), p. 35.

360 The texts here are numerous. See "Theology and the Interpretation of Narrative," pp. 96-100; "The 'Literal' Reading of Biblical Narrative," pp. 146-149; and *Types of Christian Theology*, pp. 4, 12-13, 22, 54, 112-113. See also Campbell, *Preaching Jesus*, p. 69. At several points Campbell ascribes D.Z. Phillips's position on Christian self-description to Frei. See ibid., p. 69, nn. 20 and 22.

361 *The Identity of Jesus Christ*, p. 14.

362 Karl Barth, *Homiletics*, trans. Geoffrey W. Bromiley and Donald E. Daniels (Louisville, 1991), pp. 65-66.

sum, I remain highly critical of any theological position in which ecclesiology takes precedence over Christology.[363]

---

363 Childs, *Biblical Theology of the Old and New Testaments*, p. 23.

Chapter 2

The Bible as Holy Scripture: Construal and Authority

In this chapter an exposition and critical examination of James Barr, Paul Ricoeur and Hans Frei on the Bible as Scripture is undertaken. Two primary features of the Bible as Christian Scripture in any articulation are (1) the manner in which the biblical corpus is construed as a whole canon (its *unity*); and (2) the relation of this construal to an articulation of the *authority* of the Bible.[1] Christian construals of the unity and authority of the Bible as Scripture are rendered problematic by each of our primary authors and then rearticulated on historical-critical (Barr), or hermeneutic (Ricoeur) grounds or by means of literary/social-scientific (Frei) considerations. While theological motivation is not lacking in any of these articulations of the unity and authority of the Bible and, moreover, while each conceptualization of the Bible as Scripture renders itself serviceable to theological and ecclesiastic use, doctrinal considerations are either bracketed out (Barr), deferred (Ricoeur) or left tacit (Frei) within the modulations impressed upon classic Christian notions of the unity and authority of the Bible. The net effect of this move is that the properties that Scripture acquires by virtue of God's use of it, are subverted to preliminary and entirely natural accounts of texts in relation to the intention world of their production (Barr), their nature as a "work" instanciated in writing (Ricoeur), or reading conventions appropriate to a particular genre or reading community (Frei). What each accounts lacks is a fundamental sense of the Bible as "Holy" Scripture, that is, of the unity and authority of Scripture as properties the Bible acquires by virtue of its service to the Gospel, which is its content.

James Barr: The Bible as Faith-Structured Classic Model

In the previous section on revelation, it was noted that for James Barr, revelation is not confined in its application to the record of diverse events recorded in the Bible. "Revelation," in so far as Barr considers the term licit, functions as a description of the much longer "cumulative tradition" of which the Bible is a part. Indeed, revelation in the past is presumed by the texts of the Bible and, more importantly,

---

1 David Kelsey maintains that to call a text or set of texts Scripture implies, among other things that it is "authority" and to ascribe some sort of wholeness to it. In addition to these Kelsey adds that Scripture implies a community whose identity is tied up with this body of literature (a topic we take up in the next chapter). See *The Uses of Scripture in Recent Theology* (Philadelphia, 1975), pp. 89ff.

anticipated in the future—these texts "lean" toward what is yet to be unveiled.[2] The Bible, Old and New Testaments, belong to a larger and longer "history of effects" and it is this larger tradition that provides the "matrix" within which divine acts and speech have intelligibility and the "impulse" for the occurrence of further divine acts and speech. "Inspiration," again in so far as Barr is willing to use the term, specifies not only the relationship of God to biblical authors, but also God's relationship to the whole cumulative tradition, that is, to the human tradition about God. God was in contact with his people prior to inscripturation, was in contact with them during the "crystallization" of that tradition in the writings of the Bible and continues in the same mode to make himself known today.[3]

A question that arises under the terms of this depiction of "revelation" and "inspiration" is: what is the articulation of biblical unity and authority that comport with them? When theological language that in traditional doctrinal accounts functioned, in part, to undergird a specific construal of the Bible in its totality and to provide a basis for its authority in the church, is reconceived in the light of biblical and history of religions research, how does it modulate these dependent features? In other words, how can Barr configure the unity of the Bible and its unique authority for the life of the church in a manner which is consistent with (1) generalized notions of revelation and inspiration, which make the Bible a moment in these broader phenomenon; and (2) biblical research and history of religions approaches, which are primarily concerned with the properties of texts in relation to the activities of their constituting historical agents?

In what follows, an exposition of Barr's attempt to accomplish precisely this task is presented. First, an exposition is offered of the historical-critical frame within which both the unity and authority of the Bible are rendered problematic. Presented next is Barr's polemic against the attempt of Biblical Theology to rehabilitate typology as a basis for the unity of the Testaments. This polemic actually becomes a general polemic against all attempts to articulate biblical unity on the basis of typological interpretation with its implied Christocentric construal of Scripture. Third, an elucidation is offered of Barr's strategy to establish the unity and authority of the Bible on the basis of its implication in (1) the way in which salvation is achieved; (2) the fundamental structure of faith; and (3) the unity of the One God. Finally, a critique of Barr's proposal for the unity and authority of the Bible is offered. This critique is fundamentally that Barr, oriented by the methodological conviction that a critical space free from theological infringement must be opened up between faith and Bible to let the "factual" and "truthful" emerge, is maximally interested in the properties texts acquire in relation to human agents and only secondarily interested in the properties texts acquire in relation to God's speech and action. Barr's prioritizing of the socio-intentional world of a text's production and the historical world of a text's mediation mislocates the reality in terms of which the Bible has unity and authority and thus prohibits a robust doctrinal account of the same. In our critical discussion, some preliminary suggestions are made for how a number of the problems he raises might be accounted for on other terms.

---

2 Barr, *The Concept of Biblical Theology*, p. 599.

3 *The Scope and Authority of the Bible*, p. 132.

The Bible as Holy Scripture

A Historical-Critical Frame

A central problem over against which Barr works in expressing a construal of the Bible as a whole is the breakdown of its traditional typological and allegorical unity under pressure from historical-critical interpretation.[4] The "modern scholarly expositor of the Bible works primarily . . . not with the flat literary relations on the surface of the biblical text as it is, but with the intentions of the writer in his historical setting."[5] Literary readings, which abound increasingly in modern biblical study, are primarily interested in synchronic readings of the Bible, that is, in the overall shape that images and patterns resident within the text give to the Bible. This approach to Bible reading seems to have the most in common with traditional pre-critical typological reading.[6] Other readings "set the quest for the entities referred to."[7] These may be theological entities, such as God and heaven, or historical entities, like kings or governments. Barr does not wish to bifurcate historical and theological entities into two separate classes such that theologians are interested in one and not the other. Often, he notes, historical events have theological value. The third approach to the study of the Bible aims at the discovery of the intentions of authors in their historical settings. Historical criticism, which is most active at this level of biblical interpretation, wants to assist biblical interpretation through an explication of the thought world of the people who wrote the Bible. Scholars attempt, through historical research, to unfold the situations, motives and interests of the people from whom the Bible came. In this way, the range of what a text can mean is disciplined by reference to the socio-historical circumstances of its author(s).

---

4 Barr's assessment of the legitimacy of typological and allegorical exegesis as a strategy for holding together the unity of the Testaments can be found in *Old and New in Interpretation*, pp. 103-148; "Allegory and Typology," in J. Bowden and A. Richardson (eds), *A New Dictionary of Christian Theology* (London, 1983), pp. 11-15; *The Bible in the Modern World*, pp. 59, 63, 67-69, 128-129; *Holy Scripture*, p. 116; "The Authority of Scripture: The Book of Genesis and the Origin of Evil in Jewish and Christian Tradition," in G.R. Evans (ed.), *Christian Authority: Essays in Honour of Henry Chadwick* (Oxford: Clarendon Press, 1988), pp. 59-75; "The Literal, the Allegorical, and Modern Biblical Scholarship," *Journal for the Study of the Old Testament*, 44 (1989): 3-17; "Literality," *Faith and Philosophy*, 6/4 (October, 1989): 412-427; and *The Concept of Biblical Theology*, pp. 21, 186, 254. In all of these treatments of allegory and typology, Barr refers back approvingly to his initial assessment of the matter in *Old and New in Interpretation*.

5 *The Bible in the Modern World*, p. 63. See also *Old and New in Interpretation*, p. 129. In this passage Barr raises the question of how one can articulate a convincing theological argument for the connection between the Testaments after the "historical picture of the Old Testament facts has been accepted." He notes that "our historical way of looking at the meaning of texts has made it hard for us to give *direct* theological sanction to the way in which the New Testament has used the Old."

6 *The Bible in the Modern World*, p. 67.

7 Ibid., p. 62. Barr offers a chart of "Three possible processes of study of the Bible" on p. 61 and explains the implications for the division of labor where approaches to Bible texts are concerned on the following pages. All three were actually embodied in one approach in pre-critical exegesis, "it is only in the modern world that the three modes of study have broken apart." Ibid., p. 63.

82   *Revelation, Holy Scripture and Church*

This does not mean that modern biblical scholars are exclusively and primarily interested in the "literal meaning" of the Bible. For Barr, "literal" meaning is too often equated with naïve fundamentalist or conservative understanding of the Bible as a record of ostensive historical reporting.[8] Historical research has sometimes shown that biblical reports are not accurate historical accounts at all, for example, the story of the ascension, and thus not "literally true." At these points scholars have proposed that a passage may be understood at a level other than the literal, that "something like" an allegorical sense may be attributed to the Bible or a more general sense given to the story as a whole and that these readings may also be considered "true."[9] An interpreter may give up on a strict ostensive reading of the ascension story for the more pertinent question of why the author depicted Jesus ascending, given the thought forms of the author's time. But whether a literal, allegorical, or generalized sense is ascribed to the text, the ascription is made plausible by means of historical investigation into the thought world within which the text was generated. The text itself is used as a form of evidence from which the mind of the author and circumstances of its production are reconstructed. Thus Barr maintains that the historical critic is most interested in a text's "historical-theological" sense; that is "the theology that operated in the minds of those who created the biblical literature."[10] Paul Ricoeur's contention that on an historical-critical reading of the Bible, "true meaning", "the meaning intended by the author" and "original meaning" are conflated,[11] would seem an apt description of Barr's proposal.

Breakdown of Typological Unity

This constriction of meaning to the range of meanings possible within the social and cultural horizon of the author rules out traditional typological and allegorical intertextual referencing within the Bible, since these exceed the thought world of the author(s). There can be no inscribed secondary referencing or the ascription of a fuller sense to a New Testament text, which was the realization of a meaning immanent in the Old, by means of proof-texting and special pleading to God or the Holy Spirit as

---

8 "The Literal, the Allegorical, and Modern Biblical Scholarship," p. 10; "Literality," p. 413; *Fundamentalism*, pp. 120-159; and *The Bible in the Modern World*, pp. 168ff.

9 Barr distinguishes between legitimate modern allegory and medieval and ancient forms. Older allegory (1) allegorized literal texts and, what is more, (2) decontextualized small pieces of texts, "interpreted them in ways that are irreconcilable with the context within the books" and "uproot[ed] them from the culture in which they have meaning." In short, an allegorical sense seems plausible to Barr only when and where an allegorical intention can be ascribed to the author of the text through historical research. See "The Literal, the Allegorical, and Modern Biblical Scholarship," p. 14 and *The Bible in the Modern World*, p. 172.

10 "The Literal, the Allegorical, and Modern Biblical Scholarship," p. 12. The association of meaning with the intentional world of the author can be found throughout Barr's work. See, for example, *Holy Scripture*, pp. 116-118; Review of *Introduction to the Old Testament as Scripture* by Brevard Childs, *Journal for the Study of the Old Testament*, 16 (1980): 16; and *The Bible in the Modern World*, pp. 168-176.

11 Paul Ricoeur, "The Nuptial Metaphor," in LaCoque and Ricoeur, *Thinking Biblically*, p. 266.

The author of the Bible, which is what was done in "older Christendom."[12] Moreover, the appropriation of "typology" as a legitimate means for contemporary exegesis to extend the meaning pattern of the Bible to the current life and witness of the church was also inhibited. Treated as human historical accounts, the unity of the Bible, "as a seamless robe, a network of interrelated images,"[13] is torn apart and the traditional Christian understanding of the Bible draws apart from biblical scholarship.

Barr, however, does not view the breakdown of traditional typological construals of the Bible in its unity as the permanent condition of the church's understanding of Scripture. He understands the *value* of traditional pre-critical Christian use of the Bible, typologically construed, not just in the texts themselves but also in depicting all of life in terms of patterns resident within the Bible.[14] Moreover, he maintains there is good theological reason for interest in the unity of the Bible. He writes, "If in fact the Bible in some sense comes from the one God, whether inspired by him or given by him as authority, it would seem to follow that the end-product of its effect would have some sort of unity and not be absolutely self-contradictory."[15] Barr is thus theologically motivated to offer an expression of the unity of the Bible that, at the same time, maintains both the value of the Bible in guiding the church in all of life[16] and avoids negating historical biblical research.[17]

Before turning to what Barr considers to be the most promising theological/ historical manner in which to construe the unity of the Bible, after the breakdown of its typological unity as proposed in pre-critical exegesis, he first examines and rejects two alternative options for expressing the unity of the Bible: typology reinvigorated and Christological reading of Scripture. Although there is overlap between these two strategies for articulating biblical unity, they will be treated in turn.

Barr articulates his most sustained argument against efforts to maintain the unity of the Bible by rehabilitating typology, in a way that does not negate the historical study of the Bible, in *Old and New in Interpretation*. While the polemic contexts in which his criticisms of typology change, the argument initially articulated in 1966 does not: it is either rehearsed in synopsis form or the reader is referred to the relevant material in chapter 4 of *Old and New in Interpretation*. The initial context in which Barr's repudiation of a post-critical redeployment of typology occurs in a dispute with Biblical Theology; [18] Barr notes that careful attempts to articulate the

---

12 *The Bible in the Modern World*, p. 63.

13 Ibid. See also *Old and New in Interpretation*, p. 130.

14 *The Bible in the Modern World*, pp. 62-63.

15 Ibid., p. 99.

16 *Old and New in Interpretation*, p. 130. Barr is concerned with how the church "may regulate" its own exegetical practice in keeping with typological and allegorical methods found in the New Testament.

17 Ibid.."A theological statement of the connection between the Testaments must include, and not pass by, an interpretation of the historical connection."

18 The argument is initially espoused against members of the so-called Biblical Theology movement, who were trying to articulate a sense of typology congruent with the "biblical concept of history." Barr takes issue with a number of authors, including Von Rad, Lamp, Noth, Eichrodt and others, who contributed to two collections of essays: G.W.H. Lampe and K.J. Woollcombe (eds), *Essays in Typology* (London, 1957) and Claus Westermann (ed.),

84   *Revelation, Holy Scripture and Church*

difference between typology and allegory form the backdrop against which typology is renewed. Typology, in so far as it is between events, especially acts of God, in the Bible, is acceptable for those who would reinvigorate its use in biblical interpretation because such use adheres to the Bible's own emphasis on relations of historical correspondence. Where typological interpretation verges on the allegorical because the relations between persons, objects or institutions within it are "non-historical," "it runs wild and becomes an overly subtle exhibition of cleverness."[19] This distinction between typology and allegory based on "the Bible's own historical emphasis"[20] is fundamental to an approach to the Old Testament which (1) presupposes its unity with the New Testament, and (2) guides and determines interpretation as a whole.[21]

Barr rejects this attempt. On his view, the subtle distinction between typology of a very specific kind, and allegory, cannot be maintained. He demonstrates that texts, like the Song of Solomon, can be allegorized into a system—to refer to Christ and the church or God and Israel—where God's acts in history are regarded as the primary bearers of revelation.[22] Such attempts, on his view, depend less on the method of allegory than on the nature of the texts to which the allegorical method is applied. "What is important is the following: the second system, whether 'resultant' in reality or not, by its nature and content decides the sort of thing that is going to be 'found' by the interpretative process."[23] In the case of New Testament interpretation, the second system is almost always the "Christological kerygma," and thus centering on an event in the second system sends the interpreter looking for event-type correspondences in the first system (the Old Testament). This has nothing to do with New Testament writers' methodological preference for typological interpretation over allegorical;

Essays on Old Testament Hermeneutics (Richmond, 1963). In the second edition of *Old and New in Interpretation*, Barr directs his argument against Barth and Bultmann. See *Old and New in Interpretation*, 2nd edn (London, 1982), pp. 9-11, 24, 161ff. See also Nathaniel Murrell, "James Barr's Critique of Biblical Theology: A Critical Analysis," PhD dissertation, Drew University, 1988, p. 130. Barr repeats part of his argument against typology in the context of his polemic against Brevard Childs on the canon. See *Holy Scripture*, p. 116.

Biblical Theology in Barr's use of the term refers to a mid-twentieth century movement in North America, England and in Europe. It had three distinguishing characteristics: (1) the assertion of the authority of the Bible and a biblical pattern for thinking in a modern form; (2) the synthetic attempt to state the theology of Old or New Testament "within two covers"; and (3) the analytic attempt to identify and analyze "individual strata" within the Bible and to articulate the theological function of concepts and tendencies. See James Barr, "Trends and Prospects in Biblical Theology," *Journal of Theological Studies*, 25/2 (October, 1974): 265ff.

19 G. Von Rad, "Typological Interpretation of the Old Testament," in Westermann (ed.), *Essays on Old Testament Hermeneutics*, p. 36 cited in *Old and New in Interpretation*, p. 111.

20 Ibid.

21 Westermann, *Essays on Old Testament Hermeneutics*, p. 11 cited in Murrell, "James Barr's Critique of Biblical Theology," p. 130.

22 *Old and New in Interpretation*, p. 106. He repeats this emphasis on the allegorical appropriation of the Song of Songs by the New Testament in "Allegory and Typology," p. 14.

23 *Old and New in Interpretation*, p. 109.

The Bible as Holy Scripture   85

it is a question of the subject matter, which made event-centered typology a more obvious choice.

Barr also maintains that event-centered typology is too simple a distinction and too slender a basis for the interpretation of the Old Testament and the maintenance of the unity of the Bible. It is not possible using a typology of "revelational history" (1) to maintain the fine distinction between a typology of events and other kinds of typology against the actual practice of the New Testament;[24] (2) to account for the multiplicity of ways in which the Testaments are related through not only typology but allegory, *paraenesis*, fulfillments of prophecy, linguistic connections, similarities in language and style and action;[25] and (3) to afford intertestamental literature from Hellenistic Judaism the positive valuation it deserves in shaping subsequent Christian typological exegesis. In a more recent article, Barr provides an example of this last objection. He demonstrates that in the typological relation between Adam and Christ the gap between Genesis and Paul is greater if Wisdom, that is, certain non-canonical intertestamental texts of Hellenistic Judaism, "[is] left out of the reckoning, as in almost all Protestant history." [26] However, if these texts are taken into account, such that they form part of the history of the reception of the Adam narrative which mediated an understanding of Adam that made him more amenable to typological appropriation by Paul, the gap is lessened.[27]

Barr also maintains against typological interpretation that even if it is an important way in which New Testament writers made connections with the Old Testament, this method of relating the Testaments "partake[s] to some extent in the once-ness of the incarnation."[28] It was within the thought world and temporality of the first century that Jesus entered with his message and work. This first-century situation, although partly recoverable through historical research and thus subject to examination and even admiration, is not repeatable. The interpretative forms within which early Christian witnesses worked are historically situated and thus cannot be regarded as mandatory for all subsequent interpreters.

However, the heart of Barr's rejection of typology as the key to Old Testament interpretation and the unity of Scripture, lies in his critique of "the revelational character of events to which the text is said to witness."[29] A modern interpreter cannot separate "revelational events" from the continuum of human interpretation in which they are carried. Barr writes:

> In the achievement of salvation for men we do not see the Bible functioning in relation to a history done by God only, but also a history which is the history of the interpretation of

---

24 Here Barr is objecting to the proposal of Von Rad, "Typological Interpretation of the Old Testament," pp. 17-39. See *Old and New in Interpretation*, pp. 111-115.

25 Ibid., p. 115.

26 "The Authority of Scripture," p. 73.

27 Barr notes that St Paul's point of departure in the typological appropriation of the Genesis story was Jesus Christ in his life and work, forming his ultimate authority base. The approach that Barr suggests takes the Genesis text "as the authority base in itself." Ibid.

28 *Old and New in Interpretation*, p. 131; *The Scope and Authority of the Bible*, pp. 68-69; and *Holy Scripture*, p. 116.

29 Wells, *James Barr and the Bible*, p. 108.

86   *Revelation, Holy Scripture and Church*

the Bible. We could also say: if we speak of a history of salvation, the history of biblical interpretation is as much a source of continuity in that history as the sequence of God's acts are; indeed it might be possible that the continuity shifts back and forward between the two.[30]

Barr's fundamental rejection of the rehabilitation of a typology of "events" as a basis for the interpretation of the Old Testament and unity of the Bible is that it focuses too steadily on God's acts alone as the basis for that unity. In this one-sided consideration of continuity (of God's event-actions) within the history of salvation, the human side of biblical interpretation (the continuity of human interpretation) in its variable relationship with that history, is marginalized, even left out of account.

Rejection of Christological Proposals

Barr also rejects hermeneutic depictions of the Bible that are Christologically centered; that is, which make Christ "the key" to the understanding of the Old Testament and to the construal of the Bible in its unity.[31] Barr turns a critical eye on Christological depiction of Holy Scripture three times in *Old and New in Interpretation*. The first is actually a rejection of a Christocentric model of revelation.[32] He does, however, note that a Christocentric model of revelation has implications for Scripture interpretation. The interpreter, working anywhere in the Bible, interprets with an eye toward revelation, which is almost "identical with Christ."[33] Barr rejects this mode of interpretation since it disables Old Testament interpretation on its own terms. He will take this criticism up in more detail in the third part of his critique.

    The second critical examination of Christological construal of the Bible occurs in his chapter on typology and allegory. In this case, the context of the examination is properly related to how a concentration on Christ, or the New Testament as the "key" to a proper understanding of the Old Testament, can provide a basis for interpretation and the unity of the Bible. Barr rejects this proposal on historical grounds. Historically, he contends, the relation of Christ to the Old Testament was precisely the opposite to that implied. The problem was not how to understand the Old Testament in the light of Christ, but rather, for the apostles, how to understand Christ within the light of the Old Testament. Moreover, in the current situation, with its lack of knowledge and uncertainties about Christ and the Old Testament, the Christological proposal will "lead to all the bad kinds of Christologizing the Old Testament."[34]

    The more correct approach, according to Barr, is to begin with the Old Testament as something we "*have*" in the church, and then probe the ways in which it helps us to live as disciples of Christ. Moreover, contends Barr, rather than simply accepting modes (typology and allegory) for understanding the relationships between the Testaments given from earlier times, we should put our own modes of understanding

---

30 *Old and New in Interpretation*, p. 147.

31 Ibid., pp. 139-147. Barr has in mind a collection of essays edited by A. Richardson and W. Schweitzer, *Biblical Authority for Today* (London, 1951).

32 *Old and New in Interpretation*, p. 99.

33 Ibid., p. 100.

34 Ibid., p. 140.

The Bible as Holy Scripture   87

to work to establish whether and in what senses Christ "fulfills" Old Testament Scriptures. From an historical point of view that means: (1) the Old Testament must be viewed as the necessary cultural-religious matrix into which Christ came to be born;[35] and (2) the evaluation of New Testament citations of the Old must be seen not against the context from which the texts are taken, but against the context of what Christians wanted to do with them. Only in this way will we understand the amalgam of creativity and faithfulness with which Old Testament texts are taken up and used in the New in their application to the Christ. Barr eschews heavy-handed methods, even if they are Christological, because they inhibit an inductive and historical analysis of the relationships between the Testaments.[36]

The final analysis of Christological interpretation of the Bible for the sake of biblical unity takes place in a more constructive section of *Old and New in Interpretation*. For the first time Barr proposes a basis for the unity of the Bible. It is the continuity of God's identity in salvation across the Testaments, "the God of Israel is the One God and Father of the Lord Jesus Christ."[37] However, the unity of the Testaments at the level of the one God's work of salvation cannot, on the one hand, be proved (indeed attempts should not be made to do so) because this is a confession of faith. On the other hand, this confession should not take place in a manner that is indifferent to historical scholarship; for the realities to which faith relates and by which it learns and grows are the subject of historical investigation.

It is at his level that Barr again raises his protest against Christological imposition upon overall depictions of the Bible. When this is done, the Old Testament is depreciated as the "not yet" to which the New Testament is added as the fulfillment without ever seriously considering the time of our Lord-not-yet-come as the time in which the God of Israel was working out his saving purpose in real contacts with Israel. Barr, examining Old Testament texts in their own positivity, holds that Jesus Christ, while he is the culmination of God's saving purpose, does not function as the measure of the meaningfulness of God's actions before his time. In this way the unfolding of the divine purpose in salvation is Trinitarian, not just Christological. "The direction of thought is from God to Christ, from Father to Son, and not from Christ to God."[38] What is more, this movement—from the Father to the Son—while it does not prohibit Christological interpretation, does free it from the burden of searching out "highly artificial"[39] Christological interpretations of passages where the God of Israel is the subject of Old Testament texts.

The Unity of the Bible

What can be said about the unity of the Old and New Testaments then, given that Barr rejects attempts to maintain it on the basis of typology and Christology or

---

35 Ibid., p. 141. See also *Holy Scripture*, p. 11.

36 *Old and New in Interpretation*, pp. 143-144.

37 Ibid., p. 150.

38 Ibid., pp. 154-155.

39 Ibid., p. 154.

88   *Revelation, Holy Scripture and Church*

indeed on the basis of any pattern or balance *within* the Bible?[40] In general, the bases for the unity of the Bible are not located within the text of the Bible itself, but outside of it, behind it. At an empirical level, Barr proposes that the theological relationships between the Testaments ought to be pursued through an examination of: (1) Jesus' assumption of the hermeneutic processes of the people of his own time; (2) the conflict and crisis between Jesus and the interpretative traditions of his time; and (3) the relationship between Jews and Gentiles in the achievement and reception of salvation. On this last point, Barr notes the way in which Jewish and Gentile salvation are linked together, "such that the latter does not find God except through some involvement with the former . . ."[41] Moreover, Barr maintains that in the Epistle to the Ephesians, Jew and Gentile are depicted as sharing the common destiny of showing forth reconciliation to all. Soteriology is thus an important and decisive doctrine linking the Old and New Testaments, and their peoples, together.

A second basis for the unity of the Bible relates to the first. Barr writes:

> But the profoundest unity is not a unity within the Bible, on the level of common patterns of thought, or consisting in a balance we may discern between its different emphases, between its conflicting view points: it is rather the unity of the one God, which is also a unity within variety, and—dare we say?—a unity with a history.[42]

The unity of the one God—the God of Israel who is the God and Father of our Lord Jesus Christ—is the basis for the conviction that the Bible, in all its diversity, will not present us with "irreconcilable opposites."[43] However, the prospect for scriptural unity, or for at least a diversity of construals that recognize one another as related, is only sought, grasped and found in faith.[44] Such attempts at all-encompassing depictions inevitably run up against the "intransigence" of the Bible itself. The Bible with its variety of materials, patterns and its non-systematic nature resists attempts to construe it *in toto*.[45] What is more, the unity aimed at cannot be read off the continuity of divine acts that straddle the Testaments. As Barr maintained earlier, what we have in the Bible is not a series of uninterpreted divine acts which form their own continuity and unity. The human interpretation in which God's acts are described is gathered up together with the saving acts of the one God, such that the continuity (and unity) of the story of salvation oscillates between the history of interpretation as human description and as divine action.

Moreover, this kind of construal of the whole of the Bible in a unity as, for example, the story of salvation, is enabled by a prior fundamental orientation toward the Bible. The structure of faith or the fundamental faith of the believing community

---

40 *The Bible in the Modern World*, p. 181.

41 *Old and New in Interpretation*, p. 164. See also James Barr, "The Old Testament," in David Jenkins (ed.), *The Scope of Theology* (Cleveland, 1965), p. 38.

42 *The Bible in the Modern World*, p. 181.

43 Ibid.

44 Ibid., pp. 99, 118, 181. See also *Old and New in Interpretation*, p. 150.

45 *The Scope and Authority of the Bible*, p. 122.

The Bible as Holy Scripture   89

is "generatively antecedent"[46] to the Bible and even after a "canon is formed" continues to provide a theological principle, like the *regula fidei*,[47] for ordering and relating the contents of the Bible to each other in a unity. However, this previous ecclesially immanent faith structure, which enables a unity to be made of the Bible, cannot be argued for, only confessed.[48] What is more, this confession must always be alert to the ways in which critical research makes an impact on the realities which faith confesses.

Implicated Authority of the Bible

> Where does religious authority ultimately reside? It may be said to reside, most obviously, in God himself and in the deeds of salvation that he has wrought. But our knowledge of these deeds comes to us through authoritative persons, whose interpretation of them is recognized as weighty and luminous in the Church. On the other hand, our access to these persons is mediated through the texts that they have left us. And these texts themselves contain certain interpretations of still older texts, which were understood to be authoritative from before the beginnings of Christianity itself.[49]

The question of the authority of the Bible as Scripture of the church arises for Barr within the larger context of the Bible's relation to God and the work of salvation.[50] The basis for the unity of the Bible is also the basis for its authority. As the above citation indicates, involvement with the Bible means involvement, not only directly with the human witnesses whose interpretation the Bible is, but also, through them, with the one God of Abraham, Isaac and Jacob, who is the God and Father of our Lord Jesus Christ. In the process of working out salvation, Scripture is implicated, first as Old Testament, which provided the context for the intelligibility of the life and mission of Jesus, and secondly, in the lives of present Christians who find that the Bible "speaks to us" and "fits in with the problem of faith in Jesus Christ," "the doing of his will" and that the Bible "serve(s) the upbuilding of [our] faith," and "the learning of . . . obedience."[51]

---

46 Ibid., p. 120. See also James Barr, "The Bible and Its Communities," in James Mays (gen. ed.), *Harper's Bible Commentary* (New York, 1988), p. 72.

47 See *The Scope and Authority of the Bible*, p. 121.

48 Here it seems that Barr follows Von Rad. See Barr, "Trends and Prospects in Biblical Theology," p. 271. Compare *Old and New in Interpretation*, p. 150 and *The Bible in the Modern World*, p. 181.

49 "The Authority of Scripture," p. 59. See *The Scope and Authority of the Bible*, pp. 52-64 and *Holy Scripture*, p. 4, where Barr writes: "In the Bible faith was not controlled by Scripture: rather, Scripture derived from faith."

50 *The Scope and Authority of the Bible*, p. 118, Barr notes that the argument he advances for the authority of the Bible in terms of its soteriological function is "central" to his two previous books: *Old and New in Interpretation* and *The Bible in the Modern World*.

51 *The Scope and Authority of the Bible*, p. 54. See also pp. 34-35. "The essential function of Scripture [Old Testament Scripture] was to lend intelligibility to events that were to come. Its basic soteriological direction was towards the future." See also *Holy Scripture*, p. 11 in which Barr maintains that the Old Testament is "functional in salvation" in that it provides the background for the understanding of Jesus, "through the chain of events within his ministry

90   *Revelation, Holy Scripture and Church*

The church discovers that in its involvement with God and salvation, the Bible is the means, the effective means, by which the faith-relation is engendered and sustained. "Faith is Christian because it relates itself to classically-expressed models."[52] The authority of the Bible is thus instrumental as "a God-given meeting ground"[53] for our meeting God in faith. For Christians do not believe in the Bible, *per se*, but in Jesus Christ, the one through whom we encounter God, who comes to meet us through the Bible. The authority of the Bible in the church is, on Barr's view, an aspect of its soteriological function. "Scripture is fundamental to the church of God, not because it is a book of true facts about God and about past events, but because it is built into the way in which salvation was achieved."[54]

However, like the terms "revelation" and "inspiration," which have a scope of application beyond the confines of the Bible, "authority" is also a designation which stretches behind the Bible. The Bible may be properly described as having authority, but so do the persons "behind" the Bible, who offered the luminous accounts which mediate knowledge of God and his salvific deeds. Barr suggests at a number of points that the persons and communities who generated the texts of the Bible, like St Paul, must be considered "authoritative persons" sharing as they do in the history of transmission and the formation of the texts of the Bible.[55]

The one restriction on this sharing of authority, which "revelation" and "inspiration" do not enjoy, however, is that authority is confined to those people, communities and traditions in the larger "cumulative tradition" which precede the formation of the Bible as Old and New Testaments. The Bible is a "classic literary expression of the people of God's experience in their contact with God."[56] Its classic status implies that it is unsurpassed and normative for those who come after it,[57] that it will fund preaching and liturgy and Eucharist and that its resources will provide

---

and up to his passion." He concludes, "This is a theme that I made central to an earlier book, *Old and New in Interpretation*, and I still think that it cannot be sufficiently emphasized."

52 *The Bible in the Modern World*, p. 118.

53 *The Scope and Authority of the Bible*, p. 55.

54 Ibid., pp. 53-54. See also *The Bible in the Modern World*, p. 118.

55 Barr shifts slightly toward the people of God on the question of whether it is the authority of Scripture or the authority of the people of God (pre-scriptural oral and written tradition) that should be our primary interest. His answer changes over the course of his writings. See *The Scope and Authority of the Bible*, pp. 50-51, 63-64 where Barr claims both are authoritative, and *Holy Scripture*, pp. 4ff. and 48, where he leans in the direction of the authority of the people. Ben C. Ollenburger in his review of Barr's *Holy Scripture* records that this position is "odd." It is necessary because Barr argues that "since the people of the biblical period ascribed no theological importance to the canon, neither should we." Review of *Holy Scripture* by James Barr, *Theology Today*, 41 (July, 1984): 209. See also Murrell, "James Barr's Critique of Biblical Theology," pp. 234-235.

56 *The Scope and Authority of the Bible*, p. 122. See also *The Bible in the Modern World*, pp. 117-118, 120, 122, 136.

57 Barr does entertain the notion that "later exegesis could be new revelation possibly transcending or even reversing the sense of the biblical form." *The Concept of Biblical Theology*, p. 599. In what sense the Bible would remain "paradigmatic" or "classic" while at the same time transcended is not specified.

The Bible as Holy Scripture 91

"paradigmatic guidance"[58] for the problems of the church today. In none of these tasks, maintains Barr, should the Bible be taken as an infallible guide or an inerrant source of information. The Bible is not a perfect model but a sufficient one. All human language about God is imperfect and, what is more, the Bible is not constructed as a theological system given to precision. It is rather a battleground in which men and women struggle with God and with each other so that others can learn from it.[59]

Barr's interest in including "pre-scriptural" traditions and persons and communities behind the production of the Bible within his consideration of biblical authority lead him to qualify the importance of terms like "canon" and "Scripture" in so far as these terms tend to isolate a certain stage in the development of the corpus of the Bible from its larger place within the cumulative tradition, all of which is formed in congruence "with the fundamental structure of Christian faith."[60] While he does articulate a standard historical account of the criterion for canonicity, the reasons for the development of the Christian canon,[61] and, moreover, recognizes the Bible as a "crystallization" of Israel's and the church's experience of God,[62] he resists investing the term "canon" with too much importance since this encourages an understanding of biblical authority at a purely synchronic level. Barr maintains that this move abstracts the corpus of biblical writing from its diachronic development and thus neglects the authority of pre-Christian-canon persons and communities, who in effect have shaped and mediated knowledge of God and salvation to us in their interpretations of God and salvation. This extended sense of authority, attached in its most primitive sense to the fundamental form of faith, crystallized in the Bible, but extending behind it to prescriptural communities and authors, becomes a critical principle for Barr.

In a review of David Kelsey's book, *The Uses of Scripture in Recent Theology*, Barr notes the tendency in the United States to "exaggerate" the importance of terms like "Scripture" and "canon" in specifying the nature and authority of the Bible. He maintains that Kelsey avoids the real problematics of biblical authority by a "slight of hand," when he simply asserts, "Scripture 'analytically' implies authority."[63]

---

58 *The Scope and Authority of the Bible*, p. 125; *The Bible in the Modern World*, p. 136; *Holy Scripture*, p. 43; and *The Concept of Biblical Theology*, p. 602.

59 On the sufficiency of Scripture see *The Bible in the Modern World*, pp. 119, 128. Barr uses the term "adequate" to indicate the same notion in *The Scope and Authority of the Bible*, pp. 124-125. Barr employs the Old Testament term *ribh* (dispute) to indicate the nature of the Bible as an argument about God so that others can learn from it.

60 *The Bible in the Modern World*, p. 117.

61 See "The Bible and Its Communities," pp. 71-72. Here Barr identifies authorship, theological content—whether a book accords with the church's faith as expressed by authoritative persons—as criteria for canonicity. The polemic confrontation with Marcion and the Gnostics, the question of which books could be read in church, and the temporal, ethical and geographical distance opening up between the early witnesses and the subsequent expansion of the Christian tradition, are events which precipitated an interest in the formation of a written canon for the church.

62 *The Concept of Biblical Theology*, p. 282.

63 Review of *The Uses of Scripture in Recent Theology* by David H. Kelsey (Philadelphia, 1975), *Virginia Seminary Journal*, 30/3 and 31/1 (November, 1978 and March, 1979): 40. See

92   *Revelation, Holy Scripture and Church*

Moreover, Barr's reticence about the wholesale appropriation of structuralist methods for the interpretation of the Bible is also related to the manner in which these methods of interpretation tend to cut the Bible off from "extra textual" persons and events.[64] And finally, in his argument with Brevard Childs concerning the nature and function of the canon, Barr is, at least partly, motivated by what he understands to be Childs' attempts to reify the notion of canon such that the final form of the Bible becomes authoritative in abstraction from its place within a larger reality. In his review of Childs' *Introduction to the Old Testament as Scripture*, Barr notes (1) Childs' opposition to "extrinsic hermeneutic datum"[65] in the interpretation of canonical Scripture; and (2) how Childs concentrates theological "authority" in the canonical form of the text since final redactors and canonizers, in making their last touches on the text, have cut us off from the circumstances of a text's production and its prior redactive history. The authority of the people and events out of which these texts come is visible only in the way they are presented in the final canonical form of the text.

Barr rejects Childs' first assertion since the essential hermeneutic datum of the Bible is not located within the canon itself, but in the basic structure of the faith of Israel (and the church), which is "an anterior reality through which Scripture as a secondary product was generated."[66] Barr thus invests "canon" as *regula fidei*, the faith structure by which the books of the Bible are construed, with a greater theological significance and authority than "canon" as a list of books. He contends that "canon" as theological grid makes "canon" as accepted books relatively unimportant. Whether or not a few books were added or taken away from the collection of the Bible would not alter the identity of the church, since all books are construed by the structure of faith itself,[67] or some part of it, and on this construal some books

---

also *Holy Scripture*, pp. 41ff. for a more charitable reading of Kelsey.

64 "Biblical Language and Exegesis—How Far Does Structuralism Help Us?" *King's Theological Review* 7/2 (Autumn, 1984): 52. Barr links structuralism and Childs together as proposing a hermeneutic which minimizes the historical dimension of the Bible. See *The Scope and Authority of the Bible*, pp. 45-47

65 Review of *Introduction to the Old Testament as Scripture* by Brevard Childs, p. 16. See also *Holy Scripture*, pp. 116-118 and *The Concept of Biblical Theology*, pp. 37-39, 49-51, 378-438. Barr notes in this last section that Childs so absolutizes the canon that considerations of the history and comparison of religions and biblical mentalities are ruled out of his "canonical theology." See ibid., pp. 429-431. Barr maintains that his distance from Childs on the importance of the canon lies in the distinct ways in which they conceive of the relation between biblical theology and history of religions, Barr giving a higher valuation to the later particularly with respect to "the period of the biblical books themselves." See "Trends and Prospects in Biblical Theology," pp. 273-275, 281. The quotation is from p. 281.

66 Review of Childs' *Introduction to the Old Testament as Scripture*, p. 16.

67 Barr remarks, "[T]he canon is not very important. Scripture itself in its content makes it clear to us that the boundary of the canon does not necessarily or always express precisely the horizon of authority in Christian believing." *Holy Scripture*, p. 126. See also Review of *The Uses of Scripture in Recent Theology*, p. 40; *The Scope and Authority of the Bible*, p. 61; and *Holy Scripture*, pp. 41-42. Barr appreciates that, for biblical Christianity, the concept of authoritative "Scripture," that is, of certain texts which bear religious authority, is important but canon, as a list of books, is not. *Holy Scripture*, pp. 63-64. Barr remarks elsewhere that it

The Bible as Holy Scripture   93

are more central and some are "marginal details." He also rejects Childs second assertion. Barr maintains that redactors do not, in the clear and decisive manner that Childs suggests, intend to cut interpreters off from the precanonical forms of biblical texts and thus concentrate authority in the final form of the text. It may well be that they intend for us to extend authority to the people or events out of which the text came by "anti-hermeneutical" maneuvers.[68] When a redactor resists smoothing the text, adding links, and instead leaves contradiction and difficulty open to plain view, it may well be that we readers are invited to ask what went on behind the text, before the text, in the history where God was active in Israel.[69]

In sum: the canonical books of Holy Scripture have authority in the church, on Barr's account, in so far as they are an instantiation of and implicated within the fundamental faith structure of the Christian church, which precedes them. However, authority also belongs to the persons and communities who lie behind the Bible, who in effect authored and shaped and transmitted the Bible since "the church is founded upon 'the foundation of the apostles and prophets' . . . not upon the foundation of the books named after them."[70]

Critique

"It is a main concern of both scholarship and theology that the Bible should be soundly and adequately interpreted."[71] As a means to this goal, Barr proposes that a critical space should be opened up between "faith and the Bible" to permit the "natural" and "factual" sense of the Bible to emerge free from theological infringement. Both Samuel Balentine and John Barton, contributors to and editors of a Barr *Festschrift*,[72] maintain that the freedom of biblical research from controlling theological presuppositions is, for the sake of critical inquiry, a fundamental feature of Barr's interpretative program. Barr's polemic against an understanding of the unity of Scripture that is based on typological (and/or allegorical) intertextual referencing and his understanding of the authority of canonical Scripture, reveal his determination to hold theological construals of the Bible as Holy Scripture subject to a prior historical-critical/history of religions[73] depiction of their "factuality."

---

is the "Gospel" that is supremely authoritative and that this Gospel is "lodged within inspired Scripture but not identical with it." The remark implies that the authority of the Bible is related to the message of the Gospel that calls people to faith and salvation. However, the relation between the Gospel and the formation of the canon, as something more than a list of books, never finds its way into Barr's musings.

68 Review of Childs' *Introduction to the Old Testament as Scripture*, pp. 17-18.

69 Ibid.

70 *Holy Scripture*, p. 48.

71 James Barr, *The Semantics of Biblical Language* (London, 1961), p. vii.

72 Balentine, "James Barr's Quest for Sound and Adequate Biblical Interpretation," pp. 5-7, 12-13; and Barton, "James Barr as Critic and Theologian," pp. 18-20. See also Barton, "Historical-Critical Approaches," in John Barton (ed.), *The Cambridge Companion to Biblical Interpretation* (Cambridge, 1998), pp. 16-19.

73 Levenson, "Negative Theology," p. 60. Levenson notes that Barr is interested in a history of religions approach to the Old Testament, which while related, he tries to distinguish

94 *Revelation, Holy Scripture and Church*

While confessions of the unity of Scripture and its authority are made in faith, and thus are not, for Barr, debatable on the level of evidence, the realities implicated in such confessions are subject to critical examination. "Faith itself learns and grows from studies in historical and other planes, and these in fact affect and build up its content."[74] Theology, if it wants to be a truth-seeking enterprise, must respect critical deliberations on the nature of the Bible in so far as these encroach on articulations of the unity and authority of the Bible since "truth"—and not relevance—wherever and whenever it is found, must always constrain theological construction.[75] This move on Barr's part effectively brackets out the primacy of Christian theological description of the Bible in its unity as Scripture of the Church admitting, in the end, those theological proposals that biblical research will sponsor once it has depicted the field in non-theological terms for the sake of "criticism." The central problem with this move is that it refuses, by means of a methodological preference for the properties of texts in their relation to human agents, a consideration of the special status of the Bible as Canon of and for the Church and the properties the Bible acquires by virtue of its relation to God's speech and action.[76] R.W.L. Moberly maintains, "Barr's way of conceptualizing issues of theology in relation to the Bible too easily transposes the question of God into questions about the history of religious ideas and practices."[77]

Typology and Christocentric interpretation   What Barr does not consider in his rejection of typological and Christocentric reading of the Bible is theologically warranted "retrospective reading."[78] And he does not consider reading the Old

---

from *Biblical Theology*. Levenson maintains that Barr is less than convincing in his own efforts to prevent Biblical Theology from collapsing into the history of Israelite (and Christian) religion.

74 *Old and New in Interpretation*, p. 151. Barr continues, "This is not just because faith has to pay attention to scholarship. More deeply, it is because it was in the nature, structure and historical development of the people and the tradition, the Scriptures and the religion, of Israel that the actual relations, to which faith applies itself, came into existence."

75 *Holy Scripture*, pp. 116-118. See also Review of Childs' *Introduction to the Old Testament as Scripture*, p. 16.

76 John Webster notes that the methodological preference for the properties of texts in relation to human agents "constituting a cultural and religious world" is ingrained in the manner in which theorists in cultural and religious studies and "more than a handful of modern theologians," treat Scripture. The Bible as "Holy" Scripture, that is, the Bible in its relation to God's communicative activity, is left out of these accounts. See *Holy Scripture*, p. 1. Barr indicates throughout his work that his account of the Bible as Scripture and its use in the church is framed in "very much human terms" and as such requires no reference to God in terms of inspiration or the choice of canonical books. See *The Bible in the Modern World*, pp. 118-119. See also Christopher Seitz, *Figured Out: Typology and Providence in Christian Scripture* (Louisville, 2001), p. 7.

77 R.W.L. Moberly, *The Bible, Theology, and Faith: A Study of Abraham and Jesus* (Cambridge, 2000), p. 37.

78 The phrase is used by Richard Hays, "Reading Scripture in the Light of the Resurrection," in Richard Hayes and Ellen Davis (eds), *The Art of Reading Scripture* (Grand Rapids, 2003), p. 224 and n. 19; and "The Conversion of the Imagination: Scripture and

The Bible as Holy Scripture 95

Testament in terms of the New Testament because the theological rationale for doing so is excluded from an historical-critical and history of religions approach to the Bible.[79] Barr does note that it was the Christological kerygma, not methodological preference, which encouraged New Testament writers to emphasize a typology of events with respect to the Old, but he does not develop the plain theological implication that typology (refiguring[80] Old Testament events and texts in terms of the Christ event) is rooted in the eschatological density accorded the life, death and resurrection of Jesus. This extension of the meaning of the Old Testament beyond its historical or original sense through a typologically configured and Christ-centered reading is, however, warranted by a theological judgment about what God has wrought in the world in Jesus. Richard Hays makes this very point concerning Paul's first letter to the Corinthians. He writes; " . . . Paul was not promulgating a linear *Heilsgeschichte* in which Gentiles were simply absorbed into a Torah-observant Jewish Christianity. Rather, the 'Israel' into which Paul's Corinthian converts were embraced was an Israel whose story had been hermeneutically reconfigured by the cross and resurrection."[81] The life, death and resurrection of Jesus exert hermeneutical pressure on the reading of Israel's Scripture such that they take on "resonances beyond those perceptible to its earlier readers."[82] In this way, meaning is not exclusively oriented by reconstructed historical/original/ literal sense, but expanded beyond it by means of the incorporation of Israel's story into a new story that evokes unexpected

---

Eschatology in 1 Corinthians," *New Testament Studies*, 45 (1999): 395. See also Berkouwer, *Holy Scripture*, pp. 232-233; Moberly, *The Bible, Theology, and Faith*, p. 70; and Childs, *Biblical Theology of the Old and New Testaments*, pp. 719-727.

79 James Smart notes that Barr's "dissent against all attempts to find in the New Testament witness to Jesus Christ the key to the understanding of the Old Testament" due to his narrow conception of revelation leads him to be quickly dismissive of substantial efforts to relate the Testaments around the figure of Christ and leaves the relationship between Jesus and the Old Testament "very foggy." This in spite of the fact that one of the express purposes of *Old and New in Interpretation* is to articulate the relation between the Testaments. James Smart, *The Past, Present, and Future of Biblical Theology* (Philadelphia, 1979), p. 34.

80 "Refiguring" is a term used by Richard Hays to describe two movements in the early church. First, it is used to depict the shaping of Gentile identity in the light of gospel of Jesus Christ—"a gospel message comprehensible only in relation to the larger narrative of God's dealing with Israel." Second, "refiguring" relates to the shaping of Jewish identity, the practices and beliefs of which are now figured in "critical confrontation with the gospel story." See "The Conversion of the Imagination," pp. 395, 396. Hays' use of the term is derived from Terence Donaldson, *Paul and the Gentiles: Remapping the Apostle's Convictional World* (Minneapolis, 1997), p. 236.

81 "The Conversion of the Imagination," p. 395.

82 "Reading Scripture in the Light of the Resurrection," p. 224. Hays remarks (p. 233) that one of the implications of the resurrection for biblical hermeneutics is that

we cannot confine the meaning of the Old Testament to the literal sense understood by its original authors and readers, for these ancient texts have been taken up into a new story that amplifies and illumines their meaning in unexpected ways. The New Testament writers insist that we are to read Israel's story as a witness to the righteousness of God, climactically disclosed in Jesus Christ. They insist that Israel's Scriptures, understood in the fullest and deepest way, prefigure Jesus.

and expanded senses from these ancient Scriptures. The fuller sense (*sensus plenior*) of the Old Testament, which testifies to God's gracious activity, is realized when it is put alongside the New Testament in figural relations that do not evacuate the content of the Old Testament but rather "specify [its] reference." Kevin Vanhoozer continues, "Jesus Christ—the fullest embodiment of God's gracious activity in Israel and in the world—is the literal referent of biblical testimony."[83]

Moreover, this ascription of a fuller sense to the Old Testament in the light of the death and resurrection of Jesus does not depend on the ascription of a secondary referent to the intentionality of the original author.[84] The fuller sense is elicited not by clever hermeneutical inquiry into veiled secondary intentions of human authors but by the action of God in Jesus Christ, the reality implications of which are articulated within New Testament writings through typological and figural interpretation of the Old and observed in the gathering together of Old and New Testaments together in one canon. Berkouwer writes:

> In the new situation of salvation that had appeared, and in the broad context of fulfillment, "a word [from the Old Testament] might light up based on the word and work of Jesus." Connections and context are indicated, and the words are isolated or quoted in a chain of connections; they are modified and applied in view of the one great purpose: to testify to the reality of salvation in Christ.[85]

What is more, retrospective reading engendered by the reality of Jesus Christ, his death and resurrection, does not erase either a consideration of the history of text reception or the historical specificity of what is read. Insights gained from the study of Wisdom writings of Hellenistic Judaism need not be excluded from biblical study. They help to fill in historical gaps in our understanding. However, dependence on their explanatory power in narrowing the gap between Christ and Adam in Pauline typology, for example, is qualified by the practice of a retrospective reading of Adam in the light of Christ. In other words, the use of specific typology will also have to be accounted for in terms of the "hermeneutical current" that flows between type and anti-type and the way in which "the meaning of each pole in the typological correlation is enhanced by its relation to the other."[86] Moreover, the specificity of

---

83 Vanhoozer, *Is There a Meaning in This Text?*, p. 314. See also George Lindbeck, "The Story-Shaped Church: Critical Exegesis and Theological Interpretation," in Garrett Green (ed.), *Scriptural Authority and Narrative Interpretation* (Philadelphia, 1987), p. 164. Lindbeck maintains that "the narrative meaning of the stories about Jesus was [and should be] the unique *sensus literalis* of the whole of Scripture for the groups by and for whom these stories were composed."

84 This move does not preclude some articulation of divine authorship and the attribution of an intended reference to God, which is the fuller meaning, beyond the immediate historical context of a given biblical book or passage. Kevin Vanhoozer is interested in just such a move, although on his account "the meaning associated with divine authorship—emerges only at the level of the whole canon." See *Is There a Meaning in This Text?*, pp. 264-265 and 314. See also John David Dawson, *Christian Figural Reading and the Fashioning of Identity* (Berkeley, 2002), p. 6.

85 Berkhouwer, *Holy Scripture*, p. 233.

86 Hays, "Reading Scripture in the Light of the Resurrection," p. 224, n. 19.

The Bible as Holy Scripture   97

Old Testaments texts is also maintained in typological interpretation since both type and anti-type retain their particularity even as they mutually condition and illumine one another.[87] Retrospective reading in no way excludes the full acknowledgement of the Scriptures of Israel as providing the matrix of intelligibility into which Christ came: "It will not treat the Old Testament as superseded or obsolete." For the Old Testament "has an indispensable role in bearing witness to the Gospel."[88] Retrospective reading does, however, insist on the typological (and more broadly figural) reading of the two Testaments in a unity since this is warranted by the practice of the New Testament itself in its interpretation of the central events of the life of Jesus and is thus a practice which teaches contemporary readers to remain alert to figural senses and latent meanings yet to be developed.[89]

However, Barr also makes the case that this sort of reading is too Christological, that is, it is not sufficiently Trinitarian. Retrospective reading, on Barr's account, thus suffers the same malady as attempts to rehabilitate typology in Biblical Theology. Barr maintains that his non-typological reading of the Old Testament in terms of its own positivity and salvific efficacy, where Christ is not made the measure of the meaningfulness of God's actions before his time, accords more closely with the manner in which divine salvation unfolds both in history and in the Bible. "The movement is from God to Christ, from Father to Son, and not from Christ to God."[90]

Three points can be made here. The first is that this doctrinal point is introduced into Barr's critical analysis of the typological unity of the Bible in a place subordinate to a previous historical-critical/history of religions construal of the relation between the Testaments. In short: "a Trinitarian reading" of the unfolding of divine salvation in the Bible correlates better with a critical/history of religions approach—"which respects the intentions which were present in the religion, the tradition, the prophets and the writers at the times of the various texts and of their ensuring interpretations"[91]—than with one theologically and typologically centered in Christ. Barr quite explicitly maintains that understanding texts in their socio-historical world preempts understanding them in terms of their witness to the ultimate purpose of God in the sending of his Son in the fullness of time. He argues there is "no actual prediction or prophecy" of which "Jesus is the intended content" and that however these Old Testament texts are related to God's ultimate salvific purposes "our use of these texts should relate to their intended content . . ."[92] Timothy Ward notes that history of religions approaches to the Bible tend to flatten out any sense of God

---

87 Ibid. and Frei, *The Eclipse of Biblical Narrative*, pp. 1-37. Frei is dependent on Eric Auerbach's *Mimesis*, pp. 44ff., for his understanding of typological and figural interpretation.

88 Hayes, "Reading Scripture in the Light of the Resurrection," p. 233.

89 "Jesus taught the disciples on the Emmaus road that *all* the Scriptures bore witness to him." Ibid., p. 234.

90 *Old and New in Interpretation*, pp. 154-155.

91 Ibid., p. 153. See also James Barr, *History and Ideology in the Old Testament: Biblical Studies at the End of a Millennium* (Oxford, 2000), pp. 24-25. Barr continues to give history of religions a high valuation for filling in "interpretative gaps."

92 Ibid.

98 *Revelation, Holy Scripture and Church*

as increasingly revealed through time "in the course of a teleological process of salvation worked out in history . . ."[93]

What is more, classic Christian Bible reading was Christological, since typology centers in the person of Christ, and this feature was not contrasted to but accompanied by a Trinitarian rule of faith.[94] Barr harnesses together human knowledge of the divine persons (as Father in the Old Testament and then as Son in the New) and the actual life of the divine persons, and thus confines his account to the economic Trinity. He fails to account for the immanent Trinitarian life of God in which the Father elects the Son from all eternity for the salvation of the world.[95] Gabriel Fackre makes the point that a "sequential" understanding of the Trinity is Sabellian, a position exposed and rejected by the church as insufficiently appreciative of *perichoresis*, the coinherence of the members of the Trinity.[96]

And finally, a related point is that Barr works with a conception of temporality that is not construed in any adequate relation to the Gospel. Robert Jenson writes, "Time, as we see it framing biblical narrative, is neither linear nor cyclical but perhaps more like a helix, and what it spirals around is the Risen Christ."[97] In this way, Jenson maintains, the unity of the Bible is "tighter" than we may have thought, since wherever the word of the Lord is spoken Jesus is speaking. We can, on the one hand, find out about the historical Jesus from Isaiah, Zechariah and David and, on the other, we can understand what Isaiah meant from the story of Jesus.

Behind all of these objections to Barr's proposal for a "Trinitarian" unity between the Testaments based on successive divine salvific acts and their human interpretations, there is a common claim: the unity of the Testaments is ontological and teleological.[98] Childs' points to this when he asserts that typology extends meaning beyond an original event and "finds in it an adumbration of the one consistent purpose of God within history."[99] Thus, while the unity of the Testaments

---

93 Ward, *Word and Supplement*, pp. 249-250.

94 See George Lindbeck, "Scripture, Consensus, and Community," in Richard John Neuhaus (ed.), *Biblical Interpretation in Crisis* (Grand Rapids, 1989), p. 77; Paul M. Blowers, "The *Regula Fidei* and the Narrative Character of Early Christian Faith," in *Pro Ecclesia*, 6/2 (1997): 199-228; Hans Von Campenhausen, *The Formation of the Christian Bible*, trans. J.A. Baker (Philadelphia, 1972), p. 329 and Seitz, *Figured Out*, p. 6.

95 See Childs, *Biblical Theology of the Old and New Testaments*, p. 14 and *Isaiah*, pp. 420-423. See also Thomas F. Torrance, *Reality and Evangelical Theology: A Fresh and Challenging Approach to Christian Revelation* (Philadelphia, 1997), p. 24.

96 Gabriel Fackre, *The Doctrine of Revelation: A Narrative Interpretation* (Grand Rapids, 1997), pp. 27-28. Fackre maintains, "The economy of the divine doing is rooted in the ontology of the divine being." Ibid., p. 26.

97 Robert Jenson, "Scripture's Authority in the Church," in Hays and Davis (eds), *The Art of Reading Scripture*, p. 35. See also Seitz, *Figured Out*, p. 9; and Frei, *The Eclipse of Biblical Narrative*, p. 8.

98 Barr rejects as "exaggerated" Ricoeur's claim that "the kergyma is the rereading of an ancient Scripture." See Ricoeur, "Preface to Bultmann," p. 51.

99 Brevard Childs, "Jesus Christ the Lord and the Scriptures of the Church," in Ephraim Radner and George Sumner (eds), *The Rule of Faith: Scripture, Canon, and Creed in a Critical Age* (Harrisburg, 1998), p. 12.

The Bible as Holy Scripture 99

is born witness to in successive salvific acts, it would be a failure to regard these acts as unrelated or related only in the sense that the same God performs them. The One God, the God of Israel who is the God and Father of our Lord Jesus Christ, planned, before the foundation of the world, the salvation of all creation through Jesus Christ, to which the Scriptures of the Old and New Testament in their typological unity bear witness. Childs' maintains, "I am far from convinced that Barr's analysis has really touched the heart of the theological problem related to biblical typology." He continues:

> The issue turns on the nature of the biblical referent and the effort of both the Old and New Testament authors to extend their experience of God through figuration in order to depict the unity of God's one purpose. Barr's own treatment of the relation of the testaments (*Old and New in Interpretation*, 149ff), correctly emphasizes the role of the Old Testament as a testimony to the time before Christ's coming, but fails to deal adequately with the theological claim of an ontological as well as a soteriological unity of the two testaments, which lies at the heart of the New Testament's application of the Old (cf. John 1.1-5; Col. 1.15-20; Heb. 1.2-3).[100]

But perhaps Barr would argue that while this typological reading of the Bible in its unity was the one early Christians employed, it is limited by its historical conceptuality and thus cannot be regarded as decisive for all subsequent interpreters. Typological interpretation as a method of relating the Testaments, writes Barr, "partakes to some extent in the once-ness of the incarnation,"[101] and thus modern interpreters, while respectful of it, do not need to make this practice their own. We must deploy our own mode of inquiry for articulating the unity of the Bible since previous rationales for doing so are time-bound, relative to their own historicality.

James Smart notes that Barr manifests in his work on the Bible "too much of a tendency to make concessions to the mood of the time."[102] And John Macquarrie notes the liability of such a tendency: "If our thinking at any given time is so strictly determined by the prevailing historical and cultural conditions, does not this imply a skepticism that is eventually self-destroying and takes away the possibility of rational discrimination and new departures of thought?"[103] Indeed the New Testament and, following its example, patristic exegesis of the typological and figural variety have pointed to renewed departures of thought in contemporary biblical scholarship. Brian Daley, in "Is Patristic Exegesis Still Useable?,"[104] maintains:

---

100 Childs, *Biblical Theology of the Old and New Testaments*, p. 14. See also Smart, *The Past, Present, and Future of Biblical Theology*, p. 34.

101 Barr, *Old and New in Interpretation*, p. 131 and *Holy Scripture*, p. 116.

102 Smart, *The Past, Present, and Future of Biblical Theology*, p. 36.

103 John Macquarrie, "Postscript: Christianity without Incarnation? Some Critical Comments," in Michael Green (ed.), *The Truth of God Incarnate* (London, 1977), pp. 141-142. See also Berkhouwer, *Holy Scripture*, p. 235: "Scripture does not conceal this time-relatedness but makes it possible because it serves the central proclamation of salvation."

104 Brian E. Daley, "Is Patristic Exegesis Still Useable? Some Reflections on Early Christian Interpretation of the Psalms," in Hays and Davis (eds), *The Art of Reading Scripture*, pp. 69-88. The emphasis is Daley's. See also Joseph Fitzmyer, *Scripture, The Soul of Theology*

100   *Revelation, Holy Scripture and Church*

> [A] positive perception of early Christian exegesis not merely as pre-modern but as
> thoroughly and—in some cases, at least—successfully *theological* can open our eyes
> to the other, less fulfilled need in biblical interpretation today: the need to recapture an
> understanding of interpretation's own role within the church and of its centrally theological
> task as reading, not just texts, but sacred and normative texts, texts that relate to the
> overarching story of Jewish and Christian faith.[105]

In other words, patristic exegesis, following the New Testament example to which
typology is so central, reminds contemporary critical interpretation that while
it excels at relating texts to historical contexts in which they are generated and
transmitted (and thus to the character of texts, including biblical texts, as temporally
located human products) has neglected to articulate the relation of these texts to God
and the life of God's people in any direct fashion.[106]

One of the partial ways in which Barr might exploit this option is through
a reconsideration of the theological force of his contention that typological
interpretation of the kind observed in the New Testament shares in the "once-ness" of
the incarnation. Alongside an understanding of typology in its relation to a particular
ancient social-historical world, he might also consider how the employment of this
strategy for canonical unity acquires normativity, even authority, in terms of its
relation to the "once-ness of the incarnation" and indeed, "the once-for-allness" of
the crucifixion as eschatogical fulfillment. For while the Bible must be approached
with a sense of history, and of the historical context of all meaning, the interpretative
and unitive strategies it employs acquire precedence by virtue of their relation to
God's once-for-all action in Jesus Christ.[107] In other words, the Bible, typologically
and figuratively construed in relation to Jesus Christ, is none other than Holy
Scripture, which serves the Word by the power of the Spirit to announce a new
time and reality to which the church is summoned to comport itself. As such, there
is an irreducibility and normativity to the typological (or more generally, figural)

(New York, 1994), pp. 65-66; Frei, "The 'Literal' Reading of Biblical Narrative," p. 39; and
Jaroslav Pelikan, *The Christian Tradition: A History of the Development of Doctrine, vol. 1:
The Emergence of the Catholic Tradition (100–600)* (Chicago, 1971), pp. 11-27.

105 Daley, "Is Patristic Exegesis Still Useable?, p. 87. For other positive appropriations
of elements of patristic exegesis see Moberly, *The Bible, Theology, and Faith*, pp. 39-44;
Seitz, *Figured Out*; and Dawson, *Christian Figural Reading and the Fashioning of Identity*.

106 Ephraim Radner asks whether the Christian churches can maintain a vision of the
reality of God, of God's presence and agency in the world, apart from maintaining faith in
God's providence in the world and a figural approach to Scripture like that of the Fathers. See
"The Discrepancies of Two Ages: Thoughts on Keeble's "Mysticisms of the Fathers," *The
Anglican*, 42 (2000): 10-15.

107 Indeed Richard Hays suggests that typology is employed by Paul in 1 Corinthians
to indicate that the Corinthians are included in the eschatological "once-for-all" act of God in
Jesus Christ. "He is summoning the Corinthians to reconfigure their self-understanding and
conduct in light of Jesus Christ crucified (2:2), the figure to whom Scripture (Old Testament)
points." See "The Conversion of the Imagination," p. 406.

The Bible as Holy Scripture 101

construal of the Testaments since this construal has been placed in the service of what it helps to depict—the once-for-all time of fulfillment in Jesus Christ.[108]

Authority and regula fidei   Barr's depiction of the implication of the Bible, its unity and authority in the fundamental structure of faith, by concentrating solely on the production of biblical texts as human products, misconstrues the relationship between the Bible and God's saving economy in a number of ways. The first has to do with his argument that something like a *regula fidei*, as *extrinsic* to the canon, pre-existed the formation of the New Testament in a *generative* role and that this faith structure continued to serve as the theological principle by which the overall contents of the Bible as "Scripture," more so than as canon, are construed. A difficulty with this formulation is that the rule of faith was not extrinsic to the forming canon. While it is the case that the "rule of faith" projected a kind of "plan of salvation" framework within which the concrete interpretations of the church took place and that the rule of faith was not extracted from the Bible, in a simple way, this rule was not regarded as imposed upon the Scriptures from without either.[109] In conflicts with the Gnostics, Irenaeus argued that it was the Gnostics who imposed an extrinsic grid on the Bible, while the rule of faith or "canon of truth" as an intrinsic guide "bears out the true dramatic narrative of Scripture within the church universal, which is its ever contemporary context."[110] Both Tertullian and Irenaeus regarded the rule of faith as specifying not only the content of revelation but also the overarching and irreducible (Christological and Trinitarian) plot of God's saving economy. This plot, articulated in the canon of truth, is . . ."irreducible," "properly basic to Scripture and apostolic tradition"[111] and "*always* associated with Scripture itself."[112]

---

108 It is in the time, depicted by this story (of Scripture), that we live. Jenson writes:

the Bible is not about some other folk, and not even the very beginning steps of biblical exegesis may suppose that it is. Send not to know for whom the shofar sounds, or who will experience what the prophet foretells: *tua re agitar*—it is your thing that is at issue. ("Scripture's Authority in the Church," p. 30)

109 Von Campenhausen maintains that the canon of truth "is not a norm placed over the sacred Scriptures: it shares a common origin with the latter in the original preaching of the apostles, and is therefore in material agreement with it." See *The Formation of the Christian Bible*, p. 329.

110 Blowers, "The *Regula Fidei*," p. 210. See also Von Campenhausen, *The Formation of the Christian Bible*, pp. 209ff. and 288ff. Von Campenhausen maintains that "a canon within a canon" is the closest modern analog to "the rule of faith" since the rule was more about guidance for reading and not a critical principle by which to scrutinize the Scriptures. Ibid., p. 290. See also Seitz, *Figured Out*, p. 6; R. Greer, *Broken Lights and Mended Lives: Theology and Common Life in the Early Church* (University Park, 1986); and K. Greene-McCreight, *Ad Litteram: How Augustine, Calvin and Barth Read the "Plain Sense" of Genesis 1-3* (New York, 1999).

111 Blowers, "The *Regula Fidei*," p. 210.

112 Ibid., p. 202. Blowers' emphasis. Blowers maintains that the contest with the Gnostics is thus not just at the level of "atomistic" doctrinal positions held. The contest is at the level of a collision between metanarratives, "our story versus theirs." The church maintains that it has discerned the plot within the Bible and that its performance is continuous with the scriptural plot "as belonging under the same larger economy, or within one overarching 'context' that

102 *Revelation, Holy Scripture and Church*

Moreover, Barr overstates the temporal precedence of the rule of faith over canonical formation and its generative role in relation to the New Testament. For the rule of faith was nascent alongside the formation of the New Testament canon and grew to maturity as the boundaries of the New Testament canon were defined.[113] George Lindbeck remarks, "As time went on, an explicit rule of faith and an enlarged canon came into existence. The two developments were synchronically interrelated."[114] Thus to speak of the rule of faith as antecedent to and generative of Christian Scripture is in some measure to overstate the case. What is more, this argument risks confusing the generative with the generated and thus misplacing the locus of biblical authority. What generates both the "rule of faith" and the New Testament canon is, first of all, antecedent revelation and, from an ecclesiastical point of view, the desire and need for ongoing and faithful proclamation of this revelation. Put in slightly different terms, revelation "incites" the New Testament canon as its witness, and by this witness continues to incite speech and action congruent with it.[115] The rule of faith, while it was embedded in liturgical practices and in Trinitarian and Christological readings of Hebrew Scripture, only achieves full articulation as guidance for reading the canon that formed alongside of it. Moberly writes, "The purpose of the rule of faith . . . is to guide readers so that they may discern that truth of God in Christ to which the Church, through its Scriptures, bears witness."[116]

There are two important consequences of the realization that the rule of faith only acquires full articulation alongside the canon of Scripture whose reading it rules. The first is that it concentrates "authority" of the Bible in the final form of the text. It is this text, read this way, that is authoritative; that is, it is the canonical text that the church receives as generative of, as capable of quickening the people of God to "truthful speech and righteous action."[117] It is not the whole of the

---

comprehends the whole history of God's self-disclosure from creation to judgment." Ibid., p. 211.

113 David S. Yeago makes a persuasive case that part of what constitutes a creed is the attempt to identify "unifying common judgments" in the variety of their articulation across the scope of the biblical canon. Creeds, the Nicene in particular, are an attempt, on Yeago's view, to render the same judgment about the person of Christ as does the Bible, in a conceptuality other than that of the Bible. One could argue that the "rule of faith," which grew up alongside the development of the canon, was formulated in terms of the same dynamics. It was an attempt to identity the "unified common judgments" (the plot or story line), implicit in the Bible, as the standard by which the texts should be read together as a unified story. See "The New Testament and the Nicene Dogma: A Contribution to the Recovery of Theological Exegesis," p. 96. Blowers notes that "the catholic creeds, like the Rule of Faith on which they were built, sought to capture the narrative wholeness of Scripture in a coherent story-line or plot." "The *Regula Fidei*," p. 220.

114 Lindbeck, "Scripture, Consensus, and Community," p. 77. See also Moberly, *The Bible, Theology, and Faith*, p. 42 where he argues, "The rule of faith was formulated in the early church concurrently with the process of canonical recognition."

115 On revelation as "generative" and "inciting" see Rowan Williams, *On Christian Theology* (Oxford, 2000), pp. 133-135.

116 Moberly, *The Bible, Theology, and Faith*, p. 42.

117 Webster speaks of this generative capacity of the Bible as "spirit-bestowed." *Holy Scripture*, p. 52.

The Bible as Holy Scripture

"cumulative tradition" of text transmission, texts related to the socio-historical world of their origin or luminous church personalities that are authoritative, as Barr maintains, but these texts read in relation to each other in a *particular* fashion. Lindbeck writes:

> (The use, and therefore meaning, of the text, be it noted, was the one it had in the canon-forming situation, not in some putative historically reconstructed one.) Thus a certain way of reading Scripture (viz., as a Christ-centered narrationally and typologically unified whole in conformity to a Trinitarian rule of faith) was constitutive of the Christian canon and has, it would seem, an authority inseparable from that of the Bible itself.[118]

A second consequence of the recognition of the relation between canon formation and the articulation of the rule of the faith is, contra Barr, the canon of Scripture must be appreciated as more than a list of books without exegetical consequence. Barr wants to restrict the term to a list of books,[119] but in the light of the canon's ordered development alongside the rule of faith, it would seem negligent of interpreters not to take into account the structured relationships within the canon (the grouping of Gospels at the beginning of the New Testament, for example) as in some measure implying the manner in which the Bible, as Christian Scripture, is to be read. In the context of a dispute with James Barr on the meaningfulness of the term "canon" to biblical exegesis, Francis Watson argues:

> Structured relationships are, however, integral to the concept of canon: someone who has merely memorized a list of titles, from Genesis to Revelation, without (for example) understanding the rationale of the division into two parts or the relative weight assigned to some books in comparison with others, has a very imperfect understanding of the canon.[120]

Finally, while Scripture, as a "crystallization" of Israel's and the church's experience of God, is said to be a "divinely appointed meaning place" between readers and God, no account is given that would lead one to believe that anything other than "the people of God's experience"[121] is encountered in the Bible. Once again, we have a partial, "natural account," of the basis of scriptural authority, that is, in its relation to persons of authority whose experiential accounts (of God and salvation)

---

118 Lindbeck, "Scripture, Consensus, and Community," p. 77.

119 See Barr, *Holy Scripture*, p. 49.

120 Francis Watson, *Text and Truth: Redefining Biblical Theology* (Grand Rapids, 1997), pp. 271-272, n. 29. See also Von Campenhausen, *The Formation of the Christian Bible*, pp. x, 103ff.

121 *The Scope and Authority of the Bible*, p. 122, See also *The Bible in the Modern World*, pp. 117-118, 120, 122. An exception to this can be found in an early review in which Barr maintains that "God calls forth the word of his people, Israel and the Church, in a response of witness and worship and that this Word coalesces in the Scripture." In subsequent generations, "God makes that Word of his people his own Word." However, in a footnote in *The Bible in the Modern World*, p. 180, n. 12, Barr says that this view of the matter "includes some ideas which I have now abandoned." The original article was in the *Scottish Journal of Theology*, 11 (1958): 92.

104 *Revelation, Holy Scripture and Church*

are recognized as weighty and luminous. There is no robust theological account of the authority of the Bible in relation to the subject matter of the Bible: God's saving action in the life, death and resurrection of Jesus. God is extrinsic, implied in crystallized religious experience. While Barr speaks of the content of the Bible as "the crystallization of Israel's experience of God,"[122] and as such a classic (authoritative) model for understanding God, on his articulation of the matter it would seem more just to say that the Bible is authoritative for understanding "experience of God." Brevard Childs notes that in the formation of the Christian Bible, "The authority assigned to the apostolic witnesses derived from their unique testimony to the life, death and resurrection of Jesus Christ."[123] And Karl Barth, while denying any "mysterious special privilege" for theological hermeneutics maintains, "[T]he object of the biblical texts is quite simply the name Jesus Christ, and these texts can be understood only when understood and determined by this object."[124] There is no question that the Bible is a human account, that it is a contingent historical interpretation of complexity and variety. However, concentration on the Bible as a religious, historical and literary artifact removes from sight, says James Smart, "the one element in the Bible that has been responsible for its centrality and authority in the church."[125] Jesus Christ, "concealed under the name Israel in the Old Testament, revealed under his own name in the New Testament,"[126] is the One whom the Bible is about and from whom, in his speaking, it receives its luminous and generative role in the church.

To sum up: it was argued against Barr that "sound and adequate interpretation" requires an account of the canonical Scriptures of the church, which, while it does not neglect the Bible as a human artifact, takes into account its unity and authority in relation to the primary reality by which it was engendered, shaped, and to which it bears witness.

Paul Ricoeur: The Bible as Polyphonic Intertext that Names God

When depicting the field and problem of biblical interpretation as well as articulating a notion of canonical authority, Ricoeur moves from a "general" philosophical

---

122 On the relation between the Bible as a crystallization of experience and Romanticism see Webster, *Holy Scripture*, p. 49 and Lindbeck, *The Nature of Doctrine*, p. 31.

123 Childs, *Biblical Theology of the Old and New Testaments*, p. 64.

124 Barth, *Church Dogmatics*, 1/2: 727.

125 James Smart, *The Strange Silence of the Bible in the Church: A Study in Hermeneutics* (Philadelphia, 1970), p. 78.

126 Barth, *Church Dogmatics*, 1/2: 720. See also Von Campenhausen, *The Formation of the Christian Bible*, pp. 327-328. He writes:

The Christian Bible—and this is the first and absolutely unshakeable fact that we know about it—comes into existence from the start as *the book of Christ*. The Scriptures of the Lord testify to the Lord—the Old Testament prophetically, the New Testament historically. Christ speaks in both testaments and is their true content.

The Bible as Holy Scripture   105

hermeneutic to its regional application.[127] He construes the Bible in its genric variation, the task of interpretation, the hermeneutic situation of the Christian church and the authority of the canon of Scripture in terms of categories derived from a hermeneutic of poetic texts—speech and writing, work and world of the text, distanciation, appropriation—and assumes not only the competence of this general philosophy of discourse for the direction, depiction and performance of biblical interpretation but also its necessity to the preservation of the subject matter of the Bible. The Bible is thus properly and necessarily a site for the regional application of a general literary-philosophical hermeneutic. And yet, argues Ricoeur, in the process of applying a general hermeneutic to the specific text and intertext of the Bible, general hermeneutics "becomes the organon of biblical hermeneutics."[128] For while the Bible is one particular text among many, and so permits the regional application of general hermeneutic categories, it "presents features that are so original" that the relationship between general philosophical and biblical hermeneutics is "gradually inverted, and theological hermeneutics subordinates philosophical hermeneutics to itself . . ."[129]

In his regional use of a general philosophy of discourse in the construal of the Bible as a whole and the hermeneutic situation of the church, it is really not original features, but a single common original feature of biblical texts that serve to subordinate philosophical to theological hermeneutics. This feature, however it might be refracted into other parts of Ricoeur's endeavor to apply general literary-philosophical interpretative theory to the Bible, is singular: it is the naming of God[130] throughout the polyphony of biblical discourse, the unfolding of the "thing" of the biblical world before the text. Biblical hermeneutics is a unique case," writes Ricoeur, "because all the partial discourses are *referred* to a name that is the point of intersection and the index of incompleteness of all our discourse about God,

---

127 See "Philosophy and Religious Language," pp. 43ff.; "Philosophical Hermeneutics and Biblical Hermeneutics," pp. 89ff.; "Naming God," pp. 224ff.; and Paul Ricoeur, "The Canon between the Text and the Community," in Petr Pokorny and Jan Roskovec (eds), *Philosophical Hermeneutics and Biblical Exegesis* (Tübingen, 2002), pp. 7-26. For the actual performance of exegesis congruent with the abstract depiction here described see "The Nuptial Metaphor," pp. 265-303.

128 "Philosophical Hermeneutics and Biblical Hermeneutics," p. 95. On the matter of a general hermeneutics serving as the "organon" of biblical hermeneutics *and vice versa*, what Ricoeur calls "mutual enveloping," see *Critique and Conviction*, p. 151, where Ricoeur likens his method to Schleiermacher's.

129 "Philosophical Hermeneutics and Biblical Hermeneutics," p. 90. Gregory Laughery maintains that biblical hermeneutics "surpasses" but does not "efface" philosophical hermeneutics in this inversion. *Living Hermeneutics in Motion: An Analysis and Evaluation of Paul Ricoeur's Contribution to Biblical Hermeneutics* (Lanham, 2002), p. 45.

130 Whenever Ricoeur begins to speak of the "inversion" which theological hermeneutics affects, vis-à-vis philosophical hermeneutics, he is verging on discussion of the "thing" of the text; the way a particular genre of biblical literature names God. See "Philosophical Hermeneutics and Biblical Hermeneutics," pp. 90, 91-93, "Philosophy and Religious Language," p. 46; and "Naming God," p. 221.

106   *Revelation, Holy Scripture and Church*

and because this name has become bound up with the *meaning-event* preached as resurrection."[131]

However, before ever we arrive at this feature, the text and intertext of the Bible, the interpretative situation of the church and canonical authority are first depicted with the help of literary and philosophical discourse. Indeed, on Ricoeur's account, it is only by a long detour through structural and hermeneutical analysis that the reality of the biblical text is properly configured, the specificity of the Bible's subject matter properly guarded and the problem of canonical authority rightly located and expressed. Without the conceptual assistance of general hermeneutics the performance of biblical interpretation and the "thing" of the text are jeopardized by either a rush to existential signification[132] or a psychologized theory of inspiration.[133] What is more, the rationales for canonical authority in the church can appear circular and their expression authoritarian. Ricoeur writes:

> The path I have followed has, therefore, been that of the "application" of a general hermeneutic category to biblical hermeneutics, considered a regional hermeneutic. My thesis is that this is the *only* path that leads at the same time to a recognition of the specificity of the biblical "thing."[134]

An exposition of Ricoeur's application of general hermeneutics to the text and intertext of the Bible follows in which Ricoeur (1) applies structural categories to the whole constellation of biblical texts (objectification through structure), which construe the Bible in terms of particular genre and each genre's role in shaping the confession that the text bears; (2) offers an assessment of the hermeneutical situation of the church, through an analysis of the relationship between speech and writing (distanciation by writing); and (3) considers the central referent God – and the density added to the word by Christ – by which general hermeneutics is made the organon of biblical hermeneutics. A description of Ricoeur's analysis of the need for and authority of the canon, articulated within his general structuralist-philosophical hermeneutic, completes the expository section of Ricoeur on the Bible as Scripture. Finally, a critique of Ricoeur's application of a general hermeneutic to

---

131 "Philosophy and Religious Language," p. 46. Here Ricoeur distinguishes himself from structuralist hermeneutics which claim that writing severs the connection between a text's sense ("a network of relations purely internal to the text") and reference ("discourse character of relating itself to an extralinguistic reality"). His hermeneutic thesis is that "the difference between speech and writing in no way abolishes the fundamental function of discourse (which encompasses these two variations: oral and written)." Discourse is always about something and writing does not expunge reference from discourse. Written discourse, however, differs from face-to-face discourse, which has available to it an ostensible shared common world. The world to which written discourse refers is "the world of the text and yet is not in the text. . . . I call this "the "thing" or issue of the text. It is neither behind the text as the presumed author nor in the text as its structure, but unfolded in front of it." "Naming God," pp. 220-221.

132 "Philosophical Hermeneutics and Biblical Hermeneutics," pp. 95-96.

133 See ibid., and "Philosophy and Religious Language," pp. 43-44.

134 "Philosophical Hermeneutics and Biblical Hermeneutics," p. 97. My emphasis. See also "The Canon between the Text and the Community," p. 8.

The Bible as Holy Scripture 107

the Bible is offered. The central protest raised against Ricoeur's project is that poetic description, which translates the specifics of this text into a general conceptuality, lacks theological density. His formalistic and preliminary handling of the Bible by means of a general hermeneutic minimizes (1) the importance of the subject matter of the Bible itself for a construal of the text in its unity and the hermeneutic situation of the church and the authority of the Bible as canon, and (2) the ways in which God is "involved" with the Bible, not only as subject matter but as author. Ricoeur's fundamental description of the Bible, and the various hermeneutic problems surrounding its construal and interpretation in terms of a general "poetics," sits in tension with a theological construal of the Bible as Scripture in which the Bible's relation to God's work and word is determinative.

Genric Inscription

Ricoeur attempts to prove his thesis through a consideration of the subject matter of the Bible by way of the detour he suggests. He travels through the application of structural analysis to the genric diversity of the Bible and moves to show the relevance of a consideration of the passage from speech to writing for the Christian hermeneutic situation. Only after these moves are made do we arrive at a consideration of the thing proposed or projected by texts of the Bible.

In terms of a structural analysis of the biblical documents, Ricoeur notes that "profession of faith"[135] is inseparable from the forms of discourse that contain it. Wherever God is named in the constellation of texts called the Bible, a specific literary modality bears the profession, which gives genric and temporal shape to the profession itself.[136] Narrative texts recount events of God's deliverance and are often arranged around a central event, like the Exodus, which "possesses at once a historical significance and a kerygmatic dimension."[137] These texts do not record the speech of God so much as they emphasize events as bearing the trace of God's founding and delivering action in a linear movement through time.[138] Profession takes place by narration and the focus is not on who is speaking but on the action that is narrated. The focus of exegesis thus falls not on the narrator and his motivation behind the text but on the events recounted within the text. Theologies that follow the narrative form of profession would thus be obliged to announce the God of Israel

---

135 Ricoeur oscillates between "profession of faith," "confession of faith" "discourse of faith" and "kerygma." See "Toward a Hermeneutic of the Idea of Revelation," p. 74; "Philosophical Hermeneutics and Biblical Hermeneutics," p. 92; and "Naming God," p. 224.

136 See "Philosophical Hermeneutics and Biblical Hermeneutics," pp. 91-92; "Toward a Hermeneutic of the Idea of Revelation," pp. 73-95; and "Naming God," pp. 224-235.

137 "Philosophical Hermeneutics and Biblical Hermeneutics," p. 91.

138 See "Biblical Time" in *Figuring the Sacred*, pp. 171-173. In this essay Ricoeur correlates the various genres of the Bible, not with the unique shape each gives to its "confession of faith," but to the way they order time and to the confrontation between genres "from the point of view of [their] temporal implications . . ." Ibid., p. 174. See also "The Hermeneutics of Testimony" in *Essays on Biblical Interpretation*, pp. 119-120.

108   *Revelation, Holy Scripture and Church*

as one who acts in human history and might take the form of a *Heilsgeschichte* (history of salvation).[139]

Each genre of the Bible in turn gives rise, as does narrative, to its particular mode of confession and, in this way, structural analysis helps interpreters avoid construing the polyphonic nature of confession of faith in the Bible in monolithic terms. This observation on Ricoeur's part shows its critical value in at least two instances. The first relates to the misconstrual of the *whole* of Scripture as "The Word of God" under the influence of prophetic discourse in which the author speaks for God.[140] The other target of Ricoeur's critique is "Narrative Theology," which in some of its forms attempts to reduce Scripture to "*the* biblical narrative" thereby thinning out the rich diversity of literary genres, each with its unique confession of faith and mode of temporality in canonical Scripture.[141] "The literary genres of the Bible do not constitute a rhetorical façade which it would be possible to pull down in order to reveal some thought content that is indifferent to its literary vehicle."[142] The Bible's various literary styles are irreducible because the content of religious discourse is tied to the type of discourse used to make a particular profession of faith.

While there is particularity to professions of faith within the Bible because of the literary vehicles that bear and shape them, this does not mean that the diversity of genres and confessions are unrelated. First, Ricoeur uses the term "testimony" broadly to refer to a variety of texts, the prophetic texts of Isaiah and particularly those of the New Testament, to indicate their common ability "to attest an intention, an inspiration, an idea at the heart of experience and history which nonetheless transcends experience and history."[143] The character of biblical texts to testify, not primarily to the materiality of events in a naïve fashion, but to the fact that the foundation of humanity identity transcends itself, contra Kant, and the sensible world in the absolute, is a common transgeneric feature of Old and New Testaments. Testimony is, however, related to the historical in the sense that it transfers "things seen to the level of things said"[144] in a manner that moves from confession-testimony to narration-testimony, what Ricoeur elsewhere calls following the trace of God in history. "The confession that Jesus is the Christ constitutes testimony par excellence."[145] Thus testimony cuts across the generic variation of the Bible,

---

139 "Philosophical Hermeneutics and Biblical Hermeneutics," p. 92.

140 See "Toward a Hermeneutic of the Idea of Revelation," pp. 74-77; "Philosophical Hermeneutics and Biblical Hermeneutics," p. 93; and "Naming God," p. 225. In this last source, Ricoeur speaks of the "hypostasis" of prophetic writing as an act which is forgetful of other genres in which God is named.

141 See "Toward a Narrative Theology: Its Necessity, Its Resources, Its Difficulties," in *Figuring the Sacred*, p. 238 and "Biblical Time," pp. 167-180. Wallace notes that, for Ricoeur, "any attempt to short-circuit this variety with a predetermined focus on one particular genre and one particular character—the category of narrative and the identity of Jesus, as in Frei's case—violates the text's built in plurality of expression." Mark I. Wallace, *The Second Naiveté: Barth, Ricoeur, and the New Yale Theology* (Macon, GA, 1990), p. 44.

142 "Toward a Hermeneutic of the Idea of Revelation," p. 74.

143 "The Hermeneutics of Testimony," pp. 119-120.

144 Ibid., p. 123.

145 Ibid., p. 134.

The Bible as Holy Scripture   109

emphasizing the common confessional feature of the Bible as contingent human historical witness to the manifestation of the absolute in history.[146]

Second, Ricoeur draws attention to tensions between and within genres and their temporalities: the prophetic and narrative, wisdom and hymnic discourse, must confront one another by way contrast, mutual enrichment and challenge. Narrative presents the action of God through time in a way that assures the people of God's faithfulness. Prophetic discourse, on the other hand, disrupts and disturbs as it lays before the people "the threat of the deadly event."[147] On the level of temporality, narrative can remain past historical accomplishment, tracing God's action in another time unless it is repeated in the "today" of hymnic discourse, which takes up the narration and repeats it as praise in the present. In this way the whole range of confessions and temporalities embodied in various genres are brought into play in the vast intertext that is the Bible. Mark Wallace makes that point that, for Ricoeur, "It is only as one biblical genre is interanimated by its cross fertilizations with the medley of other modes of discourse that the biblical texts effectively generate meaning."[148] The closure of the canon of Scripture marks the space within which the various forms of discourse confront one another with their professions of faith and particular temporalities and the canon sets limits on the possible configurations that can result from intercanonical generic play. Ricoeur suggests that "global configurations of meaning,"[149] which are the result of reflection on the whole of the literary corpus of the Bible, are possible. However, this total construal of the field of biblical interpretation in which no particular genre or confession of faith reigns over the others in a hierarchy[150] would seem inevitably fluid.[151] Ricoeur speaks of one genre's "playing freely" with another, and of us allowing texts "to project themselves on one another" and finally of interpreters "gather[ing] up those sparks of meaning that fly up at their points of friction."[152] Mark Wallace seems correct in his assessment of Ricoeur's construal of the Bible:

---

146 True testimony to the absolute proves itself by occasioning new experiences of the absolute. See Vanhoozer, *Biblical Narrative in the Philosophy of Paul Ricoeur*, p. 260 for an enlightening discussion of the role of testimony in the biblical hermeneutic of Paul Ricoeur.

147 "Philosophical Hermeneutics and Biblical Hermeneutics," p. 92. See also "Naming God," pp. 225-226, where Ricoeur writes, "the day of Yahweh" announced by the prophets . . . "will not be a day of joy, but of terror."

148 Mark I. Wallace, "From Phenomenology to Scripture? Paul Ricoeur's Hermeneutical Philosophy of Religion," *Modern Theology*, 16/3 (July, 2000): 310-311.

149 "Philosophical Hermeneutics and Biblical Hermeneutics," p. 91.

150 "The Nuptial Metaphor," p. 303. Ricoeur maintains that "figures" of love found throughout the Bible "intersignify one another instead of arranging themselves in some hierarchy."

151 Anthony C. Thiselton in *New Horizons in Hermeneutics: The Theory and Practice of Transforming Biblical Reading* (Grand Rapids, 1992), p. 369 notes that while any interpretation of the Bible, global or not, would, for Ricoeur, have to be argued based on intra-linguistic and intra-textual criteria, this approach to biblical texts recalls Schleiermacher's emphasis on the "corrigibility of all interpretation."

152 "The Nuptial Metaphor," p. 303.

110 *Revelation, Holy Scripture and Church*

In this approach, the Bible emerges as a polyphonic and heterogeneous intertext of oppositional genres—genres that alternately complement and clash with each other—rather than a stable book unified by a particular discourse, including prescriptive discourse (*pace* Levinas).[153]

Distanciation through Writing

The first application of general hermeneutics to biblical hermeneutics concerns the identification of the genric variety and intertextuality of the Bible and its implications for interpretation. The second part of the application of general hermeneutics to biblical interpretation helps to depict the "hermeneutic situation of Christianity."[154] In this case, biblical hermeneutics is encouraged to linger a while to consider the dynamics of the passage of speech into writing before constructing theologies centered on the Word. Christian theology has, of course, good reason to champion the "Word" above writing since all of its speech—concerning the origin, object and expression of its faith—presses toward orality in preaching, witness, a word-event (*Wort-Geschehen*).

However, the primal "hermeneutic situation" for Christian proclamation is located in the relationship between speech and writing. At every stage, historically and presently, Christian speech involves an interpretative relationship to a previous writing. Jesus interpreted the Torah in his preaching. Paul and the author of Hebrews interpreted the meaning of Jesus as the Christ through the accumulation of prophecies, institutions and titles to him taken from the Old Testament and Hebrew culture. "Preexisting significations already inscribed"[155] are taken up and provide the background and basis for the intelligibility of the new event. "In this sense," writes Ricoeur, "Christianity is, from the start, an exegesis (one has only to recall the role of 'figures' and 'types' in Paul)."[156]

What is more, "new preaching" not only interprets previous writing, the new preaching itself becomes new writing. Early Christian reflection on the meaning of Jesus' life, death and resurrection becomes, in turn, the New Testament, that is, the effect of rereading the old in terms of the new is the addition of new documents within what amounts to an extended corpus for present and future intelligibility. The two Testaments are held together through a contrast, Old and New, which at the same time sets the Testaments into a framework of harmony and intelligibility. The Christ-

---

153 Wallace, "From Phenomenology to Scripture?," p. 311. He suggests "prescriptive discourse" here since Emmanuel Levinas maintains against Ricoeur that on a "Jewish reading of the Bible . . . prescriptive lessons occupy a privileged position within Jewish consciousness, as far as the relationship with God is concerned." Emmanuel Levinas, "Revelation in the Jewish Tradition," in Sean Hand (ed.), *The Levinas Reader* (Oxford, 1989), p. 193, cited by Wallace in "From Phenomenology to Scripture?" p. 310.

154 "Philosophical Hermeneutics and Biblical Hermeneutics," p. 95. This essay marks Ricoeur's return to a theme taken up in "Preface to Bultmann," pp. 49-72.

155 Ibid., p. 95.

156 Ibid. See "Preface to Bultmann," pp. 49-51.

The Bible as Holy Scripture 111

event is "made to appear,"[157] not as an interruption to the Old Testament, but through rereading, the "fulfillment of a meaning which remained in suspense."[158]

With the close of the canon, Old and New Testament, a fixed body of witnesses is established which provides the "guide" for future speech and action and making sense of the world. "To interpret Scripture is at the same time to amplify its meaning as sacred meaning and to incorporate the remains of secular culture in this understanding."[159] Subsequent Christian speech which is generated by this activity might become new writing, but it is not added onto the canon; it is tradition—the transmission of a message through time—enabled by the chain speech–writing–speech (early Christian preaching–the Gospels–subsequent Christian preaching).[160] The New Testament then, must be interpreted; it is an object of hermeneutics (1) with regard to the Old, (2) with regard to life and reality as a whole, but also (3) in its own right since it is not itself the word of God but an apostolic witness to (an interpretation of) Jesus Christ that needs to be deciphered. "We are related to the object of its faith through the confession of its faith. Hence by understanding its witness, I receive equally, in its witness, what is summons, kerygma, 'the good news.'"[161] Writing is crucial in this, the church's hermeneutic situation, since through "distanciation," the objectification of a message through writing separated from the circumstances of its production, its initial speaker and audience the message of the Bible reaches us (the present community of readers) through its "sense" and the subject matter it professes,[162] and can be actualized or restored to speech in our reading and preaching.[163]

On Ricoeur's account, a central technique by which biblical texts have been actualized in subsequent contexts by readers within the church is through "allegorical transference."[164] In the patristic age, interpreters would cite or paraphrase a biblical

---

157 Ibid., p. 51.

158 Ibid. He goes on (pp. 51-52):

The event itself receives a temporal density by being inscribed in a signifying relation of promise to fulfillment. . . . This signifying relation attests that the kerygma, by this detour through the interpretation of an ancient Scripture, enters into a network of intelligibility . . . Jesus Christ himself, exegesis and exegete of Scripture, is manifested as logos in opening the understanding of the Scriptures.

159 Ibid., p. 53.

160 See *Thinking Biblically*, p. xii where Ricoeur writes, "Cut off from its ties to a living community, the text gets reduced to a cadaver handed over for autopsy."

161 "Preface to Bultmann," p. 56. For Ricoeur, apart from our spatial and temporal distance from the world of the New Testament, there is a unique distance which is distinctly modern—or at least that has become visible in the modern period. We have become aware through form criticism that "the text conceals" a first level of interpretation. The New Testament as we read it is already an interpretation—"we believe only by listening and by interpreting a text which its itself already an interpretation." It is this distance in particular in the face of which Ricoeur offers the dynamics of distanciation as a solution. Ibid., p. 54.

162 Ibid., pp. 94-95.

163 "Naming God," p. 219. Ricoeur likens texts that need reading to be actualized to "a musical score that requires execution" to be heard. See also Karl Simms, *Paul Ricoeur* (London, 2003), p. 132.

164 "The Nuptial Metaphor," p. 276.

text (reuse it) in a context analogous to the one in which the cited text was given. Without evacuating the specifics of the text as given, figures within the text were assimilated to figures in the present such that the gap between text and present situation was filled in. Ricoeur uses the Song of Songs as an example. He notes that the use of the Song of Songs in early Christian catechesis for baptism attests to a transference of meaning from the text to "a new speech situation." While the rite of baptism has an initial gap[165] between it and the poem of the Song of Songs, the poem is reframed in a new situation of discourse. The space between the text and the practice of baptism is then filled by the adoption of a metaphorical sense of a nuptial text, which the new situation engenders and which poetic discourse allows. Following Paul,[166] who uses the nuptial metaphor for the love between Christ and the church (Ephesians 5:25 and 2 Corinthians 11:2), and thus encourages the adoption of the language of Song of Songs into Christian speech, the words and attitudes and moves, are transferred in the liturgy from the lover and beloved of the Song of Songs to the baptized and Christ. Ricoeur cites catechetical instructions to the baptized from Ambrose in *De Sacramentis*, IV. 5:

> Following this, you must approach the altar. You have begun to move forward. The angels are watching, they have seen you approaching . . . Thus they have asked, "Who is this who rises so white from the desert?" You approach the altar. The Lord calls you or calls your soul or the church, and says, "Let him kiss me with the kisses of his mouth."[167]

In this way, interpretation of the meaning of the texts gives birth to meanings "in front of the text" as possible trajectories are realized in new readings framed by new speech situations.

However, it is Ricoeur's contention that the subsequent or "amplified" effects of reading in a new speech situation through allegory breaks down when one wants to make the claim that these meanings pre-existed the text or were intended by the author—even if the author is the Holy Spirit.[168] In such cases, claims Ricoeur, the similitude of situation which gives rise to the transference of meaning from one context to another and which is "the hermeneutical key to allegorical explication,"[169] gives way to concocted schemes "to become an arbitrary exercise, guided by mere co-occurrence of the same words within a work that is taken to be indivisible and

---

165 This gap is spatial, contextual and historical. See ibid and "Preface to Bultmann," p. 56.

166 "The Nuptial Metaphor," pp. 279, 282, 283. Ricoeur notes (p. 282) that

the typological interpretation applied by Paul to the relationship between the two covenants (the economy of the Hebraic structure with its characters, events, and institutions) as a prefiguration of the Christian economy of salvation . . . brings into equilibrium the existential distance that separates the two modes of love and make possible the assumption of the language of the Songs of Songs into Christian discourse.

167 Pelletier, *Lecture du Cantique des Cantiques*, 157, n. 33, cited in "The Nuptial Metaphor," p. 280, n. 17.

168 See "The Nuptial Metaphor," pp. 283, 286, 295.

169 Ibid., p. 285. This represents a development from Ricoeur's earlier depiction of the Christian hermeneutic situation.

The Bible as Holy Scripture 113

coherent."[170] Like their "naturalist" opponents, modern allegorists too often take their stand, not with a believing attitude within what were and are the "privileged places"[171] of liturgy and *cultus* and meditation, which allow for the transference of meaning by a similarity of situation, but in an "unmarked" or "nonobjective"[172] place from where they propose to discern hidden double meanings resident within the depths of text. Modern allegorists thus make the text an "object" of interpretation rather than, as was the case in patristic exegesis, "an interpretant"[173] in a situation where some similitude between the text's initial linguistic setting and the present situation of re-use obtains. These efforts inevitably fall prey to a threefold criticism of allegory: the arbitrary nature of literary comparisons, the constant resort to a prior theory and the imposition of allegorical meanings by church authority.[174]

In the place of this, Ricoeur wants to restore allegory through reconceptualizing it as "an effect of reading," that is, as the creation of new meaning through reinterpretation in a new context. Allegorical sense is not rooted in the intentions of authors behind the text but in the re-use of the texts of the Bible in new situations of discourse where the book's use through "metaphorization"[175] creates "a new 'use' for itself."[176] In the case of the nuptial bond, it is capable of freeing itself from its literal or obvious sense to perform metaphorical duty, with the figural encouragement of Paul, to depict the love of Christ and the baptized in the context of baptismal catechesis. This articulation comports more easily with "scientific" (i.e. historical-critical) interpretation of the Bible since the strategy by which meaning is transferred from one context to another is not resident, immanent, in the text *per se* as the intended spiritual meaning or in the world behind it, but in the similitude of a new situation "before the text," which permits or encourages the displacement. Moreover, this transference of meaning to a new situation, without the erotic overtones resident within the obvious sense of the poem, is made possible through the dynamics of poetry by which the primary sexual-body referent in the Song of Songs is suspended in a verbal-euphemistic word play that "tends to dissociate the metaphorical network from its support in the body."[177] Ricoeur's rehabilitated

---

170 Ibid., p. 283.

171 Ibid., p. 280. "Privileged places" enable us to "catch sight of the augmentation of meaning at work in certain forms of the reception of the biblical text." These places are thus sites for the "theological production" of new meaning through reuse of old texts.

172 An unmarked place is one that is indifferent to the "conditions of restatement of the canonical text." Ibid.

173 Ibid., p. 286.

174 The critical analysis of allegory with which Ricoeur works is found in T. Todorove, *Symbolism et Interprétation* (Paris, 1978) and A. Compagnon, *La seconde main ou le travail de la citation* (Paris, 1979). Cited by Ricoeur in "The Nuptial Metaphor," p. 289, n. 31.

175 Walter Brueggemann, *An Introduction to the Old Testament: The Canon and Christian Imagination* (Louisville, 2003), p. 325.

176 Robert Louis Wilken, Review of *Thinking Biblically* by André LaCocque and Paul Ricoeur, *First Things*, 93 (May, 1999): 68-71. The citation is from p. 70.

177 "The Nuptial Metaphor," p. 273. Here Ricoeur draws on the work of Robert Alter, *The Art of Biblical Poetry* (New York, 1986), pp. 185-203. See also Ricoeur, *The Rule of Metaphor*.

114   *Revelation, Holy Scripture and Church*

notion of "analogical transference" thus skirts the pertinent criticisms of modern allegory. However, neither "allegory" nor analogical transference is the category in which Ricoeur finally expresses the dynamic by which biblical texts generate new meanings in new situations of similitude. Ricoeur claims:

> It is to the general phenomenon of intertexuality, as an effect of reading, rather than allegory, as allegedly immanent within Scripture, that we may appeal in order to generate theological readings of the Song of Songs, setting out, almost like sparks of new meaning, points of intersection among texts that belong to the biblical canon.[178]

The Referent God and Christic Density

The first two applications of general hermeneutics to the interpretation of the Bible, objectification by structure and distanciation through writing, anticipate (are the prior conditions for) the one feature of biblical writing that makes possible the subversion of general to theological hermeneutics: the central place held by the referent "God,"[179] and the "density"[180] given to this word by the cross and resurrection of Christ.[181] By treading the course he does to get to the "world" or "thing" of the text, placing it in the last position, Ricoeur resists the premature imposition of the self on the process of interpretation, via his examination of objectification through structure, and at the same time avoids getting bogged down in the "excavative"[182] quest for authorial intentions, original audiences and situations in the world behind the text, via his proposal of distanciation. The reader is thus prepared to consider the Bible in its objectivity; that is, to let its unique world unfold through the medley of its originary and multi-structured texts. In this process the uniqueness of the Bible, the specificity of its discourse, comes to light.

"God . . . is the ultimate referent in these texts. God is in some manner implied by the issue of these texts, by the world—the biblical world—that these texts unfold."[183] One might say God is the coordinating center of the Bible, around which the significations produced by the varieties of biblical discourse gather. This is not to say that the naming of God is univocal in the Bible; rather in these originary expressions of faith, the naming of God is indirect and multiple, as polyphonic as the genres in which God is named. However, all the partial discourses of the Bible converge around the referent God.

At the same time, God is not enclosed by this discourse. The one to whom the texts of the Bible refer, while he speaks in prophetic discourse, is traced in narrative, commands in prescription, is sought in wisdom and invoked in the second person in praise, is nonetheless, "infinitely regressive" . . . "utterly beyond

---

178 "The Nuptial Metaphor," p. 295.

179 "Philosophical Hermeneutics and Biblical Hermeneutics," p. 97.

180 Ibid., p. 98.

181 Put more abstractly, it is the "thing" or "world of the text" that constitutes the uniqueness of biblical discourse. Ibid., p. 97.

182 The term is taken from Alter, *The World of Biblical Literature*, p. 133.

183 "Naming God," p. 221.

The Bible as Holy Scripture 115

our grasp."[184] Ricoeur helps to establish his point through an examination of the language of parables, hyperbolic proverbs and proclamatory sayings, which name God only indirectly, disruptively, and thus "shatter all attempts to replace them with theological significations."[185] He also offers an exegesis of Exodus 3:13-15. In this narrative God is both named and not named. The name God gives is enigmatic: God is named as the one who cannot be named. "I am whom I am," does not present God in language for human control "authorizing a positive ontology capable of capping off the narrative and other namings, instead it protects the secret of the 'in-itself' of God . . ."[186] Thus the Bible, a particular instance for the application of a general hermeneutic, is able to turn philosophical-literary inquiry into its own service by its unique subject matter, God, whose name is the point at which biblical literature both converges and eludes our grasp.

However, the question arises: what role does the Gospel depiction of Jesus Christ play in the naming of God in the polyphonic intertext of the Bible? In other words, is Ricoeur able to offer a construal of the Bible that is Christian, that takes seriously not only Jesus' preaching and parables, but the preaching of Jesus as the Christ, the content of the good news which is announced? Moreover, what weight do the Gospels have, as one genric mode of naming God in Jesus Christ, the fulfillment of the Old Testament, in his overall construal of Scripture? In answer, Ricoeur says two things: first, the New Testament continues to name God.[187] Thus, Gospel and Epistle texts about Jesus have a contribution to make in the polyphonic naming of God in the overall intertext of the Bible. Second, these texts have the role of adding a "density"[188] to the word "God", which philosophical notions of "being," medieval or modern, do not contain. "Christ," maintains Ricoeur, offers a specific plus to our understanding of God:

> [The term has] the power to incarnate all the religious significations in one basic symbol: the symbol to a sacrificial love, of a love stronger than death . . . In its signification [the teaching of the cross and resurrection] there is contained the notion of *his* relation to us freely given and of *our* relation to him as "absolutely concerned" and as fully "re-cognizant of our gratitude."[189]

---

184 John B. Webster, "Response to George Hunsinger," *Modern Theology*, 8/2 (April, 1992): 130-131. See Ricoeur, "Naming God," p. 228 and Hays, "Reading Scripture in the Light of the Resurrection," p. 236.

185 Fodor, *Christian Hermeneutics*, p. 242. See "Naming God," p. 229. There is thus an irreducibility to the genric naming of God.

186 "Naming God," p. 228. See also "Philosophical Hermeneutics and Biblical Hermeneutics," pp. 97-98; "Philosophy and Religious Language," p. 45; and "From Interpretation to Translation," in *Thinking Biblically*, pp. 331-363 where Ricoeur offers an extended explication of Exodus 3.

187 "Naming God," p. 230.

188 See "Philosophical Hermeneutics and Biblical Hermeneutics," p. 98; and "Philosophy and Religious Language," p. 46. The most involved discussion of what this density implies for naming God is offered in his essay by the same name, pp. 230-232.

189 "Philosophical Hermeneutics and Biblical Hermeneutics," p. 98. Ricoeur's emphases.

116   *Revelation, Holy Scripture and Church*

Thus the density that Christ adds to our understanding of God is *as* a symbol[190] and the density added *is* that of love and graciousness. However, the more pertinent issue here is this: when Ricoeur declares that, like the term "God," Christ has the power to gather to itself "all religious significations," does he mean all of the religious significations in the entirety of the canon or just the Gospels or New Testament?

The question is not easily resolved. On the one hand, Ricoeur ascribes to "Christ" the same double power he does to "God"; that is, the name marks the place of coordination of religious signification and at the same time its vanishing point. What is more, in his essay, "The Hermeneutics of Testimony," Ricoeur links "testimony to the absolute" in history to the testimony of the Gospels to Jesus as the Christ.[191] He also notes in an essay from 1968, "the Christ event is hermeneutically related to all of Judaic Scripture in the sense that it interprets this Scripture."[192] On the other hand, he is adamant that the naming of Jesus Christ in the gospels does not displace the accent of the Bible from the naming of God. He "resists with all his strength"[193] substituting the naming of one (God) for the naming of another (Jesus Christ). The teaching of Jesus, together with his cross and resurrection, only attain intelligibility with reference to the broader naming of God throughout Holy Writ. For Jesus refers to the Kingdom of *God*, cites Psalm 22 from the cross, which names God, and his resurrection is an act of God "homologous" to the Exodus.

On Ricoeur's view, any Christology that does not take into account the larger context, in which God is named, would "be diluted into an individual or collective anthropology, one that would be entirely horizontal and stripped of its poetic power."[194] To resist this tendency, Ricoeur champions a Christology "from below", which begins with the historical figure of Jesus of Nazareth and intersects with all the partial discourses of the Bible in their naming of God including Jesus and his message about God. This dialectical task, circular as it is, should be courageously taken up—avoiding both the simple logic of difference or identity. Ricoeur concludes, "The doctrine of the Trinity did this labor for one epoch of thought. A similar labor ought to be undertaken today, one that would take up the whole space of the naming of God and its discordant concordance."[195]

---

190 *Critique and Conviction*, p. 148. Ricoeur registers his agreement with Kant, his preferred philosopher of Religion, "who speaking of the figure of Christ as being the man pleasing to God . . . declares that he could not have drawn that figure out of himself, and that he found it inscribed in a sort of imaginary, or a schematism constitutive of the religious." See also Paul Ricoeur, "A Philosophical Hermeneutics of Religion: Kant," in *Figuring the Sacred*, pp. 83-85 and "The Summoned Subject in the School of the Narratives of the Prophetic Vocation," in *Figuring the Sacred*, pp. 267-268.

191 "The Hermeneutics of Testimony," pp. 134-142.

192 "Preface to Bultmann," p. 50. This position is ascribed to the interpretative situation of the early church. Whether it is Ricoeur's own position is difficult to tell.

193 "Naming God," p. 230.

194 Ibid., p. 231.

195 Ibid., p. 232.

The Bible as Holy Scripture

Canon and Authority

In his essay, "The Canon between the Text and the Community,"[196] Ricoeur considered the question of the authority of the Bible, the canon, within the life of the church. He sets the issue of authority within the familiar framework of his application of a general hermeneutic to a question about the specifics of the Bible and its import for ecclesial life. He notes that in the passage from speech to writing, a text—including the text of the Bible—acquires a threefold independence, from the author, from the initial audience and from the initial ostensible world of its production, and a shape through genric configuration. This textually mediated world proposes to subsequent readers a possible world, which the reader may inhabit. The reader may then appropriate the modality of life commensurate with the suggested world. However—and here Ricoeur locates the space within which the issue of authority arises, in the space between distancing through writing, where the text acquires a certain objectivity, and appropriation—possibilities for different understandings creep into the interpretative process. "A different proposition of meaning, a different world of the text has been opened up by a different reader/hearer. A situation of conflict is created . . ."[197] A conflict of interpretations opens up which needs to be arbitrated, and the question becomes how to do so without suppressing conflict or controlling it. "These are," writes Ricoeur, "the conditions of textual authority."[198]

Ricoeur enumerates four conditions that constrain conflicts of interpretation. The first, which is minimal, is the collecting together of texts. Some books are assembled and others are left out. Historically, this occurred in the Christian church against the backdrop of crisis, in persecution from without and heresy from within. The apostolicity and catholicity of a book—and ultimately the reference of a particular book to the authority of the Lord—were key factors in its being recognized as authoritative. These three together, Ricoeur maintains, constituted the rule of recognition, "so as to recall the Latin *recipere*."[199] The second condition that constrains conflict of interpretation involves traditions of reading and interpretation. In the case of the Bible, historically this meant that certain traditions and books, including connection to an Apostle and the writings of Paul, were established as the backdrop against which other books were recognized and received. The third condition has to do with a presumed superiority of some work over other work. Some texts, by common recognition, accrue to themselves the status "magnum opus," that is, of a great works capable of being read again and again in various contexts "without any major semantic loss."[200] This took place in the life of the church in the decisions made concerning which books were worthy to be read in worship, to be used in education and preaching, as part of its lectionary. The fourth condition sets the terms of arbitration in conflicts of interpretation is an historical community, and takes charge of the process of making sense of writings and settling conflicts. Based

---

196 "The Canon between the Text and the Community," pp. 7-26.
197 Ibid., p. 13.
198 Ibid.
199 Ibid., p. 20.
200 Ibid., p. 24.

118   *Revelation, Holy Scripture and Church*

on the recognition that guides the collection of books into a canon, the institution has a secondary power to turn recognition into obedience. What was instituted through common recognition or reception now is instituted as "an authorized quantity."[201]

Ricoeur gathers up from this discussion of canon two historical-conceptual notions that guide him to the construction of an acceptable idea of authority. He articulates what is to him an acceptable understanding of the authority of the canon against the backdrop of two complaints. The first relates to the circularity of the argument that the church establishes the canon.[202] How can it be that the church makes a decision to establish a textual authority, all the while basing its authority to do so on the text that it establishes? On Ricoeur's view, this problematic is ameliorated by the idea of "recognition." Through successive crises, the need arose for self-identity against heresy and preservation, through time against distortion. The community came to recognize itself "by these texts" . . . "as this community." In the common recognition of these texts as the basis for the arbitration of differences between contemporaries and in the ongoing recognition of these texts as the basis for the passing on of identity through time, canonical Scripture functions authoritatively in the church.

The second objection, over against which Ricoeur articulates his understanding of the authority of the canon, is that of authoritarianism, that is, the authority of the canon in the church as imposition. Ricoeur first notes that he protests the use of the term "canonical" to designate post-scriptural accretions—that is, "dogmatic teaching, together with the controls exercised over morals on the basis of the ethical content transmitted with the orthodoxy of the faith."[203] Ricoeur wants to separate the term "canon" as it is used of the New Testament from its application to subsequent accretions of imposed dogma since, on his view, these accretions belong to the political sphere and are a form of domination. The canon of the New Testament is not imposed on the church but "recognized" or "received." These terms introduce a sense of freedom and consent into the notion of authority. "From that point on," once the canon is recognized as authoritative, "we think according to, but we think freely, that is to say: we think."[204] Moreover, what the church recognizes in the lectionary it receives—for public reading alongside sermons and the celebration of the Eucharist—is "superiority." In these texts, "greatness" is recognized and received on analogy with the way great texts and great authors are received. The superiority of canonical Scripture over the recognizing church is, contends Ricoeur, a "symbolic figure" of the same relationship as that between master and disciple. There is no

---

201 Ibid., p. 15.

202 Ricoeur contemplates this hermeneutic circle between church and Scripture, one that he never understands as vicious, at a number of points in his considerations of biblical hermeneutics. The most extended considerations takes place in LaCoste and Ricoeur, *Thinking Biblically*, pp. xv-xix; Ricoeur, "Naming God," pp. 217-218; *Critique and Conviction*, pp. 142-145; and "The 'Sacred' Text and the Community," in *Figuring the Sacred*, pp. 68-72.

203 "The Canon between the Text and the Community," p. 23. In the same essay, Ricoeur reiterates that he is discussing the canon of the New Testament and not "the profusion of texts that, like heavy alluvia, have been deposited on the scriptural subsoil . . ." In this he is entirely consistent with his earlier essay, "Toward a Hermeneutic of the Idea of Revelation," p. 74.

204 "The Canon between the Text and the Community," p. 25.

The Bible as Holy Scripture 119

domination and obedience in it; rather, "Here 'following' means neither 'imitating' nor 'submitting.' It is a *Nachfolge Christi* that is proposed by the biblical Scripture in the New Testament."[205]

Critique

In this section a critique of Ricoeur's application of a general hermeneutic to the Bible is offered. The central issue raised against Ricoeur's project, as noted above, is that through a methodological preference for a poetic, natural depiction of the specifics of the Bible's construal, the hermeneutic situation of the church and attendant interpretative concepts, he debilitates a consideration of the Bible and the hermeneutic field in terms of its relationship to God's communicative action. Ricoeur fails to consider privileged genres within the Bible as the terms in which others are to be read, because he is not sufficiently attentive to theological density at the level of formalistic depiction. This move, as well as his tendency to eschew second-order dogmatic language, renders problematic his attempts to relate the naming of God to the naming of Christ in a theologically subtle fashion. Moreover, Ricoeur attributes to textual dynamics, "effects of reading," what properly belongs to the action of God. This is attributable to the hermeneutical confinement of divine reality to a final stage of hermeneutical depiction, in which God is the point of intersection, the implicated subject, of all biblical discourse. However, where God is acknowledged as both appropriating "subject" and object of biblical discourse, the author as well as the central character, the whole hermeneutical field needs to be reconfigured and the role of "distanciation," as the means by which the Bible speaks, encorporated into a thicker theological account of divine agency. Finally, Ricoeur's account of the formation and authority of the canon, while it is descriptively satisfying, lacks constructive and normative persuasiveness since it articulates the nature of biblical authority in terms of the natural category of "classic" rather than in primary relation to what the Bible is about. In sum: like Barr, Ricoeur's account of the Bible as canon, Scripture of the church, gives insufficient attention to the assets which belong to the Bible as Scripture because of its complicity in God's saving activity in Jesus Christ.

Genre and content   In his essay, "Revelation in the Jewish Tradition,"[206] Emmauel Levinas writes with appreciation of the genric taxonomy Ricoeur introduces into his discussion of the modes of discourse in the Old and New Testaments. He calls Ricoeur's essay, "Toward A Hermeneutic of the Idea of Revelation," "magisterial,"[207] and as such appreciates that it gives him a fitting context within which to initiate his own discussion of revelation. However, Levinas introduces a caveat. He writes:

> But perhaps, for a Jewish reading of the Bible, these distinctions cannot be established quite as firmly as in the pellucid classification we have been offered. Prescriptive lessons—found in the Pentateuch, the part of the Torah known as the Torah of Moses—

---

205 Ibid., p. 26.
206 Levinas, "Revelation in the Jewish Tradition."
207 Ibid., p. 193.

120 *Revelation, Holy Scripture and Church*

occupy a privileged position within Jewish consciousness, so far as the relationship with God is concerned. Every text is asked to produce such lessons; the psalms may allude to characters and events, but they also refer to prescriptions: Psalm 119:19 says, notably, "I am a sojourner on earth: hide not thy commandments from me!" The texts of the Wisdom literature are prophetic and prescriptive. Cutting across the "genres" in all directions, then, are allusions and references which are visible to the naked eye.[208]

Levinas point is that within a "Jewish" reading of the Bible more than genric variation—each with its unique mode of confession—is formative for the construal and reading of the Bible in its entirety. For "Jewish consciousness," what Ricoeur calls "prescriptive discourse," is privileged; it weighs more than the other forms of discourse even if these other forms of discourse are more voluminous. Levinas explains that Jewish reading looks for prescriptive lessons in non-prescriptive material, since prescriptive lessons have precedence: they provide the terms in which the rest of the Bible, including poetry and Wisdom literature, are read. Mark Wallace describes Levinas' position: "Biblical revelation centers on prescriptive teachings . . . to the degree that even in seemingly unlegal [*sic*] genres such as the Psalms and sapiential literature, Levinas argues that there are prescriptive upheavals where God's commanding voice to the reader breaks through the literary surface of the text."[209] Levinas does not suggest that prescriptive lessons are absent in the Psalms and Wisdom literature; prescriptive lesson reading is not an act of projection into texts. However, "in terms of relationship with God," Jewish consciousness looks for prescriptive lessons as definitive of what it means to read the Bible as a Jew.

Levinas' observation with respect to the necessary exception to Ricoeur's formal taxonomy necessary for Jewish reading of the Bible is pertinent to the reading of the Bible, Old and New Testament, as Scripture of the church. For his observation implies that what constitutes canon, and the rules for reading it, are local, that is, related to a community of readers. A sophisticated analysis and genric classification of biblical texts for Christian reading does not indicate the relative weight that the subject matter of a particular discourse has, vis-à-vis the rest of the canon. Thus the caveat Levinas makes against Ricoeur's "pellucid classification" could also be raised with respect to reading the Bible for Christological sense. In other words, a tension can be found between Ricoeur's construal of the Bible in a formal structuralist manner—as an interanimating genric intertext that names God—and the Bible read in a traditionally Christian manner—in which every text is asked to produce Christological "literal" sense, or is read in relation to Christological "literal" sense.

This tension in Ricoeur seems to arise out of his movement from general to special hermeneutics in the treatment of the Bible. Before a consideration of "local" rules for reading[210] that is, of the special weighting of biblical texts in terms of their relationship to God's communicative activity, Ricoeur first takes the long detour through structural and hermeneutical analysis in which the genric diversity of the

---

208 Ibid.

209 Wallace, "From Phenomenology to Scripture?," p. 310.

210 On the problem of the usefulness of general hermeneutics for local reading see Francis Watson, "The Scope of Hermeneutics," in Colin Gunton (ed.), *The Cambridge Companion to Christian Doctrine* (Cambridge, 1997), pp. 65-80.

The Bible as Holy Scripture   121

Bible is identified and the hermeneutic situation of the church depicted. Privileging any part of the Bible has to wait on a prior "general hermeneutic" construal of the text in its genric variety. On Ricoeur's view, this is not just a judicious procedure; it is the "only path that leads at the same time to a recognition of the biblical thing."[211] However, Levinas maintains that Ricoeur's structural taxonomy precludes just such a result. The biblical thing, or perhaps it is more felicitous to say, the content in terms of which the biblical thing is ordered, is "God's commanding voice" for Judaism, and it is set-aside in structural/hermeneutic genric depiction, in favour of "plurality of expression." The privileged sense "in terms of relationship with God," which may be a local hermeneutical concern, is preempted by formally related scriptural genres. In the same way, Christocentric "Word of God" construals[212] or Christocentric "narrative" depictions of the story line of the whole Bible as the privileged Christian sense could be jeopardized, subverted or qualified by a prior formal construal of the contents of the Bible in terms of genre and genric interplay. Mark Wallace, in describing the triangle within which meaning is generated in Biblical discourse (between author, work and audience) on Ricoeur's account, writes:

> In this triangle the Bible emerges as a complete intertwining of narrative and non-narrative forms of expression (such as prophecy and wisdom) so that any attempt to short-circuit this variety with a predetermined focus on one particular genre and one particular character—the character of narrative and the identity of Jesus, as in Frei's case—violates the text's build in plurality of expression.[213]

Wallace does not spell out the sense of "predetermined" in detail, except to say that an example of such a "predetermined focus" can be found in the work of Hans Frei, in which narrative, as a genre, and Jesus, as an individual, are privileged with respect to the rest of the Bible. However, this criticism of Frei's work from Ricoeur's perspective fails in two respects. The first way in which it fails is that it separates genre from identity. Frei does not privilege narrative and Jesus: he privileges realistic narrative *because of* Jesus. To paraphrase Luther, "realistic narrative is the manger in which Jesus Christ is laid." A central point of *The Identity of Jesus Christ* is that readers simply cannot have the subject matter, Jesus, of the Gospel narratives, apart from his storied depiction.[214] Thus Frei privileges "realistic" narrative because it is

---

211 "Philosophical Hermeneutics and Biblical Hermeneutics," p. 97.

212 "Word of God" construals of the whole of the Bible in which the prophet speaks for God acquire some initial priority in Ricoeur since he takes prophetic discourse as "a basic referent." See "Toward a Hermeneutic of the Idea of Revelation," p. 75. However, this move is minimized by two further considerations: (1) "Word of God" theologies are too abstract without Wisdom and Narrative which give attention to the nonverbal nature of revelation and roots it in history; and (2) Ricoeur's persistent concern that a concentration on prophetic speech as the measure of other forms of discourse is based on psychologized notions of inspiration.

213 Wallace, *The Second Naiveté*, p. 44. See also "From Phenomenology to Scripture?," p. 310. In this article Wallace writes, "singular attention to any one discourse—including legal discourse—runs the risk of homogenizing the Bible's semantic polyphony."

214 Frei writes, "In other words, whether these stories report history (either reliably or unreliably), whether or not the Gospels are other things besides realistic stories, what they

122   *Revelation, Holy Scripture and Church*

the genre, which through its "ascriptive literalism,"[215] renders the identity of Jesus Christ.

The second point to be made here is that Frei's focus on narrative, as the genre within which Jesus' unsubstitutable identity is rendered, is not arbitrarily imposed. In so far as Wallace's charge is that the character of Frei's "predetermined focus" is arbitrary or extrinsic, which the phrase, "violates the text's build in plurality of expression," would seem to imply, he has not grasped Frei's emphasis. Frei justifies privileging the narrative depiction of the identity of Jesus in the Gospels as the story in terms of which the whole corpus of biblical writing ought to be construed, based on the built-in figural patterns of the New Testament by which the whole of it, and the Old Testament, are related to Jesus Christ:

> Jewish Texts are taken as "types" of the story of Jesus as their common "antitype," an appropriating procedure that begins in the New Testament, notably in the letters of Paul, the letter to the Hebrews, and the synoptic gospels, and then becomes the common characteristic of the Christian tradition of scriptural interpretation until modern times."[216]

Arguments can be mounted against Frei's claims, indeed arguments have been mounted as in the previous section; but it can hardly be maintained, on Ricoeurian terms against Frei, that he violates "plurality of expression" via an extrinsic predetermined grid imposed upon the genric diversity of the Bible. Indeed, the case made by Frei suggests, as does Levinas, that a general structural construal of the Bible in its genric diversity sits in tension with the unique weight that accumulates to particular genres because of the privileged position assigned to them by the textual ensemble and the communities that read them "so far as the relationship with God is concerned." Even though Ricoeur anticipates "global configurations of meaning" arising from the vast intertextual genric friction created by texts projecting "themselves on each other," no particular genre or confession of faith may reign over others in a hierarchy. Texts "intersignify one another instead of arranging themselves in some hierarchy."[217] A general structural hermeneutical construal of the Bible as interanimating genric intertext sits in tension with local theological construals of the Bible as typologically related, Christ-centered Scripture of the church.

The Bible and message transmission   While Ricoeur's depiction of the hermeneutic situation of the church, in terms of a general philosophical hermeneutic, identifies the inevitably exegetical nature of its existence from the beginning, it lacks persuasive power for the local practice of interpretation within the church since the hermeneutic depiction he offers lacks theological weight. The question of God, his action and

---

tell us is a fruit of the stories themselves. We cannot have what they are about (the "subject" matter) without the stories themselves." *The Identity of Jesus Christ*, p. xiv. See also *The Eclipse of Biblical Narrative*, pp. 13-14.

215 By this phrase Frei points out that what the Gospels say of Jesus they mean to ascribe to him. "The story of Jesus is about him—not about someone else, or about nobody in particular, or about all of us." *Types of Christian Theology*, p. 140.

216 "The 'Literal' Reading of Biblical Narrative," p. 120.

217 "The Nuptial Metaphor," p. 303.

redemptive purposes in Jesus Christ—deferred as it is to the stage at which the question of what the texts are about—does not arise within the generic application of a philosophical hermeneutic to the constellation of interpretative tasks that belong to the church. The hermeneutic situation of the church is depicted such that the *constitutive* relation between the Bible and proclamation, the *possibility* of message transmission, and the *availability* of the subject matter of the Bible, are accounted for in general, non-theological, terms. Interpretative gaps (between Old Testament and the Christ-event, between the Bible and particular historical contexts of the church and between the first witnesses of the Christ-event and the secondary hearing of the Gospel in the church) are overcome, to be sure, thanks to writing, but surely this lacks theological dimension in terms of a persuasive account of "the church's hermeneutic situation."

"Biblical interpretation could not even get going if we did not, as a sheer minimum, presuppose that God speaks consistently."[218] Here Nicholas Wolterstorff identifies what is lacking in Ricoeur's depiction of the church's hermeneutical situation. Theological language and expectations, with respect to the interpretative situation of the church, cannot be deferred to a later stage in which the subject matter of the Bible is considered, as though the import of the subject matter of the Bible is not already present in the depiction of the hermeneutic situation of the church. This lack of theological realism—or conversely, this naturalist ontological assumption— turns up in Ricoeur's account of the hermeneutic situation of the church in the hypothetical nature of his language when it veers on theological description. He asserts that the Christ-event is interpreted in such a way to make it "appear to be" the fulfillment of Scripture and maintains that Christian preaching has thereby "chosen" to be hermeneutic. This general philosophical depiction of the hermeneutic situation of Christianity, which assumes that "a text's being is defined by reference to its occupation of a space in a natural field of communicative activity,"[219] lacks theological density; it ascribes to human creative initiative what is, in effect, a human response to God's prior action in Israel and in Jesus Christ. The New Testament accumulates Old Testament texts, images and events to Jesus because he *is* the fulfillment of them. Christian preaching does not choose to be hermeneutic; it is made hermeneutic in relation to an existing corpus, not of texts but of Scripture, by virtue of the life, death and resurrection of Jesus as the promise to which they point. God's prevenient saving action in Jesus Christ (1) encourages retrospective reading of the Old Testament, (2) situates the church within the "story" such reading engenders, and (3) appropriates lucid (clear, sufficient and effective) apostolic witness to it. The hermeneutic sites to which Ricoeur points in his analysis of writing become speech and speech become writing, and the means to address interpretative challenges these sites imply, leave

---

218 Nicholas Wolterstorff, "The Importance of Hermeneutics for a Christian Worldview," in Roger Lundin (ed.), *Disciplining Hermeneutics: Interpretation in Christian Perspective* (Grand Rapids, 1997), p. 46.

219 Webster, *Holy Scripture*, 29. "Dogmatically, the assumption is to be controverted because of its claim that a "natural" understanding of the text is more basic than an understanding of the text as scriptural."

124 *Revelation, Holy Scripture and Church*

completely out of account the radiant context of God's saving action within which the people of God take up these interpretative challenges.

For instance, Ricoeur maintains that the interpretation of life and the interpretation of the Book are drawn into a relation in which they "decipher each other" and are "mutually adjusted"[220]—a hermeneutic circle. This modern problematic, observed especially in Bultmann, is created by Paul's insistence that the hearer of the Word "decipher the movement of his own existence in the life of the Passion and Resurrection of Christ." However, while Ricoeur properly locates this as a site for hermeneutic endeavor, his "general philosophical" depiction of the hermeneutic situation does not grant noetic priority to the Bible as Scripture in the interpretation of life such that the Bible seems to end up in a conversation between equals, and it is left to the church's own interpretative genius to moderate "mutual adjustment." Ricoeur risks a vicious hermeneutic circle between the Gospel and existence. Berkhouwer writes, "Only when the aim is a correlation between kerygma and existence, in which existence itself, despite every accent of the text, is made the final 'canon' for its understanding, will such a particularly vicious circle be created."[221]

Text sense and appropriated discourse Ricoeur's account of "analogical transference" as "an effect of reading" in his examination of the Song of Songs is another context in which an interpretative "gap" between the text in its original sense as nuptial celebration and its later churchly application in baptismal catechesis is construed and bridged by means of "the general phenomenon of intertextuality." In this account, while the historical-descriptive phase of Ricoeur's investigation includes an appreciation of churchly context—a privileged site of reading—and that Paul's "attachment of nuptial signification to Christian initiation" encourages "allegorical" reading of the Song of Songs in the context of baptismal instruction, his own proposal for a theological reading, which "relocate[s] the nuptial bond in non-erotic figures of love," is rooted in a general theory of intertextuality. Here Ricoeur returns to the Bible construed as a literary constellation of interanimating genres in which all the figures of love inter-signify each other in a non-hierarchical manner. Poetic reference or metaphorization are the literary phenomena by which first order reference is suspended, and texts are free to project a secondary sense, which a new situation (the world before the text) engenders free of authorial intentionality, even if the author is God. This natural account effectively neutralizes the Bible as Scripture of the church by genericizing liturgical context as "new situation" and

---

220 Ricoeur is not consistent in the language he uses to depict the nature of the hermeneutic relation between the interpretation of the Bible and the interpretation of life. He speaks of the amplification of the meaning of the Bible as sacred meaning to incorporate all of life, but most of the metaphors he uses seem to indicate a conversation between equals. See "Preface to Bultmann," pp. 52-54. For a critique of the "conversation" model as it applies to Scripture interpretation see David L. Bartlett, *Between the Bible and The Church: New Methods for Biblical Preaching* (Nashville, 1999), pp. 13-14.

221 Berkhouwer, *Holy Scripture*, pp. 119-120. The circle is not vicious when, on Berkhouwer's account, the encounter posits "the *a priori* of the text over against all of the interpreter's baggage and presuppositions."

The Bible as Holy Scripture 125

by construing intra-canonical Christocentric typological referencing and its extra canonical interpretative extension as "metaphorization of meaning."

Wolterstorff notes that Ricoeur's hermeneutic is a "text-sense" hermeneutic since interpreting at a distance (from author, audience and intentional world) can, Ricoeur claims, only be thus.[222] An upshot of this approach is that it only ever allows God to be the object of "text-sense," never the intentional author of text-sense. God's involvement with the Bible is primarily as its main character. This is demonstrated procedurally in Ricoeur's depiction of the hermeneutic field in terms of a general philosophical hermeneutic of text-sense, and in his contention that biblical hermeneutics only makes its mark, an inversion, once the content of the Bible, God, is under discussion. However, what if God is not only a character in the story, but its author,[223] not in the sense of "insufflation" but in terms of saying something to us by means of (appropriation of) the texts of the Bible?[224] Wolterstorff, in another context, considers it "eminently plausible construal"[225] that God commissioned the apostles to be witnesses, and that from this commission a body of literature about Jesus and his teachings arose, which by the process of canonization under the providence of God,[226] became "a single volume of divine discourse,"[227] that is as a book by means of which God says something. A theological reading of the Song of Solomon, on this account, involves more than a consideration of the "poetics of metaphorization," "genric taxonomy," "intergenric friction" and "new situations of similitude"; instead the context of the Song in the Christian canon[228] leads the church to consider what God said and is saying "allegorically" thereby. Dan Stiver misses the interpretative implications of Wolterstoff's reconfiguration of the hermeneutic field, when he maintains that the Bible, even if the whole of it is construed as divine discourse, still has to be interpreted and, he insists, this is where Ricoeur's genric typing and the like, excel.[229] However, interpretation that

---

222 Wolterstorff, "The Importance of Hermeneutics for a Christian Worldview," p. 41 and Stiver, *Theology after Ricoeur*, p. 131.

223 See Jenson, "Scripture's Authority in the Church," p. 33.

224 Wolterstoff notes that there is a position between Romanticism and Structuralism, which allows that authors say things by means of texts—authors makes promises, for example. See "The Importance of Hermeneutics for a Christian Worldview," p. 44. See also *Divine Discourse*, pp. 183-222, where Wolterstorff develops a hermeneutic for the interpretation of mediating human discourse and mediated divine discourse.

225 Wolterstorff, *Divine Discourse*, p. 295.

226 Ibid. See Brevard Childs, *The New Testament as Canon: An Introduction* (Philadelphia, 1985), pp. 28, 39-40.

227 Wolterstorff, *Divine Discourse*, p. 235.

228 Wolterstorff, "The Importance of Hermeneutics for a Christian Worldview," p. 46. See also *Divine Discourse*, p. 214. Here Wolterstorff makes the point that when Song of Songs is read as appropriated divine discourse, the human author is the one allegorized, and God is the allegorizer.

229 Stiver, *Theology after Ricoeur*, p. 128. Stiver maintains that Ricoeur and Wolterstorff agree that a text takes on "a life of its own beyond the intentions of its human author." However, the life that a text takes on, as appropriated discourse gathered to the canon and authorized as a medium of divine discourse, is not "a life of its own." See ibid., p. 133.

126   *Revelation, Holy Scripture and Church*

aims at what God is saying by means of appropriated human discourse set within the ordered relations of a Christocentric canon, and the prior complex of what an interpreter believes about God,[230] renders Ricoeur's genric taxonomy of secondary value since an ordered canon resists preemption by a prior, general, hermeneutic-leveling construal of the field for a variegated theological one. On Wolterstorff's account, the whole hermeneutic field—human speech become human writing and human writing become appropriated divine speech, the formation of Scripture and its collection in the canon as God-authorized commission and the interpretation of the content of the Bible as one book in which interpreters discern what God intends by means of it—are implicated. Distanciation through writing, and mediation through a communicative chain—writing–speech–writing—are too thin an account of the hermeneutic situation of the church to set them as the necessary and sufficient conditions for the text to "say something."[231]

Naming God   However, one might ask, are there *intrabiblical* criteria[232] by means of which one can *emphasize* certain biblical names for God? Presuming that the Bible is a polyphonic collection of multi-genred literature, each with its accompanying confession of God—either as the voice behind the voice in prophetic discourse, as the one whose activity is traced in narrative and so on—is it possible, on Ricoeur's account, that the Bible as canon should itself privilege a particular naming of God such that other genric namings of God are understood and construed in relation to it? This is, in many ways, a test of Ricoeur's contention that biblical hermeneutics subverts general hermeneutics at the level of the specificity of its referent God and the unfolding of a world before the text which correlates to it. What does Ricoeur make of the density added to the naming of God by the teaching, the life, death and resurrection of Christ?

The density added to the word "God" by Christ is one that "being" does not contain. By this Ricoeur points out that the Gospels, for example, speak of sacrificial love and love stronger than death, "hope in spite of." The naming of Christ enables us to appreciate God as one who freely relates to us to evoke from us a sense of our relation to God as dependent and grateful.[233] The Gospels, as testimony to Christ,

---

230   Wolterstorff, in terms that are amenable to Hans Frei's insistence that the Bible ought to be read giving priority to the Gospels, and in keeping with the "rule of faith," notes that "we bring into play our knowledge of God" when we interpret for divine discourse. See *Divine Discourse*, pp. 218-222 and "The Importance of Hermeneutics for a Christian Worldview," p. 46.

231   "Philosophical Hermeneutics and Biblical Hermeneutics," p. 95.

232   On Ricoeurian terms, perhaps it would be more accurate to ask whether there are inner biblical criteria. The difference between the two ways of putting the question has to do with whether and to what degree one conceives of the Bible as a single book, a canonical unity. Intratextual would be the term most appropriate when working with the Bible as a single text, intertextual more appropriate to the Bible conceived of as a diverse collection of texts. The use of the language here is "theologically laden." See Ward, *Word and Supplement*, pp. 235-236.

233   "Philosophical Hermeneutics and Biblical Hermeneutics," p. 98. See also "Naming God," pp. 230-232.

The Bible as Holy Scripture 127

are thus implicated in naming God; they qualify and relate to God as named in other forms of discourse, a specific plus is added, a density beyond "being" is added to the naming of God in the polyphonic inter-text of the Bible. This density does not displace the accent of the Bible from naming God to naming Christ. What is more, the relation between the naming of God and the naming of Christ is circular—they are understood in terms of each other. Christ requires the context of the larger whole, naming of God for intelligibility. Finally, while Christ adds density to the naming of God, the density added is as a symbol. Christ is symbolic of sacrificial love, a love stronger than death. Christ functions in the Gospels in Kantian terms—as a figure, a particular instantiation of a pattern, a model—one that Ricoeur claims he could not draw out of himself.[234] Thus, the resurrection is conceived symbolically as the "resurrection in the Christian community, which becomes the body of the living Christ. The resurrection would consist in having a body other than the physical body, that is to say acquiring an historical body."[235]

The point made by Levinas regarding Ricoeur's taxonomy of biblical genres, that is, that the taxonomy is too formal to account for privileged discourse and actual communal use, would seem to hold even at the stage when biblical hermeneutics is supposed to render philosophical hermeneutics its organon. James Fodor makes the general point and asks the pertinent question:

> Perhaps the most troublesome feature that Ricoeur's hermeneutics presents to theology concerns the relative priority given to the world of philosophy over theology. Are hermeneutical or methodological questions capable of being displayed independently of the particular texts in question or are they internal to the practices of biblical exegesis, commentary, exposition, and proclamation?[236]

The naming of Christ is incorporated into the overall project of naming God in the polyphonic discourse of the Bible, and yet the formal poetic/philosophical depiction of the hermeneutic field renders certain forms of relating the different genres of the Bible problematic. Theological constructs like Old and New Testament, canon, covenant and Christocentric typology (or more generally figuration) are not included within the depiction of the Bible as a member of a class of poetic, metaphoric, texts. A circular relationship exists between naming God and naming Christ, in which Christ does not displace the centrality of the naming of God and yet this specification of the relationship lacks theological subtlety and mass. What about the naming of God in Jesus Christ and the retrospective light that casts over the various forms of genric confession as fulfillment? And why not employ the second-order language of Trinity and incarnation, not as "opaque" and "authoritarian" imposition, but as a means of helping exegesis to identify the manner in which the naming of Christ is,

---

234 *Critique and Conviction*, p. 148. See also Vanhoozer, *Biblical Narrative in the Philosophy of Paul Ricoeur*, p. 230.

235 Ricoeur, *Critique and Conviction*, p. 152. Kevin Vanhoozer argues that Ricoeur attends to the Bible for religious symbols and that this makes him vulnerable to transposing Jesus into a cipher for human experience. See *Biblical Narrative in the Philosophy of Paul Ricoeur*, pp. 227-239.

236 Fodor, *Christian Hermeneutics*, p. 302.

128 *Revelation, Holy Scripture and Church*

at the same time, the naming of God and humanity? In what appears to be an attempt to maintain formal genric integrity and polyvalent confession, a Christocentric and Trinitarian reading of the Bible according to a rule of faith is not considered. This move would not, as feared, expunge polyphonic confession from the biblical witness; it would uncover the Bible's polyphonic testimony to the redemptive action of God in Jesus Christ. As Barth writes, "theology confronts in Holy Scripture an extremely polyphonic . . . testimony to the word and work of God,"[237] and yet this observation does not forbid Barth from also maintaining the unity of the Bible, Old and New Testaments, as witness to Jesus Christ. Fodor concludes: "*How* and *where* and *by whom* God is named—i.e., ecclesial location, the particular linguistic habits and forms of life that constitute a Christian naming of God demand a more detailed exposition, greater material specification, than Ricoeur is either able or willing to provide."[238]

Classic authority Finally, we arrive at Ricoeur's recent articulation of the formation and authority of the canon in the life of the church. In this endeavor, even though Ricoeur frames the discussion and locates the problems of canon and its authority in terms of general hermeneutics in articulating a sense of the nature of "canonical authority," more historical *descriptive* attention is given to Christian reading patterns where the canon is concerned. The canon as conflict manager[239] for the church involves appeals not only to particular books, but to particular books read in a certain, even Gospel centered, pattern.[240] Ricoeur avoids the circularity of "the church authorizing texts which authorize the church's doing so" by an appeal to the notion of reception. Understood in this way, the church did not confer authority on the canonical texts of the Bible, it recognized and received them. In this way, Ricoeur reflects a traditional Protestant account of the relationship between the church and the canon. The church approves the canon, but "such an act of approval is, properly understood, a receptive rather than an authorizing act."[241]

However, when Ricoeur comes to articulate the nature of biblical authority, where he might develop a theological account in relation to the same realities by which Christian reading patterns developed and to which the canon testifies, he turns aside to literary description and Enlightenment protest. The theological realities which warranted the reception of the canon and its ruled reading as authoritative, on Ricoeur's descriptive account, are now minimized in his *normative* theological construal of the nature of biblical authority. In other words, Ricoeur develops his account of biblical "authority" against the foil of apologetic concern with the help of literary categories, rather than in primary relation to the theological realities to which the

---

237 Karl Barth, *Evangelical Theology: An Introduction*, trans. Grover Foley (Grand Rapids, 1963), p. 33. See also Lindbeck, "Critical Exegesis and Theological Interpretation," p. 170.

238 Fodor, *Christian Hermeneutics*, p. 324. Fodor's emphasis.

239 "The Canon between the Text and the Community," p. 23.

240 Ibid., pp. 14-15, 17, 19.

241 Webster, *Holy Scripture*, pp. 61-62. Here Webster is describing Calvin's position on the matter. Compare Ricoeur, "The Canon between the Text and the Community," p. 25. See also Berkouwer, *Holy Scripture*, pp. 90-91, 105ff.

The Bible as Holy Scripture 129

Bible testifies. The authority of the Bible is recognized, but the nature of its authority is articulated as a "classic,"[242] since this articulation of authority is amenable to "the protest against authority established on principle, in the name of reason," which "has become an obligatory cultural point of reference for the whole of the Western World since the Enlightenment."[243] The Bible has the property "authoritative," the nature of which is defined not in terms of its role in God's communicative action, but in terms of its participation in a natural, albeit superlative, class of human artifacts. In more traditional accounts of the nature of biblical authority, terms such as "clarity", "sufficiency" and "efficacy" are used to point to the manner in which the Bible is authoritative in matters pertaining to salvation. These qualities are all related to the doctrine of God, since they are functions of God's involvement with the Bible, ways in which the Bible, by virtue of its testimony to the saving action of God in Jesus Christ participates in its radiance.[244]

In sum: what James Barr achieves by disengagement, Ricoeur effects by delay. Barr disengages the Bible as Scripture in order critically to examine the Bible for the benefit of churchly exegesis and theological construction; Ricoeur, for the sake of guarding the unique subject matter of the Bible, defers a consideration of subject matter, and its potential for the depiction of the hermeneutic situation, until the realities of text and interpretative situation are offered first in general (poetic) terms. It was argued against Barr that "sound and adequate interpretation" requires an account of the canonical Scriptures of the church, which, while it does not neglect the Bible as a human artifact, takes into account, at a fundamental level, its unity and authority in relation to the primary reality by which it was engendered, shaped, and to which it bears witness. In the same way, against Ricoeur, we argued that maintaining the integrity of the Bible's subject matter requires an account of canonical Scripture which, while attentive to the genric shape of and hermeneutical challenges related to the Bible, takes as fundamental to construal and authority the primary reality by which the Bible was engendered, shaped, and to which it bears witness. The assumption that, in order correctly to be construed in its unity and authority, the Bible must first of all be depicted in non-scriptural terms, is challenged in both cases since Scripture (ordered texts in relation to the God who uses them) is fundamentally what the Bible is.

---

242 "The Canon between the Text and the Community" p. 24. Ricoeur develops the literary analogy in terms of the Bible's "greatness and superiority." A problem with the notion of a "classic" is that the category defeats what it is supposed to protect. One cannot maintain singularity or even uniqueness by means of membership in a general class of objects. See Fodor, *Christian Hermeneutics*, p. 254, n.57.

243 "The Canon between the Text and the Community," p. 23. See Fodor, *Christian Hermeneutics*, p. 302 and Berkhouwer, *Holy Scripture*, pp. 105-138.

244 See Karl Barth, *Church Dogmatics*, 1/2: 538. "Holy Scripture attests to the church . . . the revelation of God, Jesus Christ, the Word of God. The power in which it does so is the power of the object to which it bears witness and which has also made and fashioned it as that witness." See also Swinburne, *Revelation*, pp. 192-193; and Vanhoozer, *First Theology*, pp. 9-10, 45-126.

130   *Revelation, Holy Scripture and Church*

Hans Frei: The Bible Read 'Literally'

Hans Frei's constructive hermeneutic proposal for the reading of the Bible as Scripture is in effect an argument for a post-critical retrieval of pre-critical Bible reading by means of literary theory and then social-scientific "thick description." In order properly to attend to Frei's positive proposal, it is helpful first to articulate (1) his historical, descriptive account of pre-critical interpretation of Biblical narrative as a single story; (2) the hermeneutic developments beginning in the late eighteenth century, which rendered such reading of the Bible in its unity problematic; and then to offer (3) an account of his proposal for a nuanced retrieval of the classic mode of Christian Bible reading.

Hans Frei's overall hermeneutic project is best understood as an attempt to undo the Eclipse of Biblical Narrative and to reverse the direction of biblical interpretation[245] such that Christian Scripture is restored in its unity as a single story, held together through figuration around the ascriptively literal stories of Jesus which, in turn, provides the authoritative reality-description in terms of which Christians interpret the extra-textual world. It will be argued in the critical analysis of Frei's program to retrieve the authority and unity of the biblical materials as a single story that while the motivation of his retrieval is theological, doctrinal resources that would lend intelligibility to his constructive proposals are either left tacit or expressed in the idioms of literary or social-scientific analysis.

Pre-Critical Frame

The dominant mode of Christian Bible reading "until modern times" was, on Frei's view, born in "the appropriating procedure"[246] by which the Christian church made the Old Testament its own. By means of typology and figuration, the whole of the Hebrew Scripture in its genric variety is taken into Christian Scripture as "Old Testament." Legal and prophetic texts as well as Wisdom literature point beyond themselves to "their fulfillment in the "New Testament."[247] This procedure begins in the New Testament itself in the writings of Paul, Hebrews and the Synoptic Gospels. Two features of the manner in which the Old Testament is appropriated for Christian use were particularly decisive for Christian reading of the Bible as a whole. The first is that the full meaning of Old Testament practices, laws and regulations are derived by relating them to the central sacred story of the life, death and resurrection of Jesus. "This narrative thus has a unifying force and a prescriptive character in both the New

---

245 See Nicholas Wolterstorff, "Inhabiting the World of the Text," in Giorgy Olegovich (ed.), *Ten Year Commemoration of the Life of Hans Frei* (New York, 1999), pp. 66-68 and Dawson, *Christian Figural Reading and the Fashioning of Identity*, pp. 141-142.

246 "The 'Literal' Reading of Biblical Narrative," p. 120 and "Theology and the Interpretation of Narrative," p. 111. See also *The Eclipse of Biblical Narrative*, pp. 3-4 and Hans Frei, "'Narrative' in Christian and Modern Reading," in Bruce D. Marshall (ed.), *Theology and Dialogue: Essays in Conversation with George Lindbeck* (Notre Dame, 1990), pp. 150-151.

247 "The 'Literal' Reading of Biblical Narrative," p. 120.

The Bible as Holy Scripture

Testament and the Christian community . . ."[248] The second important hermeneutic feature implicit in this appropriative move, is that by means of the centrality of the story of Jesus, Christian tradition in the West assigns hermeneutic priority to the literal sense in reading the Bible. The normal or plain sense of the church's reading of its central texts became by consensus, the literal sense. Frei writes:

> The creed, "rule of faith," or "rule of truth" which governed the Gospels' use in the church asserted the primacy of their literal sense. Moreover, it did this right from the beginning in the *ascriptive* even more than the *descriptive* mode. That "Jesus"—not someone else or nobody in particular—is the subject, the agent, and patient of these stories is said to be their crucial point, and the descriptions of events, sayings, personal qualities, and so forth, become literal by being firmly predicated of him.[249]

Other non-literal modes of Bible reading are employed—tropological, allegorical and anagogical—but these are controlled and in the service of "literal interpretation, with Jesus the center or focus for the coherence of these readings."[250]

Moreover, through typology, extra-biblical life and events were held together with the Old Testament as incomplete figures, which while real and meaningful in their own right, stood in tensive relation to their fulfillment "in the story of Jesus or in the universal story from creation to *eschaton*, of which it was the effectually shaping masterpiece."[251] In this way, not only were Old and New Testament held together in a single cumulative story by means of figures and types fulfilled in the Gospels, literally read, but also the whole of life and reality, of extra-biblical thought and experience, were interpreted into the one real world "detailed and made accessible by the biblical story."[252] Earlier biblical stories are read as figures or types of the Gospels stories drawing the whole constellation of Scripture into a one grand story of promise and fulfillment and providing the reality in terms of which the reader made sense of present life, experience and world.

Frei, drawing on the work of James Preus,[253] does note that in practice there were at least two dominant manners in which typology and allegory were used in Christian interpretation of the Old Testament. In the first,[254] the Old Testament was interpreted

---

248 Ibid.

249 Ibid., pp. 122-123. See also *The Identity of Jesus Christ*, p. xiv and *Types of Christian Theology*, p. 5.

250 "The 'Literal' Reading of Biblical Narrative," p. 121. See also *The Eclipse of Biblical Narrative*, p. 1 and *Types of Christian Theology*, pp. 5, 140-143. Other ways of reading portions of the Bible, for example, in a spiritual or allegorical sense, were permissible, but they must not offend against a literal reading of those parts which seemed most obviously to demand it.

251 "The 'Literal' Reading of Biblical Narrative," p. 121. Frei attributes this position to Augustine. See *The Eclipse of Biblical Narrative*, p. 1.

252 Ibid., p. 3. See also "The 'Literal' Reading of Biblical Narrative," p. 121 and "'Narrative' in Christian and Modern Reading," p. 151.

253 James Preus, *From Shadow to Promise: Old Testament Interpretation from Augustine to the Young Luther* (Cambridge, MA, 1969).

254 Frei says that designating Old Testament reading a "shadow," of the New is giving it "derogatory sense." See "The 'Literal' Reading of Biblical Narrative," p. 121. Frei seems

132 *Revelation, Holy Scripture and Church*

as shadow, carnal, mere letter, over against which the New Testament is spiritual. On this reading of the Old Testament "spiritual" and "literal" coincide, since it is by means of the literal meaning of the stories of Jesus that the spiritual meaning of the Old Testament is uncovered. This elevation of meaning and reality to a "spiritual" level dissolves the distinction between typology and allegory, collapsing the former into the later. After all, why would the meaning of an event or person in its own right, as carnal reality, be preserved (by means of typology) against the spiritual density of its fulfillment in Christ? The second way of relating the Testaments in the history of Christian reading works less in terms of shadow and reality and more in terms of promise and fulfillment. "The Old Testament could be understood as *promise*, that is, as pointing to a state of affairs literally meant but only incompletely or not yet actualized at the time it was written . . ."[255] In this way, the Old Testament and the New are set in a single temporal and teleological relationship with the events and persons of the Old Testament retaining reality and meaningfulness, but one which is incomplete and anticipatory of fulfillment in Jesus Christ.[256]

This second manner in which Old and New Testament are related, as promise and fulfillment through typological and figural relation, while typical of Christian practice until modern times, is exemplified for Frei in John Calvin. Calvin's procedure for extracting meaning from the Bible embodies the three features of pre-critical realistic biblical interpretation, which also "served as the foci for the rebellion against it."[257] First, Calvin, like most pre-critical interpreters of the Bible demonstrated that, read literally, the biblical story was also a description of actual historical occurrences. True historical reference was directly and obviously implied in making literal-explicative sense of the narrative at hand. "Calvin," maintains Frei, "simply did not separate in principle the literal or for that matter the figural meaning of a text from its historical reference or its religious use, not even for purposes of arguing that they belong together."[258] Like Luther before him, for Calvin there was an identity, "a naturally appropriate coherence,"[259] between literal/grammatical sense and a text's subject matter, understood as its historical reference. No procedure for independent access to the historical realities "behind the text" were employed by Calvin since the text itself was believed to be a vehicle fit to render what it talked about. Read literally or figuratively, rather than allegorically, the Bible rendered the reality it narrated to the reader, that is, the Bible made its subject matter accessible through its cumulative narrative depiction. In this way the reader could comprehend what the Bible was about and shape life in congruence with it. However, the fundamental point is that: "The identity between the explicative sense and the historical reference of texts rested largely on the narrative rendering constituting that identity and not

---

to have Origen in mind as an exemplar of this sort of reading. See ibid and "'Narrative' in Christian and Modern Reading," p. 151.

255 "The 'Literal' Reading of Biblical Narrative," p. 122. Frei's emphaisis.

256 Ibid.

257 *The Eclipse of Biblical Narrative*, p. 1.

258 Ibid., p. 23.

259 Ibid., p. 24.

The Bible as Holy Scripture 133

on a linguistic theory of reference."[260] No independent access to or independent depiction of the historical world behind the text was deemed necessary in Calvin, since the Bible, by means of its cumulative narrative rendering, sets forth what it is about with perspicuity.

The second feature of pre-critical biblical interpretation exemplified by Calvin, is that if the real historical world described in the many stories of the Bible was one world of a single chronological sequence, then there must be a single cumulative story to portray it. The interpretative means for drawing together the diverse stories of the Bible into this single cumulative story is found in typological and figural interpretation. The theological warrant for the extension of literal meaning by means of typology is the Christological conviction that "the canon is one because the meaning of all of it is salvation in Jesus Christ."[261] Thus in reading the Old Testament, even where the literal sense does not specifically refer to Christ, as in Genesis 3:15, it is nevertheless, as part of Scripture, related in an indirect (figural) way to the overarching Christological meaning of the Bible. Frei does not find a theory of typology or figuration in Calvin, rather he notes that "the figural procedure was exhibited more in application than in the abstract,"[262] by means of the luminescence of sheer juxtaposition between figures such that a bond was established between identical patterns of meaning and a "mutual enhancement"[263] effected. Frei notes that while Calvin, under the influence of Platonism, tended toward figuration between patterns of meaning across different temporal sites, "his sense of figural interpretation remained firmly rooted in the order of temporal sequence and the depiction of temporal occurrences, the links between which can be established only by narration and under the conviction of the primacy of the literal, grammatical sense."[264] Thus, his use of figural interpretation never lost its connection with the literal sense. He was not waylaid by allegorical reading, and because of the amenability of figural reading to literal reading he was able to exploit its interpretative potential in rendering the two Testaments as one canon, a single story of creation, fall and of salvation in Jesus Christ.

Finally, Calvin's interpretative procedure embodies the pre-critical conviction that the one true world, rendered in the overarching figurally-related story of the Bible, encompasses the life and experience of any age and reader. Indeed, for Calvin there is no gap between the world depicted, the reality cumulatively rendered, in the Bible and the current life of the reader. Thus for Calvin, as for classic Christian readers, one had a duty to fit into this world, of which one was a member, and to comport oneself to this depiction. A reader's personal life as well as the events of the era were construed as figures of the storied world of the Bible and thus interpretative stance is given to the reader vis-à-vis that world.

---

260 Ibid.

261 Ibid., p. 27.

262 Ibid., p. 30.

263 Ibid., p. 27. Frei characterizes the relationship between figural and literal reading as "mutual supplementation" and "family resemblance." He writes, "They belong together, though they are on the one hand not identical nor, on the other, a substitute for each other." Ibid. For a splendid account of Frei's reading of Calvin on this point see Dawson, *Christian Figural Reading and the Fashioning of Identity*, pp. 145-149.

264 *The Eclipse of Biblical Narrative*, p. 31.

134   *Revelation, Holy Scripture and Church*

Two caveats are important to Calvin's account. First, neither the reader nor "tradition" make a material contribution to the cumulatively rendered world of the Bible. The patterns of meaning, which are inherent in the Bible in a teleological pattern within an unfolding historical narrative, while they enclose the reader, do not require any material contribution or unique interpretative perspective for their completion. The reader does not interpret the Bible by means of extra-biblical experience or interpretative stance rather the direction of interpretation is that of "encorporating extra-biblical thought, experience and reality into the one real world detailed and made accessible by the biblical story—not the reverse."[265] Indeed to "imprint" on the text is to interrupt the actual reading of the overarching narrative, in which literal (and figural) reading offer a temporal and teleological unfolding of the Bible's cumulatively rendered world on its own terms, for an arbitrary and forced pattern.[266] Second, the Holy Spirit does not make a material contribution to the cumulatively rendered world of the Bible. The internal testimony of the Holy Spirit is not, for Calvin, to be conceived of apart from the narrative and cumulative depiction of the world with which the Bible is concerned. The setting forth of the real world rendered in the Bible is simultaneously the basis for its effective rendering by the Holy Spirit to the reader. The Spirit does not add to the "intrinsic clarity" of the Bible in its own right; rather the Holy Spirit overcomes the blindness of the reader, so that "he will discern the written biblical word to be God's own Word . . ."[267]

Critical Problematic

Frei traces the fracturing of classic Christian Bible reading to developments in the eighteenth century: "First in England and then in Germany the narrative became distinguished from a separable subject matter—whether historical, ideal, or both at once—which was now taken to be its true meaning."[268] Whereas in Calvin, subject matter, cumulative narrative depiction, true historical reference and religious significance all coalesced in a literal/figural reading of the one story of the Bible, this unity is fractured by means of a bifurcation between subject matter, now available by means of independent description, and narrative depiction.

The conjunction between the biblical story read literally, and reference to actual historical occurrence, was dissolved in disputes with Deism. In the context of apologetic debate about miracles and revelation, the question of independent confirmation of the events reported in the Bible was raised. The plausibility of events reported (the factuality of revelation) and the credibility of New Testament writers (the historical reliability of their reports) were defended by "Supernaturalists"[269] by

---

265 Ibid. See also "The 'Literal' Reading of Biblical Narrative," p. 121 and "'Narrative' in Christian and Modern Reading," p. 151.

266 *The Eclipse of Biblical Narrative*, pp. 34-35. See also Frei's constructive "Remarks in Connection with a Theological Proposal," pp. 32-33.

267 *The Eclipse of Biblical Narrative*, pp. 21, 24, 34. Citation from p. 21.

268 Ibid., p. 51. See also *The Identity of Jesus Christ*, p. xiv and *Types of Christian Theology*, pp. 138-139.

269 Frei uses this term to specify a group of eighteenth-century German thinkers who defended biblical and theological conservatism by means other than biblical literalism or

The Bible as Holy Scripture

means of placing the Bible within a broader context of rational canons of meaning and submitting narrative to general tests of factual probability. In this way the reliability of biblical accounts, the integrity of the apostles, the possibility of miracles and the fulfillment of Old Testament prophecies in the New, were demonstrated to be in accord with rational religion. "Liberal" or deistic commentators, on the other hand, submitting biblical accounts to similar canons of historical reliability, were less persuaded that the Bible could be treated as "a factually reliable repository of divine revelation."[270] The important point for Frei in this conflict is that both sides were increasingly veering toward the position that the explicative meaning of a given biblical text was its ostensive/historical referent. The Bible makes sense in so far as it can be demonstrated accurately to refer to the events recorded. No longer is the Bible a coherent world of discourse, whose cumulative narrative depicts reality in its own right, one to which readers were obliged to adjust themselves. "Hermeneutics," writes Frei, "is clearly on its way toward a notion of explicative interpretation in which a biblical narrative makes sense in accordance with its author's intentions and (before long) the culture he exemplifies. And the meaning of the narrative is the subject matter to which the words refer."[271]

Frei identifies three further repercussions of the Supernaturalist move to justify the integrity of biblical narrative by means of general canons of rationality and historical facticity. First, the basis for the unity of the Bible read as one book is shifted. Whereas for Calvin, the unity of the Bible is at the level of a single cumulative story within the text, held together by figuration around the literal meaning of the stories of Jesus, "Supernaturalists" argue, initially, for the unity of the Bible by means of fulfillment of prophecy as a historical fact. They add to this the more existential argument that the Bible is a unity because it produces a similar effect in all its parts in the minds of pious readers. Moreover, some develop a historical-theological notion of the unity of the Bible based on the development of religious ideas within the Bible tied to a conviction concerning God's presence in this religious history. However, the unity conceived on this account is not at the level of a single cumulative story told in the Bible itself but in the actual occurrence of the supernatural events reported by the biblical writers. It is a unity of "outer biblical history as well as a supposed historical connectedness of its ideas and outlooks, they embodied."[272] In this way, the basis for the unity of the Bible shifts outside of the story of the Bible itself to be demonstrated by reference to the progression of religious ideas and supernatural events that the Bible reports.

A second consequence of the "Supernaturalist" move to apply to the Bible general canons of rationality and historical probability is that it resulted in the dominance of historical inquiry in biblical interpretation. The Bible construed as a narrative

---

theories of inspiration. "Commentators of the supernaturalist persuasion argued the literal truth of Scripture, demonstrating what they thought to be the specific nature of its inspiration and also setting forth reasons for the factual reliability of its reports." *The Eclipse of Biblical Narrative*, p. 86. See also *Types of Christian Theology*, p. 138.

270 *The Eclipse of Biblical Narrative*, p. 87.

271 Ibid., p. 91.

272 Ibid., p. 92.

136   *Revelation, Holy Scripture and Church*

whole over a temporal sequence looked very much like an historical narrative. Thus it was entirely fitting that the Bible should be subjected to historical inquiry and verification. "For whatever happened must surely be the meaning of the narrative texts."[273] Moreover, interpretative procedure, like all procedures at the time of the late eighteenth century in Germany, "obeyed the slogan: dare to think."[274] Frei makes the case that this climate, together with a methodological predilection on the part of Supernaturalists, refused to allow biblical interpretation to continue under privileged theological rules. General theories of interpretation which involved subjecting the content of the Bible to established criteria of grammar, logic, moral and religious analysis, "seemed to go hand in hand with an historical analysis for which credible historical explanation was a function of uniform and natural rather than suddenly and miraculously disrupted historical experience."[275] While there were some dissenting voices to the assumptions implicit in the move to include biblical hermeneutics within a general theory of interpretation and much debate regarding the historical reliability of the Bible, by the middle of the eighteenth century, Frei maintains, there was widespread agreement that the meaning of the biblical narratives was the ostensive events to which they referred and thus a corresponding interest in historical inquiry as the dominant mode of biblical interpretation followed.[276]

The three distinguishing features of classical Christian Bible reading break up under the pressure of the twin interests of apologetics and historical investigation in eighteenth century hermeneutics. First, the unity of literal-grammatical sense, subject matter and true historical reference comes apart for the sake of apologetic defense.[277] What the Bible is about becomes logically separated from the cumulative narrative pattern in which it is depicted such that the explicative sense of the Bible is no longer the literal/figural but ostensive/historical sense. Moreover, the basis for the unity of the Bible as a single story, from creation to *eschaton*, held together through typology around the "literal" Gospel narratives of the life, death and resurrection of Jesus, shifts outside the text to historical facts, the experience of the reader or the development of religious ideas. In this environment, figural reading appears "a rather preposterous historical argument" and loses its credibility both as a manner

---

273 Ibid., p. 90.

274 Ibid., p. 94.

275 Ibid., p. 93.

276 See ibid., p. 95. See also *The Identity of Jesus Christ*, p. xiv and "'Narrative' in Christian and Modern Reading," p. 152. In this last essay, Frei notes that literal reading is continued and transformed in both fundamentalism and historical-critical analysis. For both the meaning and significance of the literal sense were judged to reside in the distinction between positive correspondence between the depiction of the narrative text and its true "referent," i.e., what had actually, historically, and in that sense literally transpired. When the two matched, the text literally read made literal sense precisely because it was isomorphic with its actual referent; when they did not, the literal-actual referent was substituted as the true meaning of the text for the literal-written form, and the latter turned instead into a detective's clue to the discovery of that referent.

277 Frei notes that before the eighteenth century it was possible "to read texts literally and at the same time to leave the referential status of what was described in them [biblical texts] indeterminate." *Types of Christian Theology*, p. 138.

The Bible as Holy Scripture 137

of reading and as "an instrument for uniting the canon."[278] Finally, the question of applicative sense arises. Here we arrive at the third consequence of the hermeneutic shift of the eighteenth century. In Calvin, explicative sense already included applicative sense. The reader is encompassed by the story, there is no gap between the reader and the cumulatively rendered world of the Bible. The reader has a duty to behave in the real world of which the reader is a part. For the "Supernaturalists" says Frei, for whom explicative sense is taken to be ostensive reference, a different path is taken. They affirmed that the Bible means, literally what it says, although here "literal" means ostensive. Thus because the Bible is a factual historical depiction of the world, all the miracle stories are true, God shaped the earth, and man, Adam and Eve fell as described with dire consequences for us all. All of these things happened as described, and thus doctrines based on them are true descriptions of the human condition, of our condition, with permanent religious significance.[279]

Before bringing this section to a conclusion, Frei describes a second option with respect to the breakdown of the literal reading of Bible narrative that arises in the eighteenth century. Under the influence of the rationalism of Christian Wolff, another version of meaning as reference arises. What if those who adopted the meaning as reference view proceeded to explore the ostensive dimension of biblical narrative by means of historical inquiry? And what if they discovered that the pursuit of meaning as ostensive reference resulted in the text under consideration making no sense at all—either because it did not refer to an actual event, person or happening or because it vaguely referred or incorrectly referred? At least two positive apologetic options are open. The first, Frei notes, is to reconstruct the historical situation more accurately than does the Bible and then to use that reconstructed fact or event as the basis for ongoing religious significance. Sometimes it could be the reconstructed fact itself that is the abiding significance of the text, at other times some feature closely related to it. In either case, says Frei, biblical texts, "retain their significance because they refer to an inherently plausible rather than (as in the literal-historical reading) to a most unlikely or even inconceivable event."[280] The other option, still within a frame of reference in which meaning is reference, is to idealize the referent of the text. Here, Frei traces the influence of Wolff for whom meaning is equated with "the transconceptual essence of possible reality to which a concept and word refer."[281] Where the Bible obviously does not have an historical referent in view, the story told is interpreted as an eternal truth about God or human nature. Conyers Middleton (1683–1750) in his allegorical interpretation of the Genesis story goes in this direction. He extracts from the story an "ideal meaning," "a metaphysical truth" which, while it does not divest the story of any factual reference or historical sequence, renders the textual account somewhat superfluous to the doctrinal content it conveys. The story is about the world having a beginning in God, human inhabitants and happiness forfeited by opposition to the will of God.[282] "[W]hether or not the

---

278 *The Eclipse of Biblical Narrative*, p. 7.
279 Ibid., p. 119.
280 Ibid., pp. 119-120.
281 Ibid., p. 101.
282 Ibid., pp. 120-122.

138 *Revelation, Holy Scripture and Church*

story is true history," writes Frei, "its meaning is detachable from the specific story that sets its forth."[283]

In conclusion: While this account of Frei's study of eighteen- and nineteenth-century hermeneutics restricts itself to the first part of his book, *The Eclipse of Biblical Narrative*, the material reviewed is sufficient to illumine Frei's contention.[284] The breakdown of the literal reading of biblical narrative is directly related to the apologetic-interpretative move that places the Bible within a larger more comprehensive interpretative context for investigation and adjudication. Where once the Bible in its narrative, figurally-related, unity depicted the reality within which extra-textual events and occasions and lives acquired their intelligibility, the eighteenth-century apologetic interest in historical inquiry (and the nineteenth-century interest in consciousness), whether hostile or friendly to the Bible, fractured this unity by locating explicative meaning outside the text in an historical or idealized referent upon which applicative meaning depended. A principal effect of this relocation of meaning is that the direction of interpretation is reversed: the Bible no longer interprets extra-textual reality, extra-textual reality under some general depiction interprets the Bible. The meaning of biblical narrative is effectively eclipsed and the authority of the Bible as Scripture is diminished twofold: its reliability is either affirmed or reconfigured via a larger interpretative scheme and its narrative unity and interpretative potential for all of life undercut.[285]

Post-Critical Retrieval

> [T]he issue which concerns us is the extent to which the Bible can be profitably read in our day as a canonically and narrationally unified and internally glossed whole (that is, self-referential and self-interpreting) whole centered on Jesus Christ, and telling the story of the dealing of the Triune God with his people and his world in ways which are

---

283 Ibid., p. 6. Frei notes that "first allegory and then myth came to be the non-historical classifications into which realistic narratives were fitted." *The Identity of Jesus Christ*, p. xiv. See also, "David Friedrich Strauss," in Ninian Smart (ed.), *Nineteenth Century Religious Thought in the West* (Cambridge, 1985), vol. 1, pp. 215-260. Here Frei notes the same apologetic pattern in Strauss's nineteenth-century *The Life of Jesus*. In this work Strauss aims (1) to distinguish fact from fiction in the Gospels on the basis of general criteria (historical-critical research); (2) to offer the most likely shape of the historical core given; and (3) to employ a category, "myth," which is most appropriate to "supernatural accounts." In this way Strauss employs a general meaning as reference theory in both its ostensive and ideal forms to articulate the meaning of the Gospels. See ibid., pp. 233-238.

284 Frei contends elsewhere that the hermeneutic shift that is decisive for the breakdown of pre-critical hermeneutics, or at least of the reading of the Bible as realistic narrative, starts at the "beginning of the eighteenth century" and continues "at an accelerating pace with the development of historical criticism." *The Identity of Jesus Christ*, p. xiv.

285 See Wolterstorff, "Inhabiting the World of the Text," p. 67. See also Dawson, *Christian Figural Reading and the Fashioning of Identity*, p. 141. Dawson, like Wolterstorff, notes that Frei's work to reverse the eclipse of biblical narrative is aimed at preserving the authority of the Bible.

The Bible as Holy Scripture   139

typologically (though not, so at least the Reformers would say, allegorically) applicable to the present.[286]

George Lindbeck identifies the positive project of Hans Frei as what is in effect a post-critical retrieval of pre-critical hermeneutics. In other words, Hans Frei aims at undoing the eclipse of biblical narrative and reversing the direction of biblical interpretation so that the unity and authority of the Bible as sacred text[287] for the life of the church is restored. Frei is not interested in securing such a retrieval by means of obscurantist tactics such as attributing unity or authority to the Bible as a result of "any inherent divinized quality" but rather, he proposes that both unity and authority are attributable to the Bible when it is read as Scripture, that is, as a unified whole typologically centered on Jesus Christ, and thus as a witness to "The Word of God."[288]

While the low-level theoretical resources Frei employs to effect a credible retrieval of this construal of the Bible are revised in the course of this project,[289] the relative direction of Frei's historical-hermeneutic-theological program is not: he aims at restoring a chastened version of classical Christian Bible reading which grants priority to the ascriptive literalism of the Gospels (Christology) and their centrality for construing the whole of the Bible.[290] Frei maintains that his *Types of Christian Theology* and other "more recent work,"[291] are both "a continuation as well as a revision of his two previous efforts," that is, *The Eclipse of Biblical Narrative* and *The Identity of Jesus Christ*. They are a continuation in the sense that Frei consistently maintains that, "the conceptual issue of Christology, that is, the nature of the unitary ascriptive subject ought to have priority over the historical one . . ." (against David Friedrich Strauss, and historical-critical research which follows his lead) and that literal sense reading is incompatible with phenomenological hermeneutics (as a general "foundational" theory in Ricoeur).[292] Frei's project of restoring "literal reading" is articulated against general versions of meaning as ostensive historical or ideal (mythic-symbolic) reference. The revision in his program, as noted, is primarily that the conceptual resources employed to argue that the Bible ought to be read

---

286 Lindbeck, "Scripture, Consensus, and Community," p. 75.

287 Frei is reticent about the term "sacred text" although he does use it. He indicates that the Bible is "sacred" because it "comes to focus around a sacred story." One community's text is taken over by another community and the sacredness of the whole story is related to the appropriating procedure. In specific terms, the whole of the Bible is "sacred text" because of its relation to the central sacred story of Jesus. The citation is from *Types of Christian Theology*, p. 12. See also "'Narrative' in Modern and Christian Reading," pp. 149-150.

288 "Conflicts in Interpretation," p. 163. Frei, like Ricoeur, aims at "a postcritical naiveté." See "Theology and the Interpretation of Narrative," p. 107.

289 See "The 'Literal' Reading of Biblical Narrative," pp. 139-149 and *Types of Christian Theology*, p. 12.

290 See Dawson, *Christian Figural Reading and the Fashioning of Identity*, p. 144 and Frei, "The 'Literal' Reading of Biblical Narrative," p. 142.

291 "The 'Literal' Reading of Biblical Narrative" and "David Friedrich Strauss," pp. 215-260.

292 *Types of Christian Theology*, pp. 6-7 and "The 'Literal' Reading of Biblical Narrative," pp. 129-139.

140   *Revelation, Holy Scripture and Church*

in keeping with the ascriptive literalism of the Gospel accounts changes. The shift is from construing the Bible as an instance of "realistic narrative" which warrants literal reading as a convention appropriate to that genre, to "thick description" which justifies reading the Bible literally in keeping with the common-sense conventions of the community for which it functions religiously.[293]

Frei's attempt to offer an account of the unity and authority of the Bible in continuity with pre-critical Bible reading is from the beginning and throughout anti-apologetic. Frei eschews attempts to make sense of the texts of the Bible and to construe the content of the Bible in terms of general theories since such broad theories are either (1) not interested in reading the text as *text* but as *source*, in the case of historical-critical research,[294] or (2) reduce the subject matter of all texts to some form of self-understanding before the text, in the case of phenomenological hermeneutics.[295] In both cases, the question "to what does the text refer," either behind the text or in front of it, preempts a patient reading of the text in keeping with its most appropriate conventions. These broad conceptually laden hermeneutic approaches to the specific texts of the Bible are not helpful because they "overwhelm exegesis and subject matter in the case of at least one kind of text."[296]

Frei argued in *The Eclipse of Biblical Narrative* and *The Identity of Jesus Christ* that there is a literary feature of the Gospels often noticed in eighteenth-century biblical interpretation but seldom taken into hermeneutic account: the Gospels are "realistic narrative." Frei appropriates the category "realistic" from Eric Auerbach, who in his monumental work *Mimesis* noted that while Homer "does not need to base his story on historical reality, his reality is powerful enough in itself" and, moreover, Homer's "reality" is not reducible to allegory.[297] Recognizing the same realistic feature in the Gospel accounts, Frei made both a critical and constructive case. First, Frei argued that "realistic narrative" while reading very much like history is not rightly considered identical to it. It is a "category error" to conflate the literal realistic depiction of the Gospels with "depiction as an accurate report of actual historical facts."[298] This is the error into which eighteenth-century apologetics, in attempts to defend the historical reliability of the Bible, were drawn. Realistic

---

293 Shannon Craigo-Snell maintains that Frei's later articulation of literal reading does not tell us to read the text differently; it

"is not focused on *how* to read the text in a particular way but *why* we should read it that particular way . . . Frei no longer says that the structure of the stories themselves demand a certain kind of reading . . . He now warrants the *sensus literalis* on the basis of Christian community and tradition.

See "Command Performance: Rethinking Performance Interpretation in the Context of Divine Discourse," *Modern Theology*, 16/4 (October, 2000): 487-488.

294 See *Types of Christian Theology*, p. 1.

295 *The Identity of Jesus Christ*, pp. xiii-xvii. This claim is at the heart of Frei's running critique of the hermeneutic approach of Ricoeur. See *Types of Christian Theology*, pp. 6-7; "'Narrative' in Christian and Modern Reading," pp. 158-159; and "The 'Literal' Reading of Biblical Narrative," pp. 126-139.

296 *The Identity of Jesus Christ*, p. xvi.

297 Auerbach, *Mimesis*, p. 13.

298 *The Identity of Jesus Christ*, p. xiv.

The Bible as Holy Scripture

narrative, whether or not it reports history reliably, has a specific quality about it that is preempted when is it is simply counted as a species of historical discourse. Frei maintained that realistic narrative ought to be read in keeping with the kind of literature that it is:

> Realistic narrative reading is based on one of the characteristics of the Gospel story, especially its later part, viz., that it is history-like—in its language as well as its depiction of a common public world (no matter whether it is the one we all think we inhabit), in the close interaction of character and incident, and in the non-symbolic quality of the relation between story and what the story is about. In other words, whether or not these stories report history (either reliably or unreliably), whether or not the Gospels are other things besides realistic stories, what they tell us is a fruit of the stories themselves. We cannot have what they are about (the "subject matter") without the stories themselves. They are history like precisely because, like history-writing and the traditional novel, and unlike myths and allegories, they literally mean what they say. There is no gap between the representation and the thing represented by it.[299]

In the case of the Gospel depictions of Jesus, Frei made the specific point that as realistic narrative what these texts say about Jesus they mean to predicate of him, and not of humanity in general or of no one in particular. The texts render the subject matter with ascriptive literalism; what they say about Jesus becomes literal by its application to him.[300] The meaning of a realistic narrative *is* the story it tells; not the historical or idealized references it makes. Meaning is literary-literal not ostensive-literal. Frei's application of Auerbach's category of "realistic" to the Bible enabled him to notice the "category" mistake of historical-critical readings of the Bible and so to argue for the retrieval of classic Christian Bible reading in which one reads for "meaning" (which realistic narrative bears in its own right) apart from theories of reference, which tend to eclipse attending to biblical narrative.

Frei employed two other observations made by Auerbach with respect to biblical literature. The first is a comment in which Auerbach notes the difference between Homer and the Old Testament:

> Far from seeking, like Homer, merely to make us forget our own reality for a few hours [the Bible] seeks to overcome our reality: we are to fit our own life into its world, feel ourselves to be elements in its structure of universal history . . . The Bible's claim to truth is not only more urgent than Homer's, it is tyrannical—it excludes all other claims.[301]

In their function as "realistic narratives" the Bible claims to offer a framework into which all other events must be fitted. Auerbach makes no claim that the world the Bible offers is in fact the one true description of the real world, only that at the level

---

299 Ibid.

300 See "The 'Literal' Reading of Biblical Narrative," p. 122. In a relatively early essay, 1967, Frei acknowledges his appreciation of New Criticism and Auerbach for their help in assisting biblical interpretation which is normative. "Remarks in Connection with a Theological Proposal," pp. 32-33 (quotation from p. 32).

301 Auerbach, *Mimesis*, p. 15.

142   *Revelation, Holy Scripture and Church*

of meaning that this is what the texts do. This observation concerning the appeal of biblical narrative at the level of realistic depiction enabled Frei to rehabilitate one of the fundamental features of pre-critical Bible reading. The Bible read as realistic story, literally, defines, in a way that is not possible by means of literal ostensive reading, "the one common world in which we all live and move and have our being."[302] Here Frei finds, by means of Auerbach, what he knew in more theologically realist terms in Barth.[303]

The other way in which Auerbach's reflections assist Frei is in recovering a sense of typological and figurative interpretation that is compatible with literal reading, that is, one that does not lapse into allegory. If literal meaning is to be extended across the entire canonical corpus, in a way that guards the intrinsic connection "between time-bound picture and the meaning represented by it,"[304] allegory, with its tendency to detach meaning patterns from their temporal narrative rendering, will not work. Frei noticed that Auerbach, along with Calvin, was able to make a convincing argument that figural interpretation was a means of extending literal sense across the whole of the biblical corpus. Auerbach writes:

> Figural interpretation establishes a connection between two events or persons in such a way that the first signifies not only itself but also the second, while the second involves or fulfills the first. The two poles of a figure are separated in time, but both, being real events and person, are within a temporality . . . The connection between occurrences is not regarded as primarily a chronological or causal development but as a oneness within the divine plan, of which all occurrences are parts and reflections. Their direct earthly connection is of secondary importance, and often their interpretation can altogether dispense with any knowledge of it.[305]

Frei claimed that this understanding of figural reading guards against its collapse into figurative non-literality. [306] In figuration, the connection between two events, persons, or occasions in their own right is made without dissolving one into or by means of the other. Moreover, both the first and the second poles of a figure are rooted in a temporal providential flow in a manner, which does not depend on "a

---

302 Frei, "An Afterword: Eberhard Busch's Biography of Karl Barth," p. 161.

303 In the preface to *The Eclipse of Biblical Narrative*, p. viii, Frei identified Barth as an author who was particularly influential on his thinking, although he writes: "In his [Barth's] hands theology becomes an imperious and allegiance-demanding discipline, *and he might well have rejected out of hand the external treatment it receives in the present essay*." My emphasis.

304 *The Eclipse of Biblical Narrative*, p. 29. Frei defines what he means by allegory: "Allegory is the attachment of a temporally free-floating meaning pattern to any temporal occasion whatever, without any intrinsic connection between sensuous time-bound picture and the meaning represented by it." Dawson notes that Frei strengthens Auerbach's association of meaning with its sensatory base by referring to its "intrinsic connection." See Dawson, *Christian Figural Reading and the Fashioning of Identity*, p. 149.

305 Auerbach, *Mimesis*, p. 73, cited in *The Eclipse of Biblical Narrative*, pp. 28-29.

306 *The Eclipse of Biblical Narrative*, p. 29. Compare to "The Nuptial Metaphor," pp. 276-295, where Ricoeur conflates typology and figuration with allegory and designates them all means of "analogical transference."

The Bible as Holy Scripture

nonprovidential, scientific-historical understanding of the historical relation between events."[307] In conversation with Auerbach (and New Criticism), then, Frei (1) established the unity of subject matter and narrative depiction by drawing attention to the ascriptive literalism of realistic narrative, (2) drew attention to the imperious claim of biblical narrative to be the framework into which all other events must be fitted, and (3) recognized a species of interpretation, figural reading, which extends literal meaning without abstracting meaning patterns from their temporal narrative rendering.

However, Frei became concerned that his attempt to promote a classical Christian mode of Bible reading, and to provide a Christocentric construal of the canon of Scripture, might be jeopardized by its resting or appearing to rest too heavily upon the literary theory of New Criticism[308] and the work of Erich Auerbach[309] in conversation with whom he had proposed "realistic narrative reading." In place of this literary context for "realistic" reading of the Bible, Frei shifted the weight of his argument back onto ecclesial practice (that is, the consensual manner of Bible reading in the Western Christian tradition which he had noticed early on[310]) as the basis for reading the Bible in a "literal" mode. Under the influence of some of his colleagues at Yale,[311] Frei found in the social-scientific work of Clifford Geertz[312] the kind of low-level theory that would account for reading the Bible in keeping with classical Christian conventions for handling Holy Scripture. Working at "thick description"[313] in a manner analogous to the anthropologist, who wants to grasp details of a "culture" in their connection with the whole way of life and in the terms of the participants (a cultural-linguistic view of religion),[314] Frei maintained that one could discover within the Christian West a consensus concerning how the Bible

---

307 Dawson, *Christian Figural Reading and the Fashioning of Identity*, p. 148.

308 See "The 'Literal' Reading of Biblical Narrative," pp. 140-143 (quotation from p. 143). It is in this essay that Frei develops his preference for "literal" over "realistic" reading.

309 Frei acknowledged his debt to Auerbach in the preface of *The Eclipse of Biblical Narrative*, p. vii; a greater degree of caution is exercised in "The 'Literal' Reading of Biblical Narrative," p. 139.

310 See "Remarks in Connection with a Theological Proposal," p. 32. See William Placher, "Introduction," pp. 16-18.

311 William Placher identifies the work of Kelsey, *The Uses of Scripture in Recent Theology* and Lindbeck, *The Nature of Doctrine: Religion and Theology in a Postliberal Age* as of particular importance in the development of Frei's thinking on realistic reading become literal sense. See also Vanhoozer, *First Theology*, p. 218; Dawson, *Christian Figural Reading and the Fashioning of Identity*, pp. 143-144; Woltertorff, *Divine Discourse*, pp. 219-220; and Marguerite Abdul-Masih, *Edward Schillebeeckx and Hans Frei: A Conversation on Method and Christology* (Waterloo, 2001), pp. 32-33.

312 Clifford Geertz, *The Interpretation of Cultures* (New York, 1973).

313 The term is Gilbert Ryle's, but it is used by Geertz. The approach is "thick" in that it attempts to see behavior, for example, as a part of the dense world or semiotic system in which it is intelligible, and it is "descriptive" in the sense that it resists theorizing tendencies for the actors" or participants" point of view. Ibid., pp. 13, 27. See Frei, "The 'Literal' Reading of Biblical Narrative," pp. 146-147.

314 "The 'Literal' Reading of Biblical Narrative," p. 147.

144 *Revelation, Holy Scripture and Church*

should be read. This manner of reading Frei calls "literal reading." Apart from the diverse senses of this designation, Frei maintains that there is a "basic ascriptive Christological sense" to "literal" reading. This means "that the subject matter of these [Gospel] stories is not something or someone else, and that the rest of the canon must in some way or ways, looser or tighter, be related to this subject matter or at least not in contradiction to it."[315] What is more, "The literal ascription to Jesus of Nazareth of the stories connected with him is of such far reaching import that it serves not only as focus for inner-canonical typology but reshapes extra-textual language in its manifold descriptive uses into a typological relation to these stories."[316] Once again Frei was able, using a different set of low-level tools, to maintain the ascriptive literalism of the Gospel(s)' depiction of the identity of Jesus without heavy investments in general literary theory, to construe the Bible as a whole as a single temporal sequence through figural interpretation and to extend this interpretative context to incorporate extra-biblical thought. Frei returns to a chastened version of the "three elements in the traditional realistic interpretation of the biblical stories"[317] with which his hermeneutic program began.

This move, however, raises an obvious question. Has Frei traded literary theory for social-scientific theory? Is Frei simply cashing in Auerbach and New Criticism to purchase Geertz and "thick description"? It would seem, however, that such social-scientific proposals are only an *occasion*[318] for a recovery of the "literal reading" of the Bible that Frei proposes.[319] For if inquiry is made into the internal logic whereby the literal as opposed to say, the allegorical sense, of the Bible became the plain sense[320] for the church, a theological logic is readily apparent. Literal reading, on Frei's view, became the plain sense of the Bible within the church, not on a priori grounds or as a logically necessary development but "largely by reason of

---

315 *Types of Christian Theology*, p. 5. See also pp. 15-16.

316 "The 'Literal' Reading of Biblical Narrative," p. 147.

317 *The Eclipse of Biblical Narrative*, p. 1.

318 "Occasion" here is in distinction to "grounds" or "justifying reason." In *Types of Christian Theology*, p. 41.

319 This raises the further question of whether the same thing might be said with respect to the literary theories in conversation with which Frei initially made his proposal for reading the Bible as "realistic" narrative. Frei suggests an answer to this question when he writes, "The kind of theology I like best is the kind that is closer to this outlook" [Geertz's thick description] "than to philosophy, or to historiography" or, notes William Placher, "to literary criticism." Hans Frei, *Types of Christian Theology*, p. 13 (my insertions). See also Placher, "Introduction," *Theology and Narrative*, p. 18.

320 The "plain" sense for Frei is the normative or "consensus" sense which the Bible came to have in the Christian community. See "The "Literal" Reading of Biblical Narrative," p. 122. In his essay, "Theology and the Interpretation of Narrative: Some Hermeneutical Considerations," p. 104, Frei cites Charles Wood with approval: "This literal sense—the natural, plain, obvious meaning which the community of faith has normally acknowledged as basic, regardless of whatever other constructions might also properly be put upon the text—is grounded in the community's own experience with the text." From Charles Wood, *The Formation of Christian Understanding: Theological Hermeneutics* (Philadelphia, 1981), p. 43.

The Bible as Holy Scripture 145

the centrality of the story of Jesus . . ."[321] Stated within a context in which Frei is offering a kind of "thick description" of the formation of the canon and of the hermeneutic by which the early church came to read the Bible, Frei identified the Christological grounds around which Scripture was and is construed. He remarks, "[I]n the universal story from creation to *eschaton*" the story of Jesus "was the effectually shaping centerpiece."[322]

While Frei's use of "thick description" yielded a "descriptive" account of the Western tradition of Bible reading, the mode of Bible reading he describes is also one which he prescribes for the present life of the Christian church if it is to recover from the eclipse of biblical narrative. With the exception of the naïve historical dimension of pre-critical Bible reading (which conflates entirely history-like with historical-ostensive reading), Frei proposes that the church retrieve its consensual tradition of reading the Bible literally as Scripture (as an authoritative whole); although the viability of a successful retrieval rests in great measure upon "the actual fruitful use religious people continue to make of it [literal reading] in ways that enhance their own and other people's lives."[323] In any case Frei suggests that "literal" reading be the primary mode of Bible reading for the life of the Christian church since this became, under the influence of the Gospel's depictions of the life, death and resurrection of Jesus, the plain sense[324] of the Bible for the church. To read Scripture *authoritatively* in the community for which it functions then, is to read it in a manner which is governed by the "literal" sense of the Gospel stories of Jesus and their interpretative potential for the whole of the canon typlogically/figurally construed in relation to him.

Critique

In the critique that follows, an analysis of Hans Frei's hermeneutic is offered that treats, in order, his attempt to retrieve the first two central features of classical biblical interpretation.[325] First, a critical review of his attempt to restore the concept of "literal sense," together with the conceptual tools he appropriates to articulate its viability, is undertaken. Next, we undertake an examination of Frei's deployment

---

321 "The "Literal" Reading of Biblical Narrative," p. 121. "[A]llegory tended to be in the service of literal interpretation, with Jesus the center or focus of coherence for such reading." Ibid.

322 Ibid., p. 121.

323 "The 'Literal' Reading of Biblical Narrative," p. 119. See also Craigo-Snell, "Command Performance: Rethinking Performance Interpretation in the Context of Divine Discourse," p. 477.

324 Perhaps it would be better to say "controlling" sense or "authoritative" sense of the Bible. For Frei does not wish to say that "literal" is the only mode in which one reads the Bible for the life of the church. He wants to suggest that the ascriptive literalism of the story of Jesus controls allegorical, tropological and anagogical readings. "The "'Literal' Reading of Biblical Narrative," pp. 120-124. See also *Types of Christian Theology*, p. 5 and "Conflicts in Interpretation," pp. 164-166.

325 An analysis of intratextual interpretation will be a part of the critical review undertaken in the next chapter on church and biblical interpretation.

146   *Revelation, Holy Scripture and Church*

of figural reading as the means by which reading the Bible as a single cumulative story is accomplished. In both cases, the contention is made that Frei's account of the justification of literal reading, while it is oriented to the most fitting reading of the Gospels, and of Scripture as a whole, and though motivated by theological concern, suffers from a lack of theological density in its execution. Frei does not specify the fundamental doctrinal grounds upon which the literal, ascriptive reading of the Gospels and figural extension of literal meaning to the whole of the Christian Scriptures, are warranted. He thereby leaves tacit the ways in which the unity and authority of Scripture are related to the content and witness of Scripture itself for the more mediate discussion of genric type (realistic narrative) and semiotic system (church decision). A fuller account of the hermeneutic field and the theological warrants for "literal" reading and its figural extension is required, in which such reading is fundamentally related to radiance of the Gospel and the single scope of Holy Scripture, Jesus Christ.

The Justifications for Literal Reading

> What remains perplexing, however, is just how Frei thinks text and tradition, formal narrative structure and communal *sensus literalis*, are finally related in the justification of how the church reads Scripture.[326]

One of the central aims of Frei's hermeneutic program is to achieve a restoration of the literal reading of the Bible. The literal reading he wants to retrieve is fundamentally related to Jesus as the ascriptive character of the Gospels; what the Gospels say about Jesus they mean to predicate of him. Jesus and the Gospel(s)' depiction of him are intertwined to the extent that we cannot have what the Gospels are about, independent of the narrative depiction of Jesus. *Jesus* as ascriptive subject narratively rendered, *not* the text's putative historical or idealized referent, is what the Gospels are about. Initially, Frei articulated this notion of literal sense by means of the genric type within which Jesus is depicted. The Gospels are realistic narrative and as such, whether they report history reliably or not, they mean what they say, their subject matter is a fruit of realistic depiction; there is no gap between their form of representation and the thing (person) represented by it. Anxious that he may have caught himself in a general theory,[327] such that the Bible became an instance of the general class, "realistic texts," Frei moved to a more social-scientific basis to articulate and justify "literal" reading. The justification for the same sort of "literal" reading of the Gospels that he defended by means of realistic narrative is now accomplished by means of "thick description," sympathetic socio-anthropological portrayal of communal practice. How do these texts function for the community that

---

326 Hunsinger, "Afterword: Hans Frei as Theologian," p. 259. Hunsinger's comment is directed at Frei's essay, "The 'Literal' Reading of Biblical Narrative."

327 Wolterstorff notes that the argument from realistic narrative also lacks prescriptive persuasiveness. It may well be that the Bible is realistic narrative, but why *must* this quality be honored? The movement to community consensus as the basis for how the canon ought to be read has, potentially, greater prescriptive force for the community in which in functions. See *Divine Discourse*, p. 220.

The Bible as Holy Scripture   147

makes religious use of them? The consensus of the Western Christian interpretative tradition is to read the whole textual constellation in relation to the ascriptive realism of the Gospels—the whole of the Bible is read in congruity with its central story, "its effectually shaping centerpiece."[328] Literal reading, then, is the plain sense, or normative reading, within the Christian church from very early on: therefore, plain sense reading is authoritative for the Christian church.

However, Frei also curiously maintains that there was no a priori reason, or logically necessary development, that lead to the ascendancy of the "literal" reading he champions.[329] And yet, has Frei not already affirmed "literal" reading as "plain" sense reading for the church based on the centrality of the story of Jesus? Does not this imply that "literal" reading is a logically necessary Christological development? It does not seem to be the case, since Frei maintained that it was entirely possible that spiritual reading could have become the consensus or plain reading of the stories about Jesus for the church; indeed, the temptation to do so was strong.[330] Mike Higton argues that Frei moves from "dubious literary theory" to "Church [practice] and Christology" to justify narrative reading of the Gospels.[331] However, Higton does not reckon with the passage in which Frei maintained that literal reading was a logically contingent development. Christology is central for Frei, to be sure, but he asserted that even with the centrality of the stories about Jesus, the plain sense reading of the Bible could have become "spiritual" rather than "literal" reading. Literal reading is a contingent (not an a priori or logically necessary) theological development that is determined, on Frei's account, not by Christology—which would make the Gospels central on either a literal or spiritual reading—but by ecclesiastical decision. Nicholas Wolterstorff contends that, for Frei, the *sensus literalis* emerged as the *senus fidelium* because the reading community over the long run judged it the most "beneficial." But he concludes, "What exactly that benefit might be, remains open to discussion . . ."[332]

Frei notes elsewhere that the Western Christian consensus on the priority of the literal sense over all other senses in the interpretation of Scripture is strongly connected to (and perhaps derivative of) its application to the figure of Jesus. The fact that the church came to read the Gospels such that Jesus is the ascriptive subject of the stories about him exalts the literal sense over other legitimate readings.[333] However, the choice of the church to read the Gospels "literally" as their authoritative plain sense is warranted neither by the genre of the literature as realistic narrative (Frei has by this point rejected that option), nor by the reality status of the subject

---

328 "The 'Literal' Reading of Biblical Narrative," p. 121.

329 Ibid., p. 122.

330 Ibid.

331 See Mike Higton, "Frei's Christology and Lindbeck's Cultural Linguistic Theory," *Scottish Journal of Theology*, 50/1 (1997): 91-92.

332 Wolterstorff posits that behind Frei's interest in the literal sense is "his Barthian theology—that the great benefit of thus interpreting the Gospels is that Jesus' enactment of his identity as Messiah and Son of God is then presented to us." *Divine Discourse*, p. 220. See also Poland, "The New Criticism, Neoorthodoxy, and the New Testament," p. 469.

333 *Types of Christian Theology*, p. 5.

148   *Revelation, Holy Scripture and Church*

matter of the Gospels, since literal reading is "not referentially univocal."[334] The question as to what the church was up against in its decision to authorize literal reading as plain sense reading is thus an open one.

Frei seems to suggest a Christological direction: "In that [Christian] tradition, the ascriptive literalism of the story . . . of the singular agent enacting the unity of human finitude and divine infinity, Jesus of Nazareth, is taken to be itself the ground, guarantee, and conveyance of the truth of the depicted enactment . . ." [335] And yet, the force of "in that tradition" and "is taken to be," when read in the light of his previous remarks concerning how there was "no *a priori* reason" or "necessary logical development" that made literal ascriptive reading plain sense reading for the Church, appears to grant the church the role of *deciding*, in an almost arbitrary fashion, what would be the logic of plain sense reading, instead of the role of developing a consensus which *recognized* that ascriptive literal reading was the mode of reading most coherent with, and intelligible on the basis of, the "singular agent enacting the unity of human finitude and divine infinity, Jesus of Nazareth."[336] Higton is right to want to take the more theologically realist position, that the interpretative tradition proceeds in the direction of "literal" reading of the Gospel stories about Jesus, because to read them otherwise is to misread them. One cannot separate Jesus (as subject matter) from the ascriptive literalism of the Gospels because that is who Jesus *is*. Frei's later position would have been strengthened had he affirmed that "spiritual reading" does not become the plain sense of the Christian interpretative tradition because it dissolves the incarnational particularity of Jesus the Messiah as the ascriptive subject of the Gospels, and read without that ascriptive particularity, it is no longer Jesus the Messiah about whom one reads. Wolterstorff comments: "In principle, Frei could have argued for it [*sensus literalis* interpretation] by starting from his theological convictions and argu[ed that] those convictions presuppose this style of interpretation. But that is not what he did—not most of the time, anyway."[337]

Frei's resolve to proceed in the direction of articulating "literal" reading as the plain sense consensus reading of the interpretative tradition is bound up with the social-scientific model by means of which he offers a descriptive account of Scripture reading in the church.[338] "Thick description" yields an account of Bible reading which terminates at the level of "rules for reading" operable within the

---

334 Ibid.

335 "The 'Literal' Reading of Biblical Narrative," p. 143.

336 Ibid. George Hunsinger, commenting on the developments within Frei's thought in *Types of Christian Theology*, writes:

Although it may seem strange for the *sensus literalis* to take precedent over Christology in the evaluation of the various types [of theology] (as though Christology developed for the sake of the *sensus literalis* rather than the reverse!), that is perhaps precisely Frei's point . . . It seems fair to say, that by increasingly focusing on the *sensus literalis*, Frei effectively arrested any further development in his own proposal about the person and work of Christ. ("Afterword: Hans Frei as Theologian," p. 261)

337 Wolterstorff, *Divine Discourse*, p. 219.

338 See Vanhoozer, *First Theology*, pp. 218-219.

The question is where such rules come from. Are they authoritative for the community because the texts themselves require to be understood along these lines, or are they authoritative because the community has arbitrarily decided to read the text in certain ways and to exclude other readings that might appear to be equally plausible in themselves?[339]

Frei, by choosing a social-scientific model as the means by which to articulate Christian reading conventions, necessarily terminated the discussion of the basis for literal reading at the level of communal practice. This articulation prematurely closes off discussion and can, as Watson suggests, appear to ground Christian reading conventions on a form of ecclesiastic voluntarism[340] and thus render them vulnerable to interpretative tyranny. What is more, by blurring the distinction between authoritative text and interpretative tradition, the critical potential of the Bible over against the church is muffled. The problem inherent in this move is that it is overly optimistic with regard to the believing community. As Vanhoozer notes, "the believing community is all too often portrayed . . . as unbelieving or confused, and subsequent church history has not been reassuring either."[341] What Frei's account of "literal reading" requires is a fundamental sense of the Bible as Holy Scripture in which "literal reading" is a convention required, not by the mediate constraints of either genric type (in his earlier work) or reading public (in his later work), but by virtue of the Bible and the church's relation to God's salvific activity. John Webster writes, "[B]y treating Scripture as a semiotic *positum* in the culture of the church as visible social entity, it risks severing the transcendent reference of both church and Scripture."[342]

An opportunity for greater theological realism in his account of "literal" reading presents itself in Frei's brief consideration of the Reformational notion of scriptural perspicuity. Frei maintains that the priority of the "literal sense" enshrined in the "rule of faith" and the "rule of truth," was up until the Reformation authorized by ecclesiastical tradition. He writes, "Not until the Protestant Reformation is the literal sense understood as authoritative—because perspicuous—in its own right, without

---

339 Watson, *Text and Truth*, p. 125, n. 11.

340 Timothy Ward argues that like Stanley Fish, "by privileging as the plain sense the sense which the church has chosen, Frei brushes up against . . . the solipsistic dangers inherent in locating meaning in the reading-community." See *Word and Supplement*, p. 158. See also Vanhoozer, *First Theology*, p. 219.

341 Vanhoozer, *First Theology*, p. 219. He cites Kathryn Tanner, who affirms that on Frei's view, there is no longer "any absolute distinction between the text's proper sense and the contributions of an interpretative tradition." Kathryn Tanner, "Theology and the Plain Sense," in Garrett Green (ed.), *Scriptural Authority and Narrative Interpretation* (Philadelphia, 1987), p. 63. Cited in *First Theology*, p. 219.

342 Webster, *Holy Scripture*, p. 49. Frei maintains that the descriptive context for the literal sense is the "religion of which it is part, understood at once as a determinate code in which beliefs, ritual, and behaviour patterns come together as a common semiotic system . . ." "The 'Literal' Reading of Biblical Narrative," p. 146.

150 *Revelation, Holy Scripture and Church*

authorization from the interpretative tradition."[343] Apart from the fact that Frei had previously maintained that it was the Reformers who offered "a drastic alternative," that is, a grammatical-historical "literal alternative," to the "multiplex" mostly non-literal, readings of the Bible that had developed in "traditional theory of scriptural interpretation,"[344] Frei does not exploit the theological potential of "perspicuity" in the Reformers for his own interpretative retrieval. Frei made three claims: (1) "Literal" reading is authoritative reading of the Bible in the Reformers; (2) it is not authorized by the interpretative tradition; and (3) it is warranted because "perspicuous—in its own right." Claims (1) and (2) seem substantially correct, provided the historical and referential dimensions are assumed, as Frei notes, in the Reformers' notion of "literal sense." Claim (3) however, could be usefully spelled out in relation to a larger theological matrix. The perspicuity or clarity of the Bible "in its own right" could read as though this property of Scripture's literal sense was an *en se* literary property of the Bible as a human product. James Fodor notes that Frei has a tendency to blur "certain structuralist insights with claims regarding the perspicuity and sufficiency of Scripture."[345] However, for the Reformers, clarity is a feature of the relationship of the Bible to the luminous work of God in the Gospel. Luther wrote:

> For what still sublimer thing can be hidden in the Scriptures, now that the seals have been broken, the stone rolled away from the door of the sepulcher, and the supreme mystery brought to light, namely, that Christ the Son of God has been made man, that God is three and one, that Christ has suffered for us and is to reign eternally? Are not these things known and sung even in the highways and byways? . . . The subject matter of the Scriptures, therefore, is all quite accessible, even though some texts are still obscure owing to our ignorance of their terms. Truly it is stupid and impious, when we know that the subject matter of Scripture has all been placed in the clearest light, to call it obscure on account of a few obscure words.[346]

While biblical interpretation required exegetical effort, knowledge of "obscure words," of custom and syntax, the Reformers were preoccupied with the "emanating light" of the message of salvation in Christ and in a confession of faith "praised the Word in its clarity and power."[347] Literal sense reading of the Bible, then, in so far as it is related to Reformation notions of the clarity of Scripture, would be authorized, not by interpretative tradition, which often stands in need of reform, but as a convention endorsed by the luminous message of salvation which is the content of Holy Scripture. "According to the Reformers . . . the confession of perspicuity is not a statement in general concerning the human language of Scripture, but a confession concerning the perspicuity of the gospel *in* Scripture."[348] The primacy of

---

343 "The 'Literal' Reading of Biblical Narrative," p. 123.

344 *The Eclipse of Biblical Narrative*, p. 19.

345 Fodor, *Christian Hermeneutics*, p. 283.

346 Martin Luther, in Jaroslav Pelikan and Helmut T. Lehmann (gen. eds), *Luther's Works*, vol. 33: *Career of the Reformer III*, Philip Watson (ed.), "The Bondage of the Will," trans. Jaroslav Pelikan (Philadelphia, 1972), pp. 25-26.

347 Berkhouwer, *Holy Scripture*, p. 273.

348 Ibid., p. 275.

The Bible as Holy Scripture 151

literal reading of the Gospels, and the rest of Scripture in relation to them, does not then rest on the *sensus fidelium* but is required by the *lumen evangelium*.

The Bible as a Single Story   A second aim of Frei's hermeneutic retrieval, which is central in his effort to undo the eclipse of biblical narrative, is to restore a sense of coherence to the Bible as one story through figural extension of the ascriptively literal stories about Jesus over the whole of the canon. For Frei the authoritative *mode* of reading is literal and the authoritative *construal* of the Bible as a unity is narrative. In *The Eclipse of Biblical Narrative*, Frei offers a sympathetic description of Calvin's use of figural interpretation to extend the literal meaning of the stories about Jesus as a means of securing the unity of the Testaments. Frei maintains that Calvin is able to extend literal meaning through the "logic of intensification rather than supersession."[349] While figural interpretation takes persons and events into another context where they prefigure what is to come, this move does not downgrade the reality and truth of their original occurrence. Figural interpretation extends, gives an additional "new" meaning: it does not efface but intensifies. This use of figural reading gives rise, not to shadow and reality, in which the shadow dissolves in the light of reality, but to promise and fulfillment such that the Testaments read in a forward direction in a state of perpetual complementarity. Frei's interest in Calvin's use of figural interpretation is, of course, theologically motivated. Frei wants to maintain or preserve the authority of the Bible, particularly its capacity as a whole to render an "authoritative" and unified identity description of God. This motivation is not spoken on the surface, but the unity of the Bible is crucial to his other project, *The Identity of Jesus Christ*.[350]

However, in an interesting move, once Frei offers his theologically motivated descriptive account of Calvin's use of figuration, he turns to Auerbach's literary analysis to "characterize the threats to figural extension in a way that shows how Calvin's conception of literal and figural reading successfully resisted them."[351] That is, it appears that while theology motivates Frei to historical and literary descriptive analysis, the idiom he chooses to "characterize" threats against and "successful" performance of figural interpretation is distinctly non-theological. In some respects, it must be said that Frei, in deploying a "system of ideas" for the construal and interpretation of the Bible, is following Barth. "In attempting to reflect on what is said to us in the biblical text, we must first make use of the system of thought we bring with us, that is, of some philosophy or other."[352] However, Frei's use of Auerbach and New Criticism in this case appear not as tools used in making sense of what is said in biblical texts, but as the idiom within which the figural reading and

---

349 Dawson, *Christian Figural Reading and the Fashioning of Identity*, p. 150. Dawson is drawing on Frei's discussion of Calvin's *Institutes*, 2.11.2 in *The Eclipse of Biblical Narrative*, p. 33.

350 See Francis Watson, *Text, Church and World: Biblical Interpretation in Theological Perspective* (Grand Rapids, 1994), p. 23.

351 Dawson, *Christian Figural Reading and the Fashioning of Identity*, p. 147.

352 Barth, *Church Dogmatics*, 1/2: 729. He goes so far as to say that to "dispute this" is "to dispute the grace and finally the incarnation of the Word of God, we cannot basically contest the use of philosophy in scriptural exegesis." Ibid., p. 730.

152 *Revelation, Holy Scripture and Church*

the unity of the Bible are conceived. Frei notes that his book, "falls into the almost legendary category of analysis of analyses of the Bible in which not a single text is examined, not a single exegesis undertaken."[353] Moreover, he exhibits a certain dis-ease about how Barth, whose figural interpretation he commends, would receive the argument he makes: "In his hands [Barth's] theology becomes an imperious and allegiance demanding discipline, and he might well have rejected out of hand the *external* treatment it receives in the present essay."[354] Francis Watson summarizes the discussion to this point:

> [A]lthough Frei's motivation is clearly theological, the theological dimension is held in abeyance and literary-critical judgments determine the analysis. These literary-critical judgments—on "realistic" narrative, on "figuration" as a means of incorporation into the biblical world, and so on, serve as surrogates for theological concerns that never explicitly appear yet constantly make their influence felt.[355]

Frei's use of Auerbach's literary analysis to defend the intelligibility and coherence of figuration as an extension, not a violation, of literal reading, is indeed most masterful. It does provide a helpful and necessary support to his conception of biblical unity and authority and their role in offering the reader an identity-description of God. However, his account of the role of figuration in an overall construal of the biblical corpus would be considerably strengthened and gain doctrinal density were the place of figuration (and the Auerbachian defense he offers) located within a theological description of the hermeneutic field in which it is employed. In other words, some account of figurative reading and biblical unity grounded in the communicative activity of the One God in the work of salvation, or the role of figuration in reflecting the single scope of Scripture, Jesus Christ, would give it dogmatic weight. Frei may well have been motivated by some of these very concerns, but they need to be articulated, not *after* the detour through literary analysis or a social-scientific rendering of descriptive context (prolegomena) but *prior* to and *alongside* it. Without this fundamental move, Frei gives the impression that the literary conventions of the Bible find their singular constraint in "autonomous" textual works (or consenting communities) to the neglect of their determination by their content and witness.[356]

François Wendel and Randall C. Zachman set the theological context for the intelligibility of figuration as a literary device for the unity of the Testaments in Calvin. Wendel notes that Calvin deduces, "from the immutability of the divine will, that it could not express itself otherwise in the New Testament than in the Old."[357] The

---

353 *The Eclipse of Biblical Narrative*, p. vii.

354 Ibid., p. viii. My emphasis.

355 Watson, *Text, Church and World*, p. 23. Watson makes the point (p. 25), in a Ricoeurian turn of phrase, that in Frei's work "Faith seeking understanding attains it by way of a literary detour." Watson is here speaking of *The Eclipse of Biblical Narrative*.

356 See Poland " The New Criticism, Neoorthodoxy, and the New Testament," p. 469.

357 François Wendel, *Calvin: The Origins and Development of his Religious Thought*, trans. Philip Mairet (London, 1963), p. 208. For a good critical analysis of Frei's reading of Calvin see Randall C. Zachman, "Gathering Meaning from the Context: Calvin's Exegetical Method," *Journal of Religion*, 82/1 (January, 2002): 14ff.

The Bible as Holy Scripture 153

unity of the Testaments for Calvin, maintains Zachman, is first grounded in the unity of God since "God always remains like himself."[358] Moreover, this "fundamental and substantial unity of the Old and New Testaments" does not downgrade the "fundamental importance" of the work of Christ. For while the Testaments are separated by their temporal position in the one plan of salvation, "the Biblical witness as a whole is to be regarded as witness to Jesus Christ, and theology has no other purpose than the guidance of believers in this question of the Christ through all the Biblical writings."[359] Convinced that Scripture is, in its entirety, a witness to Jesus Christ, that in all of its diverse expressions the thing to look for is kergymatic content in order to "comprehend the true nature of the biblical witness,"[360] the Church Fathers and Reformers spoke of the singularity of the "scope" of the Bible. By this term they pointed not simply to the aim or purpose of a text but to the "creedal core" found within the larger context of the Bible and which in turn "delimits the purpose of any part of the Bible on the basis of the whole."[361] Figural reading (and allegorical reading), always disciplined by the literal sense, is thus properly oriented, not just by the formal features of the text as "realistic narrative", but also by the overall theological content and witness, the "scope," of the Bible, Jesus Christ. T.F. Torrance writes:

> Strictly speaking Christ himself is the scope of the Scriptures, so that it is only through focusing constantly upon him, dwelling in his Word and assimilating his Mind, that the interpreter can discern the real meaning of the Scriptures. What is required then is a theological interpretation of the Scriptures under the direction of their ostensive reference to God's self-revelation in Jesus Christ and within the general perspective of faith.[362]

In conclusion: Calvin, like Frei, did propose that Christians read Scripture as a unity through typology and figuration as extensions of literal sense. Read in this fashion,

---

358 John Calvin, *Commentarius in Epistolam ad Hebraeos*, ed. T.H.L. Parker, *Ionannis Calvini Opera Exegetica* XIX (Geneva, 1996), p. 15, lines 22-24, cited in Zachman, "Gathering Meaning from the Context: Calvin's Exegetical Method," p. 26.

359 Wendel, *Calvin*, p. 215. See also Wesley A. Kort, *"Take, Read:" Scripture, Textuality, and Cultural Practice* (University Park, 1996), p. 34.

360 Childs, *Theology of the Old and New Testaments*, p. 725. Childs speaks of the scope of Scripture as "a constant pointer, much like a ship's compass, fixing on a single goal, in spite of the many various ways of God (Heb 1.1), toward which the believer is drawn." Ibid. See also Torrance, *Reality and Evangelical Theology*, pp. 101-107.

361 Gerald Sheppard, "Between Reformation and Modern Commentary: The Perception of the Scope of Biblical Books," in G.T. Shepherd (ed.), *William Perkins: A Commentary on Galatians* (1617) (Pilgrim Press, 1989), p. lxxi. Sheppard made the interesting point that Frei "could have found even greater support in the use of scope that embodies the element of biblical realism while allowing for the multi-genre nature of Scripture." Ibid. In other words, "scope" could have released "narrative" from the over-freighted duty of holding the diverse materials of the Bible together in a single genre, and yet hold the Bible together in a Christological unity.

362 Torrance, *Reality and Evangelical Theology*, p. 107. See also T.F. Torrance, *The Hermeneutics of John Calvin* (Edinburgh, 1988), pp. 51-138 for a discussion of Calvin's use of the term "scope" in terms consistent with the above citation.

154   *Revelation, Holy Scripture and Church*

Frei established the means for reading the Bible, authoritatively, as an identity description of God. However, Calvin, unlike Frei, does not arrive at the task of theological description by means of a literary argument. Calvin began from the unity and constancy of God, whose Word, Jesus Christ, is the single scope of Scripture. Read from this center, through typology and figuration, "every doctrine of the law, every command, every promise, always points to Christ."[363]

In terms of reading the Bible as a whole through figural interpretation, Frei also raises the matter of "forward" (non-retrospective) reading as crucial to his interpretative program of retrieval. For Frei, reading the Bible as a "cumulative" narrative held together as one story through figuration, implies "directionality" (from past to present) in reading. "The meaning pattern of reality is inseparable from its forward motion; it is not the product of the wedding of that forward motion with a separate backward perspective upon it, i.e., of history and interpretation joined as two logically independent factors."[364] Garnering meaning from the Bible thus involves following the temporal sequence of the story toward fulfillment in Jesus Christ. Fulfillment is not the sole means by which events and persons are made figures. They are figures primarily in their own right, the Israelites possessed and enjoyed the land of Canaan and whether or not they knew this to be a figure of future inheritance, it *was* a figure at the time. Frei, in his reading of Calvin, is trying to guard the meaning pattern of the biblical narrative in its own right, from figure to fulfillment, against retrospective reading that gives Old Testament events and persons specificity and reality based on subsequent Christian reading patterns. This move on Frei's part grants figural events a reality status, specificity and uniqueness, that prevents their being abstracted from the narrative by allegorical pressures. Moreover, by it Frei affirmed, with Calvin, that the Christian figural reader does not stand outside the temporal framework of the story in order to read it. The framework the story provides—from figure to fulfillment—is the only framework there is since it is the temporal framework of reality itself. The teleology of the story is the teleology of reality under the providence of God. "In effect, the Christian figural reader is expected to position him or herself in the place of the ancient Israelites and not to allow subsequent awareness of Christian 'fulfillment' to displace the legitimacy of the figure's own meaning and truth."[365]

While Frei espoused a kind of realism in this appropriation of Calvin on the directionality of figural reading, there are two considerations that would make the argument he offers more persuasive. First, the rejection of retrospective Christian reading for the meaning of Old Testament figures in the light of Christ (Christian reading patterns) seems to trade on confusion between the status of Old Testament figures and events in their own right, and our knowledge of them as figures. Frei claimed that for Calvin, the Spirit does not add "a new dimension to the text" but rather "enlightens the heart and mind to see what the text says,"[366] but he does not

---

363 Calvin, *Commentary on Romans*, 10:4, cited in Zachman, "Gathering Meaning from the Context: Calvin's Exegetical Method," p. 26.

364 *The Eclipse of Biblical Narrative*, p. 36.

365 Dawson, *Christian Figural Reading and the Fashioning of Identity*, p. 142.

366 *The Eclipse of Bibical Narrative*, p. 34.

The Bible as Holy Scripture 155

flesh this discussion out in terms of what it might mean for Christian reading of the Bible. Retrospective reading is not the means whereby reality is conferred on Old Testament figures; it is the means by which their place in the cumulative story is uncovered, unveiled, shown to be what it is in the light of Christ. Calvin suggests as much when in his comparison of the differences between the Testaments he noted: "The second difference between the Old and New Testaments consists in figures: that, in the absence of the reality, it showed but an image and shadow in the place of the substance; the New Testament reveals the very substance of truth as present."[367] Here Calvin draws attention to the role of the New Testament as *revealing* the substance of truth. Likewise, both Richard Hayes and R.W.L. Moberly, in extended treatments of Luke's story of Jesus and the disciples on the road to Emmaus, make the point that while Jesus cannot be *understood* apart from Jewish Scripture, "Jewish Scripture cannot be *understood* apart from Jesus."[368] Retrospective reading is noetically required to enlighten the reader as to what is already present but not yet understood or configured properly. It might even be said to be necessary to grasp "the meaning pattern" of the Bible as a whole. Hayes argues it is the resurrection that teaches us to read the Old Testament figurally as Christian Scripture.

> In the light of the New Testament's witness, we cannot confine the meaning of the Old Testament to the literal sense understood by its original authors and readers, for these ancient texts have been taken up into a new story that amplifies and illumines their meaning in unexpected ways . . . the resurrection teaches us to read for figuration and latent sense.[369]

The other feature of Frei's discussion of directional Bible reading that needs greater theological specification is his emphasis on figures "in their own right." The cumulative pattern yielded in the from-figure-to-fulfillment movement of Bible reading, as well as the refusal to admit a backward perspective (from fulfillment to figure) seems to push in the direction of leaving space for a non-Christological reading of the Old Testament. And yet, Calvin, who regards Jesus Christ as the single scope of Scripture, the object of its common witness, would hardly want to admit a relative autonomy of the Old Testament "in its own right," as though there were a realm or time in Scripture that did not witness to Christ. In other words, there is a sense in which there can be no "in their own right" reading of Old Testament figures since these figures are never not already implicated in the *telos* to which they witness. Without further specification, while Frei seems to gain a teleological unity between the Testaments, in words that Brevard Childs originally directs at James Barr, "he fails to deal adequately with the theological claim of an ontological . . . unity of the testaments, which lies at the heart of the New Testament's application of the Old (cf. John 1:1-5; Col. 1:15-20; Heb. 1:2-3)."[370]

---

367 Calvin, *Institutes of the Christian Religion*, Library of Christian Classics, vols 20 and 21, ed. John T. McNeill (Philadelphia, 1960), II.XI.4, p. 453.

368 Moberly, *The Bible, Theology, and Faith*, p. 51.

369 Hayes, "Reading Scripture in the Light of the Resurrection," p. 233.

370 Childs, *Biblical Theology of the Old and New Testaments*, p. 14.

156   *Revelation, Holy Scripture and Church*

One of the ways in which Frei might address this lacuna in his hermeneutic would be by means of Robert Jenson's interesting suggestion that time, as it frames biblical narrative, is not linear, as Frei's project supposes. "Time," writes Jenson, "is more like a helix, and what it spirals around is the risen Christ." A transposed notion of narrative cumulation would be required on this count in which there are no readings of Scripture which are not already involved with the pre-existent Christ of the Old Testament or the incarnate Word of the New. Meaning patterns would not be inseparable from forward motion toward Christ, but from their circular motion around Christ. Jenson writes provocatively, "[Luther's] exhoratation to take Aaron as Christ, the great high priest (and so on for all the characters of the exodus story), and thus to read sections of the Pentateuch as something like another Gospel is simply a pointer to Exodus' plain sense."[371] Moreover, Jenson supposes that if the word of the Lord that came to Isaiah was Jesus Christ, then the "vision of the Christ that the Church has derived from the prophet, of a 'man of sorrows and acquainted with grief,' is not a mere allowable trope but is in fact a product of Christ's own testimony to his own character given by the mouth of the prophet."[372]

In sum: the argument was made that Frei's account of the justification of literal reading, while it is oriented to a fitting reading of the Gospels and of Scripture as a whole, suffers from a lack of theological density in its execution. Frei does not specify the fundamental doctrinal grounds upon which the literal ascriptive reading of the Gospels and figural extension of literal meaning to the whole of the Christian Scriptures are warranted. He thereby leaves tacit the ways in which the unity and authority of Scripture are related to the content and witness of Scripture itself for the more mediate discussion of genric type (realistic narrative) and semiotic system (church decision). A richer account of the hermeneutic field and the theological warrants for "literal" reading and its figural extension are required in which such reading is fundamentally related to radiance of the Gospel and the single scope of Scripture, Jesus Christ.

---

371   Jenson, " Scripture's Authority in the Church," p. 35.
372   Ibid.

Chapter 3

The Church and the Bible Critically Read

In this chapter an exposition and examination of James Barr, Paul Ricoeur and Hans Frei on the nature and function of the critical reading of the Bible for the life of the Christian church is undertaken. The focus of attention in each case is given to their respective characterizations of the nature of Bible reading as critical, and the manner in which such readings modulate the reading and hearing of the Bible by the church, in and for faith, as Scripture. The procedure is first to provide a descriptive overview of the various modes of Bible reading proposed and to show how they are related in the thought of each interpreter for the sake of a more truthful (Barr), less ideological and thus more authentic (Ricoeur), or more conventional/faithful (Frei) reading of Scripture for the life of the church. There is no question that each thinker is convinced that when the church reads Holy Scripture with a view to putting it into practice, its reading *must* be critical. Negatively, this implies that when Scripture is interpreted for the life of the church it may not circumvent the iconoclastic potential of historical-critical research (Barr), the hermeneutics of suspicion (Ricoeur), or reading conventions demanded by genre type or embedded communal convention (Frei). It should be noted that none of these thinkers maintains that the critical mode of reading they espouse excludes other kinds of reading, terminates in skepticism regarding the subject matter of the Bible, or disables hearing Scripture in a believing mode. Rather each proposal is in effect an argument for how reading the Bible critically ought to order other modes of Bible reading, and especially the church's listening to and reading of the Bible as Scripture. Each author is engaged in a project that aims at the felicitous reading of the Bible for the life of the Christian community.

While each interpreter is invested in a variant of critical reading with a view to the benefit of the church, the preponderant character of the term "critical" is derived apart from a consideration of the force and shape that it acquires in relation to God's communicative activity by means of the Bible. The term "critical" acquires its primary nature and substance for the thinkers we consider from: (1) Enlightenment notions of "free critical inquiry" in which interpreters "bracket out" theological conviction and ecclesial context in order to achieve readings that can cut against received tradition (Barr); (2) the essential critiques of religion as economic, philosophical or psychodynamic distortion offered by Marx, Nietzsche and Freud, in which proposed "religious" interpretation is subjected to iconoclastic interrogation in order to gain renewed authenticity (Ricoeur); or (3) embedded genric and religious conventions appropriate to particular texts or religions in order to achieve readings which retain their integrity over against a panoply of explanatory interpretative strategies (Frei). In each case, the critical potential of the Bible as a witness to the Gospel, as that means which God uses to accost, interrogate, create and sustain the people of God,

158 *Revelation, Holy Scripture and Church*

is displaced from primacy by the relatively "objective" evidentiary considerations of the scholarly guild (Barr), muted through correlation with the critique of religion rendered by the masters of suspicion (Ricoeur), or left tacit by means of a terminal consideration of genric or ecclesial convention (Frei). While Barr's emphasis on the semantic and evidentiary aspects of biblical interpretation is invaluable in establishing the text, disambiguating historical and linguistic obscurity, and in rendering interpreters responsible to those interpretations that the text will bear, and while Ricoeur provides important insight into the potential for the distortion of authentic biblical interpretation rooted in false consciousness, and while Frei helps interpreters to envisage biblical interpretation in its concrete relation to the embodied life of the Christian church, what is lacking in each description of the critical interpretation of the Bible as Scripture for the life of the church is a thoroughly theological account of the radical *kritikos* of God's Word, that is, of the fundamental nature and force of the term "critical" in relation to God's use of Holy Scripture in the life of God's people. "The Church lives solely because day by day, it is newly called and upheld, confronted and governed by its Lord."[1]

James Barr: Critical Biblical Research and the Listening Church

Three hermeneutic convictions are central for James Barr in the critical reading of the Bible for the life of the Christian church. Critical interpretation implies, first, that the church's reading of Scripture must be open to the contributions of historical-critical investigation.[2] In this mode of reading the doctrinal relation of the Bible to church and tradition is reconstrued such that the Bible is viewed under them. The Scriptures, while they represent a fixed form of the tradition, must not conceal that they are the crystallization of a long process; they are a product of the believing community. Historical-critical investigation re-expands Scripture into its many layers resisting the temptation to read the Bible as a "fixed metaphysical entity" and enabling a greater understanding of it in terms of its theological function for the church.[3] In order to pursue this kind of biblical research, however, the interpreter of the Bible must be able to suspend traditional theological convictions so that meanings other than these may be derived from the biblical tradition where warranted. For Barr, such critical freedom in biblical research should be granted by the church in order for it to honor (1) the doctrine of justification by faith, by which the interpreter is set

---

1 The Düsseldorf Thesis (Thesis 5, 1933), in William Niesel, *Reformed Symbolics* (Edinburgh, 1962), pp. 355-356.

2 Barr prefers "critical biblical research" to the more common designation "historical-critical method." The reason for this is that the latter places too much emphasis on the historical component of critical research, and not enough on its linguistic and literary components. See *Holy Scripture*, pp. 105-106.

3 Historical-critical research thus is more closely aligned with "pure" theology than imagined. For many of its practitioners have valued it precisely for the theological results that it has enabled for the church. Barr resists the "common opinion" that biblical theology arose as a protest against historical-critical non-theological study of Scripture. See *The Concept of Biblical Theology*, pp. 8-9.

The second hermeneutic conviction, which overlaps with the first, concerns the shared social locus of biblical interpretation. To the question, "Does Biblical Study Still Belong to Theology?"[4] Barr answers yes and no. While it is true that "when the study of Scripture is undertaken as a theological task, then it must be done in the context of the church and with a personal involvement related to that context," this by no means proves that "no valid biblical study can be undertaken except in that context."[5] In order to guard the freedom of biblical research, an institutional setting free from ecclesial tutelage is important. For not only does the scholarly guild maintain the freedom needed for critical biblical inquiry, it also "has had a considerable degree of scientific objectivity."[6] The reality of the academy, predicated as it is on the objectivity of critical biblical research, is of crucial importance for the church's use of the Bible. For the work of this community prevents the imprisonment of the Bible in the categories and language of the present religious community, and positively enables the Bible to speak afresh to the church through "insights and arguments that come from beyond itself."[7]

The third conviction is both negative and positive. It relates to the service that critical biblical research performs in mediating the church's hearing of the Scriptures. On Barr's account, critical biblical research does not include a hermeneutic strategy for overcoming the historical and existential distance created by such inquiry. Such distance is already overcome, on Barr's view, by the church's actual use (hermeneutical updating) of the Bible in its own life of prayer and praise (the frame of reference for understanding the Scriptures). However, as the church listens for the "Word of God" in its hearing of the canon of Scripture, it is also responsible to modulate this hearing in the light of critical biblical research. Moreover, in its conversation with the academic community of biblical scholars, the church is positively enabled to hear the Scriptures speak a fresh word, which it might not otherwise hear within the confines of its solitary life.

In the critique that follows a case is made against Barr that his construal of the mode, institutional locus and use of the Bible by the church as dependent upon historical criticism within the scholarly guild (where theological conviction and Christian faith even where they exist are bracketed out for the sake of criticism), is problematic both in terms of the coherence of the proposal and its compatibility with and practical usefulness to the life of the Christian church. On the one hand, Barr deploys confessional warrants (justification by faith, the authority of Scripture)

---

4 *The Scope and Authority of the Bible*, pp. 18-29.

5 Ibid., p. 26.

6 *Holy Scripture*, p. 113.

7 James Barr, "The Bible as a Document of Believing Communities," in Hans Deiter Betz (ed.), *The Bible as a Document of the University* (Chico, 1981), p. 37. Kevin Vanhoozer, in a review of Francis Watson's *Text, Church and World*, paraphrases James Barr's question: "Does Biblical Study Still Belong to Theology?" with the following question: "Is the Bible a document of faith, to be interpreted only in the community of faith," he asked, "or do faith traditions inevitably distort the true meaning of the Bible, in which case the saint had better give way to the scholar." *Pro Ecclesia*, 7/3 (Summer, 1998): 365.

160 *Revelation, Holy Scripture and Church*

and theological constructs (the Bible) for his "non-theological" critical interpretative program within the academy. Nevertheless, it seems that he cannot maintain with consistency either that (1) critical reading of the Bible, free from controlling theological convictions, is at the same time warranted by and the instantiation of these convictions; or (2) that there is a subject matter, an artifact for critical study, called the Bible, existing apart from specific Christian theological convictions and practices without which the "Bible" is an optical illusion. On the other hand, when Barr successfully brackets out theological constructs and faith commitment from critical biblical research, the interpretative disposition (mastery) and deflation of the interpretative field (to the facts of a materialist ontology) are at such odds with Christian interpretative practice and "the great things of the Gospel"[8] that the results may not engender a fresh or new hearing of it in the church. Moreover, such an account verges on ascribing to a conversation between communities of interpretation what belongs to God. For while the church does seek a Word from beyond itself, it is God to whom the church looks for this saving Word. In short, Barr's construal of the hermeneutic field in which theological conviction and faith commitment are suspended in the interpretation of the Bible for the sake of the church is not consistently and thoroughly oriented to the object which faith confesses and upon which it fundamentally depends for the critical hearing of Holy Scripture as the Word of God.

Interpretation in the "Critical" Mode

The primary sense in which the Bible ought to be read critically[9] concerns the role of historical-critical analysis of Scripture. Although the fixation of tradition in the formation of the Bible sometimes hides it from view, the Scriptures emerged as the product of an extended historical period of formation and redaction. For Barr, this implies that the doctrine of Scripture should not be placed such that it follows the doctrine of God and revelation—as though it were in a privileged place outside of and antecedent to church and tradition. Rather Scripture is positioned under the doctrine of the church, the people of God and tradition. "Scripture follows tradition as a special case within the totality of tradition . . ."[10] Historical-critical investigation, where it is not barred by fundamentalist concepts of holy writ, has enabled the multi-

---

8 The phrase is taken from Alvin Plantinga, "Two (or More) Kinds of Scripture Scholarship," *Modern Theology*, 14/2 (April, 1998): 243. Plantinga uses the term to refer to the main lines of Christian Christological thought: "that Jesus was really the pre-existent second person of the divine trinity who was crucified, died, and then literally rose from the dead the third day."

9 For Barr, the Bible ought also to be read critically in relation to the structure of faith, something like the *regula fidei*. This relation was a central topic in the discussion of Barr on the Bible as Scripture.

10 *The Scope and Authority of the Bible*, p. 48. Barr writes, "We have seen that the traditional 'Catholic' argument, that the Bible derived from the church, is entirely valid as against the traditional 'Protestant' position which refused to see the Bible as deriving from the church and which therefore sought to give Scripture priority over the church in the *ordo revelationis*."

The Church and the Bible Critically Read 161

dimensional and historical nature of the Bible to come to view, so that interpreters approach it "more like tradition than it first appeared to be."[11] By working against the foreshortening of tradition in the fixation of the Bible, historical reading has "restore[d] to Scripture the same sort of status that we apply automatically to the history and tradition of the church."[12] In other words, by interpreting the Bible "historically" (i.e. within the process of tradition) and not as a fixed metaphysical entity, critical reading has helped to increase the "understanding of Scripture in its proper theological role."[13] Scripture is thus not isolated as authoritative books, but rather is authoritative with reference to the life, experience and thinking of the people of God from whom the Scriptures came.[14]

However, in order to enable the historical-critical interpreter to render service to the church, the interpreter, argues Barr, ought to be "free" to follow the dictates of modern interpretative methods—even where treading this path may lead the interpreter into conflict with accepted theological interpretation. It is in this sense that biblical criticism is "critical"—free to derive from the Bible meanings other than those that are traditional.[15] In this case, Barr is referring to post-biblical tradition over which, on his view, the Bible is privileged. According to Barr, freedom from the oversight of post-biblical tradition, accorded the interpreter, is rooted in the logic of Protestantism. Justification by faith means, on Barr's interpretation, that Christians justified freely in Christ have no other religious obligations which must be fulfilled in order to carry out their calling as Christians. And in the case of the biblical scholar, this means that they are free to carry out the critical examination of Scripture "whether it is in agreement with the confession of faith, or whether church authorities will find it agreeable."[16]

Another warrant whereby Barr grounds his conviction concerning the freedom of the biblical scholar to carry out critical work, unhindered by accepted theological doctrine, is that such a freedom will enable theological construction to be more faithful to its confessed authority (Scripture). For Barr, one of the consequences of

---

11 Ibid., p. 50.

12 Ibid. For Barr, "Protestantism was right in claiming Scripture as its authority and in denying that tradition (after Scripture) could be placed on the same level as Scripture . . ." *Holy Scripture*, p. 31. The plain implication here is that pre-scriptural tradition (oral and textual) stands on the same level, in terms of authority, as Scripture in its final form.

13 *The Scope and Authority of the Bible*, p. 50.

14 See ibid., pp. 50-51, 63-64 and *Holy Scripture*, p. 48.

15 James Barr, "Modern Biblical Criticism," in Bruce Metzger and Michael Coogan (eds), *The Oxford Companion to the Bible* (New York, 1993), p. 318. See also *Holy Scripture*, p. 34. The possibility that post-biblical doctrinal construction is an attempt to honor the authority of Scripture does not seem to arise here. And thus accepted, theological doctrine and the dogma of the church are consistently understood as obfuscating to the critical work of the biblical scholar on text of the Bible.

16 *Holy Scripture*, p. 35. See also James Barr, "Exegesis as a Theological Discipline Reconsidered and the Shadow of the Jesus of History," in Donald G. Miller (ed.), *The Hermeneutical Quest: Essays in Honor of James Luther Mays on his Sixty-Fifth Birthday* (Allison Park, 1986), pp. 17-18. This represents a break with his earlier view in *The Scope and Authority of the Bible*, pp. 48-49.

162   *Revelation, Holy Scripture and Church*

the Protestant "isolation" of Scripture as a criterion of sound Christian belief was that it secularized Scripture[17] so that existing theological belief is set over against its exegesis (suspended) in order "to overthrow" if necessary "the concepts of recent, standard and customary theology and lead . . . to reformation."[18] This is not to say that Protestants have always practiced this freedom to which they are in principle committed.[19] But where the Protestant principle of biblical authority is practiced, it requires the freedom, on the basis of sound scriptural exegesis, says Barr, "to question, to adjust, and if necessary to abandon prevailing doctrinal traditions." He continues, "Where this freedom does not exist, however much the Bible is celebrated, its authority is in fact submitted to the power of a tradition of doctrine and interpretation."[20]

Under oppressive circumstances, where "Christian" freedom is withheld by the churches, then, counsels Barr, "secularism as the best approximation (of such freedom) is to be welcomed and embraced."[21] The understanding of critical freedom, of the unencumbered liberty "to come to exegetical results which may differ, or even contradict, accepted theological interpretation,"[22] not only has theological roots in the Reformation, it is also a child of the Enlightenment. Thus it would seem that where scholarship runs up against ecclesiastical censure, it can find freedom of a secular variety, rooted in the Enlightenment, in institutions outside the church.

Interpretation in Two Institutions

In his discussions of the institutional locus of biblical interpretation, James Barr recognizes the existence of two interpretative communities. The first is the "believing community," which designates those places where exegesis is carried out under theological presuppositions and in a mode congruent with personal faith. The other context, broadly speaking, is the academy, where documents of faith are examined, without supposing that they are valid or true, by those that are not necessarily adherents to the faith. Individuals may well work between these communities, and indeed these communities learn from the work of each other, but these do exist as distinct locales with distinct contributions to make to biblical interpretation.

---

17 Where Scripture is used as "the criterion" of faithful theological belief, then it is theological belief that is "secularized"—placed over against the content of Scripture—in the critical moment Barr describes. Elsewhere Barr suggests this very thing. "Modern Biblical Criticism," p. 318.

18 See "Exegesis as a Theological Discipline Reconsidered," p. 18.

19 "The facts of Scripture" have often been "obscured through the imposition of a [Protestant] tradition." *Holy Scripture*, p. 31. See also pp. 108-109 for some examples of how confessional traditions have overrun the "facts" of the text.

20 Ibid., pp. 31-32. See also *History and Ideology in the Old Testament*, p. 45. In this context Barr quotes Barton who speaks of historical criticism as an "iconoclastic movement" which "refuses to allow people to mean anything they want by their sacred texts." Barton maintains that this movement has "scarcely even arrived there" (in the church). The Barton citation is from "Historical-Critical Approaches," pp. 17-18.

21 *Holy Scripture*, p. 35.

22 Ibid., p. 34.

The Church and the Bible Critically Read 163

Bible study, where it is undertaken as a theological task, must be done in the "church," with a faith commitment appropriate to that context. It is a critical task, as we noted, but the operative critical "canon" is the faith structure of the community. By reading the Bible as a document ordered by a theology, that is, by reading the Bible as a document of faith,[23] important new insights in biblical study may well take place.[24] Theologians have been correct to note that where "theology is excluded from the study of the Bible"[25] questions of theological relevance to the church are not asked, and non-theological assumptions have rushed in to fill the void left by their absence. It is Barr's experience that the second of these liabilities, the absence of reflection on the theological dimension of Scripture, is more likely in an academic context.[26] In response to the objection that theological commitment is likely to lead to a skewing of the evidence in Bible study, Barr notes that in several cases such commitment has stimulated and supported research. "Strong theological commitment can coexist with and rejoice in a very high degree of objectivity."[27]

However, the overall thrust of Barr's position is that all too often "religious conviction is far more powerful than biblical data."[28] The history of both Catholicism and Protestantism demonstrates the constant interposing of a doctrinal heritage over the facts of the Bible.[29] Barr maintains, therefore, that a non-churchly "institutional context" for the critical interpretation of the Bible is needed to protect the integrity of the freedom of "critical research." In order to guard the freedom of biblical interpretation from a tradition of doctrine and interpretation (from ideology) such that the believing community is able to remain open to the impact of critical research, Barr suggests that the institutional locus of biblical interpretation and research not be confined to the believing community, but be willingly shared with a broader academic world. "Unless this is done," says Barr, "the Bible will be imprisoned in the categories of the present religious community and will cease to have any new message to deliver."[30] All too often, claims Barr, Christians have engaged in a

---

23 In *The Bible in the Modern World* Barr makes the point that it is impossible to read the Bible as a document of faith without a theology. For reading the Bible in a non-theological mode would be to practice interpretation on a "purely historical or literary level." He continues, "The task of a theology is to guide, to inform and to discipline the affirmations of faith made by Christians." Ibid., p. 133.

24 While Barr does affirm that discoveries may take place in the confessional reading of Scripture, there can be no doubt that, for him, the critical (non-confessional reading that takes place in the atmosphere of scholarly freedom) is far more promising. *Holy Scripture*, p. 108.

25 *The Scope and Authority of the Bible*, p. 25.

26 Ibid.

27 Ibid., p. 24.

28 "Exegesis as a Theological Discipline Reconsidered," p. 13.

29 *Holy Scripture*, p. 31. Barr construes this failure to listen to the Bible over a doctrinal heritage as a failure of constructive theological imagination. See "Exegesis as a Theological Discipline Reconsidered," p. 14.

30 "The Bible as a Document of Believing Communities," p. 37. John Barton writes, "Biblical critics . . . are not people who attack or diminish the text, but those who let the text speak, removing the wrappings which ecclesial authority or personal piety have placed around it." "James Barr as Critic and Theologian," p. 21.

164   *Revelation, Holy Scripture and Church*

sectarian study of the Bible which insulates them against biblical data, even when it is quite clear or unanimous, by censoring critical inquiry. But by including the total scholarly community within the scope of biblical research, the church is positioned such that it will remain open to the consideration of new critical biblical insights, which might impinge on its accepted doctrinal tradition. In this way Scripture may also address the church "other than through the mediation of our own tradition."[31]

A second reason for the scholarly guild as a locus of biblical interpretation has to do with the relative "objectivity" Barr accords to the historical-critical study of the Bible. On Barr's view, an alliance with the academy is possible because of the "objectivity" and inter-disciplinary nature of the historical-critical method of research. For unlike theological study and exegesis, which takes place under theological convictions, the critical study of the Bible is "comparatively free" from sectarian interest, that is, its results "are not predetermined by a given authoritative ideology."[32] The work of a particular scholar is not measured, in this wider academic community, by its relation to theological presuppositions "but by the relation between his opinion and the evidence."[33]

This is not to suggest that the community of biblical scholars do not work with presuppositions or that individual scholars are not motivated in their study by personal religious commitment. But these presuppositions and commitments are not permitted to be imposed on the inductive study of the Bible in the critical community. "[T]he person of faith-commitment should, in the face of biblical material, to some extent hold his or her faith-commitment in suspense."[34] Working as it does with the "factual realities of the Bible,"[35] (i.e. the objectivities of the text itself), critical research resists broad theoretical (theological) convictions, which might skew or prohibit inquiry into the appropriate field of evidence.[36] In the world of critical scholarship,

---

31 *Holy Scripture*, pp. 110-111. Biblical study, writes Barr, "can fully serve the context of the church only in so far as it respects also the integrity of modes of study and interpretation, valid with that community [the wider academic community] over which theology as theology cannot pronounce." *The Scope and Authority of the Bible*, p. 28.

32 *Holy Scripture*, p. 114.

33 *The Scope and Authority of the Bible*, pp. 27-28. Barr is aware of the criticism that there are no facts without interpretation. However, he calls this a "comforting half truth," and insists that "it remains perfectly possible, even if difficult, to distinguish between factual and nonfactual." Barr continues, "[T]he distinction is essential for the task of weighing and evaluating what purport to be interpretations." See "Exegesis as a Theological Discipline Reconsidered," p. 40 and *History and Ideology in the Old Testament*, pp. 49-50.

34 *The Concept of Biblical Theology*, p. 205. See also *History and Ideology in the Old Testament*, pp. 47-48.

35 "Modern Biblical Criticism," p. 319. These factual realities consist of the style, genre, form, historical frame, overarching theme, use of language, etc., of a given biblical passage. For a reading to be regarded as a legitimate reading, a scholar must marshal evidence from these realities, without special pleading to a theological conviction or broad theoretical considerations.

36 The more that research into various fields became important as "the standard and criterion for judging the validity of exegesis," says Barr, "the more the context of biblical understanding broadened beyond the church to include the total academic community—the humanities and sciences. For it was to these fields that questions raised by biblical scholarship

The Church and the Bible Critically Read   165

a biblical exegete must make a case based upon a persuasive appeal to the relevant evidence critically reconstructed apart from confessional special pleading. While this is always a more or less probable enterprise, it does provide an "objectivity" which sets biblical study free from "denominational allegiance as a criterion or test of validity."[37]

In response to the argument that the analysis of biblical literature must always begin from a position of religious commitment, "which would perceive the material as canonical Scripture, authoritative in the community," Barr responds that this would divide scholars into two distinct groups—"one working from religious commitment and the other not."[38] It is very unlikely that those who espouse this point want this result. Moreover, Barr claims that having worked in both theological institutions and university departments, "I cannot see that there is any fundamental difference in exegetical method, logic or criteria of relevance between one case and the other."[39] The only commitment which is requisite for participation in the critical study of the Bible is, according to Barr, "an interest in doing this sort of critical work."[40]

The Listening Church and Critical Scholarship

One of the ways in which the central task of modern biblical hermeneutics has often been put, under the influence of the historical-critical study of the Bible is this: given our knowledge of the "original historical" meaning of the Bible rooted in the conditions of its production, how do we move to a sense which is relevant and meaningful for the life of the church today? There is in the critical study of the Bible an historical gap that is opened up and intensified by rooting meaning in the circumstances of a text's production. The challenge for the interpreter is thus to bring this meaning forward out of the world of a text's production and into the present life of the church. However, although this may be "the great question as posed by twentieth-century biblical hermeneutics,"[41] it is not Barr's way of addressing the issue of the churchly application of the critical study of the Bible.

On Barr's view, this understanding of the hermeneutic challenge is forgetful of the fact that in practice "the church establishes the network of familiar relations within which its Scriptures are known and understood."[42] Because these books are

---

and to which traditional church doctrine had no answer, that criticism turned." *Holy Scripture*, pp. 108-109.

37 Ibid., p. 113.

38 *Holy Scripture*, p. 111. Barr has Brevard Childs' "Canonical Criticism" in view here, although it is doubtful that Childs actually holds this view. See Childs, *The New Testament as Canon*, pp. 31ff.

39 "Exegesis as a Theological Discipline Reconsidered," p. 19.

40 *Holy Scripture*, p. 111. Barr echoes these same words with respect to whether faith commitment is necessary to participate in the biblical theology enterprise. He maintains that based on what has been written in biblical theology, no more than "an *interest* in theology and an *empathy* with it" are required of its practitioners. Emphasis is Barr's. *The Concept of Biblical Theology*, p. 194.

41 *Holy Scripture*, p. 45.

42 Ibid., p. 43. See also *The Bible in the Modern World*, p. 138.

166   *Revelation, Holy Scripture and Church*

accorded a special status (as canonical Scripture) they have not, and are not, left "encapsulated within their original culture"[43] but are constantly given a hermeneutical updating by their continued use within the church. As the church reads, studies, expounds and uses the Scriptures in its liturgical life, this set of texts continues to provide "the frame of reference for understanding" such that every person who takes "their religion seriously" will know that "it is these books, 'the Bible', that have a clear and special association with their own present day church."[44] Only in the case of canonical Scripture is there the expectation that the Word of God will be heard within the contemporary church. And thus the supposed distance between the world of a text's production and the present life of the church is closed, not by a hermeneutic method, but by the church's continued and expectant use of the Bible as Holy Scripture.

And yet, given Barr's account of the hermeneutic updating of the Bible through the church's continuing use of it as canonical Scripture, what are we to make of the free and therefore critical inquiry into the meaning of the Bible by the scholarly guild? Is the meaning of the Bible now "uncritically" rooted in the church's use of Scripture ruled by inherited theological doctrine? Not at all. In the first place, the church needs to give the primary place in its preaching, thinking and meditation to the careful and detailed interpretation of the Bible. In its preaching, for example, the church must make sure that it does not let contemporary theological questions, the topical treatment of biblical texts, and especially the mere rehearsal of traditional religious convictions, displace preaching which is in some sense related to biblical texts. "First place," writes Barr, "should be given to the search for the meaning of Scripture itself; this is what the community needs, and wants, to hear."[45]

In the second place, the believing community, as it listens for the Word of God for today in the canonical Scriptures, is still responsible to listen also to free critical scholarship. The way in which Barr construes the hermeneutic situation is thus: "given the church's readiness to hear the Scripture as the Word of God for today, how is that hearing to be modified, refined, and clarified through our knowledge of the actual character of the biblical text, as mediated through critical, historical and other sorts of knowledge?"[46] Here we have come full circle with Barr. For this critical mode of inquiry, intent as it is upon investigating the factual realities of the Bible that ground its meaning, can modify, refine and clarify the churchly interpretation and use of the Bible, such that they are not simply overrun by "traditional doctrine" or churchly use. Indeed, Barr goes so far as to claim that "the effectiveness of the Bible as a document of the believing community is related to the extent to which the

---

43 Ibid.

44 Ibid. "Indeed part of belonging to the Christian community is a continual reading of Scripture, especially in worship." See also John Barton, *People of the Book? The Authority of the Bible in Christianity* (Louisville, 1993), p. 60.

45 "The Bible as a Document of Believing Communities," p. 36.

46 Ibid., p. 46. Here Barr is pointing to the way in which "truth" (linguistic analyses, the perception of diverse sources, sociological situations behind the text, which in effect generate a text, etc.) is always the "final criterion for theology" (as opposed to relevance). *Holy Scripture*, p. 118.

study of it is shared by the believing community with the academic world."[47] For the Bible's ability to "speak afresh"[48] and deliver a "new message"[49] to the Christian church is, at least in part, dependent upon the church's openness to listening to and participating in the conversation of biblical critics in the academy.

In sum: in order to facilitate the work of the biblical scholar, the doctrinal heritage of the church must be suspended. The freedom of the interpreter to follow research wherever it may lead directly implies, for Barr, the suspension of received meanings, which may otherwise circumscribe the derivation of non-traditional ones. Second, the reading of Scripture has at least two social loci. When read as a document of the believing community the Bible is ruled by theological presuppositions. These presuppositions enable the church to construe the Bible in ways that guide, inform and discipline the claims of faith made by believers. Biblical scholars within the church have shown, in many cases, that firm conviction is compatible with a close listening to the texts of the Bible. However, it is the scholarly guild—where there is freedom to follow research wherever it may lead—that gives relative objectivity to the process of biblical interpretation. In this social locus, sectarian denominational prejudice has little sway, since proposed readings stand or fall by their relation to the evidence. While the church does carry on biblical interpretation which serves its own doctrinal heritage, it falls to critical scholars to ensure that denominational prejudice does not run over the text.

Third, Barr proposes that the use of the Scriptures by the church within its own life is to be "modified, refined and clarified" by the deliverances of critical research if such use is to be licit. For while the use of Scripture within the church provides the means whereby they are brought into the present as living texts, the use of the Bible must be regulated by the actual nature of the texts. The church's use of biblical texts is dependent therefore upon the deliverances of the scholarly guild if such use is to be responsible to the factual realities of the Bible. Hearing a "new message" from the Scriptures, letting the Bible "speak afresh" in the church, is related to the measure in which the church will share its study of the Bible with the academic world.

Critique

In the critique that follows a case is made against Barr that his construal of the mode, institutional locus and use of the Bible by the church as dependent upon historical criticism within the scholarly guild (where theological conviction and Christian faith even where they exist are bracketed out for the sake of criticism), is problematic both in terms of the coherence of the proposal and its compatibility with and practical usefulness to the life of the Christian church. The cogency of Barr's proposal is problematic since he maintains that confessional warrants, which are the grounds for his critical approach, at the same time requires their suspension. Moreover, the subject matter, "the Bible," is a confessional construct, which no longer presents itself as a whole when it is divorced from its doctrinal construal. What is more,

---

47 "The Bible as a Document of Believing Communities," pp. 36-37
48 Ibid., p. 37.
49 Ibid.

168   *Revelation, Holy Scripture and Church*

when Barr successfully brackets out theological constructs and faith commitment from critical biblical research, the interpretative disposition (mastery) toward the text of the Bible sits in tension with a listening to the Bible as Holy Scripture. Moreover, such an account can tend toward ascribing to a conversation between communities of interpretation, academic and ecclesial, what belongs to God. In short, Barr's construal of the hermeneutic field in which theological conviction and faith commitment are suspended in the interpretation of the Bible for the sake of the church is not consistently and thoroughly oriented to the object which faith confesses and upon which it depends for the hearing of Holy Scripture as the Word of God.

A theological argument for the suspension of doctrine?   Barr's justification for the "free" historical-critical examination of the Bible as a licit and indeed helpful mode of reading for the life of the church verges on a conceptual tangle. The justification he provides for the suspension of theological belief in order critically to read the Bible is theological. "[I]n turning to the Bible in itself, critical scholarship was still following what the churches had professed, namely that the interpretation was subject to the biblical text."[50] Based on the authority of Scripture and justification by faith, both of which are central to Protestant confessional standards, interpreters ought to suspend such beliefs for the sake of iconoclastic "free" reading. Presumably, then, historical-critical reading does not suspend all theological belief; for confessional standards operate at the level of warranting the very practice said to bracket them out for the sake of their application. It is difficult to imagine how a coherent case could be made on Barr's terms.[51] A coherent account would require either that Barr dispense with a theological justification for non-theological reading altogether or that he render his account of historical-critical reading in such a way as to put it in the service of what faith confesses. In the case of the latter, an examination of biblical texts might be undertaken critically to examine the faithfulness and integrity of a particular theological conviction in the service of faith, but not by means of the suspension of the entirety of the church's confession. Indeed, part of what would enable the critical examination of a particular aspect of church dogma vis-à-vis Scripture would be its coherence with a Christocentric, Trinitarian rule of faith reading and interpretation of it. Thus a critical reading of a church doctrine would take place by examining it against the "Bible," which is itself a theological construct (with Old and New Testaments in a Christocentric unity).

In Barr's deployment of a theological rationale for the critical examination of the Bible, he also conflates the Enlightenment spirit of free inquiry into the biblical materials with the Reformers understanding of Christian freedom arising from justification by faith.[52] This attempt demonstrates a failure to appreciate the degree to which the notion of freedom for the Enlightenment differs in great measure from

---

50 *History and Ideology in the Old Testament*, p. 49. Barr's emphasis.

51 See Moberly, *The Bible, Theology, and Faith*, p. 5. Moberly makes the point that critical exegesis stands in a "curious situation;" that is, in order to render a critical account of biblical texts for Christian belief and practice, one excludes Christian belief and practice from the interpretative process.

52 See *Holy Scripture*, p. 35.

The Church and the Bible Critically Read

that of the Reformers. Luther's most radical comments about the content of the canon, for example, when he designates James as "an epistle of straw," are not made in the spirit of Kantian free critical inquiry; rather, this is a theological judgment made in the light of his understanding of the canonical centrality of the doctrine of justification by faith. Paul Althaus writes, "It was particularly within the canon that Luther practiced theological criticism of its individual parts. The standard of this criticism is the same as his principle of interpretation, that is, Christ: the gospel of free grace and justification through faith alone."[53] Barr has proposed a similarity between Luther and the Enlightenment spirit of free inquiry, which, at best, is too forcefully put. Moreover, by pointing to Luther's theologically critical reading of the Bible founded on the centrality of Christ and the freedom which justification by faith engenders, Barr has pointed to a species of "free" and "critical" inquiry that, unlike his own proposal, does not bracket out central Christian dogmatic convictions in the reading of Holy Scripture, but rather relies on them for both its "critical" and "free" character.

What is more, Barr's suggestion that the Reformers' notion of Christian freedom stands in close proximity to the Enlightenment's tradition of free-critical inquiry obscures the degree to which "critical methods can generate what by theological standards is a false stance toward Scripture as a field of divine communication."[54] In the critical mode of reading that Barr promotes, which will resort to the approximate equivalent of secular freedom if the church will not offer the liberty toward the text that historical-critical method requires, a certain alienating distance from the context of the church is opened up. No longer is the Bible Holy Scripture, that is read as a single Christocentric book under a Trinitarian rule of faith—an orientation *reflected in* the church's direct involvement with the Bible in its "normed norms" of liturgical, devotional, catechetical and homiletical practice—but as fragments of ancient middle eastern literature. However, to read the Bible in a manner in which "the gospel is not followed" is not to read the Bible as Scripture at all. Robert Jenson comments, "We will either read the Bible under the guidance of the church's established doctrine, or we will not read the Bible at all. When we attempt dogmatically rebellious or ignorant readings of the Scripture, we will find only *dissecta membra* in our hands."[55] Moreover, read "critically," as Barr uses the term, the deference and humility toward

---

53 Paul Althaus, *The Theology of Martin Luther*, trans. Robert C. Schultz (Philadelphia, 1966), p. 82. See also Brevard Childs, Review of *Holy Scripture: Canon, Authority, Criticism* by James Barr, *Interpretation*, 38 (January, 1984): 70. Childs writes:

His call for freedom in research is certainly not wrong, but the issue lies in whether one can so easily identify the biblical understanding of freedom in Christ with the concept of freedom espoused by the Enlightenment. Have we not learned anything from the struggle of Augustine with Pelagius or Luther with Erasmus? Or how convincing is the appeal to the Pauline doctrine of justification by faith as a warrant for the use of modern biblical criticism . . . to have it now echoed from Oxford's bastions of rationality seems strangely incongruous, to say the least.

54 Webster, *Holy Scripture*, p. 104.

55 Robert Jenson, "Hermeneutics and the Life of the Church," in Carl E. Braaten and Robert Jenson (eds), *Reclaiming the Bible for the Church* (Grand Rapids, 1995), p. 98. See also Moberly, *The Bible, Theology, and Faith*, pp. 11-12. "It [the Bible] is a collection whose

170   *Revelation, Holy Scripture and Church*

the subject matter of the Bible, again reflected in the church's direct involvement with the Bible in its liturgical, devotional, catechetical and homiletical use, are replaced by an anthropology of competence and mastery.[56]

For Christian readers and hearers of Scripture, who comport themselves in a manner appropriate to the subject matter of the Bible, one listens in the spirit of receptivity and passivity with a teachable spirit; reading the Bible is a matter of discipline and devotion and dependence upon the mercy of God.[57] Because of God's effective agency by means of the church's use of the text, Bible reading is "inexhaustibly fecund" and the Bible can never be "discarded nor dominated."[58] In the monastic practice of *lectio divina* in which three different kinds of Bible reading are practiced (worship, prayer, and reading or hearing the Bible for nourishment) the unity of spiritual reading, that is, reading deferential to and dependent upon the grace of God, is witnessed.[59] Reading is likened to eating, such that *lectio* is inseparable from rumination or *meditatio*, understood as prayer and contemplation.[60] Barr, however, tends to minimize this orientation to Holy Scripture in the church for the sake of "criticism" in which the Bible is submitted to non-scriptural reading. A liability of this approach, as Webster notes, is that because of the anthropology of mastery that underlies it, "the professional interpreter transcends the event of God's self-communication, and so is not a part of the same spiritual economy as church and Scripture."[61] Instead of assisting the church in its task of Scripture reading and interpretation under God, it may be that critical readings, as envisaged by Barr, in so far as they search for a standpoint for biblical interpretation outside the purview of the one given by God in Jesus Christ, could be construed as acts of resistance against it.

Factual realities and faith commitment   There are at least two important points to be made against Barr's understanding of the relationship of the biblical scholarly

---

coherence depends on the assumption that the texts relating to Jesus of Nazareth belong with, and interpret, the antecedent Scriptures of Israel." Ibid., p. 12.

56 See Webster, *Holy Scripture*, pp. 104-105.

57 See Kort, "*Take, Read*," pp. 19-36. See also Paul J. Griffiths, *Religious Reading: The Place of Reading in the Practice of Religion* (Oxford, 1999), pp. 42-54.

58 These phrases are taken from James Fodor, Review of *Religious Reading: The Place of Reading in the Practice of Religion* by Paul Griffiths, *Modern Theology*, 17/4 (October, 2001): 529.

59 See Kort, "*Take, Read*," p. 23; Griffiths, *Religious Reading*, pp. 18-19.

60 Kort, *Take, Read*," p. 23. Kort is here describing the tradition of *lectio divina* as appropriated by Calvin. He makes the point that by focusing on reading as eating, "the most intimate concepts of Scripture are not addressed to the "rational" intellect, but to an understanding derived by taste (Ibid., p. 140, n. 13) such that "by reading one receives the text with the *palatum cordis*." Ibid., p. 23.

61 Ibid., pp. 104-105. See also Francis Watson, "The Quest for the Real Jesus," in Markus Bockmuehl (ed.), *The Cambridge Companion to Jesus* (Cambridge, 2001), p. 160. Watson writes, "From that perspective [the historian's], one cannot speak of God; from the other perspective [Christian faith], one cannot but speak of God. The common ground between the two perspectives—which is sometimes very striking—should not be allowed to mask this fundamental difference."

The Church and the Bible Critically Read 171

guild to the church in the interpretation of Holy Scripture. The first relates to an issue of coherence. Moberly writes, "Barr's brief allusion to confessing theology, and his depiction of it as optional within biblical study which can thus flourish without it, could leave his reader wholly innocent of the fact that the Bible is itself a confessing construct."[62] In other words, Barr's account of the academic study of the artifact "Bible" presupposes a subject matter quite impossible apart from the relation of these texts to the communities for which they function. These texts were given shape and contour by Jews and Christians who collected them together for religious life. Barr assumes a Christian Bible, Old Testament and New Testament, to be studied independent of confessional "ideology," which is itself shaped by Christian ideological confession. "It is a collection whose coherence depends on the assumption that the texts relating to Jesus of Nazareth appropriately belong with, and interpret, the antecedent Scriptures of Israel."[63] Moreover, in addition to the implication of a "delimited canon" and a "particularistic community," the very concept of the Bible implies "reading according to its own transcendentally based conventions in accordance with its own identity-conferring structures."[64] In other words, bracket out the confessional life, "the religious conviction" of the community upon whom these texts have imposed themselves, and there is no self-defined object "Bible" present for critical inquiry. It is an "optical illusion" to suppose that there is a book, the Bible, "which can self-evidently stand on its own . . ."[65] Taken out of the church, all that is left of the Bible are fragments of ancient religious movements.[66] Without the deployment of a fundamental faith construct, which Barr wants to avoid for the sake of critical objectivity, biblical studies sits uneasily poised between the faculties of Theology and Near Eastern Studies.

However, consistency can be purchased at the expense of those features implicit in the theological construct "Bible" that are central to the community for which the Bible functions. The same series of texts can be construed and studied on a reconfigured interpretative field. The "ideological" construal of the Bible as a unity around Jesus of Nazareth as the fulfillment of the Scriptures can be subverted to other construals in which a "faith commitment" or constructs of faith (doctrine and creeds) are not operative. Barr seems to move in this direction. "By dispensing with a need for a faith commitment, Barr casts his lot not with traditional religious communities of interpretation, but with that community that is the modern pluralistic university."[67] Barr believes that in this space, under a non-theological construal of

---

62 Moberly, *The Bible, Theology, and Faith*, p. 11.

63 Ibid., p. 12.

64 Levenson, "Negative Theology," p. 60.

65 Moberly, *The Bible, Theology, and Faith*, p. 12. Moberly writes (p. 14):
There is thus a nice irony in the fact that the recurrent rhetoric on the part of biblical scholars about freeing the Bible from ecclesiastical and dogmatic presuppositions so that it can speak for itself, tends to coexist largely uncomplainingly with the preservation of that ecclesiastical and dogmatic construct, the Bible itself.

66 Jenson, "Hermeneutics and the Life of the Church," pp. 89-90. See also "Scripture's Authority in the Church," pp. 27-28.

67 Levenson, "Negative Theology," p. 60. Alvin Plantinga notes that for historical-critical research, "one theme that seems to command nearly universal assent . . . is that in

172   *Revelation, Holy Scripture and Church*

the interpretative field, edifying results for the church will obtain; new and fresh readings of the Bible for the life of the church will emerge.

The second issue for consideration is that of cooperation. Is the relationship of dependence of the church upon a non-confessional "critical" reading of the Bible within the academy, one which escapes ideology and is comparatively free from sectarian interest, really as Barr depicts it? Barr seems to assume that within the church the interpretation of the Bible can be held captive to "present ideologies" whereas in the university scholars work exclusively with "the factual realities." However this is a false picture of the interpretative field; for as Francis Watson maintains against Barr, "there is no such thing as a pure description of a neutral object; description always presupposes a prior construction of the object in terms of a given interpretative paradigm."[68] In other words, what counts as a "factual reality," and its meaning and place on the interpretative field, is determined by the interpretative paradigm (ideology) with which interpreters work. And, on an historical-critical depiction of the hermeneutic field (one from which theological conviction and faith commitment is expunged), biblical texts are "historical artifacts—chance remnants of a previous stage in human history—whose meaning is wholly determined by their historical circumstances of origin."[69]

However, this construal of the reality of the Bible by virtue of its non-confessional nature (its naturalist ontology) leaves out of consideration precisely those features of the text (by virtue of its relation to God) that shape specifically Christian interpretative habits and practices and render the Bible vital to the life of the church. While there is some overlap of "factual realities" which impinge on the interpretation of the Bible, shared by confessional and non-confessional readings, and thus a measure of cooperation and learning that ought to be shared,[70] the failure of "critical" method to take account of all the "evidence" due to its deflationary presuppositions renders it of limited value to the church's task of Scripture interpretation. Alvin Plantinga notes that various forms of the practice of historical-critical study (all of which are

---

working at this scientific project (however exactly it is to be understood) you do not invoke or employ any theological assumptions or presuppositions." "Two (or More) Kinds of Scripture Scholarship," p. 251.

68 Watson, *Text, Church and World*, p. 33. See also Barr, *The Concept of Biblical Theology*, pp. 201-202. Here Barr offers no material criticism of Watson's position, only *ad hominem* comments. Jon Levenson, in his review of Barr's book, maintains that while Barr complains that Watson's observation about observation being theory-laden is one "proclaimed a hundred times" and an "unoriginal thought," it ought to be repeated. Levenson writes, "Perhaps in a field in which scholars strive to differentiate sharply between 'what it meant' and 'what it means'—even assigning the question to different disciplines—the thought needs to be proclaimed a hundred and one times." "Negative Theology," p. 61.

69 Watson, *Text, Church and World*, p. 33.

70 Jenson remarks that "the Church may happily receive any and all insights such [historical-critical] investigations stumble across or information they make available. But such activity is not and cannot be *exegesis* of texts from the volume we call the Bible . . . What justifies churchly reading of Scripture is that there is no other way to read it, since 'it' dissolves under other regimes." "Scripture's Authority in the Church," p. 28. Emphasis Jenson's.

proceed on the basis of reason alone, without employing theological assumptions or anything known by faith) are insufficiently realist, imperiously delimiting the field of inquiry by a prior declaration regarding the realities with which the Bible is concerned and how best to account for them.[71] The church ought therefore to be cautious about the degree to which its reading is "shared" with the academy since the assumptions operative in many forms of historical-critical reading exclude from the outset the action of God—Father, Son and Holy Spirit—by which the Bible as Holy Scripture and the church as a creature of the Word are evoked, sustained and reading conventions appropriate to them engendered. Stephen Fowl writes:

> Christians [ought to be cognizant] . . . that their particular interests and concerns with Scripture, as well as their specific interpretative convictions and habits, are not the same as, if not directly opposed to, those of the profession of biblical studies. There may not be outright enmity, but there is not much fruitful cooperation either . . . As a result, the work of biblical scholars must always be appropriated in an *ad hoc* way, on a case-by-case basis.[72]

A new hearing   Barr holds to the position that the church's actual use of the Bible sets the frame of reference for the ongoing meaningfulness of the Bible to the life of the church. Barr is not especially troubled by the distance opened up between the historical world of the Bible's production and the present circumstances of the community for which it functions since "the church establishes the network of familiar relations within which its Scriptures are known and understood."[73] In other words, the distance between the world of a text's production and the present life of the church is closed, not by a hermeneutical method, but by the church's expectant use and diligent search of the Bible for what "the community needs, and wants, to hear."[74] Hermeneutical updating of Scripture is a function of communal use. Barr does not introduce a doctrine of the Holy Spirit into his ecclesial account of "hermeneutical updating" and thus, in keeping with his immanentist construal of the hermeneutic situation, his depiction is a human/communal one. The text of the Bible is made relevant to the present circumstances of the life of the church by interpretative communal action. Moreover, in its listening to the Bible, the church must also listen to the deliberative results of the academic study of the Bible and modify its hearing of Scripture accordingly. Indeed, the "effectiveness" of the Bible, by which Barr means the ability of the Bible to "speak afresh" and deliver a "new

---

71 Plantinga, "Two (or More) Kinds of Scripture Scholarship," pp. 250-274.

72 Stephen E. Fowl, *Engaging Scripture: A Model for Theological Interpretation* (Oxford, 1998), p. 183. In a footnote, Fowl cites Jon Levenson who remarks that the myth of cooperation between church and the scholarly guild of biblical interpreters "is almost always perpetrated by those who have already seriously, albeit unconsciously, compromised their specific Jewish or Christian convictions." See Levenson, "Theological Consensus or Historicist Evasion: Jews and Christians in Biblical Studies," in *The Hebrew Bible, The Old Testament and Historical Criticism* (Louisville, 1993) cited in *Engaging Scripture*, p. 183, n. 13.

73 *Holy Scripture*, p. 43.

74 "The Bible as a Document of Believing Communities," p. 36.

174   *Revelation, Holy Scripture and Church*

message," "is related to the extent to which the study of it [the Bible] is shared by the believing community with the academic one."[75]

Barr properly points to the importance of the church's attention to matters pertaining to the humanity of Scripture. The Bible is a human product whose compositional features—languages, syntactical structures and genre—as well as the history of its development, are realities about which interpreters must be informed in order adequately to interpret it. Should the church isolate itself from critical learning about such matters, it would impoverish its interpretative skill and render visible a docetic view of the Bible. Plantinga writes:

> Clearly, we are indebted to HBC [historical-biblical criticism]; it has enabled us to learn a great deal about the Bible we otherwise might not have known. Furthermore, some of the methods it has developed can be and have been employed to excellent effect in various studies of interest and importance, including traditional Biblical commentary.[76]

However, in so far as Barr renders an account of the Bible, which ascribes agency to it (an ability to speak afresh) and relates the effectiveness of this agency to "critical inquiry" he presents an incomplete picture of hearing the Word of God.

In the first place, there are theological questions as to what sort of "new message" would be delivered from a social location by means of an interpretative methodology that assumes, for example, the real Jesus must be rescued from the church, that objects of critical study must be free from theological contamination, that God does not intervene in history, that incarnation, resurrection and judgment are mythological, that resurrection narratives are legendary.[77] Karl R. Donfried, unlike Barr, is not persuaded that the study of Scripture in two locations (church and academy) has had or will have the edifying consequences for the church that Barr suggests. He writes:

> What has happened today is a shift in the context in which Scripture is interpreted, a shift from the church to the academy. This social shift has often forged a new alliance with the academy in opposition to the classical expressions of the Christian faith. In the name of history, which often is a pretense for an ideological theology, classical and normative expressions of Christian faith are frequently attacked, at times overtly and at times more invidiously and subtly.[78]

While critical scholars, like Barr, are sometimes concerned that the church in its life and preaching has been slow on the uptake where it comes to the results of

---

75 Ibid., p. 37.

76 Plantinga, "Two (or More) Kinds of Scripture Scholarship," p. 250. See also Childs, *Isaiah*, pp. 3-5 and Watson, *Text, Church and World*, pp. 227-228. Watson notes the positive function of historical understanding against an "over-anxious, defensive biblicism."

77 See Watson, *Text, Church and World*, p. 228; "The Scope of Hermeneutics," pp. 73-74; and Hays, "Reading Scripture in the Light of the Resurrection," p. 237.

78 Karl Donfried, "Alien Hermeneutics and the Misappropriation of Scripture," in Braaten and Jenson (eds), *Reclaiming the Bible for the Church*, p. 19.

critical examination of the Bible, [79] they should also be aware that this may simply be the result of the marginal implications of "the latest historical-critical hypothesis" to the task of preaching,[80] or that the "alleged results" of historical-critical inquiry "rest upon epistemological [and ontological] assumptions that [the church] does not share."[81] While Barr is correct in his contention that passing interpretation through the sieve of historical-critical inquiry from which theological conviction and faith commitment are bracketed out will yield "new" readings, the question is whether such readings will be congruent with the truth by which the church is created and sustained. Richard Hays notes, for example, that many preachers and New Testament scholars are "unwilling partisans of the Sadducees" since, "dogmatics does not permeate the whole course of their historical work,"[82] and thus, even though they are believers, they do not ask "how the resurrection—if it is true—ought to affect our methods for studying the history of the Synoptic traditions."[83]

Finally, Barr's sense of the effectiveness of the Bible as a "document of the church," that is, its ability to speak afresh to the church, is over-invested in the church's listening to and participating in the conversation of biblical critics in the academy and under-invested in the action of the sovereign and free God, who renders the Bible a vehicle of his own speech. While one needs a thorough knowledge of creaturely realities implicated by the fact of the Bible, it is God, who by a miracle of grace, transforms this human witness into a living and effective Word for the church:

> The Word of God is God himself speaking in Holy Scripture. For God once spoke as Lord to Moses and the prophets, to the Evangelists and apostles. And now through their written word He speaks as the same Lord to His Church. Scripture is holy and the Word of God, because by the Holy Spirit it became and will become to the Church a witness to divine revelation.[84]

---

79 See Plantinga, "Two (or More) Kinds of Scripture Interpretation," pp. 260-261. The section is entitled, "Why are not most Christians more Concerned?" i.e., about historical-critical interpretation of Scripture.

80 Watson, *Text, Church and World*, p. 228:

The frequent complaint that preachers do not show sufficient zeal in communicating to their hearers the results of historical-critical scholarship, fearful of the outrage they would cause were they to do so, is only justified in a limited sense; for this reticence also betrays an awareness that in this context the Bible and its interpretation is expected to offer something different than the latest historical-critical hypothesis.

81 Plantinga, "Two (or More) Kinds of Scripture Interpretation," pp. 244, 260. Plantinga maintains that Christians ought to maintain their acceptance of the "great things of the Gospel" and "anything else they accept on the basis of biblical teaching" since there are "good reasons for a traditional Christian to ignore the deflationary results of HBC" [historical-biblical criticism].

82 Adolf Schatter, "The Theology of the New Testament and Dogmatics," in R. Mogan (ed. and trans.), *The Nature of New Testament Theology: The Contribution of William Wrede and Adolf Schlatter*, SBT 2/25 (Naperville, IL, 1973), p. 126.

83 Hays, "Reading Scripture in the Light of the Resurrection," p. 238.

84 Barth, *Church Dogmatics*, 1/2: 457.

Paul Ricoeur: Suspicious Hermeneutics and Submissive Communities

Paul Ricoeur is alert to the fact that when one approaches the world of biblical interpretation, it is crucial to spell out the type or mode of reading one undertakes. For different approaches to reading the Bible, while they are not mutually exclusive, have different goals, serve distinct objectives and work with presuppositions that are specific and even opposite. While there are a great variety of hermeneutical aims and interests, in his own writings the interests of the hermeneutical philosopher and of one who belongs to a Christian tradition confront each other in the interpretation of the Bible. It is on the basis of these two "affiliations" that Ricoeur enters the world of biblical interpretation.[85]

In the first instance, Ricoeur's affiliations confront one another in his deployment of the hermeneutics of suspicion in the interpretation of the Bible by and for the community of faith.[86] Ricoeur maintains that the believer's confrontation with alternate "de-mystifying" readings of religion and religious texts provided by Marx, Nietzsche and Freud, while they are unavoidable in the modern world, need not engender cynicism. Indeed, for Ricoeur the confrontation is mutually enriching; that is, neither party will emerge intact from such an engagement. Moreover, maintains Ricoeur, it is not necessary that believers jeopardize their fundamental relationship of belonging to an historical community of faith in order to engage in a "suspicious" moment. Through the objectification of language in writing and the dynamic of distanciation—the freedom of texts from authorial intentions, readers and everyday description—a space is opened up within the interpretative drive toward appropriation into which the critique of ideology can enter. Where the masters of suspicion are engaged to unmask idols in the process of interpretation, believers are divested of false self-understandings, and a more authentic appropriation of the matter of the text is permitted.

Ricoeur's twin affiliations confront one another again when he considers the ways in which the believing community may read the Bible and how far philosophical thought may follow. On his assessment of the matter, there are a variety of modes in which historic communities of faith read their texts. There are comprehensive readings that aim at large construals of biblical thought using philosophical notions of cogency and involving philosophical concepts and language. Here the philosopher may follow since this is a "mixed mode" of thought. Canonical readings of the Bible aim at the intelligibility that these texts have for the community that has gathered, transmitted and uses them. It is at this stage that religious and philosophical readings begin to go their own ways. For here the idea of a privileged authoritative text and a dependent engendered community first arises. Philosophical thought can only follow with a sense of wonder at this stage. At the level of kerygmatic reading, the community is involved in self-definition as it deciphers and listens to the Bible.

---

85   See Ricoeur, *Critique and Conviction*, p. 139. See also Wallace, "From Phenomenology to Scripture?" p. 302.

86   See "Two Essays by Paul Ricoeur: The Critique of Religion and The Language of Faith," in *Union Seminary Quarterly Review*, 28/3 (Spring, 1973) and *Freud and Philosophy*, trans. Denis Savage (New Haven, 1970).

While there are critical internal moments actualizing one reading and suppressing another, there is no question of the asymmetry between founding text and founded community. This reading may be followed by "outsiders," who can empathetically enter the unique relation between text and community, but it most properly belongs to religious readers who venture that this textual ensemble contains a liberating word.

When Ricoeur reaches the level of kergymatic reading within a profession of faith, he notes that what distinguishes this style of reading from philosophical reading is finally a question of disposition and a willingness to put the text into practice. Kerygmatic reading is one which readily acknowledges its dependence on a founding word, its adherence to a word from beyond itself and its openness to comport itself to that word. To the "outside" reader dependence on a textually-mediated founding word—passed on within competing interpretative traditions—may appear circular, to the adherent it proves itself in the self-understanding and form of life it engenders. This transfer from "text to life" is guided by preaching and enacted in liturgy. The responses solicited by kergymatic reading and listening should not, however, be conflated to "the obedience of faith." The plurivocity of scriptural texts and kergymatic readings provoke modes of response equally diverse.

Following the exposition of Ricoeur's hermeneutic proposal for the critical and kergymatic reading of the Bible within the life of the church, a critique is offered. The critique consists in the contention that Ricoeur mutes the appropriative value of those critical features, which accrue to Holy Scripture by virtue of their relation to the Gospel, through a compulsory methodological correlation of them with the masters of suspicion (and the background anthropological commitments implied by suspicion). This correlation, while Ricoeur maintains that it takes place within a relationship of belonging, and that it is mutually purifying of both suspicious critique and proposed Scripture reading, nevertheless can subvert the integrity the scriptural reading of the Bible since it establishes "suspicious reading" as a *sine qua non* for Christian Bible reading and appropriation. Moreover, because kergymatic reading gains its integrity solely by way of interpretative clash with the masters of suspicion, that is, it must be achieved by iconoclastic interaction, such reading is over-invested in the idea that meaning must be "wrestled" from the text, won by human interpretative skill. Thus the perspicuity of Scripture, and meaning as a gift of the grace of God the Holy Spirit, do not figure predominantly in Ricoeur's consideration of the critical interpretation of the Bible for the life of the church.

Suspicious Reading

The deconstruction of prejudice and illusion constitute a crucial and distinctive aspect of the hermeneutic work of Ricoeur. For while he belongs to the hermeneutic school in which "understanding" necessitates belonging to an historical tradition, Ricoeur introduces the critical moment of "explanation" into his interpretation theory itself.[87]

---

87 A number of commentators regard this as among Ricoeur's most important contributions to philosophical and biblical hermeneutics. See for example John E. Smith, "Freud, Philosophy, and Interpretation," in Lewis E. Hahn (ed.), The Library of Living Philosophers, vol. 22: *The Philosophy of Paul Ricoeur* (Chicago, 1995), p. 156; Anthony

178 *Revelation, Holy Scripture and Church*

Located within the hermeneutic movement of interpretation toward the appropriation of meaning is the move to unmask or smash idols by way of structuralist-linguistic and socio-critical analysis.

Appropriating the external critique of the "masters of suspicion," Ricoeur is able to move hermeneutics toward a critically refined interpretation and appropriation of texts. On the one hand, the critique of religion by Marx, Nietzsche and Freud (as economic, philosophical or psychodynamic distortion), has the force of an outside critique, which "is not to be assimilated and baptized by force . . ."[88] These masters of suspicion have nurtured the modern context to the point that religion and religious interpretation will, without ever abolutizing the art of suspicion, have to face the challenge they represent. We are hereafter, as modern religious subjects and believing communities that desire mature faith, required to do business with the iconoclastic panoply of interpretation generated in work of Marx, Nietzsche and Freud. Ricoeur writes:

> What we have appropriated to ourselves is first, the critique of religion as a mask, a mask of fear, a mask of domination, a mask of hate. A Marxist critique of ideology, a Nietzschean critique of resentment and a Freudian critique of infantile distress, are hereafter the views through which any kind of mediation of faith *must* pass.[89]

Ricoeur does not want to imply that this external critique of religion functions in a purely negative fashion as a critical sieve through which the faith of the believer must pass to be legitimate. In the interaction between the "suspicious" interpretation of religion and the believer's appropriation of the meaning of texts of faith there is a critical exchange. For while "the faith of the believer cannot emerge intact from this confrontation . . . neither can the Freudian concept of reality."[90] This interaction is thus mutually purifying. The mechanistic, causal world-view, which is implicit in Freudian metaphors of interpretation, for example, comes under assault in Ricoeur.[91] On the other hand, writes Thiselton, "With regard to the biblical writings, this clearly implies that no appropriation is earned if it has not engaged with possible seductive explanations of the text."[92]

Thiselton, "Biblical Studies and Theoretical Hermeneutics," in John Barton (ed.), *The Cambridge Companion to Biblical Interpretation* (Cambridge, 1998), pp. 105-107; Anthony Thiselton, *New Horizons in Hermeneutics*, pp. 344ff.; Wallace, "Introduction," in *Figuring the Sacred*, pp. 7-10; Werner G. Jeanrond, *Theological Hermeneutics: Development and Significance* (New York, 1991), pp. 74-76; and Garrett Green, *Theology, Hermeneutics, and Imagination: The Crisis of Interpretation at the End of Modernity* (Cambridge, 2000), p. 11.

88 "Philosophical Hermeneutics and Biblical Hermeneutics," p. 100.

89 "Two Essays by Paul Ricoeur," p. 209. See also Erin White, "Between Suspicion and Hope: Paul Ricoeur's Vital Hermeneutic," *Journal of Literature and Theology*, 5/3 (November, 1991): 312.

90 *Freud and Philosophy*, p. 551.

91 Thiselton, "Biblical Studies and Theoretical Hermeneutics," p. 105.

92 Thiselton, *New Horizons in Hermeneutics*, p. 361. Ricoeur makes the case that the masters of suspicion offer a common critique of religion, which he calls de-mystification. The force of their critique of religion is not so much about the content thereof but more about the

The Church and the Bible Critically Read

The purpose of this explanatory moment of suspicion is, for the believing community, in the end, edifying. Ricoeur understands the work of the three masters of suspicion as positive for a post-critical faith. They enable religious interpretation to "destroy the idols,"[93] "to clear the horizon for a more authentic word, for a new reign of Truth"[94] or, as he writes in an earlier essay, "to smash the idols . . . to let the symbols speak."[95] In other words, each of these masters unmasks what is false in the interpretation of religion and religious texts for the sake of uncovering the true meaning of religion. David Stewart writes, "Far from being an attack on religion that explains it away, such critiques are purifying, even essential to religion."[96] Suspicion is in this way differentiated from skepticism in the sense that it is meant to clear away self-interested or erroneous interpretations (i.e. interpretation rooted in false-consciousness) for the sake of greater authenticity and expanded possibility. Criticism chastens naïve interpretation, but it works toward a second naïveté;[97] that is, re-reading in the mode of conviction.

The transposition of the external critique of religion into an *internal* one is, on Ricoeur's account, enabled by distanciation. The world of the poetic text, through inscription in writing, its genric shape and style, and its distance from everyday description and reality, has an "objectivity" over against the subjectivity of its authors and readers. Its alien matter or meaning, if it is to be appropriated, will thus entail "the critique of ideology," that is, the questioning of those prejudices, which prohibit the matter of the text from coming to be. For in order to appropriate the matter of a text, the prejudices of the reader, indeed the self of the reader, must be de-realized before the text so that the matter of the text is allowed emerge and present its fresh possibilities for the self.[98]

Ricoeur maintains that this critical moment *within* text interpretation does not supplant the fundamental relationship of belonging to tradition. Attentive to Gadamer's criticisms of alienating distance, which sits askance of belonging to and participation in an historical tradition for the sake of objectivity,[99] Ricoeur maintains

---

origin. They offer powerful and perceptive counter explanations for the origin of religion—in false consciousness—in order to restore "man's positivity." "Critique of Religion," p. 208.

93 *Freud and Philosophy*, p. 54.

94 Ibid., p. 33.

95 "Critique of Religion," p. 209.

96 David Stewart, "The Hermeneutics of Suspicion," *Journal of Literature and Theology*, 3/3 (November, 1989): 298.

97 The term is Ricoeur's. In the context of its use in *Freud and Philosophy*, p. 28, Ricoeur is making the point that hermeneutics has a double motivation: "willingness to suspect, willingness to listen." The suspicious mode enables faith on the far side of criticism, a post-critical faith. Ibid., p. 27. See Jeanrond, *Theological Hermeneutics*, p. 74.

98 See "Philosophical and Theological Hermeneutics," p. 100.

99 In a number of important essays, Ricoeur considers how he can introduce a critique of ideology into hermeneutics without destroying the "fundamental and primordial relation whereby we belong to and participate in the historical reality that we claim to construct as an object." "The Hermeneutical Function of Distanciation," p. 131. See also "Hermeneutics and the Critique of Ideology," pp. 63-100; "Phenomenology and Hermeneutics," pp. 101-128; and

180 *Revelation, Holy Scripture and Church*

that his text-based notion of distanciation is properly conceived of as a moment of belonging. Ricoeur writes:

> The concept of distanciation is the dialectical counterpart of the notion of belonging, in that sense that we belong to an historical tradition through a relation of distance which oscillates between remoteness and proximity. To interpret is to render near what is far (temporally, geographically, culturally, spiritually).[100]

As adherents interpret the texts of their traditions, texts that give them mediated access to their founding events, and respond to the matter before them in the text, they engage in a suspicious reading of the self in front of the text. For if they are to appropriate what is unfamiliar, novel, at variance with their subjectivity ("render near what is far"), they must disappropriate a fixed self-understanding to do so. Into the space opened up by the distanciation of poetic texts from their authors and readers and everyday description, there enters a challenge to, a critique of, the illusions of the subject. And it is here that the critique of ideology, in a Marxist, Freudian, Nietzschean manner, enters into a hermeneutic of self-understanding before the text. For the tools of deconstruction are usefully employed to expose, smash and overturn in order that the "matter" of the text can have its way with the subjectivity of the reader.

Shared Readings

Not all readings of the Bible involve, aim at, presuppose or are receptive to the moment of "non-violent" appeal to the imagination of the reader before the texts, that is, to what Ricoeur calls "revelation." On Ricoeur's account there are comprehensive, canonical and kergymatic readings of Scripture. Each of these readings works with a specific goal in view and with a particular disposition toward the text. Comprehensive reading, or descriptive theology, is more or less oriented to the large construal of biblical thought.[101] It is in greater conversation with philosophical thought than either canonical or kergymatic readings since questions of cogency and the use of conceptual language from philosophy (and other fields) make it a mixed mode of thought.[102] Comprehensive readings are multiple since, as historical critics have shown, they have been and are ruled by different norms. In any case, descriptive (or dogmatic) theology, maintains Ricouer, "consists in a conceptual and discursive ordering of predication, which relates a word held to

---

"Science and Ideology," pp. 222-246; all in John B. Thompson (ed.), *Hermeneutics and the Human Sciences* (Cambridge, 1981).

100 "Phenomenology and Hermeneutics," pp. 110-111.

101 See "Toward a Narrative Theology: Its Necessities, Its Resources, Its Difficulties," pp. 247-248.

102 See LaCocque and Ricoeur, *Thinking Biblically*, pp. xvii-xviii where Ricoeur maintains that the conceptualization of early Christian Trinitarian and Christological discussion in Greek philosophical terms is neither "misfortune" nor "perversion." However, he notes that the "trajectory" of the readings of the Bible in which he engages in *Thinking Biblically* has "a broader range" and "embraces the whole history of reception." Ibid., p. xviii.

The Church and the Bible Critically Read   181

be founding with a circumstantial judgment on the present and the future of the communities of faith."[103]

Canonical readings of the Bible mediate between kerygmatic and comprehensive readings. They function to alert the reader to the fact that historical-critical method is only one mode in which religious texts may be explored.[104] Canonical reading aims at the intelligibility of the received version of the texts that function for the community that has transmitted, sanctioned and uses them. Ricoeur contends that at the level of canonical reading, philosophical and religious readings begin to go their own ways. For implicit within the canonical reading of the Bible by a community which has received it, are the ideas of authority and privilege and their counterparts, dependence and submission. In the recognition and reception of these texts, apart from other texts and even faithful commentary, we verge on a "non-philosophical moment."[105]

The kind of reading, in which the reading community recognizes itself "as comprised, in every sense of the word, in and by this particular body of texts,"[106] and moves toward putting the texts into practice (i.e. kerygmatic reading), belongs most properly to those for whom this text functions religiously. That is to say, it belongs to those who have wagered that within this textual ensemble are contained the "figures of my liberation"[107] and/or the summons to authentic selfhood.[108] However people enter a religion,[109] it is constitutive of religious readers to privilege a word beyond themselves (i.e. a revealed word), as it is mediated through texts and understood within interpretative traditions.[110]

If "outside" readers want to follow the movement of biblical interpretation to the meaning these texts have for the communities in which they function religiously, Ricoeur indicates that they must enter, through "imagination and sympathy,"[111] the relationship that obtains between these founding texts and the communities founded by them. There is, maintains Ricoeur, a unique relationship between the texts of the biblical corpus and historical communities, Christian and Jewish, for whom these are founding texts, that is, in the interpretation of their Scriptures these communities

---

103 Ricoeur, *Critique and Conviction*, pp. 142-143.

104 See Thiselton, *New Horizons in Hermeneutics*, p. 368.

105 *Critique and Conviction*, p. 143. Ricoeur is attentive to "schools of thought" in philosophical circles, but maintains that the philosophical community "knows nothing comparable to the reception of a religious text by a historical community like that of the Jewish or Christian communities." *Thinking Biblically*, p. xvi.

106 *Thinking Biblically*, p. xvii.

107 "Philosophical Hermeneutics and Biblical Hermeneutics," p. 101.

108 See "The Summoned Subject in the School of the Narratives of the Prophetic Vocation," pp. 263ff. See also Wallace, "From Phenomenology to Scripture?," p. 302.

109 According to Ricoeur, some of the ways in which people enter into a religion are through birth, or transfer "by exile or hospitality." *Critique and Conviction*, p. 145.

110 Ibid. The religions he has in view are Judaism and Christianity, and occasionally Islam. See ibid., p. 146.

111 *Thinking Biblically*, p. xvii. This kind of empathy, according to Ricoeur, is the "minimum condition" for "outside" readers to gain access to the meaning of these (biblical) texts.

182
Revelation, Holy Scripture and Church

interpret themselves. "A kind of mutual election takes place here between those texts taken as foundational and the community we have deliberately called a community of reading and interpretation."[112] Religious or kerygmatic reading requires that the reader enter into this unique relation, a hermeneutic circle,[113] between a specific engendered community and a privileged engendering text in order to gain access to the meaning of these texts.[114]

This circle, however vicious it may appear in the philosophical domain,[115] is not, for the faithful, a partnership between equals. The founded community that reads and listens recognizes that there is an asymmetry between itself and its founding texts. It acknowledges itself as assembled, brought together, and held together by this particular group of texts in their partial and multiple readings.[116] Ricoeur notes that religious communities acknowledge the "authority"[117] that their texts have over them in their submission, reception and crediting of them, that is, in their kerygmatic use of them. He writes: "Even when this relation surpasses that between authority and obedience to become one of love, the difference in altitude between the word that teaches with authority and the one that responds with acknowledgement cannot be abolished."[118]

Kergymatic reading within the community of faith, although it works from the standpoint of adherence and acknowledges an asymmetry between itself and its founding texts, does include and generate "internal" critical discussion. Ricoeur notes that readings of faith have always been shaped by the expectations of readers and the spirit of the times.[119] This fact has generated critical discussions within communities of faith concerning licit conceptualizations and cultural shapings of the biblical kerygma in confessional theologies. Moreover, faith readings of founding texts always involve a prioritizing of canonical texts in relation to each other. Ricoeur uses the example of Luther construing the Bible in relation to the book of Romans and of Martin Luther King Jr's attempts to make the passage out of Egypt

---

112 Ibid. Elsewhere Ricoeur calls this "reciprocity" between community and text. See "The 'Sacred' Text and the Community," p. 69.

113 See *Critique and Conviction*, p. 145 and "Reply to David Detmer," in Hahn (ed.), *The Philosophy of Paul Ricoeur*, pp. 495-496.

114 Although Ricoeur is here referring to the Bible and access to its meaning by "sympathy and imagination," this would be the case of any outside reader of "any historical community that bases itself on any sacred corpus whatever." *Thinking Biblically*, pp. xvii.

115 It appears vicious, "a source of astonishment, even of perplexity" to the philosopher, maintains Ricoeur, since in the philosophical domain, "criticism carries the day over conviction." *Thinking Biblically*, p. xvi. See also "Reply to David Detmer," pp. 494-497.

116 *Thinking Biblically*, p. xvii.

117 See "The 'Sacred' Text and the Community," p. 70.

118 *Thinking Biblically*, p. xvii. See also "The 'Sacred' Text and the Community," p. 69.

119 *Critique and Conviction*, p. 144. Ricoeur writes, "kerygmatic interpretations are also multiple, always partial . . . varying according to the expectations of the public, itself shaped by a cultural environment bearing the imprint of the epoch."

the "supreme paradigm."[120] In each case, critical judgment is at work opening some possibilities and suppressing others.

Submissive Reading

"Outside" readers may follow, with no little astonishment, members of historical communities that read the Bible as a privileged text to gain the meaning that these texts have for the communities that use them. However, within the communities themselves, where a clearly delineated (canonical) Scripture is read and heard as an "authoritative text," readers, according to Ricoeur, are involved both in an act of self-definition and in a call to "pu[t] the texts into practice."[121] This kerygmatic (religious) reading of faith acknowledges its dependence on a earlier founding word, mediated through writing within a history of interpretation, and it involves judgments concerning how properly to comport oneself to it. While this mode of reading is not bereft of discriminating moments, its predominant ethos is not one of critique but, on Ricoeur's view, one of conviction, adherence, crediting a word "reputed to have come from further and from higher than myself."[122] In the reading and hearing of faith, it is the case that the reader (or community) is constituted by the subject matter of the definite textual ensemble of the Bible and that the reader (or community) listens to it in order to transfer text to life.

The difference between philosophical and religious reading is, for Ricoeur, largely a matter of attitude. As we have previously noted, within historical communities that read Scripture as authoritative, the predominant disposition toward the textual ensemble is submissive.[123] Religious readers "agree to enter or have already entered into this vast circuit involving a founding word, mediating texts and traditions of interpretation."[124] They regard as healthy, not vicious, says Ricoeur,[125] three hermeneutic circles in which they are complicit as listeners of Scripture. The first is between the Word of God and Scripture—God makes himself known by his Word and the Word is mediated only in the Scriptures. The second is between the canon of Scripture and the ecclesial community—the community establishes its identity by receiving and interpreting these texts and these founding texts are held to be the very ones upon which its identity is based. The third is between the community and the believer—the community recognizes itself as founded by these texts and the individual believer belongs by receiving an interpretation proposed by one of various communities interpreting these founding texts.[126] The attitude of personal reception or adhesion to this whole constellation of the self-presentation of the Word,

---

120 Ibid., pp. 144, 149. Kerygmatic readings thus involve "choices and decisions" about "the priority among the texts that 'speak to us.'" Ibid., p. 149.

121 Ibid., p. 149. See also "Reply to David Detmer," pp. 494-495.

122 *Critique and Conviction*, p. 144.

123 Ibid.

124 Ibid., p. 145.

125 See "Reply to David Detmer," pp. 494, 497; *Critique and Conviction*, p. 145; and *Thinking Biblically*, p. xvii.

126 See "Reply to David Detmer," pp. 494-495; *Critique and Conviction*, pp. 144-145; "Naming God," p. 217; and *Thinking Biblically*, p. xvii.

184 *Revelation, Holy Scripture and Church*

the attestation of Scripture and the recognition of the community as the source of its identity, are definitive of religious reading.

The reliance of the community of faith upon a carefully circumscribed body of founding texts, which transmits the self-presentation of God, is clearly observed in preaching.[127] Preaching, on Ricoeur's view, is "the permanent reinterpretation of the text that is regarded as grounding the community . . ."[128] As such, preaching resorts only to those texts which transmit the events recognized by the community as founding, that is, canonical Scripture:

> You preach on canonical texts, but not on profane; the community would be completely changed if you chose a modern poet to do a sermon, or if you took the Bhagavad Gita into the church. This is a crisis of the community because its own identity relies on the identity of the text . . .[129]

The religious community finds itself, therefore, prepared to listen to (wager on) only these texts. They assume that Scripture is worth hearing in the hope that what is risked in submissive listening will be "returned a hundredfold as an increase in comprehension, valor, and joy."[130] Proclamation thus turns to the "sacred texts"[131] of Scripture for a kergymatic reading within a profession of faith that fulfills the community's desire to hear and be guided to a self-understanding and life congruent with its founding events.[132]

In a dispute about atheism and evidence for belief in God, Ricoeur responds to David Detmer's request for evidence[133] by maintaining that there is "no evidence in a verificationist sense of the term."[134] However, Ricoeur continues his response by transposing the request for evidence into his construal of the relation between text and community. What there is, he writes, "is self-understanding on the level of the community and the individual, correlative to transcendent self-presentation."[135] Of course, transcendent self-presentation is textually mediated as we have noted, and

---

127 See "The 'Sacred' Text and the Community," p. 69.

128 Ibid., p. 70.

129 Ibid.

130 "Naming God," p. 217.

131 Ricoeur prefers to speak of "authority" over "sacred" when specifying the status that sacred texts have in Christianity. "I am frightened by this word 'sacred.'" Ricoeur, "The 'Sacred' Text and the Community," p. 72. At least part of what is at stake for Ricoeur in his hesitancy to use the term sacred with respect to biblical texts is the increased awareness of the permeable boundaries between sacred texts (canonical texts) and non-sacred texts (non-canonical texts).

132 See "Science and Ideology," p. 225, where Ricoeur notes that for an historical community to be sustained after its founding act "'ideology' must perpetuate the initial energy beyond the period of effervescence." In this sense, preaching from Scripture might be said to be an ideological act in the church.

133 David Detmer, "Ricoeur on Atheism: A Critique," in Hahn (ed.), *The Philosophy of Paul Ricoeur*, pp. 477-493.

134 "Reply to David Detmer," p. 496.

135 Ibid. There is, in other words, the history of the reception of the text. See *Thinking Biblically*, pp. xii-xiv.

The Church and the Bible Critically Read

the traditions of interpretation surrounding these mediating texts are multiple. There is pluralism, even a competition between interpretative traditions that receive these texts within Judaism and Christianity.[136] Nevertheless, in the above response Ricoeur indirectly identifies a goal of Christian preaching as the ongoing interpretation of founding texts; that is, the guiding of the community and individual into a self-understanding that is aligned with the textually mediated subject matter.

While in the context of this dispute, Ricoeur notes that it is the self-understanding of the individual or community that is correlative to transcendent self-presentation, his sense of Scripture reading and listening by the communities for which it functions religiously is that there is also action and experience that is correlative to transcendent self-presentation. Indeed, on Ricoeur's view, the "verification" of the text is accomplished with the guidance of preaching in "the transfer from text to life."[137] Put in more poetic terms, the possible world disclosed in the interaction of hearing community and text not only engenders a corresponding self-understanding, but also invites the audience (the church?) to act in ways oriented to this disclosed world. Ricoeur writes, "It is mainly in the reception of the text by an audience that the capacity of the plot to transfigure experience is actualized."[138]

Kerygmatic reading, within what seems a liturgical context, thus works toward "putting the text into practice."[139] Ricoeur is somewhat reluctant to call this putting into practice "the obedience of faith," since his notion of what the text requires of readers is broader than an appeal to the will for obedience. The genric range of Scripture engenders kergymatic readings that invite various sorts of conformity. Ricoeur writes:

> Kergymatic reading . . . is multiple: I mean that it is not reduced to a call to obedience . . . but that it is also a call to reflection, meditation . . . even to study, as the rabbis like to say, reading, discussing, interpreting the Torah, then held to be a lesson. This is clearly the case for sapiential writings, as well as for many narratives.[140]

The call that issues from a given historical community's kerygmatic reading of the Bible in the transfer from text to life is thus modulated by the genric variety of holy writ, even as it is guided in the transfer by preaching.

---

136 *Critique and Conviction*, p. 145. This plurality of interpretative communities engendered by one and the same series of texts in the long history of its reception bears witness to the "irreducible plurivocity" of the biblical corpus.

137 "Naming God," p. 217.

138 "Toward a Narrative Theology: Its Necessity, Its Resources, It Difficulties," p. 240. In this context Ricoeur speaks of "displaced" readers before the world displayed in front of the text. They are displaced from the actual world into a possible world with new horizons of possible experience.

139 *Critique and Conviction*, p. 149.

140 Ibid.

186 *Revelation, Holy Scripture and Church*

Critique

In the following section a critique of Ricoeur's proposal for critical and kergymatic Bible reading and appropriation in the life of the church is offered. The main objection to Ricoeur's understanding of Bible reading is that both modes, while helpfully depicted as distinct though related hermeneutical orientations, are not critically subordinated to the Gospel. Critical reading, as Ricoeur understands it, is Bible reading passing through the iconoclastic fires of the masters of suspicion by which it is purified. While Ricoeur notes that there is mutual purging in this process, he nevertheless establishes suspicious reading as a *necessary* condition; it is the means by which a second naïveté is earned. Bible reading in the form of conviction requires interaction with the masters of suspicion to earn the right of legitimacy, of post-critical faith, on the far side of criticism. Theological difficulties with this hermeneutic strategy are: (1) it submits the integrity of Christian interpretative practice to the background knowledge of the masters of suspicion in rudderless correlation; (2) it overlooks the degree to which Gospel interrogation of the church by means of Word and Sacrament has a critical and primary hermeneutic function for the church; and (3) it undervalues the appropriative logic by means of which external critique is rendered useful to Christian life and practice.

In the second section of the critique an examination of kergymatic reading within the church, as depicted by Ricoeur, is undertaken. Ricoeur maintains that in the hermeneutic struggle with the masters of suspicion, and through construals of the canon related to the time and place in which the Bible is interpreted, the church wrestles meaning from Holy Scripture. Church and Bible are, for Ricoeur, related through mutual election. The submission of the community to the text is a source of bewilderment to philosophers whose primary mode toward all texts is critical rather than submissive. While the community that listens to the Bible grants a certain formative precedence to the Bible in its listening, the call that issues to the community of faith—moderated by genre and heard in preaching—Ricoeur is hesitant to understand primarily in terms of obedience. It is argued that because Ricoeur does not relate interpretation in a thorough-going manner to the Gospel, his depiction of the hermeneutic situation of the church is insufficiently realist. Too much emphasis falls on meaning as established and won by hard-fought human interpretative effort and too little on meaning as a gift of grace, achieved through the action of God in Jesus Christ—of which the Bible is a fit and perspicuous inscripturation made effective for the church by the Spirit.

Critical Reading

> In all analysis of "criticism," a radical view of this *kritikos* of God's Word must be preserved, whereby a sharp distinction is made between criticism *of* the word and criticism *by* the Word . . . Even though the term "positive criticism" or "criticism in love" is used in this connection, this criticism is clearly a testing and sifting by means of a norm that is above the church . . . It is not possible to exalt oneself above God's speaking, nor criticize it.[141]

---

141 Berkouwer, *Holy Scripture*, pp. 355-356.

In some ways Ricoeur's proposed suspicious reading of sacred texts, by means of the iconoclastic panoply provided by the masters of suspicion, takes the place given to historical-critical analysis in the work of James Barr. The fundamental similarity is that the submission of biblical texts and churchly interpretation of biblical texts to these critical moments—enabled by either historical-critical or suspicious reading—is iconoclastic to the end of the edification of the life of the church. The church takes into its own life the results of submitting its texts and their interpretation to "critical" reading and thus its use and appropriation of the Bible is enriched and made more authentic. A major difference is that for Barr, "critical" reading, if it is to maintain its critical and relatively objective nature, ought to take place in institutional and theological independence from the church and its confession. One of the problems with this move is that the preponderant weight of criticism is thereby placed outside of the life of the community for which the Bible functions as Holy Scripture. Criticism can be alienated from the life and practice of the Christian community, that is, from the relationship of belonging.

Ricoeur, on the other hand, though equally interested in avoiding biblicism of a naïve and uncritical nature, locates the moment whereby Bible reading is rendered "critical" within the relationship of belonging. While proposed readings of the Bible (any kind of mediation of faith) "must" pass through the critique of religion (as economic, philosophical or psychodynamic distortion) in order to be purged of interpretative self-interest rooted in false consciousness, the dynamic of distanciation through writing enables suspicious reading to become internal to the relationship of belonging. In order for readers to appropriate what is other, at a distance (temporally, culturally, spiritually) from them in the tradition to which they belong, the self in front of the text disappropriates a fixed self-understanding in order to receive alien meaning. Into this de-realized moment of the self before the otherness of the distanciated world offered by the texts of my predilection, the critique of ideology enters in, to question and challenge seductive self/community-serving interpretations so that the true matter of the text will be appropriated.

Ricoeur also insists, in a more thoroughgoing manner than Barr, that the critique engendered by the engagement of the masters of suspicion in the interpretation of the Bible (or more generally the mediation of faith) cuts both ways. The overall thrust of Barr's hermeneutic discussion leans hard in the direction of the church's responsibility to appropriate the results of critical inquiry into its own interpretation and use of the Bible with minimal critical rebound from the theological and faith commitment of the church on the critical work of biblical scholars; indeed doctrine and faith are bracketed out for criticism's sake. For Ricoeur, however, the engagement with Marx, Nietzsche and Freud cuts both ways; it is mutually purifying. While appropriations of readings of the Bible must pass through the critiques of religion offered by these masters of suspicion, the point is not to engender cynicism or atheism on the part of the Christian interpreter; that is, it is not to render them converts to suspicion. (There is a rejection, on the part of Ricoeur, of the atheistic and mechanistic world-view implied in Freud's critique of religion, for example.) The goal in the interplay

188 *Revelation, Holy Scripture and Church*

between church reading and the masters of suspicion is to emerge on the other side, with a "post-critical faith . . . a second naïveté."[142]

While Ricoeur will arrive at readings of the Bible characterized by the relationship of "submission" (he remains suspicious of "obedience") by the church to these founding texts (the second naïveté), readings characterized as "critical" have appropriated to themselves (as an internal critique) the suspicious critiques of religion as that through which the mediation of faith "must pass."[143] In a manner analogous to the hermeneutic/poetic (non-theological) detour required properly to articulate and restore the concepts of "revelation" and "Scripture," an engagement with suspicion is required to render proposed church readings of the Bible authentic. Ricoeur's account of critical reading, like his development of the concepts of revelation and Scripture, is articulated on the basis of a construal of the hermeneutic field within which the idea of criticism gains force apart from a fundamental consideration of those critical features which accrue to Holy Scripture as it is related to God's communicative activity within the fellowship of the Holy Spirit. In other words, at a fundamental and primary level Ricoeur establishes that Scripture readings proposed to the de-realized self in front of the text must be appropriated only after they have been subjected to the purification of interaction with the masters of suspicion and thus earned their integrity. While Ricoeur does acknowledge the mutual criticism involved in such reading, and that suspicious reading takes place within the oscillating movement of belonging, the primacy of place establishes suspicious reading (or at least frictive interaction of proposed biblical reading with the masters of suspicion) as an interpretative *sine qua non* for critical ecclesial reading and appropriation. This move subverts critical features that, on a theological account, ought to be primary: (1) the critical judgment of God in Jesus Christ (the Gospel) borne witness to and made effective in Word and Sacrament by the Holy Spirit; and (2) the centrality of the Gospel, not only as that to which the entirety of Scripture stands in ordered relationship, but as that by which external critique is measured and converted to Christian use.

Garrett Green makes the observation that suspicious reading always implies trust. The trust implicit or explicit in the suspicious reading of sacred texts is in the background knowledge (the anthropology or understanding of reality) by means of which suspicion is raised.[144] While Ricoeur maintains that suspicious reading of sacred texts always involves mutual purification, he does, however, render Christian

---

142 *Freud and Philosophy*, p. 28. Following Ricoeur's suggestion regarding the purifying role of the hermeneutics of suspicion, Merold Westphal suggests devotional reading of Marx, Nietzsche and Freud for Lent. See Merold Westphal, *Suspicion and Faith: The Religious Uses of Modern Atheism* (Grand Rapids, 1993), pp. 3, 10-13.

143 "Two Essays by Paul Ricoeur," p. 209.

144 Green, *Theology, Hermeneutics, and Imagination*, pp. 21, 200-202. Dan Stiver makes the point that Ricoeur, while he does not want to baptize them, understands the insights of "the critical enemies" of Christian faith, "as compatible, even helpful, to the Christian awareness of the universal pervasiveness of distortion and even depravity." However, Stiver does not appreciate the degree to which a recognition of the compatibility of such criticism is dependent upon a prior critical evaluation of the masters of suspicion by means of the Gospel. In this sense, it is only by means of their "baptism" that the insights of the "critical enemies"

readings of the Bible vulnerable to the assumptions of alien and even hostile understanding of reality, since such assumptions in the hermeneutic he proposes do not function in a relation *subordinate* to the sources and norms of Christian faith itself, but in a relationship of critical *correlation*. "At their worst," those forms of theology that import Marxian and Nietzschean forms of suspicion and critique into the reading of Christian texts and communal life "subject theology and the church to alien criteria derived not from the Gospel of Jesus Christ but from modern autonomous humanism."[145] And, even at their best, holding alongside the Gospel an alien criteria of suspicion for the sake of smashing the idols which stand in the way of interpretation and appropriation of Holy Scripture breaks all idols but one. For a hermeneutic implication of the first commandment, "You shall have no other gods before (or besides) me," is that the Gospel (faith in the God of Jesus Christ) provides the fundamental orientation for the critical interpretation of the Bible for the church, and the basis for the critical appropriation of extra-scriptural schemes of thought.

Green, while he questions the basis of trust behind a hermeneutics of suspicion on theological grounds, does not dispense with suspicious-critical reading of Holy Scripture. Readings of the Bible can and have been ordered to serve the wealthy, patriarchy and false-consciousness of various sorts. However, the fundamental trust by which critical suspicion is oriented, for Christians, is "that trust, which we call faith in the God of Jesus Christ. This trust commits us to a form of suspicion more radical than the secular kinds because it is the hermeneutical expression of God's judgment."[146] A critique of patriarchy and of the interpretative practices which justify it, while occasioned by cultural movements, requires a hermeneutics "whose suspicion stems from an underlying trust in the crucified Messiah and the God who raised him from the dead."[147] Christian readings of Scripture, and the forms of life assumed by the community of faith, are rendered suspicious and interrogated by this Gospel, which is the measure of their faithfulness. By means of preaching and prayer and the sacramental life of the church, practices normed and warranted by the

---

of Christianity can be appropriated for Christian use. See Stiver, *Theology After Ricoeur*, p. 159.

145 Green, *Theology, Hermeneutics, and Imagination*, p. 190. Green maintains that: "Theological appropriations of the hermeneutics of suspicion have been naïve at just this point. They have wanted to root out bad faith without taking responsibility for the implicit grounds of that suspicion." Ibid., pp. 200-201. See also G.D. Robinson, "Paul Ricoeur and the Hermeneutics of Suspicion: A Brief Overview and Critique," *Premise*, 2/8 (September, 1995): 18 and Rowan Williams, "The Suspicion of Suspicion: Wittgenstein and Bonhoeffer," in R.H. Bell (ed.), *The Grammar of the Heart: New Essays in Moral Philosophy and Theology* (San Francisco, 1988), pp. 36-53. The argument that the hermeneutics of suspicion ought to be more suspicious, bears striking similarity to Barth's argument that the "critical historian needs to be more critical." Both recognize that the "naturalism" often implicit in the critique threatens to subvert what the Bible is about, i.e., "the Word in the words." See Barth, *The Epistle to the Romans*, 2nd edn, p. 8.

146 Green, *Theology, Hermeneutics, and Imagination*, p. 22. Green is careful to avoid an understanding of faith or trust which leads to philosophical foundationalism.

147 Ibid., p. 203.

190 *Revelation, Holy Scripture and Church*

Gospel and made effective by the Spirit, the community of faith undergoes a regular and continual interrogation (reformation).

Rowan Williams, for example, offers a critical analysis of the "false anthropology" [148] of human rights and achievement at work in much of North Atlantic society and the way in which, if taken into the church, threatens to constrict the integrity of sacramental action rooted in the Gospel. In baptismal liturgy a child's condition is first described as one of peril, of liability to divine wrath. After baptism, the child is said to be grafted into Christ by grace. Neither of these conditions, belonging with Adam or belonging to Christ, are "things over which the subject has any control."[149] In the same way, the liturgy of the Eucharist—by focusing on the identity of Jesus—transforms the identity of those who gather for the meal from "betrayers to guests, whose future betrayals are already encompassed in the covenanted welcome enacted by Jesus."[150] In both of these rites, choice and self-construction are pushed to the margin as determinative of human identity; that is, they are rendered suspicious by an understanding of human identity with others on the basis of the common regard of God. "Sacramental practice," writes Williams, "seems to speak most clearly of loss, dependence and interdependence, solidarities we do not chose: none of these themes is particularly welcome or audible in the social world we currently inhabit as secular subjects."[151] Williams does not intend to found a social program on the sacramental practice of the church; he does note, however, that sacramental practice faithfully performed "hold[s] up a mirror to other forms of sociality and [says] that these are at risk and under judgment."[152] And if sacramental, and analogously homiletic practice, rooted in the Gospel, hold up a mirror to external forms of life at odds with the Gospel, no less is the case with internal hermeneutic and ecclesial practice that is adverse to God's judgment on human life in Jesus Christ. Witnessed in the power of the Holy Spirit in Word and Sacrament, the Gospel constantly threatens ideologies of self-construction and achievement, even as it calls into being forms of life (including interpretative practice) in congruence with it.

Faith and Philosophy The deliberately hermetic relationship between faith and philosophy within Ricoeur's later hermeneutic program may well be at the root of his refusal to "baptize"[153] the critique of the masters of suspicion. For Ricoeur does not want either to ground theology and biblical interpretation in philosophy—what he calls the "cryptophilosophical" temptation[154]—or to ground philosophy in faith or theology—what he calls "ontotheological amalgamation."[155] At times, Ricoeur even erects a methodological partition between faith and philosophy, as a thoroughgoing

---

148 Rowan Williams, "Sacraments of the New Society," in *On Christian Theology* (Oxford: Blackwell, 2000), p. 221.

149 Ibid., pp. 210-211.

150 Ibid., p. 216.

151 Ibid., p. 219.

152 Ibid., p. 220.

153 Webster maintains: "Baptism is the origin and permanent condition of theological reason." *Holy Scripture*, p. 134.

154 Ricoeur, *Oneself as Another*, p. 25.

155 Ibid., p. 24.

The Church and the Bible Critically Read   191

Kantian.[156] This is particularly the case in *Oneself as Another* from which he excluded the lectures concerning God and biblical hermeneutics, originally a part of the 1986 Gifford Lectures, for the sake "asceticism of argument" and "agnosticism in method."[157] While Ricoeur acknowledges that his interest in various philosophical problems and biblical interpretation may well be motivated by "the convictions that bind me to biblical faith,"[158] these convictions are barred from autonomous philosophical discourse. Indeed Ricoeur works at biblical interpretation, not as a Christian, but as a philosopher, a "curious inquirer," all the while convinced that he can bracket out "his biblical and Christian convictions in order to do philosophy"[159] and formulate arguments "which are aimed at all rational beings capable of discussion, no matter what their position on the question of religion."[160] A difficulty with this approach, like that of James Barr who also wants to bracket out Christian conviction, is that it pushes in the direction of hermeneutic schizophrenia.[161] For the sake of rendering biblical interpretation, "the mediation of faith" more authentic for the community of faith, one holds in methodological suspension the whole of theological conviction or holds it against a methodologically agnostic critique. Not only does this procedure engender criticism from both theological and philosophical sides for covert inconsistency,[162] and raise questions about the degree to which

---

156 See Wallace, "From Phenomenology to Scripture?" p. 303; and Pamela Sue Anderson, "Agnosticism and Attestation: An Aporia concerning the Other in Ricoeur's *Oneself as Another*," *Journal of Religion*, 74/1 (1994): 65-76.

157 Ibid. See also Ricoeur, "Intellectual Autobiography," in Hahn (ed.), *The Philosophy of Paul Ricoeur*, p. 50. Pamela Anderson argues that the insistence that philosophy remain agnostic, independent of religious and theological commitments, which one finds in *Oneself as Another* and in Charles Reagan, "Interview avec Paul Ricoeur: Le 8 juillet 1991," *Bulletin de la société américaine de philosophie de langue française*, 3/3 (Winter, 1992): 157-159, represents a change in direction in the thought of Ricoeur. In "Toward a Hermeneutic of the Idea of Revelation" he wants to develop a hermeneutic of revelation that will avoid an unbridgeable gap between the truths of faith and the truths of reason. See " Agnosticism and Attestation," pp. 69-70, n. 21.

158 *Oneself as Another*, p. 34. See also "Intellectual Autobiography," p. 41 where Ricoeur notes that his interest in narrative is sponsored, in part, by his work in biblical exegesis.

159 Fodor, *Christian Hermeneutics*, 247, n. 4.

160 Charles E. Reagan, *Paul Ricoeur: His Life and His Work* (Chicago, 1996), p. 126.

161 Compare Fodor, *Christian Hermeneutics*, p. 247, n. 3 and Fowl, *Engaging Scripture*, p. 187. Both note the liability of a methodological schizophrenia when "one's professional life is sealed off from one's confessional commitments." Ricoeur writes, "I prefer the risk of schizophrenia to the bad faith of a pseudo-argument." Reagan, *Paul Ricoeur: His Life and His Work*, p. 126.

162 See Fodor, *Christian Hermeneutics*, pp. 246-247. Fodor writes, "Despite his well placed fears concerning ontotheology's resurgent powers, one wonders whether Christians can really have it both ways, i.e., embrace both an agnosticism and meaningful belief. After all, affirming both agnosticism and attestation leaves us with an aporia concerning the other." See also Christian Bouchindhomme and Rainer Rochlitz (eds), *Temps et récit de Paul Ricoeur en débat* (Paris, 1989); Glenn Whitehouse, "Ricoeur on Religious Selfhood: A Response to Mark Wallace," *Modern Theology*, 16/3 (July, 2000): 315-317; and Anderson, "Agnosticism and Attestation," pp. 65-76. Here Anderson concludes by challenging Ricoeur on the idea of

192 *Revelation, Holy Scripture and Church*

such critique can be internal to the relation of belonging, it renders vulnerable the integrity of Christian faith to a rudderless correlation between faith and philosophy. Thiselton's suggestion, that for Ricoeur it is "the work, but not the world view"[163] of the masters of suspicion that is adopted to root out interpretation rooted in false consciousness, is not adequate. For no criteria or hermeneutic orientation for sorting out "work" from "world view" is offered; indeed, in so far as Ricoeur assigns a priority faith is the object of criticism. We need, "faith that has undergone criticism, *postcritical* faith . . . it is a rational faith, for it interprets; but it is faith because it seeks, through interpretation, a second naiveté . . . Believe in order to understand, understand in order to believe."[164]

One does not need to ground the whole of philosophy in an ontotheology in order to deploy the conceptual language and criticism of philosophy and other disciplines in biblical interpretation. No such thoroughgoing relationship is necessary between them. On an *ad hoc* basis the use of external language and argument can be adjudicated for its usefulness to Christian faith and Scripture interpretation as it is submitted to scriptural interrogation. Offering a description of this procedure in Barth and Anselm, Hans Frei writes:

> [T]he rule is that that language [of philosophical schemes] must be highly formal, in the sense that the use of the conceptual scheme must be firmly governed by the specific Christian descriptions that such schemes are asked to render in second order re-descriptions. . . The subordinating assignment is made unsystematically or asymptotically. How it is done is a matter of seeing the application in a given context.[165]

The appropriation of human schemes of thought is a subordinating assignment, that is, of the scheme of thought to Christian description, and thus the manner by which external critique of the mediation of faith may be made internal to Christian interpretative practice could properly be designated conversion. Augustine makes the point that "knowledge collected from the books of the pagans . . . should be seized and held to be converted to Christian use." This is accomplished by the "censure" of Holy Scripture.[166]

---

autonomous philosophical discourse since in his work "belief remains the ultimate, however covert, foundation for attestation—for his hermeneutical method of truth." She maintains that attestation (faith) "serves surreptitiously against decisive doubt." Ibid., p. 76.

163 Thiselton, "Biblical Studies and Theoretical Hermeneutics," p. 108.

164 Ricoeur, *Freud and Philosophy*, p. 28. The difference between this essentially correlationist method and that of Anselm's faith seeking understanding, what Frei calls *ad hoc* correlation, is obvious. See *Types of Christian Theology*, p. 41.

165 Frei, *Types of Christian Theology*, p. 41. See also ibid., p. 79, and "An Afterword: Eberhard Busch's Biography of Karl Barth," pp. 160-162.

166 Augustine, *On Christian Doctrine*, trans. with an introduction by D.W. Robertson, Jr (New York, 1958), Book 2, XL: section 60, p. 75. Compare Barth, *Church Dogmatics*, 1/2: 734. He writes:

> We can say, therefore, that the use of a human scheme of thought in the service of scriptural exegesis is legitimate and fruitful when it is a critical use, implying that the object of the

Grace and Critical Meaning Ricoeur's careful appreciation of the different modes and ends of biblical interpretation and the degree to which philosophical thought may follow ecclesial use of the Bible is another locus for the confrontation for his two affiliations. Moreover, his attention to the ends toward which Bible reading may be directed and the overlap between reading publics in various modes of reading has the promise of ameliorating certain kinds of hermeneutical conflict. He does, nevertheless, overestimate the degree to which global, what he calls "comprehensive" or "descriptive" theological reading, is shared (a mixed mode of thought) between philosophical and confessional communities through a lack of appreciation for the Anselmian logic by which philosophical concepts and notions of cogency are employed in descriptive theology. Even at this level of Bible reading, such borrowed concepts and notions are subordinated to and rendered intelligible in relation to the kerygma of the confessing community in a manner that would garner no little astonishment in those "bewildered" by submission.[167] In what follows, a critique of the cogency of Ricoeur's depiction of the church in its relationship to the reading of the Bible as Holy Scripture particularly at the level of what he calls kergymatic reading is undertaken. The depiction of this relationship, because it lacks a thorough account of divine grace in relation to both human interpretative effort and the ongoing efficacy of Holy Scripture in the life of church, is too formal. More specifically, in his account of kergymatic reading, Ricoeur tends to ascribe to the text of the Bible or the action of the church what is, most properly, the action of God or human action enabled by God.

Ricoeur is clear that founding texts relate a founded community to a word that comes from higher than myself. Within a relationship of "mutual election" between text and community, submissive readers of their sacred texts wager that the texts of their predilection can guide them via the act of preaching to forms of life (self-understandings) that are correlative with the transcendent self-presentation mediated via their texts. "It is mainly in the reception of the text by an audience that the capacity of the plot to transfigure experience is actualized."[168] Two features of this summary of Ricoeur's construal of the church's relationship to Holy Scripture lack theological realism. The first is Ricoeur's tendency to ascribe to "plot capacity," an immanent textual feature, the ability to transfigure experience. Presumably, one could make a case that Ricoeur does relate "plot capacity" to subject matter, "transcendent self-presentation," such that transfigurative capacity is related to the founding events which founding texts mediate to guide and shape the life of the church. And yet, even then his account is too beholden to a natural account of mediacy; "what is far is rendered near" by means of interpretative effort. Only after interpretation has endured

---

criticism is not Scripture, but our own scheme of thought, and that Scripture is necessarily the subject of this criticism.

See also Berkhouwer, *Holy Scripture*, p. 364.

167 See Barth, *Church Dogmatics*, 1/2: 468-469.

168 "Toward a Narrative Theology: Its Necessity, Its Resources, Its Difficulties," p. 240. Ricoeur recognizes that ascribing agency to texts is problematic. "There is a sort of mutual choice between being chosen—*if I can say this*—by a set of writings and by the interpretation which follows from these writings and choosing them." Reagan, *Paul Ricoeur: His Life and His Work*, p. 126. Emphasis mine.

194 *Revelation, Holy Scripture and Church*

"the terrible battle for meaning,"[169] that is, been through engagement with the masters of suspicion, has it arrived at a second naïveté. The resultant interpretation, a self-transfiguring word, is thus shaped by the multiple meanings made of founding texts in a particular time and place through an ordering of canonical texts. The impression, then, is that "meaning" is extracted from founding texts for human transformation by interpretative effort in conjunction with textual dynamics alone.

While there is an interpretative struggle to make sense, Ricoeur's natural account of meaning made mediate by human effort and textual configuration does not speak of meaning as a gift of God's grace, apart from works, and thus "places the reader in a disturbed relation to the text, one in which the clarity of Scripture as divine self-communication has to prove itself . . ."[170] Scripture exegesis is a joyous task because, while it requires interpretative effort and study and prayer, it is undertaken in the conviction that "the terrible battle for meaning" has already taken place and been won once for all. To this Holy Scripture bears witness in Old and New Testaments and, what is more, the Spirit is poured out to illumine this witness and to form and sustain a people in congruence with it. What is missing in Ricoeur is a sense of the priority and effectiveness of God's gracious action in Jesus Christ borne witness to in Holy Scripture in the power of the Spirit for the church over human interpretative effort to battle for or construct meaning.[171] Ricoeur's account of faith as "risk" or "wager" on a certain body of texts in the hope that what is risked will reap reward (a hundred-fold return in comprehension, valor and joy), it could be argued, implies a certain venturesome gamble on the part of the church that lacks an appreciation of faith both as a gift (against the Pelagian implications of meritorious or calculated choice) and as knowledge and assurance (against the implication of blind faith implied in a gamble). One means of correcting this vulnerable construal of faith would be to reconfigure "mutual election" to characterize not the relationship between text and audience, but between God and his people, realized in Jesus Christ and made effective through the instrumentality of Scripture by the Spirit.

Hans Frei: The Critical Primacy of *Sensus Literalis*

> The discussion of what constitutes a critical theological reading of the New Testament Gospels occupied the North American Theologian Hans Frei for the last 20 years of his life.[172]

Like James Barr and Paul Ricoeur, Hans Frei is interested in a critical reading of the Bible for the life of the church. Frei maintains that critical reading of the Bible requires the "bracketing out,"[173] suspension or interrogation of imposed interpretative grids for the sake of gaining a critical or authentic interpretation of the Bible for the

---

169 Ricoeur, "A Philosophical Interpretation of Freud," in Don Ihde (ed.), *The Conflict of Interpretations: Essays in Hermeneutics* (Evanston, 1974), p. 176.

170 Webster, *Holy Scripture*, p. 106.

171 See Jüngel, *God as the Mystery of the World*, pp. 163-164.

172 Lee, *Luke's Stories of Jesus*, p. 15.

173 See ibid., p. 26.

The Church and the Bible Critically Read   195

life of the Christian church. Moreover, all three seem to be of a similar mind where faith commitment is concerned. A reader need not be disposed believingly to the truth claims of the Bible in order to read the Bible in a critical mode; even though, for all three, the critical mode they sponsor is for the sake of authentic, truthful or faithful Christian Bible reading. The difference between them on the role of faith is the degree to which Barr and Ricoeur *insist* on an agnostic methodology for iconoclastic interrogation. Whereas for Frei, faith, in the sense of acquaintance with the one whose identity is depicted in the Gospels, is neither required, nor required to be suspended, in order to read them.[174] Faith or the faith relationship is not the object in view in the interpretation of the Gospels, rather it is the identity of Jesus Christ. Moreover, the ability to follow the "literal" reading of biblical narrative does not depend on privileged or esoteric forms of knowledge but on an "analytic procedure" appropriate to genre recognition[175] or "normal human sensitivity and respect"[176] for communal reading conventions rendered by means of "thick description."

A major difference between Frei and Barr is that, on Frei's depiction of the hermeneutic field, critical traffic flows in the *opposite* direction to that suggested by Barr. One does not suspend church doctrine and practice (ecclesiology) in order to submit Bible reading to a methodologically and institutionally independent analysis; rather, one suspends historical-critical discussion (of meaning and reference) in order to attend to either the literary features of the Bible (in his early work) or follow the church's ruled use of the Bible (in his later work), particularly those which govern Gospel reading in relation to the rest of the Bible and, indeed, to the rest of reality. Barr wants, on the one hand, to suspend church doctrine and faith commitment for the sake of critical interpretation since these insulate the Bible against rigorous "objective" examination. Frei on the other hand, wants to suspend historical reading in order to let the text as realistic narrative or the ruled reading of the Bible in the community for which it functions, emerge free from high-level theoretical imposition. Once a reading of the Bible most congruent with either (1) the kind of literature the Gospels are, or (2) the ruled use of the Gospels in the life of the church is established, then the theological interpreter has a means by which critically to appropriate historical-critical (and other kinds) of Bible reading.

A major distinction between Frei and Ricoeur can also be made. Whereas for Ricoeur, critical traffic in the engagement between proposed readings of the Bible and the masters of suspicion is two-way, resulting in mutual purification, for Frei, the critique of the masters of suspicion would be critically appropriated. The priority of an ascriptive "literal" sense reading of the Gospels, and the rest of the Bible in typological or figural relation to it, provides the critical point of departure for the

---

174 See Frei, *The Identity of Jesus Christ*, p. xvii. "My hope is that, no matter whether one is a believing Christian or not, one can make sense of the Gospel story in its own right . . ." However, Frei does note that an exposition of the Gospels as realistic narrative, while a purely formal procedure, is one undertaken by the believer in praise of God under the conviction that to speak of Jesus Christ necessarily involves his presence, while for the unbeliever such a claim is "meaningless" "devoid of any significance for him"; for the pilgrim [someone on the way to belief] it is a "puzzle." Ibid., pp. 1-9.

175 See ibid., pp. xiii-xiv and *The Eclipse of Biblical Narrative*, p. 10.

176 See "The 'Literal' Reading of Biblical Narrative," p. 147.

196 *Revelation, Holy Scripture and Church*

adjudication of proposed readings of Scripture. In so far as the masters of suspicion could assist in exposing false readings of the Bible as Holy Scripture, readings which do not comport to the priority of the literal sense of the stories about Jesus because they are rooted in hostile "ideologies," they might well be critically appropriated, that is, render valuable service to literal sense reading. However, in so far as reading or critical strategies are rooted in theoretically high-level explanatory literary or philosophical theory, they ought, on Frei's account, to be held in abeyance since they threaten by wholesale application to break apart what is, in effect, the scriptural reading of the Bible. Frei carves out methodological space, gained by resort to literary distinction and then ecclesial practice, from within which he can engage in a theological reading of the Bible and the critical appropriation of readings ancillary to the task. In what follows in this section, a more thorough exposition of the polemic hermeneutical strategies by means of which Frei secures the interpretative methodological space for "literal sense" reading of the Gospels as critical reading, as well as an account of the nature of literal sense reading, is offered.

Following this exposition an examination of Frei's proposal of literal sense reading as critical reading is undertaken. While Frei makes significant theological gains in comparison to Barr and Ricoeur, his critical hermeneutic option leans too heavily upon the positivity of interpretative-ecclesial action with respect to the critical use of Scripture in the church. Frei's deployment of poetic and social-scientific categories in order to protect the priority of Christocentric figural interpretation lacks theological rootage in the doctrine of God. By warranting his proposal for critical interpretation by means of embedded church practice, Frei offers an ecclesially conservative rendering of the church's use of Scripture; rather than one by which God reforms and sustains the church. Moreover, while intratextual interpretation promises a critical applicative strategy for the interpretation of all of reality in terms of a typologically construed Christocentric canon, the possibility of such extratextual critical interpretation is over-invested in an understanding of faith as an imaginative capacity and socialized skill at the expense of an understanding of faith as personal assent and trust created ever anew by God the Holy Spirit through Word and Sacrament.

Gaining Methodological Space

If Frei defers on the question of whether the Gospel narratives are true, that is, whether or not the claims they make correspond to a historical or idealized referent, it is not because he believes the Gospels do not make truth claims. Indeed, he asserts that biblical narrative makes an "urgent and imperious claim to truth."[177] However, while biblical narratives often have an historical reference, they also refer in the mode of "witness" to the Word of God, whether they are historical or not. Their adequacy (truth) as witnesses to the Word of God is enabled by grace, and this feature is missed or bracketed when truth claims are situated within large-scale monolithic

---

177 "'Narrative' in Christian and Modern Reading," p. 156.

The Church and the Bible Critically Read   197

theories of reference.[178] Frei, especially in *The Eclipse of Biblical Narrative* and *The Identity of Jesus Christ*, resists reading the Bible in terms of an epistemology in which meaning is solely ostensive (ideal or historical) reference because he believes such reading is not altogether appropriate to the literary fact of biblical narrative.

Frei's claim is that eighteenth- and nineteenth century-Christian hermeneutics, in an apologetic struggle initiated in battles with Deism, sought to defend the integrity of biblical narrative by means of offering independent confirmation or probability analysis of the intended referent of the text. The problem ingredient in this move is that the realistic narrative itself, as a literary phenomenon capable of rendering its own world, is eclipsed by an alternative or independent account of the ostensive events narratively rendered. This is the end result of large-scale interpretative projects that interpose themselves on biblical narrative in spite of the generic resistance realistic narrative presents to such efforts. Frei notes that throughout the eighteenth and nineteenth centuries "Biblical commentators again and again emphasized the simplicity of style, the life-likeness of depiction, the lack of artificiality or heroic elevation in theme in such [narrative] stories," and what is more, "that representation and depiction had a great deal to do with each other and came very close in the stories."[179] However, because they lacked the appropriate procedure for identifying and interpreting realistic narrative, interpreters all too often conflated "history-like" to ostensive "historical" narrative, or in the event of a historical discrepancy, to an idealized (allegorical or mythological) referent. Frei calls this confusion a "category error,"[180] thereby resisting the application of interpretative conventions appropriate to history or allegory or myth in the case of the Gospels. Instead he deploys the category "realistic narrative," of which the Gospels are an instance, as that to which interpretative tools and concepts must yield. In this manner, Frei gains on literary grounds the methodological space within which to attend to the literal reading of the Gospels and so preserves the critical priority of this mode of reading over appropriated ancillary readings serviceable to it. "Frei," writes David Lee, "procedurally bracketed . . . historical discussions in order to attend to the literary dimension of the Gospel texts."[181]

Frei's literary strategy to gain the methodological space within which, on a literal sense reading, the Gospels could "speak for themselves" and so gain precedence over ostensive interpretation, proved problematic, especially for Frei. While arguments at the level of poetic cogency and the relation between truth and meaning were launched against it, Frei grew suspicious that his appropriation of the category "realistic narrative" to express the history-like character and the literal reading of the Gospels was itself beholden to "general theory."[182] In other words, he grew anxious that the methodological real estate he had gained against historical or ideal ostensive

---

178 See, for example, *The Identity of Jesus Christ*, pp. 14-15, 164-165; "Conflicts in Interpretation," pp. 163-166; "Response to 'Narrative' Theology,'" pp. 209-212; and "Of the Resurrection of Christ," pp. 203-206.

179 *The Eclipse of Biblical Narrative*, pp. 10-11.

180 *The Identity of Jesus Christ*, p. xiv.

181 Lee, *Luke's Stories of Jesus*, p. 26.

182 "The 'Literal' Reading of Biblical Narrative," pp. 142-143.

198   *Revelation, Holy Scripture and Church*

reading for literal sense reading of the Gospels on their own terms, he had sold to
new-critical literary theory. In some ways, it seemed that the stories of the Gospels
were critically subordinated to a general literary class—the very thing Frei sought to
avoid. The question became, once again, how does one carve out the hermeneutical
space within which the Bible, especially the literal reading of the Gospel narratives
in particular, could maintain their critical positivity for theological construction
against over-invested interpretative concepts and tools deployed to service their
interpretation? Frei writes:

> It is the case that description of the Christian religion, especially in the West, has included
> a description of its sacred text in which at the very least certain portions regarded as
> central were to be read not allegorically or spiritually but literally. Another reading may
> be allowed, but it must not offend the literal sense of those crucial sections.[183]

Frei turns from literary theory to low-level anthropological descriptive practice[184]
to gain the methodological space within which "literal reading" of the Gospels
establishes itself as the critical standard in terms of which others modes of reading
are deployed and the rest of the Bible (and reality) is read. Unlike the use of a general
literary category, which defends literal sense reading under the rubric of "realistic
narrative" at the price of rendering it an instance of a general class of texts, descriptive
(not explanatory) social science, like literal reading itself, "governs and bends to its
own ends"[185] whatever general categories it employs to suit what the religion for
which the Bible functions religiously is actually doing with it texts. "The descriptive
context, then, for the *sensus literalis* is the religion of which it is a part, understood
at once as a determinate code in which beliefs, ritual, and behavior patterns, ethos as
narrative, come together as a common semiotic system . . ."[186] Thus, while varieties
of communities have sacred texts, the descriptive tools employed in the case of the
Christian church's reading of the Bible are used to render an account of reading
conventions particular to this text as it is read by this particular community in its
common life. This is description that is "thick"—sympathetically oriented to the
actions and conventions of the cultural insider. And the consensus pattern of Bible
reading, rendered through thick description of instanciated liturgical, devotional and
creedal use through history in the church, is literal sense reading of the Gospels
and the rest of the Bible and reality in typological relation to them.[187] Literal sense
reading, as Christian consensus or plain sense reading, is now deployed to create the
methodological space necessary to engage in theologically constructive reading of
the Bible free of the threat of eclipse by theory-laden interposition. "The customary
use to which the text has been put in the context of the community's belief and

---

183 *Types of Christian Theology*, p. 12, see also p. 14.

184 See ibid., pp. 11-12.

185 "The 'Literal' Reading of Biblical Narrative," p. 143. On the distinction between
explanatory and descriptive analysis see ibid., pp. 146-147 and *Types of Christian Theology*,
pp. 12-13. In thick description "rather than explaining the culture that one tries to look at, one
tries to describe it."

186 "The 'Literal' Reading of Biblical Narrative," p. 146.

187 Ibid., pp. 120-124, 144.

The Church and the Bible Critically Read   199

life"[188] commends literal sense reading and thus "probably sets bounds on what can and cannot be done" in so far as one interprets as "an adherent who speaks for the common community of interpretation."[189]

Literal Reading as Ruled (Critical) Reading

What then is the nature of "literal sense" reading and what critical limits does it set for the use of Holy Scripture? In his later work, Frei gives careful attention to the contours of literal sense reading and its import for theological construction. Indeed, in the posthumously published *Types of Christian Theology*, Frei examines the practice of theological construction on the basis of which approach is most amenable to literal sense reading of Holy Scripture. First, literal sense reading of the Bible, established by "the greatest degree of agreement in the use of the text in the religious community,"[190] was (and ought to be) focused on the person of Christ. He constitutes the center of literal sense reading around which the rest of Scripture is organized in typological relation. Second, literal sense as the "plain sense" for the community that uses the Bible, is "literal ascriptive," particularly in the case of the Gospels. Jesus' identity is not illustrated in his story, in the events he experiences, the things he says, the kingdom he announces; his identity is constituted by these events. Frei writes, "the literal sense is in the first instance very specifically focused on him as the specific, unsubstitutable personal subject of the stories."[191] Frei also articulates this rule less Christologically and more formally on two fronts when he maintains (1) against those (like Barr) who seek to recover "behind the written text" the meaning the author intended, that the text is "the fit enactment of the intention to say what comes to be in the text;"[192] and (2) against Ricoeur and the hermeneutic

---

188 "Theology and the Interpretation of Narrative," p. 110.

189 *Types of Christian Theology*, p. 57.

190 Ibid., p. 15. Frei draws on the work of Charles Woods and Raphael Loewe in his articulation of literal sense as the plain sense of the text for the community that uses the text. See Woods, *The Formation of Christian Understanding*, part III and Raphael Loewe, "The 'Plain' Meaning of Scripture in Early Jewish Exegesis," *Papers of the Institute of Jewish Studies in London* (Jerusalem, 1964), vol. 1, pp. 140-185. The emphasis on meaning as use is also ascribed to Wittgenstein. "Don't ask for the meaning; ask for the use." See "Theology and the Interpretation of Narrative," p. 104. Frei's extended discussions of the nature of "literal sense" reading are given in *Types of Christian Theology*, pp. 5, 14-15, 84, 140-143; "Theology and the Interpretation of Narrative," pp. 102-114; "The 'Literal' Reading of Biblical Narrative," pp. 120-124, 144-149; and "Conflicts in Interpretation," pp. 153-166.

191 *Types of Christian Theology*, p. 141.

192 Ibid., pp. 15-16. This assertion is a thread that is continuous throughout Frei's work. See "Remarks in Connection with a Theological Proposal," pp. 34-36 and "Theology and the Interpretation of Narrative," pp. 102-103. The anthropology of alienation that lies behind the quest for authorial intention, Frei critiques in "Remarks in Connection with a Theological Proposal." See also David Demson, "Response to Walter Lowe," *Modern Theology*, 8/2 (April, 1992): 148. Demson argues that this assertion on Frei's part is rooted, not in a doctrine of revelation (or inspiration), but creation. "Creation in the image of God means to be so created that there does not exist a gap in ordinary speech between what is said and what is meant."

tradition which seeks a coincidence of sense and subject matter under high powered hermeneutical theory in front of the text, that there is a descriptive fit between words and subject matter or reference already in the text.[193] Finally, Frei maintains that literal sense in the Christian West is not referentially univocal. While Jesus is the ascriptive subject of the Gospels, Frei recognizes a diversity of reality ascriptions to Jesus in the Christian tradition. For some he is the central character of a narrative plot, for others a charismatic figure, an actual historical figure, or an ascriptive subject under an ontological or metaphysical description—"such as one person in whom two natures are indissoluably and unabridgedly united."[194] A consensus position on the reality status of Jesus has not obtained within the community for whom the text functions.

To sum up, and to articulate these ecclesially based descriptive principles governing literal sense reading in prescriptive terms, Frei maintains the following minimal, flexible and "not too constrictive" rules.[195] The first, is predictable: Christian readings of the Bible must not drive a wedge between those things, events and attributes attributed to Jesus and Jesus as their ascriptive subject. Jesus is a specific person in the Gospel narratives, and thus these accounts may not be read in such a way as make someone or something else the subject of the depiction. This rule is very much at the basis of Frei's critique of "hermeneutical" construals of the Gospels, which, on his account, translate these stories into presentations of human modes-of-being in the world (possible worlds) and thus lose the specificity of the singular person Jesus, who becomes an instance of this mode-of-being rather than the single ascriptive subject of these accounts.[196]

The second rule under which the Christian Scriptures have been (and ought to be) read is, writes Frei: "no Christian reading of the Bible may deny either the unity of the Old and New Testaments or the congruence (which is not the same as literal identity) of that unity with the ascriptive literalism of the Gospel narratives."[197] The church's literal reading of the Bible—as a vast, loosely structured narrative typologically centered in the Gospel depictions of the life of Jesus—provides a critical check over the use to which the Bible can be put in the church. Here it would seem that Frei challenges the appropriateness of those readings of the Bible that

---

193 *Types of Christian Theology*, p. 16. See also "Conflicts in Interpretation," pp. 164-165 and "Theology and the Interpretation of Narrative," pp. 103-104. In this latter essay, Frei maintains that the fit between the signified and the signifier is sought at the intralinguistic or semiotic rather than the epistemological level. We have the reality "only under the depiction and not in a language-neutral or language transcending way." See Ibid. Here Frei connects this formal point to a theology of incarnation.

194 "The 'Literal' Reading of Biblical Narrative," pp. 142-143.

195 Ibid., p. 143.

196 Frei also resists the attempt to make metaphor (parable) primary in the Gospels such that the Passion is read through them. Parables, on Frei's view, "are descriptively metaphorical, they contribute indirectly to the identification of the person who spoke them 'with authority.' Their meaning in this procedure is primarily ascriptive (I take that to be the basic sense of what one means in the tradition of pre-critical New Testament interpretation as the "literal sense." Frei applies here his first informal rule. "Conflicts in Interpretation," pp. 164-65.

197 "The 'Literal' Reading of Biblical Narrative," p. 145.

The final rule under which the Bible has been (and ought to be) read within the community of faith is this: "any readings not in principle in contradiction with these two rules are permissible, and two of the obvious candidates would be the various sorts of historical-critical and literary readings."[199] Having challenged the imperious application of general hermeneutic theories of interpretation (which make Jesus a instance of rather than the subject of the ascriptive literalism of the Gospels) and of historicist-reductive readings of the Bible (which fracture the unity of the canon and transport the literal sense into the world behind the text), Frei now allows that they be re-admitted in a chastened form. It would seem that for Frei, the "effective shaping centerpiece" of the Bible, the history-like Gospel depictions of the life, death and resurrection of Jesus, not only holds the canon together in a unity but also disciplines the tools and methods by which this text is read. In other words, the informal rules, implicit in and established by the church's "literal" reading of the Bible, function as rules by which various techniques and hermeneutic conceptualities for reading texts are critically employed for Bible reading that is Christian.

Literal Reading and Extratextual Reality

There are, for Frei, at least three important functions that literal sense reading plays in the interpretation and use of Holy Scripture in the life of the church. In the first instance, as was demonstrated in the chapter on the Bible as Scripture, literal sense interpretation of the Gospels is the basis for the typological unity of Old and New Testaments in a Christocentric rule of faith reading. The explicative meaning of the Bible is directly related to this ruled reading of the Bible as authoritative Holy Scripture. A second feature of literal sense reading, as Christian consensus or plain sense reading, is that it is critical reading. The deployment of reading strategies and conceptualities are critically subordinated to the ascriptively literal stories of Jesus for a scriptural reading of the Bible. This feature of literal sense reading requires that historical-critical and phenomenological hermeneutic categories and modes of interpretation (among others) be bent and shaped to serve the literal sense of the Gospel stories of Jesus. Finally, literal sense reading of the Gospels, and the rest of the Bible in typological/figural relation to them, is also suggestive of an ecclesial

---

198 Ibid., p. 121. In a early essay, "Theological Reflections on the Accounts of Jesus' Death and Resurrection," pp. 92-93, n. 18, Frei reflects on the significance to faith and theological truth-claims of attempts "to reconstruct the setting of Jesus' preaching and acts in his own life and in the cultural matrix of his time." He agrees with Nils Dahl, "that faith is *relatively* uninterested in the historical Jesus research" but that this does not mean faith is "*absolutely* uninterested in it." For to draw this conclusion says Frei, "would be a kerygma-theological Docetism."

199 "The 'Literal' Reading of Biblical Narrative," p. 145.

202 *Revelation, Holy Scripture and Church*

strategy for reading extratextual reality. In other words, as in Calvin, Frei returns to a reading strategy that unites explicative and applicative senses of Holy Scripture around the literal sense reading of the stories about Jesus. This is the final step in undoing *The Eclipse of Biblical Narrative*. The direction of the flow of interpretation is that of "absorbing"[200] the extratextual universe into the descriptive framework of Scripture by means of figural construal (deliberate misreading) rather than "translating" the language of the Bible into an extrascriptural idiom. Frei writes:

> The literal sense is the paradigmatic form of such intratextual interpretation in the Christian community's use of its Scripture: The literal ascription to Jesus of Nazareth of the stories connected with him is of such far reaching import that it serves not only as focus for inner-canonical typology but reshapes extratextual language [and events] in its manifold descriptive uses in typological relation to these stories.[201]

The breakdown of this mode of reading the extratextual world, under the pressure of ostensive theories of reference that fractured the typological unity of the Bible and thus the rest of the reality in relation to it, Frei rehabilitates by means of the methodological "breathing space"[202] gained for literal sense reading, first by resort to the category, "realistic narrative" (which holds off *history* for *history-like*) and, second, by means of "thick description" (which holds off high powered *explanation* for empathetic insider *description*).

The task of extending the scriptural framework as the idiomatic framework by means of which all of life is construed, Frei believes to be a, if not the, most pressing task for the contemporary church.[203] However, this is not to suppose that applicative unanimity is the aim of such an emphasis. While Frei argues that literal sense reading of the Gospels and the rest of the Bible and reality in typological relation to them is warranted by the consensus of church practice, he does not expect that consensus on a literal sense orientation to the text will lead to a consensus explicative or applicative sense reading but rather to interpretative pluralism. Indeed, one of the advantages of identifying and construing literal sense reading in sociolinguistic terms is that while it functions descriptively to depict communal consensus at the level of orientation to the text, it allows for an appreciation of diverse interpretations rooted in various contexts and reading communities. David Lee writes:

---

200 Ibid., p. 147. Frei appropriates this term from George Lindbeck. For Lindbeck and Frei "absorbing" the extratextual world into the scriptural world typologically construed and Christologically centered is definitive of intratextual theology. "A scriptural world is thus able to absorb the universe. . . Scripture creates its own domain of meaning and . . . the task of interpretation is to extend this meaning over the whole of reality." Lindbeck, *The Nature of Doctrine*, p. 117. See also Lindbeck, "Scripture, Consensus, and Community," pp. 74-103.

201 "The 'Literal' Reading of Biblical Narrative," p. 147. See also Lindbeck, *The Nature of Doctrine*, pp. 117-118.

202 "Conflicts in Interpretation," p. 162.

203 See "The 'Literal' Reading of Biblical Narrative," pp. 148-149. Frei believes that a recovery of applicative literal sense reading may well be facilitated in conversation with various forms of Judaism.

The Church and the Bible Critically Read   203

Instead of the insistence that there is one meaning and interpretations of the text are assessed by how close they approach the single meaning, now Frei [in his sociolinguistic phase] acknowledges that a reading community can generate legitimate readings of the text and that these will inevitably differ from readings of the same text produced by other communities in other contexts.[204]

With this interpretative and applicative pluralism in mind, Frei sides with pre-modern biblical interpreters whose interest in biblical interpretation lay more with "applicative" and less with "historical" fit, since this preserves the reality-depicting function of the Bible against attempts "to substitute a philosophy of history for an intratextual interpretative scheme."[205] In the exegetical work of Augustine, for example, Frei observes a drive towards the applicative in the manner in which Augustine grants the literal sense (and the construal of the rest of the Bible and reality in relation to it) priority. Frei writes:

> Augustine, for example, understood the plain sense of Scripture to be that which conduces to faith, hope and the twofold love of God and neighbour. The *sensus literalis* therefore is that which functions in the context of the Christian life, and James Preus is right in proposing that for Augustine this edifying or normative literal sense is actually identical with the true spiritual reading of an unedifying literal sense.[206]

The viability of literal sense reading of the Bible, particularly where it concerns church reading in the mode of "absorbing" the world, Frei does not take up in great detail at a theoretical level. Frei maintains that Bible reading that interprets the world "will follow excellently from the actual, fruitful use religious people continue to make of it in ways that enhance their own and other people's lives."[207] While Frei supposes not great gains, indeed continuing losses, in terms of literal sense reading of the Bible for those who do not make "direct religious use of it,"[208] he does not consider the cultural decline of literal sense reading of the Bible definitive for religious readers. It may well be distressing to Christians that the Bible is not read in keeping with its literal sense (and here Frei wants to avoid obscurantist reading), but this fact ought not thwart the church from the practical viability of literal sense reading or the promise that such reading may well have for cultural issues of justice and freedom. If the church can rightly order its priorities, literal sense reading may entail a recovery of its vocation, as a "religion" rather than as an ideological prop for Western culture.[209]

Frei's Yale colleague George Lindbeck also argues for a rehabilitation of classic (literal sense), and yet not anti-critical, reading of the Bible for the church. Like Frei, he does not suppose that a common literal sense orientation in interpretative and

---

204 Lee, *Luke's Stories of Jesus*, pp. 83-84. See also Fodor, *Christian Hermeneutics*, p. 285.

205 "The 'Literal' Reading of Biblical Narrative," p. 149.

206 "Theology and the Interpretation of Narrative," p. 105. Frei refers to Preus, *From Shadow to Promise*, p. 14.

207 "The 'Literal' Reading of Biblical Narrative", p. 119.

208 Ibid.

209 Ibid., pp. 119, 148-149.

204 *Revelation, Holy Scripture and Church*

applicative discussion, however it alters the context of ecclesial debate, will yield unanimity on substantial matters.[210] What is more, like Frei, he wonders how and whether such reading can again come to "inform the *sensus fidelium*."[211] Lindbeck, working out of a concern for ecumenism, proposes not only that literal sense reading can provide the basis for a followable and habitable world for Christian readers in their attempt to make sense of the reality, but also a basis for Christian unity or at least the framework within which genuine church discussion can take place.[212] However, Lindbeck is not confident that literal sense reading is all together amenable to the "clamor of the religiously interested public for what is currently fashionable and immediately intelligible."[213] He notes that the church and Western culture alike are the victims of "contemporary forgetfulness."[214] Scriptural language, as it is ordered to the literal sense of the stories about Jesus, no longer functions as a shared medium for cultural discussion. While some scriptural metaphors are residually present in cultural discussion, this is altogether different from imaginatively inhabiting, "troping all that we are, do, and encounter in biblical terms."[215] Neither believers nor unbelievers see the world imaginatively through the lens of Scripture any longer since the whole notion of a privileged text has been subverted to intertextuality in which all texts are read on the same level in relation to each other. And yet, Lindbeck proposes that the recovery of literal sense reading of the Bible and the rest of reality in relation to it is not impossible. Christian communities may recover, through catechesis, "the skill to use their own tongue."[216] What is more, where preachers employ this linguistic skill, for example in the strong and imaginative misreading of present realities into the "deviant" framework of the Bible in sermons, Christian faith and theology may well become interesting again. "It is thus by the apparently

---

210 "Scripture, Consensus, and Community," p. 100:

Christians will continue to differ, not only on political questions of peace and justice and of socialism and capitalism but also on matters of direct ecclesial import such as the ordination of women. . . Retrieval of classical hermeneutics even in combination with historical criticism does not decide this issue. Yet it changes the context of the debate. Attention focuses, not on entitlements, privileges, and gender, but on the pastoral office itself as God's instrument for the nurturing of his people with word and sacrament.

211 Ibid., p. 99.

212 Ibid., pp. 100-101. In this context Lindbeck argues that a return to classical Christian reading patterns, even on the part of a remnant, "would be living proof that Scripture is a unifying and followable text." Lindbeck maintains that he is not discouraged about this possibility: "God's guidance of world and church history has sown seeds for the rebirth of the written word, and it is for believers to pray, work and hope against hope that God will bring these seeds to fruition through the power of the Holy Spirit." Ibid., p. 101.

213 Lindbeck maintains that the translation of Christian specificities into extra-scriptural frameworks, the *modus operandi* of liberal theology, seems more likely in the present intellectual climate. See *The Nature of Doctrine*, p. 134.

214 "Barth and Textuality," p. 370.

215 Ibid., p. 371.

216 Ibid., p. 372. The emphasis on recovering the linguistic facility necessary imaginatively to dwell in the world of Scripture can be found throughout Lindbeck's writings. See also *The Nature of Doctrine*, pp. 128-134 and "The Search for Habitable Texts," *Daedalus*, 117/2 (1988): 153-156.

plodding but intrinsically absorbing task of working with the Bible in one hand and the newspaper in the other (to use Barth's phrase) that the theologian can best contribute to church and society."[217] In other words, by engaging in imaginative misreadings of extratextual reality in relation to the Christocentric scriptural world, Christian preachers, theologians and disciples may well provide the greatest missionary service to our culture. The reasonableness of Christianity, on Lindbeck's account, may be best demonstrated by the "assimilative powers" of the Christian narrative, that is, by the ability of the Christian narrative to absorb extratextual reality into an interpretative framework that makes practical and "cognitively coherent sense of relevant data."[218] Thus Lindbeck, like Frei, supposes that the church may best fulfill its apostolic commission by reacquiring the skill of reading the world through the lens of a Christologically construed canon.

Critique

In this section, a critique of Frei's construal of the nature of Bible reading as critical and its relationship to the community for which it functions religiously is offered. An examination of the strategies by means of which Frei gains methodological space for the practice of the literal sense reading of Holy Scripture for the church, the character of literal sense reading as critical reading for faith and of faith and, finally, his critical strategy for absorbing extratextual reality into the world of the Bible is undertaken. While Frei's depiction of the hermeneutic situation and the integrity of the interpretative task of the Christian church offers significant theological gains over the other hermeneutic options examined, it leans too heavily upon the positivity of interpretative-ecclesial and not divine action with respect to the critical use of Scripture in the church. The methodological space gained both by Frei's deployment of poetic and social-scientific categories in order to protect the priority of Christocentric figural interpretation requires theological rootage in the doctrine of God in order to gain interpretative integrity. Moreover, by grounding his proposal for the critical interpretation of the Bible on embedded church practice, Frei potentially brackets out, not critical interpretation by the church, but critical interpretation of the church by the One who accosts, creates and sustains the church by means of the witness of Holy Scripture. Finally, while intratextual interpretation promises an applicative strategy for the interpretation of all of reality in terms of a typologically construed Christocentric canon, the possibility of such extratextual critical interpretation is over-invested in an understanding of faith as an imaginative capacity and socialized skill, at the expense of faith as personal assent and trust created ever anew by God the Holy Spirit through Scripture.

---

217 "Barth and Textuality," p. 376. In the *Nature of Doctrine*, Lindbeck call this "ad hoc apologetics."

218 *The Nature of Doctrine*, p. 131. See Bruce Marshall's development of this aspect of Lindbeck's thinking on the matter of demonstrating Christian truth claims by means of assimilative power. "Absorbing the World: Christianity and the Universe of Truths," pp. 69-102 in Bruce Marshall (ed.), *Theology and Narrative: Essays in Conversation with George Lindbeck* (Notre Dame, 1990).

Meaning, truth and subject matter   Perhaps the major thrust of Frei's interpretative proposal is to guard the integrity of the literal sense of the Gospels in an overall construal of the biblical materials. The ascriptively literal sense of the stories about Jesus provides the touchstone in terms of which all of the other biblical materials are related to an overarching story. As noted, Frei resists interpretative moves that would privilege the ascriptively literal stories of Jesus in such a way as to make their meaning dependent upon faith, that is, that takes the question of the accessibility of the subject matter of the Gospels out of the public realm. The Gospels are about Jesus, in the literally ascriptive mode, and this claim is in principle available to anyone who can make the appropriate genre distinction or, later on, to any sensitive observer of the use Christians make of Holy Scripture in their common life. Interpreters may not agree on the reality status of Jesus, that is, on whether or not or in which mode the ascriptively literal stories about Jesus are true, but the meaning of the stories in which the identity of Jesus is rendered in keeping with the genre type or reading conventions of the community for which the Bible functions religiously is in principle open to any sensitive reader.

The distinction that Frei wants to make between the meaning of the Bible and the truth of the Bible, for the sake of gaining methodological space for the task of exegesis as unencumbered by general theories as possible,[219] and the corresponding claim that the "literal meaning" of the Bible is available to any careful or sensitive interpreter, both of the Bible and of the religion to which the Bible belongs, may not be an entirely tenable. At the level of poetics, for example, Meir Sternberg maintains that Frei has tried to put to one side the "hopeless tangle that religious controversy has made of the issues of inspiration and history"[220] by focusing on the "realistic quality" of biblical narrative, which "can be interpreted in its own right without being confused with the quite different issue of whether or not the realistic narrative was historical."[221] Sternberg argues that the poetic device of the omniscient narrator in Scripture will not allow him to make this move so easily. Sternberg writes:

> Generally speaking, realism or history-likeness never has a bearing "in its own right on meaning and interpretation," because it signifies one thing in a historiographical and another in a fictional context. Even more evidently, neither the omniscient narrator nor the supernaturalness of the narrated world, for example, will read the same under these variations in narrative contract; nor will the clashes between the realistic and the nonrealistic.[222]

---

219 See Frei, "The 'Literal' Reading of Biblical Narrative," pp. 62-63; *The Eclipse of Biblical Narrative*, pp. 10-16; and *The Identity of Jesus Christ*, p. xii. Lindbeck also wants initially to bypass questions about the truth of the Bible, especially where such questions lead to a consideration of reference, in order to give priority to the question of meaning in scriptural exegesis. See *The Nature of Doctrine*, pp. 114-124.

220 Sternberg, *The Poetics of Biblical Narrative*, p. 82.

221 Ibid., p. 81.

222 Ibid., p. 82.

Sternberg maintains therefore that one must "postulate inspiration" (not necessarily believe in it) in order to make sense of the Bible "in terms of its own conventions."[223] In short, even on the poetic level, gaining methodological space by means of genre recognition involves a series of commitments that are not so benign as Frei suggests.

Moreover, a reader's relation to the central subject matter of the Bible, the reality in relation to which the Bible has meaning, as either empty or graciously present, does seems to bear on the question of meaning. Gary Comstock argues, especially with relation to Frei's work *The Identity of Jesus Christ*, that Frei prevaricates on the question of truth and meaning.[224] Comstock argues that Frei simultaneously maintains, on the one hand, that the meaning of the Bible is autonomous, that is, self-evident to anyone who reads the Bible for what it is and, on the other, that to understand the meaning of the Bible with regard to the identity of Jesus is to affirm him as present. He concludes that Frei must, therefore, recognize that meaning is unintelligible apart from reader response.[225]

While Comstock rightly locates a lacuna in Frei's interpretative proposal, his insistence that Frei provide a larger account of "reader response," apart from which meaning is unintelligible, is unsatisfactory. Theologically, the more promising direction would be to introduce a stronger sense of the work of the Spirit in making the identity of Jesus intelligible to readers (that is, in *enabling* readers to respond) and thus in forming the Christian community. In other words, if Jesus is not present in the power of the Spirit, then there is no response that will make the puzzling claims these texts make intelligible. For while there may be a formal (ideal?) level at which the subject matter of the Bible is available to the attentive reader of the text,[226] a refusal to permit, from the outset, the possibility of the absolute singularity of the task and identity of Jesus Christ as these are depicted in the gospels, that is, a refusal to regard Jesus as risen and the Bible as a living witness to the Word of God, would leave the reader with, as Barth puts it, "only an empty spot at the place to which the biblical writers point."[227]

This is not, however, to imply that the reader or the reader's or church's response to the text is itself a generative locus of textual meaning; rather it implies the Bible must be received for what it is, a witness to revelation, before an individual can be "regarded as a serious reader and exegete."[228] Although a reader might postulate that

---

223 Ibid., p. 81.

224 See Gary Comstock, "Truth or Meaning: Frei versus Ricoeur on Biblical Narrative," *Journal of Religion*, 66 (1986): 117-40.

225 Ibid., pp. 123-124, 126.

226 However, even at this formal level we need to be aware that the Bible makes an "urgent and imperious claim to truth," (Frei, "'Narrative' in Modern and Christian Reading," p. 156) and that this claim is, for Frei, part of the sense of the Bible. If therefore, an individual rejects the truth claim(s) of the Bible, another construal of the subject matter of Scripture, which is necessarily reductive from a theological point of view, would be necessary to make some sense of the Bible as a whole. In this case, we would have to wonder whether meaning, in the case of the Bible, is a general class.

227 Barth, *Church Dogmatics*, I/2: 469.

228 Ibid.

208 *Revelation, Holy Scripture and Church*

the Bible is a witness to revelation, in order better to understand it on its own terms, the luminosity of this text does not in the end rest upon the reader's or community's imaginative or sympathetic self-positioning. Robert Jenson makes the theologically realist point that if Jesus is risen then it is he himself who offers an identity description by means of Holy Scripture. Where Jesus is not

> exiled from historical agency . . . Jesus himself is the one who says in the church, through the church's tradition about him, "It is the one born of Mary and baptized by John and . . . that is risen." We are not the agents of the risen Lord's identification: he is.[229]

Hermeneutically speaking this implies that "*all*" compositional and ecclesial interpretative decisions vis-à-vis the texts of Holy Scripture "are instruments of the risen Lord to identify himself to his people, to say, 'I, the one who . . . am your Lord;' in the case of a saying, 'I, the one who said . . ., am your Lord.'"[230] Frei's interest in a neutral methodological space as a hermeneutical locale by means of which to guard the literal sense of the stories about Jesus from interpretative provincialism and to secure their place as the critical sense, whether purchased by investment in literary (realistic narrative) or social-scientific theory (thick description of embedded ecclesial reading practices), tends to sit askance of this richer account of Jesus' self-identification in and for the church.

Critical Reading by the church and of the church   On Frei's account, Holy Scripture is read critically in at least a couple of ways. The first is that the whole of the Bible is read in "critical" relation to the literal sense of the stories about Jesus. There is an ordered relation of texts within the canon of the Bible such that the mode adopted in construing and reading it as a unity is determined by the literal sense of the stories about Jesus. Non-Gospel portions of Holy Scripture may, indeed must, be read metaphorically or allegorically when and where their literal sense comes into conflict with the central story of Gospels as it is read in the ascriptive literal mode. Any reading of the Bible within which the two Testaments are read in a unity around the Gospel narratives of the life, death and resurrection of Jesus constitutes a legitimate (plain sense) reading of Holy Scripture. The interpretative conceptualities and tools employed in the interpretation of the Bible read scripturally must not usurp but service this global construal of the scriptural field. Extratextual reality is also read critically into this same framework. Using the same strategy by means of which the Bible is held together in a Christocentric unity, extratextual events and persons and situations are interpreted by means of typological configuration. Just as the inner canonical world of Scripture is critically configured so extratextual reality is critically construed—deliberately misread—into the interpretative idiom of Holy Scripture.

Frei's account of the first sense in which we employ the term "critical" or "plain sense" reading is the one to which a considered response is offered here. On Frei's account, particularly in his substantive later essays, he maintains that critical

---

229 Robert Jenson, *Systematic Theology*, vol. 1: *The Triune God* (Oxford, 1997), p. 173.

230 Ibid. Jenson's emphasis.

reading—reading the Bible as a unity of Old and New Testaments typologically and figurally construed in relation to the literal ascriptive sense of the Gospel stories about Jesus—is "plain sense" reading. It is "plain sense" since it the obvious sense to the community for whom the texts of Holy Scripture function religiously.[231] Such rules for reading, Frei maintains, are "embedded"[232] in the church's use of the Bible in its own life.

A striking feature of this account of the scriptural reading of the Bible is the degree to which it potentially immunizes "embedded" church practice from Gospel criticism. In other words, Frei articulates the basis for critical Bible reading by the church but offers no substantive theological account of the critical reading of embedded church practice by means of Holy Scripture. While Frei's account has the virtue of drawing attention to biblical interpretation as it is embodied in Christian liturgical and devotional and not just formal technical exegetical practice, he minimizes the role of Scripture as an instrument by means of which God accosts and interrogates and reforms church practice. Frei's social-scientific proposal assumes a certain stable and faithful institutional embodiment or sedimentation of the meaning of Scripture rather than a disruptive, always partial and incomplete performance of it.

Kathryn Tanner, in a defense of literal meaning as plain sense meaning along the lines Frei suggests, notes that this functionalist approach to the meaning of the Bible leaves itself open to the above criticism. She writes, "The approach itself assumes communal practices already set up and running; it does not go behind them to anything more basic from which they derive or to which they might be accountable."[233] Tanner proposes, however, that this criticism is misplaced. By drawing a distinction between communal consensus as the formal but not the material principle of the plain sense, Tanner attempts to preserve a measure of the authority of literal sense reading over against community practice. While a reader may be socialized into the church's reading practices and conventions, these skills are not themselves the plain sense reading of the Bible. When the acquired skills for plain sense reading are put into practice, they yield pluralistic readings or performances which are not of themselves (1) the rules for reading, but (2) expository or applied senses which can be measured against "what the text itself says." Indeed the privileging of plain sense reading of the Bible requires the priority of the text *qua* text over any plain sense performance of it. On Tanner's account, "the functional import of privileging the plain sense is the denial of a semantic equivalence between text and interpretation: interpretative accounts, in other words, cannot capture without remainder what the text conveys, and therefore none of them can take its place."[234] Any given plain sense reading

---

231 Like Hans Frei, whose view she defends, Kathryn Tanner understands the plain sense reading of the Bible as "a function of communal use: it is the obvious or direct sense of the text according to a *usus loquendi* established by the community in question." And again; "In sum, the plain sense is the "familiar, the traditional and hence the authoritative meaning" of a text within the community whose conventions for the reading of it have therefore already become relatively sedimented." Tanner, "Theology and the Plain Sense," pp. 62-63.

232 "The 'Literal' Reading of Biblical Narrative," pp. 147-148.

233 Tanner, "Theology and the Plain Sense," p. 66.

234 Ibid., p. 72.

210 *Revelation, Holy Scripture and Church*

distinct from the text is an interpretation and as such subject to the interrogation of the text from which it takes rise.

The success of Tanner's proposed defense of the potential self-critical nature of plain sense reading in the life of the church has been contested at a number of levels. One of the most convincing criticisms is this: to wed literal sense to the reading practices and consensus of the Christian community is "particularly inappropriate in an age when consensus is an endangered species and when many readers have fallen into bad habits."[235] Moreover, Tanner's proposal does not meet the standard she sets herself at the beginning of her essay. For even if she is successful in defending the notion that the literal sense of Scripture, as the orientation to the text engendered by socialization in the reading conventions of the Christian church, can be self-critical, her proposal "does not go behind them [communal reading conventions] to anything more basic from which they derive or to which they might be accountable."[236] While Tanner does attempt to establish a minimal notion of textual autonomy against proposed readings, Kevin Vanhoozer notes that the ability to distinguish between the formal and material senses of plain sense reading, the literal sense and the way it is conventionally read, is a "fragile conceptual distinction."[237] It would be more theologically convincing if her account, as well as Frei's, went beyond functionalist notions of plain sense reading in which self-criticism is possible to a theological account of the matter in which the reading of Scripture undertaken in faith and prayer not only challenges particular readings but threatens and overturns calcified communal practice. Neither Tanner nor Frei seem to envisage the possibility that "the sense which a reader has been socialized into treating as 'plain' may not be related at all to what the text could be construed as saying 'on its face.'"[238] Some account of Scripture as the Word of God that "is living and active and sharper than any two-edged sword" would root communal reading conventions in that from which they derive and to which they are finally accountable.

Extending the narrative   Applicative reading of the Bible as Holy Scripture by the church is also critical reading in the work of Hans Frei. The same inner canonical strategy by which the Bible is held together as a unity, functions as the interpretative lens for extratextual reality. Biblical persons, events and situations are not translated into extrascriptural idioms for the sake of "intelligibility" but rather extrascriptural reality is figurally related to the Christ-centered world of Holy Scripture. Extrascriptural reality gains intelligibility for the church by means of its rendering under the tutelage of Holy Scripture.

Anthony Thiselton makes the observation that intratextual interpretation because it reverses the direction of interpretation, "serves to question [the] tendency to give privilege to the present in a necessary way."[239] Intratextual interpretation, because it

---

235 Vanhoozer, *First Theology*, p. 224. See also Ward, *Word and Supplement*, pp. 159-160.

236 Tanner, "Theology and the Plain Sense," p. 66.

237 Vanhoozer, *First Theology*, p. 224.

238 Ward, *Word and Supplement*, p. 159.

239 Thiselton, *New Horizons in Hermeneutics*, p. 557. See also Dietrich Bonhoeffer, in Edwin E. Robertson (ed.), *No Rusty Swords: Letters, Lectures and Notes 1928-1936 from the*

The Church and the Bible Critically Read

211

moves descriptively from the priority of the biblical world (in its figural construal around the ascriptively literal stories about Jesus), saves readers from the tyranny of "relevance," in which the Bible is asked to deliver a word on pressing issues of the day. Barth's comment exposes the promise of the intratextual approach:

> It is not the case that the exposition of Holy Scripture must finally issue in the answering of the so-called burning questions of the present day, that if possible it will acquire meaning and force as it is able to give an illuminating answer to the questions of the present generation . . . In face of it, we cannot know beforehand what the real present is . . . In a very real sense this will not appear until the Bible opens up before us, to give us correct and infallible information about ourselves and our real questions, concerns and needs.[240]

Frei and Lindbeck in their common espousal of intratextual interpretation, demonstrate a formal "Anselmian"[241] similarity to Barth. However, the move from Scripture to the depiction of extratextual reality is clearly rooted for Barth in (1) the ontological priority of the realities borne witness to in the Bible, which (2) the Bible "opens up before us." Typological and figural interpretation across the Testaments and in relation to the extrascriptural world are not simply deft or imaginative hermeneutical maneuvers enabled by successful catetechical training (socialization in the religion of which these texts are a part)[242] but are rooted in the realities revealed by means of the Bible. Intratextual interpretation, which locates and specifies the identity and meaning of extratextual realities, events and persons, in relation to the Christocentric biblical world, does so because, by the action of God the Holy Spirit, this is revealed as their true identity and meaning.

Both Lindbeck and the later Frei seem to push in the direction of grounding their applicative hermeneutic strategy on the decision and action of the church. Lindbeck, in particular, appears to trace the formation of Christian imagination to what is its mediate source in the Christian community and its embodiment in biblical texts, and not its ultimate or final source in the hearing of Scripture in the power of the Spirit. To express the problem doctrinally: Lindbeck and Frei need to undergird their functionalist ecclesiology with a stronger account of pneumatology especially as this relates to the churchly task of extending the narrative.

While linguistic and imaginative training within the Christian community in the self-referencing world of Scripture no doubt contributes to the competent human

---

Collected Works, trans. John Bowden (New York, 1965), p. 306. Bonhoeffer writes, "The present is not where the present age announces its claims before Christ, but where the present age stands before the claims of Christ."

240 Barth, *Church Dogmatics*, 2/1: 738-739.

241 See Stout, "Hans Frei and Anselmian Theology." Stout maintains that Frei and Barth are of the same ontological temper in their interpretation of the Bible. Stout characterizes Frei's use of literary theology and social-scientific thick description as Anselmian *ad hoc* apologetics. However, the relationship between Barth and Frei on the matter of Anselmian interpretation is, as has been argued in the section on revelation, more formal than substantial. Frei, and Lindbeck, tend toward the transposition of the theological realism of Barth into features of the text or community.

242 See *The Nature of Doctrine*, pp. 113-124.

work of the translation of extratextual realities into the framework of Scripture, the capacity to acknowledge and dwell within this world of which Jesus Christ is the center ought to be attributed in the first instance not to churchly catechesis but to the work of the Spirit. Indeed, Lindbeck's and Frei's proposals might be strengthened (1) by employing the word "faith" instead of "imagination"; and (2) by specifying the character of faith, less in terms analogous to Aristotelian virtue or *habitus*, and more in terms of trusting assent.[243] Faith is the gift of God the Holy Spirit to the Christian community and its members whereby they are granted the vision to view contemporary circumstances and realities in the light of the "real world" of the Gospel and thus are enabled to respond in ways corresponding to the Gospel. On this view of the matter, preaching and the sacramental life of the church are not exclusively or even primarily means of "inculturating hearers more deeply into their tradition while training them in the practices of their community"; but rather they are "proclaiming the gospel by which the Holy Spirit creates faith."[244] The church, which is formed by the gift of grace, is also maintained from outside of itself by the free sustaining grace of God. Although it is charged with the real human task of extending the narrative, which I take to be the task of Christian witness, it is fundamentally dependent in this task upon the sustaining presence and activity of the Holy Spirit. Robert Jenson draws on an Old Protestant distinction which ascribes to the authority of Scripture a "double capacity: one to judge other writings and teachings . . . another to bring about the assent of faith."[245] It is the second of these capacities in particular, Scripture as the creative and sustaining *viva vox* of God for the church, that can be displaced in the intratextual applicative strategy of Frei and Lindbeck.

---

243 See Lose, *Confessing Jesus Christ*, pp. 120-121.

244 Ibid., p. 121. Lose notes that whatever the strengths of the cultural-linguistic move against "individualistic excesses of modernity . . . it undercuts the biblical understanding of *pistis* [faith] as both personal assent and trust." Ibid., p. 120.

245 Robert Jenson, *Systematic Theology*, vol. 2: *The Works of God* (Oxford, 1999), p. 273. The citation is from Johannes Musaeus, *Introductio in theologiam* (1679), 1:29n.

Conclusion

While the dominant tone of this essay has been expository and analytical, the general shape of a constructive proposal for the deployment of doctrine (revelation, Holy Scripture and church) in the depiction of the hermeneutic field has been implicit. When the aim of Scripture reading is its interpretation for the life of the Christian church, the nature and function of Bible as it is implicated in God's revelatory and salvific action is primary. What is more, creaturely realities caught up in the generation, formation, canonization and interpretation of Holy Scripture are best (truly) construed in relation to the action of God by means of the Bible. Concepts like inspiration, sanctification and election are usefully employed as descriptive of God's use, hallowing, of creaturely realities in God's one work of salvation wrought in Jesus Christ. This does not erase the humanity of the Bible or of the church and its practices within the interpretative field, but rather functions to give them theological density within the economy of salvation. Such a theological ontology of Scripture, which renders its account of the nature and function of the Bible as these are implicated within God's redemptive action, should not be taken as perspectival or as one side of a dualist account of the Bible. For while the language and conceptuality in which a theological ontology of the Bible is offered are always historically situated, and while specific historical, literary or social-scientific investigation into a limited field of inquiry may temporarily abstract parts of the Bible out of their canonical context, the implication of Holy Scripture in God's revelatory/salvific action is fundamental to what the Bible is. What is more, a theological construal of the interpretative field, in which the doctrines of revelation, Holy Scripture and church function to orient biblical interpretation at a fundamental level, is not only crucial to a theologically realist account, but also helps to highlight the human work of Scripture interpretation as a dependent act. Interpretation of the Bible as "Holy" Scripture is dependent upon the *viva vox* of God the Holy Spirit such that the appropriate corresponding human disposition is prayer for the grace of God.[1]

However, this is not to imply that historical, literary, philosophical and social scientific investigations are unimportant to the task of biblical interpretation for the life of the Christian church. On the contrary, these investigations have been and are crucial to the churchly reading of Holy Scripture. Attention to the grammar, syntax and form of the best text of the Bible we can establish is attention to the means that God uses in the life of the people of God. It is this text (the Bible), read this way (scripturally) among these people (the church) that God graciously employs to constitute and sustain a people for himself. It is only when and where interpretative tools and theoretically freighted approaches function to construe the hermeneutic terrain in a preemptive and preliminary (privileged) fashion such that an account of

---

1 See Donald Wood, "The Place of Theology in Theological Hermeneutics," *International Journal of Theology*, 4/2 (July, 2002), 169-171.

214   *Revelation, Holy Scripture and Church*

divine agency vis-à-vis the Bible (1) is conflated to human action virtually without remainder; or (2) is deferred and then transposed into an entirely natural or areligious account; or (3) is left tacit in deference to mediate human realities, that interpreters are left with a potentially deflationary account of the hermeneutic situation of the church.

The incorporation of the scholarly investigations of ancillary disciplines into the church's work of biblical interpretation thus best takes place under the logic of Anselmian appropriation, i.e., how does a particular insight or account contribute to expectant and prayerful reading of the Bible, which is determined by its subject matter. In the task of Scripture interpretation for the life of the Christian church, as the people of God listen for the voice of God, insights into the meaning of the Bible garnered by historical-critical, literary, philosophical and social-scientific studies are taken up where they overlap, contribute *and* constrain the understanding that faith seeks. Matters such as establishing the text, uncovering the theological pressures ingredient in text formation and canonization, and theological plurivocity within them, genre recognition, semantic specification, analysis of rule of faith readings in the Fathers, and even, or especially in keeping dogmatics attentive to the primary task of theology, Scripture exegesis, are all basic to the church's reading of Holy Scripture.

Robert Jenson makes the point that historical-criticism is especially pertinent to the scriptural reading of the Bible. In the history of interpretation there have been at least three ways to read the Bible: tropologically, anagogically and allegorically. While both Testaments have been traditionally read in the first two modes, in ways that point "to the end" and "to the life of faith," allegorical reading has ordinarily been restricted to the Old Testament. This is because the Gospels, and in particular Christology, establish the limits of the allegorical reading of the Old Testament. However, the Gospels, particularly as they concern the life, death and resurrection of Jesus, may not be read allegorically since it is their literality that provides control over allegorical reading in the rest of the Bible. Without this "historical" constraint, spiritual exegesis floats free of the text and Bible reading becomes arbitrary; it is no longer tethered to the text. Historical-critical investigation can render assistance against such "ahistorical associations."[2] More positively, by means of submission to the scriptural reading of the Bible as a witness to revelation and to what the grammar and sense of the story so construed will bear, historical-critical investigation becomes a sanctified human enterprise in the service of God the Holy Spirit. Scripture interpretation is a human work involving human realities; it requires training, knowledge and insightful disciplined scholarship, all of which are serviceable to the discernment of and an encounter with "the Word in the words."[3]

Theological hermeneutics is undertaken in prayer for the grace of God as genuine human work in the service of the scriptural reading of the Bible. It is also undertaken in hope. A fundamentally theological depiction of the task of Scripture interpretation is not itself the interpretation of Holy Scripture. What is more, it does not, even together with ancillary disciplines, provide anything like a fool-proof orientation to

---

2 Jenson, *Systematic Theology*, vol. 2: *The Works of God*, pp. 283-284.

3 Barth, *The Epistle to the Romans*, p. 9.

Conclusion 215

and method for garnering the meaning of the Bible for the life of the people of God. "There is no single technique able to provide the key to the secret of Scripture, not even a perfected hermeneutics."[4] Moreover, exegetes cannot force the hand of the sovereign and free God by interpretative self-positioning with respect to the text of the Bible or establish meaning in it by interpretative labor. "The object [of the Scriptural Word] is God's revelation in Jesus Christ, it is testimony of this revelation inspired by the Holy Ghost, and it can become luminous for us through the same Holy Ghost."[5]

However, interpretation takes place in prayer and as penultimate human work with hope, because God has demonstrated that in sovereign freedom God is for us in the Gospel. God's condescension in Jesus Christ, his accommodation to creaturely reality, hallows that reality, including the human speech it evokes as a fit and effective vehicle for God's communication.[6] Put in slightly different terms, the radiance of the light shed in the Gospel of Jesus Christ, by the God who is light, elicits and gives the altogether human witness of the Bible a clear, sufficient and effective witness unto salvation. "To confess Holy Scripture and its authority is to be aware of the command to understand and interpret it."[7] Interpretative effort, which gathers together insights from relevant scholarly disciplines in the scriptural reading of the Bible that aims at hearing the Word of God is thus neither a futile esoteric enterprise,[8] nor presumption, but an obedient and free act of Christian discipleship.

---

4 Berkouwer, *Holy Scripture*, p. 135.

5 Barth, *Church Dogmatics*, 1/2: 730.

6 Ronald Thiemann makes the point that where God claims (annexes) a piece of creaturely reality as his own and binds himself to it, "we are warranted in accepting the God-forged link between the human and the divine." *Revelation and Theology*, p. 95.

7 Berkouwer, *Holy Scripture*, p. 137.

8 Luther makes the point to Erasmus: "the Holy Spirit is no skeptic." Martin Luther, in Jaroslav Pelikan and Helmut T. Lehmann (gen. eds.), *Luther's Works*, vol. 33: *Career of the Reformer III*, Philip Watson (ed.), "The Bondage of the Will," trans. by Jaroslav Pelikan (Philadelphia: Fortress Press, 1972), p. 24.

Bibliography

Books

Abdul-Masih, Marguerite. *Edward Schillebeeckx and Hans Frei: A Conversation on Method and Christology*. Waterloo: Wilfred Laurier University Press, 2001.

Abraham, William. *The Divine Inspiration of Scripture*. Oxford: Oxford University Press, 1981.

Achtemeier, Paul J. *The Inspiration of Scripture: Problems and Proposals*. Philadelphia: Westminster Press, 1984.

Alter, Robert. *The Art of Biblical Narrative*. New York: Basic Books, 1981.

———. *The Art of Biblical Poetry*. New York: Basic Books, 1986.

———. *The World of Biblical Literature*. New York: Basic Books, 1992.

Althaus, Paul. *The Theology of Martin Luther*. Translated by Robert C. Schultz. Philadelphia: Fortress Press, 1966.

Auerbach, Eric. *Mimesis: The Representation of Reality in Western Literature*. Princeton: Princeton University Press, 1953.

Augustine. *On Christian Doctrine*. Translated with an introduction by D.W. Robertson, Jr. New York: Bobbs-Merrill, 1958.

Barr, James. *Biblical Faith and Natural Theology: The Gifford Lectures for 1991*. Oxford: Clarendon Press, 1993.

———. *Biblical Words for Time*, SBT 33. London: SCM Press, 1962.

———. *Escaping From Fundamentalism*. London: SCM Press, 1984.

———. *Fundamentalism*. London: SCM Press, 1977.

———. *History and Ideology in the Old Testament: Biblical Studies at the End of a Millennium*. Oxford: Oxford University Press, 2000.

———. *Holy Scripture: Canon, Authority, Criticism*. Philadelphia: Westminster Press, 1983.

———. *Old and New in Interpretation: A Study of the Two Testaments*. New York: Harper and Row, 1966; 2nd edn. London: SCM Press, 1982.

———. *The Bible in the Modern World*. London: SCM Press, 1973.

———. *The Concept of Biblical Theology: An Old Testament Perspective*. London: SCM Press, 1999.

———. *The Garden of Eden and the Hope of Immortality*. London: SCM Press, 1992.

———. *The Scope and Authority of the Bible*. Philadelphia: Westminster Press, 1980.

———. *The Semantics of Biblical Language*. London: Oxford University Press, 1961.

Barth, Karl. *Against the Stream*. London: SCM Press, 1954.

———. *Church Dogmatics* (13 vols). Edited and translated by G.W. Bromiley and T.F. Torrance, *et al.* Edinburgh: T & T Clark, 1936-1969.

———. *Evangelical Theology: An Introduction*. Translated by Grover Foley. Grand Rapids: Eerdmans, 1963.

———. *Homiletics*. Translated by Geoffrey W. Bromiley and Donald F. Daniels. Louisville: Westminister/John Knox, 1991.

218   *Revelation, Holy Scripture and Church*

——. *The Epistle to the Philippians 40th Anniversary Edition*. Translated by James Leitch. Louisville: Westminister/John Knox, 2002.

——. *The Epistle to the Romans*. 2nd edn.Translated from the 6th German edn by Edwyn C. Hoskyns. London: Oxford University Press, 1933.

Bartlett, David L. *Between the Bible and the Church: New Methods for Biblical Preaching*. Nashville: Abingdon Press, 1999.

Barton, John. *People of the Book? The Authority of the Bible in Christianity*. Louisville: Westminster/John Knox, 1993.

——, editor. *The Cambridge Companion to Biblical Interpretation*. Cambridge: Cambridge University Press, 1998.

Betz, Hans Dieter, editor. *The Bible as a Document of the University*. Chico, CA: Scholars Press, 1981.

Berkhof, Hendrikus. *The Christian Faith: An Introduction to the Study of the Faith*. Translated by Sierd Woudstra. Revised edn. Grand Rapids: Eerdmans, 1986.

Berkouwer, G.C. *Studies in Dogmatics: Holy Scripture*. Translated and edited by Jack B. Rodgers. Grand Rapids: Eerdmans, 1975.

Bockmuehl, Markus, editor. *The Cambridge Companion to Jesus*. Cambridge: Cambridge University Press, 2001.

Bonhoeffer, Dietrich. *No Rusty Swords: Letters, Lectures and Notes 1928–1936 from the Collected Works*. Vol. 1. Edited by Edwin H. Robertson. Translated by John Bowden. New York: Harper and Row, 1965.

Bouchindhomme, Christian and Rochlite, Rainer, editors. *Temps et récit de Paul Ricoeur en débat*. Paris: Cerf, 1989.

Braaten, Carl E. and Jenson, Robert W., editors. *Reclaiming the Bible for the Church*. Grand Rapids: Eerdmans, 1995.

Brett, Mark. *Biblical Criticism in Crisis?* Cambridge: Cambridge University Press, 1991.

Brown, David. *Tradition and Imagination*. Oxford: Clarendon Press, 2000.

Brown, Raymond. *The Critical Meaning of the Bible*. New York: Paulist Press, 1981.

Brueggemann, Walter. *An Introduction to the Old Testament: The Canon and Christian Imagination*. Louisville: Westminister/John Knox, 2003.

——. *Theology of the Old Testament: Testimony, Dispute, Advocacy*. Minneaoplis: Fortress Press, 1997.

Calvin, Jean. *Institutes of the Christian Religion*. Volumes 20 and 21 in the Library of Christian Classics. Translated and edited by Ford Lewis Battles. General Editors John Baillie, John T. McNeill and Henry P. Van Dusen. Philadelphia: Westminster Press, 1960.

Campbell, Charles L. *Preaching Jesus: New Directions for Homiletics in Hans Frei's Postliberal Theology*. Grand Rapids: Eerdmans, 1997.

Childs, Brevard. *Biblical Theology of the Old and New Testaments: Theological Reflection on the Christian Bible*. Minneapolis: Fortress Press, 1993.

——. *Introduction to the Old Testament as Scripture*. Philadelphia: Fortress Press, 1979.

——. *Isaiah: A Commentary*. Louisville: Westminister /John Knox, 2001.

——. *Old Testament Theology in a Canonical Context*. Philadelphia: Fortress Press, 1985.

——. *The New Testament as Canon: An Introduction*. Philadelphia: Fortress Press, 1985.

Davis, Ellen F. and Hays, Richard B., editors. *The Art of Reading Scripture*. Grand Rapids: Eerdmans, 2003.

Bibliography

Dawson, John David. *Christian Figural Reading and the Fashioning of Identity.* Berkeley: University of California Press, 2002.

Demson, David. *Hans Frei and Karl Barth: Different Ways of Reading Scripture.* Grand Rapids: Eerdmans, 1997.

Donaldson, Terrence. *Paul and the Gentiles: Remapping the Apostle's Convictional World.* Minneapolis: Fortress Press, 1997.

Dornisch, Loretta. *Faith and Philosophy in the Writings of Paul Ricoeur.* Lewis/Queenston/ Lampeter: Edwin Mellen Press, 1990.

Dulles, Avery, S.J. *Models of Revelation: A Cornerstone of Christian Theology.* New York: Doubleday, 1985.

Fackre, Gabriel. *The Doctrine of Revelation: A Narrative Interpretation.* Edinburgh Studies in Constructive Theology. Grand Rapids: Eerdmans, 1997.

Fish, Stanley. *Is There a Text in This Class?: The Authority of Interpretative Communities.* Cambridge, MA: Harvard University Press, 1980.

Fitzmyer, Joseph A. *Scripture, The Soul of Theology.* New York: Paulist Press, 1994.

Fodor, James. *Christian Hermeneutics: Paul Ricoeur and the Refiguring of Theology.* Oxford: Clarendon Press / New York: Oxford University Press, 1995.

Fowl, Stephen E. *Engaging Scripture: A Model for Theological Interpretation.* Oxford: Blackwell, 1998.

——, editor. *The Theological Interpretation of Scripture: Classical and Contemporary Readings.* Oxford: Blackwell, 1997.

Frei, Hans. "The Doctrine of Revelation in the Thought of Karl Barth, 1909-1922: The Nature of Barth's Break with Liberalism." PhD dissertation, Yale University, 1956.

——. *The Eclipse of Biblical Narrative: A Study in Eighteenth and Nineteenth Century Hermeneutics.* New Haven: Yale University Press, 1974.

——. *The Identity of Jesus Christ: The Hermeneutic Bases of Dogmatic Theology.* Philadelphia: Fortress Press, 1975.

——. *Theology and Narrative: Selected Essays.* Edited by George Hunsinger and William Placher. New York: Oxford University Press, 1994.

——. *Types of Christian Theology.* Edited by George Hunsinger and William Placher. New Haven: Yale University Press, 1992.

Geertz, Clifford. *The Interpretation of Cultures.* New York: Basic Books, 1973.

Gnuse, Robert. *The Authority of the Bible: Theories of Inspiration, Revelation and the Canon of Scripture.* New York: Paulist Press, 1985.

Green, Garrett, editor. *Scriptural Authority and Narrative Interpretation.* Philadelphia: Fortress Press, 1987.

——. *Theology, Hermeneutics, and Imagination: The Crisis of Interpretation at the End of Modernity.* Cambridge: Cambridge University Press, 2000.

Greene-McCreight, Karen. *Ad Litteram: How Augustine, Calvin and Barth read the "Plain Sense" of Genesis 1-3.* New York: Peter Lang, 1999.

Green, Michael, editor. *The Truth of God Incarnate.* London: Hodder and Stoughton, 1977.

Greer, R. *Broken Lights and Mended Lives: Theology and Common Life in the Early Church.* University Park: Pennsylvania State University Press, 1986.

Griffiths, Paul J. *Religious Reading: The Place of Reading in the Practice of Religion.* Oxford: Oxford University Press, 1999.

Gunton, Colin E., editor. *The Cambridge Companion to Christian Doctrine*. Cambridge: Cambridge University Press, 1997.

Hand, Sean, editor. *The Levinas Reader*. Oxford: Basil Blackwell, 1989.

Jeanrond, Werner G. *Theological Hermeneutics: Development and Significance*. New York: Crossroad, 1991.

Jenson, Robert. *Systematic Theology:* Volume 1: *The Triune God*. Oxford: Oxford University Press, 1997.

——. *Systematic Theology:* Volume 2: *The Works of God*. Oxford: Oxford University Press, 1999.

Josipovici, Gabriel. *The Book of God: A Response to the Bible*. New Haven: Yale University Press, 1988.

Joy, Morny, editor. *Paul Ricoeur and Narrative: Context and Contestation*. Calgary: University of Calgary Press, 1997.

Jüngel, Eberhard. *God as the Mystery of the World: On the Foundation of the Theology of the Crucified One in the Dispute between Theism and Atheism*. Translated by Darrell L. Guder. Grand Rapids: Eerdmans, 1983.

Kelly, J.N.D. *Early Christian Doctrines*. 5th edn. New York: Harper and Row, 1978.

Kelsey, David. *The Uses of Scripture in Recent Theology*. Philadelphia: Fortress Press, 1975.

Kort, Wesley A. *"Take, Read:" Scripture, Textuality and Cultural Practice*. University Park: Pennsylvania State University Press, 1996.

LaCocque, André and Ricoeur, Paul. Translated by David Pellauer. *Thinking Biblically: Exegetical and Hermeneutical Studies*. Chicago: University of Chicago Press, 1998.

Lampe, G.W.H and Woollcombe, K.J., editors. *Essays in Typology*. London: SCM Press, 1957.

Laughery, Gregory. *Living Hermeneutics in Motion: An Analysis and Evaluation of Paul Ricoeur's Contributions to Biblical Hermeneutics*. New York: University Press of America, 2002.

Lee, David. *Luke's Stories of Jesus: Theological Reading of Gospel Narrative and the Legacy of Hans Frei*. Journal for the Study of New Testament Supplement Series 185. Sheffield: Sheffield Academic Press, 1999.

Lindbeck, George. *The Nature of Doctrine: Religion and Theology in a Postliberal Age*. Philadelphia: Westminster Press, 1984.

Lose, David J. *Confessing Jesus Christ: Preaching in a Postmodern World*. Grand Rapids: Eerdmans, 2003.

Lundin, Roger, editor. *Disciplining Hermeneutics: Interpretation in Christian Perspective*. Grand Rapids: Eerdmans, 1997.

Luther, Martin. *Luther's Works*. General editors. Jaroslav Pelikan and Helmut Lehmann. Volume 26: *Lectures on Galatians 1535, Chapters 1-4*. Translated and edited by Jaroslav Pelikan. St Louis: Concordia, 1963.

——. *Luther's Works*. General editors, Jaroslav Pelikan and Helmut Lehmann. Volume 33: *Career of the Reformer III*. Edited by Philip Watson. Philadelphia: Fortress Press, 1972.

Marshall, Bruce D., editor. *Theology and Dialogue: Essays in Conversation with George Lindbeck*. Notre Dame, IN: University of Notre Dame Press, 1990.

Meeks, Wayne. *The First Urban Christians*. New Haven: Yale University Press, 1983.

Moberly, R.W.L. *The Bible, Theology, and Faith: A Study of Abraham and Jesus*. Cambridge: Cambridge University Press, 2000.

Bibliography

Murrell, Nathaniel Samuel. "James Barr's Critique of Biblical Theology: A Critical Analysis." PhD dissertation, Drew University, 1988.

Niebuhr, Richard H. *The Meaning of Revelation*. New York: Macmillan, 1941.

Neuhaus, Richard John, general editor. *Biblical Interpretation in Crisis: The Ratzinger Conference on Bible and Church*. Grand Rapids: Eerdmans, 1989.

O'Donovan, Oliver. *Resurrection and Moral Order: An Outline for Evangelical Ethics*. Grand Rapids: Eerdmans, 1986.

Olegovich, Giorgy, editor. *Ten Year Commemoration to the Life of Hans Frei 1922–1988*. New York: Semenenko Foundation, 1999.

Pecknold, C.C. *Transforming Postliberal Theology: George Lindbeck, Pragmatism and Scripture*. London: T & T Clark International, 2005.

Pelikan, Jaroslav. *The Christian Tradition: A History of the Development of Doctrine. Vol. 1: The Emergence of the Catholic Tradition (100–600)*. Chicago: University of Chicago Press, 1971.

Placher, William. *Narratives of a Vulnerable God*. Louisville: Westminster/John Knox, 1994.

——. *The Domestication of Transcendence: How Modern Thinking about God Went Wrong*. Louisville: Westminister/John Knox, 1996.

Preus, James. *From Shadow to Promise: Old Testament Interpretation from Augustine to the Young Luther*. Cambridge, MA: Harvard University Press, 1969.

Radner, Ephraim and Sumner, George, editors. *The Rule of Faith: Scripture, Canon, and Creed in a Critical Age*. Harrisburg: Morehouse, 1998.

Rahner, Karl. *Quaestiones Disputatate*. Volume 1: *Inspiration in the Bible*. 2nd revised edn. Translated by C. Henkey. New York: Herder and Herder, 1964.

Reagan, Charles E. *Paul Ricoeur: His Life and His Work*. Chicago: University of Chicago Press, 1996.

Richardson, A. and Schweitzer, W. editors. *Biblical Authority for Today*. London: SCM Press 1951.

Ricoeur, Paul. *Critique and Conviction: Conversations with Francois Azouvi and Marc de Launay*. Translated by Kathleen Blamey. New York: Columbia University Press, 1998.

——. *Essays on Biblical Interpretation*. Edited with an introduction by Lewis S. Mudge. Philadelphia: Fortress Press, 1980.

——. *Figuring the Sacred: Religion, Narrative, and Imagination*. Edited with an introduction by Mark I. Wallace. Translated by David Pellauer. Minneapolis: Fortress Press, 1995.

——. *Freud and Philosophy*. Translated by Denis Savage. New Haven: Yale University Press, 1970.

——. *From Text to Action: Essays in Hermeneutics,II*. Edited and translated by Kathleen Blamey and John B. Thompson. Evanston, IL: Northwestern University Press, 1991.

——. *Hermeneutics and the Human Sciences*. Edited and translated by John B. Thompson. Cambridge: Cambridge University Press, 1981.

——. *Interpretation Theory: Discourse and the Surplus of Meaning*. Fort Worth, TX: Texas Christian University Press, 1976.

——. *Oneself as Another*. Translated by Kathleen Blamey. Chicago: University of Chicago Press, 1992.

——. *The Conflict of Interpretations: Essays in Hermeneutics*. Edited by Don Ihde. Evanston, IL: Northwestern University Press, 1974.

222 *Revelation, Holy Scripture and Church*

——. *The Rule of Metaphor: Multi-Disciplinary Studies of the Creation of Meaning in Language*. Translated by Robert Czerny with Kathleen McLaughlin and John Costello, SJ. Toronto: University of Toronto Press, 1977.

Sanders, James A. *From Sacred Story to Sacred Text*. Philadelphia: Fortress Press, 1987.

Schleiermacher, Friedrich. *The Christian Faith*. Translated by H.R. Mackintosh and J.S. Stewart. Edinburgh: T & T Clark, 1928.

Schneiders, Sandra M. *The Revelatory Text: Interpreting The New Testament as Sacred Scripture*. New York: HarperCollins Publishers, 1991.

Seitz, Christopher R. *Figured Out: Typology and Providence in Christian Scripture*. Louisville: Westminister/John Knox, 2001.

——, editor. *Nicene Christianity: The Future for a New Ecumenism*. Grand Rapids: Baker Book House, 2001.

Simms, Karl. *Paul Ricoeur*. London: Routledge, 2003.

Smart, James D. *The Past, Present, and Future of Biblical Theology*. Philadelphia: Westminster Press, 1979.

——. *The Strange Silence of the Bible in the Church: A Study in Hermeneutics*. Philadelphia: Westminster Press, 1970.

Sternberg, Meir. *The Poetics of Biblical Narrative: Ideological Literature and the Drama of Reading*. Bloomington: Indiana University Press, 1985.

Stiver, Dan. *Theology after Ricoeur: New Directions in Hermeneutical Theology*. Westminister/John Knox, 2001.

Swinburne, Richard. *Revelation: From Metaphor to Analogy*. Oxford: Clarendon Press, 1992.

Tanner, Kathryn. *God and Creation in Christian Theology: Tyranny or Empowerment?* Oxford: Basil Blackwell, 1988.

——. *Theories of Culture: A New Agenda for Theology*. Minneapolis: Augsburg Fortress, 1997.

Thiemann, Ronald F. *Revelation and Theology: The Gospel as Narrated Promise*. Notre Dame, IN: University of Notre Dame Press, 1985.

Thiselton, Anthony C. *New Horizons in Hermeneutics: The Theory and Practice of Transforming Biblical Reading*. Grand Rapids: Zondervan, 1992.

——. *The Two Horizons: New Testament Hermeneutics and Philosophical Description*. Grand Rapids: Eerdmans, 1980.

Thompson, John B. *Critical Hermeneutics: A Study in the Thought of Paul Ricoeur and Jürgen Habermas*. Cambridge: Cambridge University Press, 1981.

——. *Studies in the Theory of Ideology*. Los Angeles: University of California Press, 1984.

Torrance, Thomas F. *Reality and Evangelical Theology: A Fresh and Challenging Approach to Christian Revelation*. Philadelphia: Westminster Press, 1982.

——. *The Hermeneutics of John Calvin*. Monograph Supplement to the *Scottish Journal of Theology*. Edinburgh: Scottish Academic Press, 1988.

Vanhoozer, Kevin. *Biblical Narrative in the Philosophy of Paul Ricoeur: A Study in Hermeneutics and Theology*. Cambridge: Cambridge University Press, 1990.

——. *First Theology: God, Scripture and Hermeneutics*. Downers Grove: Intervarsity Press, 2002.

——. *Is There a Meaning in This Text?: The Bible, The Reader, and the Morality of Knowledge*. Grand Rapids: Zondervan, 1998.

Bibliography

Von Campenhausen, Hans. *The Formation of the Christian Bible*. Translated by J.A. Baker. Philadelphia: Fortress Press, 1972.

Wallace, Mark I. *The Second Naiveté: Barth, Ricoeur, and the New Yale Theology*. Macon, Georgia: Mercer University Press, 1990.

Ward, Timothy. *Word and Supplement: Speech Acts, Biblical Texts, and the Sufficiency of Scripture*. Oxford: Oxford University Press, 2002.

Watson, Francis. *Text, Church and World: Biblical Interpretation in Theological Perspective*. Grand Rapids: Eerdmans, 1994.

——. *Text and Truth: Redefining Biblical Theology*. Grand Rapids: Eerdmans, 1997.

Webster, John B. *Holy Scripture: A Dogmatic Sketch*. Cambridge: Cambridge University Press, 2003.

Wells, Paul Ronald. *James Barr and the Bible: Critique of a New Liberalism*. Phillipsburg, NJ: Presbyterian and Reformed Publishing, 1980.

Wendel, François. *Calvin: The Origin and Development of his Religious Thought*. In *The Fontana Library of Theology and Philosophy*. Translated by Philip Mairet. New York: Collins, 1963.

Westphal, Merold. *Suspicion and Faith: The Religious Uses of Modern Atheism*. Grand Rapids: Eerdmans, 1993.

Williams, Rowan. *On Christian Theology*. Oxford: Blackwell, 2000.

Wimsatt, W.K. *The Verbal Icon: Studies in the Meaning of Poetry*. Kentucky: University of Kentucky Press, 1954.

Wolterstorff, Nicholas. *Divine Discourse: Philosophical Reflections on the Claim that God Speaks*. New York: Cambridge University Press, 1995.

Woods, Charles M. *The Formation of Christian Understanding: Theological Hermeneutics*. 2nd edn. Valley Forge, PA: Trinity Press International, 1993.

Young, Francis. *Biblical Exegesis and the Formation of Christian Culture*. Cambridge: Cambridge University Press, 1997.

Articles/Chapters

Anderson, Pamela Sue, "Agnosticism and Attestation: An Aporia concerning the Other in Ricoeur's *Oneself as Another*." *Journal of Religion*, 74/1 (1994): 65-76.

Balentine, Samuel E. "James Barr's Quest for Sound and Adequate Biblical Interpretation." In *Language, Theology and the Bible: Essays in Honour of James Barr*, pp. 5-15. Edited by Samuel E. Balentine and John Barton. New York: Oxford University Press, 1994.

Balentine, Samuel E. and Barton, John. "The Reverend Professor James Barr." In *Language, Theology and the Bible*, pp. 1-4.

Barton, John. "Historical-Critical Approaches." In *The Cambridge Companion to Biblical Interpretation*, pp. 9-20. Edited by John Barton. Cambridge: Cambridge University Press, 1995.

——. "James Barr as Critic and Theologian." In *Language, Theology and the Bible*, pp. 16-26.

Barr, James. "Allegory and Typology." In *A New Dictionary of Christian Theology*, pp. 11-15. Edited by Alan Richardson and J. Bowden. London: SCM Press, 1983.

224 *Revelation, Holy Scripture and Church*

——. "Biblical Language and Exegesis—How Far Does Structuralism Help Us?" *King's College Review*, 7/2 (Autumn, 1984): 48-52.

——. "Divine Action and Hebrew Wisdom." In *The Making and Remaking of Christian Doctrine: Essays in Honour of Maurice Wiles*, pp. 1-12. Edited by Sarah Coakley and David A. Pailin. New York: Oxford University Press, 1993.

——. "Exegesis as a Theological Discipline Reconsidered and the Shadow of the Jesus of History." In *The Hermeneutical Quest: Essays in Honor of James Luther Mays on his Sixty-Fifth Birthday*, pp. 11-45. Edited by Donald G. Miller. Allison Park: Pickwick, 1986.

——. "Jowett and the 'Original Meaning' of Scripture." *Religious Studies*, 18 (1982): 433-437.

——. "Jowett and the Reading of the Bible, 'Like any other book.'" *Horizons in Biblical Theology*, 4/2 and 5/1 (December, 1982 and June, 1983): 1-44.

——. "Literality." *Faith and Philosophy*, 6/4 (October, 1989): 412-427.

——. "Modern Biblical Criticism." In the *Oxford Companion to the Bible*, pp. 318-324. Edited by Bruce Metzger and Michael Coogan. New York: Oxford University Press, 1993.

——. "Revelation through History in the Old Testament and in Modern Theology." *Interpretation*, 17 (April, 1963): 193-205.

——. Review of *Biblical Criticism in Crisis?: The Impact of the Canonical Approach on Old Testament Studies* by Mark G. Brett. *Journal of Theological Studies*, 43 (1992): 135-141.

——. Review of *Divine Revelation and the Limits of Historical Criticism* by W. J. Abraham. *Scottish Journal of Theology*, 36 (1983): 247-250.

——. Review of *Essays on Biblical Interpretation* by Paul Ricoeur. *Theology*, 84 (November, 1981): 462-464.

——. Review of *Introduction to the Old Testament as Scripture* by Brevard Childs. *Journal for the Study of the Old Testament*, 16 (1980): 12-23.

——. Review of *Text and Truth: Redefining Biblical Theology* by Francis Watson. *Interpretation*, 52/4 (October, 1998): 438-439.

——. Review of *The Divine Inspiration of Holy Scripture* by William J. Abraham. *Journal of Theological Studies*, 34/5 (April, 1983): 370-376.

——. Review of *The Uses of Scripture in Recent Theology* by David H. Kelsey. *Virginia Seminary Journal*, 30/3 and 31/1 (November,1978 and March, 1979): 39-40.

——. "The Authority of Scripture: The Book of Genesis and the Origin of Evil in Jewish and Christian Tradition." In *Christian Authority: Essays in Honour of Henry Chadwick*, pp. 59-75. Edited by G.R. Evans. Oxford: Clarendon Press, 1988.

——. "The Bible and Its Communities." In *Harper's Bible Commentary*, pp. 65-72. General editor James L. Mays. New York: Harper and Row, 1988.

——. "The Bible as a Document of Believing Communities." In *The Bible as a Document of the University*, pp. 25-47. Edited by Hans Deiter Betz. Chico, CA: Scholars Press, 1981.

——. "The Literal, the Allegorical, and Modern Biblical Scholarship." *Journal for the Study of the Old Testament*, 44 (1989): 3-17.

——. "The Old Testament." In *The Scope of Theology*, pp. 23-38. Edited by David Jenkins. Cleveland: Meridian Books, 1965.

——. "The Old Testament and the New Crisis of Biblical Authority." *Interpretation*, 25 (1971): 24-40.

Bibliography

———. "The Theological Case against Biblical Theology." In *Canon, Theology and Old Testament*, pp. 3-19. Edited by G.M. Tucker, D.L. Petersen and R.R. Wilson. Philadelphia: Fortress Press, 1988.

———. "Trends and Prospects in Biblical Theology." *Journal of Theological Studies*, 25/2 (October, 1974): 265-282.

Bayer, Oswald. "Theology in the Conflict of Interpretations—Before the Text." *Modern Theology*, 16/4 (October, 2000): 495-502.

Blowers, Paul M. "The *Regula Fidei* and The Narrative Character of Early Christian Faith." *Pro Ecclesia*, 6/2 (1997): 199-228.

Bruns, Gerald L. "Midrash and Allegory: The Beginnings of Scriptural Interpretation." In *The Literary Guide to the Bible*, pp. 625-646. Edited by Robert Alter and Frank Kermode. Cambridge, MA: Harvard University Press, 1987.

Childs, Brevard S. "Childs Versus Barr." Review of *Holy Scripture: Canon, Authority, Criticism* by James Barr. *Interpretation*, 38 (January, 1984): 66-70.

———. "Critical Reflections on James Barr's Understanding of the Literal and the Allegorical." *Journal for the Study of the Old Testament*, 46 (1990): 3-9.

———. "Jesus Christ the Lord and the Scriptures of the Church." In *The Rule of Faith: Scripture, Canon, and Creed in a Critical Age*, pp. 1-12. Edited by Ephraim Radner and George Sumner. Harrisburg: Morehouse, 1998.

———. "On Reclaiming the Bible for Christian Theology." In *Reclaiming the Bible for the Church*, pp. 1-18. Edited by Carl E. Braaten and Robert W. Jenson. Grand Rapids: Eerdmans, 1995.

———. "Response to Reviews of *Introduction to the Old Testament as Scripture*." *Journal for the Study of the Old Testament*, 16 (1980): 52-60.

Comstock, Gary. "Truth or Meaning: Ricoeur versus Frei on Biblical Narrative." *Journal of Religion*, 66 (1986): 117-140.

———. "Two Types of Narrative Theology." *Journal of the American Academy of Religion*, 55/4 (1987): 687-717.

Craigo-Snell, Shannon. "Command Performance: Rethinking Performance Interpretation the Context of Divine Discourse." *Modern Theology*, 16/4 (October, 2000): 475-494.

Daley, Brian E., SJ. "Is Patristic Exegesis Still Useable? Some Reflections on Early Christian Interpretation of the Psalms." In *The Art of Reading Scripture,* pp. 69-88. Edited by Ellen Davis and Richard Hays. Grand Rapids: Eerdmans, 2003.

Dawson, David. "Allegorical Intratextuality in Bunyan and Winstanley." *Journal of Religion*, 70/2 (April, 1990): 189-212.

Demson, David. "Response to Walter Lowe." *Modern Theology*, 8/2 (April, 1992): 145-148.

Detmer, David. "Ricoeur on Atheism: A Critique." In *The Library of Living Philosophers*. Edited by Lewis Edwin Hahn. Chicago: Open Court Press, 1995. Vol. 22: *The Philosophy of Paul Ricoeur*, pp. 477-493.

Donfried, Karl P. "Alien Hermeneutics and the Misappropriation of Scripture." In *Reclaiming the Bible for the Church*, pp. 19-45. Edited by Carl E. Braaten and Robert W. Jenson. Grand Rapids: Eerdmans, 1995.

Fodor, James. Review of *Religious Reading: The Place of Reading in the Practice of Religion* by Paul J. Griffiths. *Modern Theology*, 17/4 (October, 2001): 529-531.

226   *Revelation, Holy Scripture and Church*

——. "The Tragic Fate of Narrative Judgment: Christian Reflections on Paul Ricoeur's Theory of Narrative." In *Paul Ricoeur and Narrative: Context and Contestation*, pp. 153-174. Edited by Morny Joy. Calgary: University of Calgary Press, 1997.

Folkert, Kendall W. "The 'Canons' of Scripture." In *Rethinking Scripture: Essays from a Comparative Perspective*, pp. 170-179. Edited by Miriam Levering. New York: State University of New York Press, 1989.

Frei, Hans W. "An Afterword: Eberhard Busch's Biography of Karl Barth." In *Types of Christian Theology*, pp. 147-163. Edited by George Hunsinger and William C. Placher. New Haven: Yale University Press, 1992. Reprinted from *Karl Barth in Re-view*, pp. 95-116. Edited by Martin Rumscheidt. Pittsburgh: Pickwick Press, 1991.

——. "Barth and Schleiermacher: Divergence and Convergence." In *Theology and Narrative: Selected Essays*, pp. 177-199. Edited by George Hunsinger and William C. Placher. New York: Oxford University Press, 1993. Reprinted from *Barth and Schleiermacher: Beyond the Impasse?*, pp. 65-87. Edited by James O. Duke and Robert F. Streetman. Philadelphia: Fortress Press, 1988.

——. "Conflicts in Interpretation: Resolution, Armistice, or Co-Existence?" In *Theology and Narrative*, pp. 153-166. Reprinted from *Theology Today*, 49/3 (October, 1992): 344-356.

——. "David Friedrich Strauss." In *Nineteenth Century Religious Thought in the West.* Volume 1: 215-260. Edited by N. Smart. Cambridge: Cambridge University Press, 1985.

——. "Eberhard Busch's Biography of Karl Barth." In *Types of Christian Theology*, pp. 147-163. Reprinted from *Karl Barth in Re-view*, pp. 95-116. Edited by Martin Rumscheidt. Pittsburgh: Pickwick Press, 1991.

——. "Epilogue: George Lindbeck and *The Nature of Doctrine*." In *Theology and Dialogue: Essays in Conversation with George Lindbeck*, pp. 275-282. Edited by Bruce D. Marshall. Notre Dame, IN: University of Notre Dame Press, 1990.

——. "H. Richard Niebuhr on History, Church and Nation." In *Theology and Narrative*, pp. 213-232. Reprinted from *The Legacy of H. Richard Niebuhr*, pp. 1-23. Edited by Ronald F. Thiemann. Minneapolis: Fortress Press, 1991.

——. "Karl Barth: Theologian." In *Theology and Narrative*, pp. 167-176. Reprinted from *Reflection*, 66/4 (1969): 5-9.

——. "'Narrative' in Christian and Modern Reading." In *Theology and Dialogue*, pp. 149-163.

——. "Niebuhr's Theological Background." In *Faith and Ethics: The Theology of H. Richard Niebuhr*, pp. 9-64. Edited by Paul Ramsey. New York: Harper and Row, 1957.

——. "Of the Resurrection of Christ." In *Theology and Narrative*, pp. 200-206. Reprinted from *Anglican and Episcopal History*, 58/2 (June, 1989): 139-145.

——. "Remarks in Connection with a Theological Proposal." In *Theology and Narrative*, pp. 26-44.

——. "Response to 'Narrative' Theology: An Evangelical Appraisal." In *Theology and Narrative*, pp. 207-212. Reprinted from *Trinity Journal*, 8 NS (Spring, 1987): 21-24.

——. "The 'Literal' Reading of Biblical Narrative in the Christian Tradition: Does it Stretch or Will it Break?" In *Theology and Narrative*, pp. 117-152. Reprinted from *The Bible and the Narrative Tradition*, pp. 36-77. Edited by Frank McConnell. New York: Oxford University Press, 1986.

Bibliography

———. "Theological Reflections on the Accounts of Jesus' Death and Resurrection." In *Theology and Narrative*, pp. 45-93. Reprinted from *The Christian Scholar*, 49 (1966): 263-306.

———. "Theology and the Interpretation of Narrative: Some Hermeneutical Considerations." In *Theology and Narrative*, pp. 94-116.

Folkert, Kendall W. "The 'Canons' of Scripture." In *Rethinking Scripture: Essays from a Comparative Perspective*, pp. 170-179. Edited by Miriam Levering. New York: State University of New York Press, 1989.

Gunton, Colin. "Historical and Systematic Theology." In *The Cambridge Companion to Christian Doctrine*, pp. 3-20. Edited by Colin Gunton. New York: Cambridge University Press, 1997.

Hays, Richard. "Reading Scripture in the Light of the Resurrection." In *The Art of Reading Scripture*, pp. 216-238. Edited by Ellen Davis and Richard Hays. Grand Rapids: Eerdmans, 2003.

———. "The Conversion of the Imagination: Scripture and Eschatology in 1 Corinthians." *New Testament Studies*, 45 (1999): 391-412.

Henry, Carl F. "Narrative Theology: An Evangelical Appraisal." *Trinity Journal*, 8 NS (Spring, 1987): 3-19.

Higton, Mike. "Frei's Christology and Lindbeck's Cultural Linguistic Theory." *Scottish Journal of Theology*, 50/1 (1997): 83-95.

———. "Hans Frei and David Tracy on the Ordinary and the Extraordinary in Christianity." *Journal of Religion*, 79/4 (October, 1999): 566-591.

———. Review of *Edward Schillebeeckx and Hans Frei: A Conversation on Method and Christology* by Marguerite Abdul-Masih. *Modern Theology*, 19/4 (October, 2003): 590-592.

Hunsinger, George. "Afterword: Hans Frei as Theologian." In *Theology and Narrative: Selected Essays*, pp. 233-270. Edited by George Hunsinger and William Placher. New York: Oxford, 1993.

———. "Beyond Literalism and Expressivism: Karl Barth's Hermeneutical Realism." *Modern Theology*, 3/3 (1987): 209-223.

———. "Truth as Self-Involving: Barth and Lindbeck on the Cognitive and Performative Aspects of Truth in Theological Discourse." *Journal of the American Academy of Religion*, 61/1 (1993): 41-55.

Jenson, Robert W. "Hermeneutics and the Life of the Church." In *Reclaiming the Bible for the Church*, pp. 89-106. Edited by Carl E. Braaten and Robert Jenson. Grand Rapids: Eerdmans, 1995.

———. "Scripture's Authority in the Church." In *The Art of Reading Scripture*, pp. 27-37. Edited by Ellen Davis and Richard Hays. Grand Rapids: Eerdmans, 2003.

Jülicher, Adolf "A Modern Interpreter of Paul," In *The Beginnings of Dialectical Theology*, pp. 72-81. Edited by James M. Robinson. Richmond, VA: John Knox Press, 1968.

Kearney, Richard. "Paul Ricoeur and the Hermeneutic Imagination." In *The Narrative Path: The Later Works of Paul Ricoeur*, pp. 1-31. Edited by T. Peter Kemp and David Rasmussen. Cambridge, MA: MIT Press, 1989.

Kelsey, David H. "The Bible and Christian Theology." *The Journal of the American Academy of Religion*, 48/3 (1980): 385-402.

228 *Revelation, Holy Scripture and Church*

Kermode, Frank. "The Argument about Canons." In *The Bible and the Narrative Tradition*, pp. 78-96. Edited by Frank McConnell. New York: Oxford University Press, 1986.

——. "The Canon." In *The Literary Guide to the Bible*, pp. 600-610. Edited by Robert Alter and Frank Kermode. Cambridge, MA: Harvard University Press, 1987.

Levenson, Jon. "Negative Theology." Review of *The Concept of Biblical Theology: An Old Testament Perspective* by James Barr. *First Things*, 100 (February, 2000): 59-63.

——. "Theological Consensus or Historicist Evasion: Jews and Christians and Historical Criticism." In *The Hebrew Bible, the Old Testament and Historical Criticism*, pp. 82-105. Louisville: Westminister/John Knox, 1993.

Levinas, Emmanuel, "Revelation in the Jewish Tradition." In *The Levinas Reader*. pp. 190-210. Edited by Sean Hand. Oxford: Basil Blackwell, 1989.

Lindbeck, George A. "Barth and Textuality." *Theology Today*, 43 (1986): 361-376.

——. "Postcritical Canonical Interpretation: Three Modes of Retrieval." In *Theological Exegesis: Essays in Honor of Brevard S. Childs*. Edited by Christopher Seitz and Kathryn Greene-McCreight. Grand Rapids: Eerdmans, 1999.

——. "Scripture, Consensus, and Community." In *Biblical Interpretation in Crisis*, pp. 74-103. Edited by Richard John Neuhaus. Grand Rapids: Eerdmans, 1989. Reprinted from *This World*, 23 (Fall, 1988): 5-24.

——. "The Bible as Realistic Narrative." *Journal of Ecumenical Studies*, 17/1 (1980): 81-85.

——. "The Church." In *Keeping the Faith: Essays to Mark the Centenary of Lux Mundi*, pp. 179-208. Edited by Geoffrey Wainwright. Philadelphia: Fortress Press, 1988.

——. "The Church's Mission to a Postmodern Culture." In *Postmodern Theology: Christian Faith in a Pluralist World*, pp. 37-55. Edited by Frederic Burnham. New York: Harper and Row, 1989.

——. "The Search for Habitable Texts." *Daedalus*, 117/2 (1988): 153-156.

——. "The Sectarian Future of the Church." In *The God Experience*, pp. 226-243. Edited by J.P. Whelan, SJ. New York: Newman, 1971.

——. "The Story-Shaped Church: Critical Exegesis and Theological Interpretation." In *Scriptural Authority and Narrative Interpretation*, pp.161-178. Edited by Garrett Green. Philadelphia: Fortress Press, 1987.

Loewe, Raphael. "The 'Plain' Meaning of Scripture in Early Jewish Exegesis." In *Papers of the Institute of Jewish Studies in London*. Volume 1, pp. 140-185. Jerusalem, 1964.

Long, Thomas G. "Committing Hermeneutical Heresy." *Theology Today*, 44/2 (July, 1987): 165-169.

Lowe, Walter. "Hans Frei and Phenomenological Hermeneutics." *Modern Theology*, 8/2 (April, 1992): 133-144.

Macquarrie, John. "Postscript: Christianity without Incarnation? Some Critical Comments." In *The Truth of God Incarnate*, pp. 140-144. Edited by Michael Green. London: Hodder and Stoughton, 1977.

Marshall, Bruce. "Absorbing the World: Christianity and the Universe of Truths." In *Theology and Narrative: Essays in Conversation with George Lindbeck*, pp. 69-102. Edited by Bruce Marshall. Notre Dame, IN University of Notre Dame Press, 1990.

McCormack, Bruce L. "Historical Criticism and Dogmatic Interest in Karl Barth's Theological Exegesis of the New Testament." In *Biblical Hermeneutics in Historical Perspective*,

Bibliography

pp. 322-338. Edited by Mark S. Burrows and Paul Rorem. Grand Rapids: Eerdmans, 1991.

——. "The Significance of Karl Barth's Theological Exegesis of Philippians." In *The Epistle to the Philippians 40th Anniversary Edition*, pp. v-xxv. Louisville: Westminister/John Knox Press, 2002.

Moberly, R.W.L. "The Christ of the Old and New Testaments." In *The Cambridge Companion to Jesus*, pp. 184-199. Edited by Markus Bockmuehl. Cambridge: Cambridge University Press, 2001.

Mudge, Lewis S. "Paul Ricoeur on Biblical Interpretation." In *Essays on Biblical Interpretation*, pp. 1-40. Edited by Lewis S. Mudge. Philadelphia: Fortress Press, 1980.

Noble, Paul R. "The Sensus Literalis: Jowett, Childs, and Barr." *Journal of Theological Studies*, 44/1 (April, 1993): 1-23.

Ollenburger, Ben C. Review of *Holy Scripture: Canon, Authority, Criticism* by James Barr. *Theology Today*, 41 (July, 1984): 207-210.

Outka, Gene. "Following at a Distance: Ethics and the Identity of Jesus Christ." In *Scriptural Authority and Narrative Interpretation*, pp. 144-160. Edited by Garrett Green. Philadelphia: Fortress Press, 1987.

Pannenberg, Wolfhart. "Revelation in Early Christianity." In *Christian Authority: Essays in Honour of Henry Chadwick*, pp.76-85. Edited by G.R. Evans. Oxford: Clarendon Press, 1988.

Pellauer, David. "Foreward: Recounting Narrative." In *Paul Ricoeur and Narrative: Context and Contestation*, pp. ix-xxiii. Calgary: University of Calgary Press, 1997.

Placher, William C. "Gospels' Ends: Plurality and Ambiguity in Biblical Narratives." *Modern Theology*, 10/2 (April, 1994): 143-163.

——. "Introduction." In *Theology and Narrative: Selected Essays*, pp. 3-25. Edited by George Hunsinger and William Placher. New York: Oxford University Press, 1993.

——. "Paul Ricoeur and Postliberal Theology: A Conflict of Interpretations?" *Modern Theology*, 4/1 (1987): 35-52.

Plantinga, Alvin. "Two (or More) Kinds of Scripture Scholarship." *Modern Theology*, 14/2 (April, 1998): 243-278.

Poland, Lynn. "The New Criticism, Neoorthodoxy, and the New Testament." *Journal of Religion*, 65/4 (October, 1985): 459-477.

Radner, Ephraim. "The Discrepancies of Two Ages: Thoughts on Keble's Mysticism of the Fathers." *The Anglican* 42 (2000): 10-15.

Reagan, Charles E. "The Dialectic between Explanation and Understanding." *Journal of Literature and Theology*, 3/3 (November, 1989): 285-295.

——. "Interview avec Paul Ricoeur: Le 8 julliet 1991". *Bulletin de la société américaine de philosophie de langue française*, 3/3 (Winter, 1992): 157-159.

Ricoeur, Paul. "A Philosophical Hermeneutics of Religion: Kant." In *Figuring the Sacred: Religion, Narrative, and Imagination*, pp. 75-92. Translated by David Pellauer. Edited by Mark Wallace. Minneapolis: Fortress Press, 1995.

——. "A Philosophical Interpretation of Freud." In *Conflicts in Interpretation: Essays in Hermeneutics*, pp. 160-176. Edited by Don Ihde. Evanston, IL: Northwestern University Press, 1974.

——. "Appropriation." In *Hermeneutics and the Human Sciences*, pp. 182-193. Edited by John B. Thompson. Cambridge: Cambridge University Press, 1981.

230 *Revelation, Holy Scripture and Church*

——. "Biblical Hermeneutics." *Semeia*, 4 (1975): 29-148.

——. "Biblical Time." In *Figuring the Sacred*, pp. 167-180. Originally published as "*Temps biblique.*" *Archivio di filosofia*, 53 (1985): 25-35.

——. "From Interpretation to Translation." In André Lacocque, and Paul Ricoeur, *Thinking Biblically: Exegetical and Hermeneutical Studies*, pp. 331-363. Chicago: The University of Chicago Press, 1998.

——. "Hermeneutics and the Critique of Ideology." In *Hermeneutics and the Human Sciences*, pp. 63-100.

——. "Intellectual Autobiography." In The Library of Living Philosophers. Volume 22: *The Philosophy of Paul Ricoeur*, pp. 3-53. Edited by Lewis Hahn. Chicago: Open Court Publishers, 1995.

——. "Interpretive Narrative." In *Figuring the Sacred*, pp. 181-199. Reprinted from *The Book and the Text: The Bible and Literary Theory*, pp. 237-257. Edited by Regina M. Schwartz. Oxford: Blackwell, 1990.

——. "Myth as the Bearer of Possible Worlds." In *Dialogues with Contemporary Continental Thinkers*, pp. 36-45. Manchester: Manchester University Press, 1984.

——. "Naming God." In *Figuring the Sacred*, pp. 217-235. Reprinted from *Union Seminary Quarterly Review* 34 (1979): 215-227.

——. "Pastoral Praxeology, Hermeneutics, and Identity." In *Figuring the Sacred*, pp. 303-314. Originally published as "Praxeolgie pastorale, hermeneutique et identité." In *L'Interprétation, un défi de l'action pastorale* (Actes du colloque 1987 du groupe de recherche in études pastorales avec la collaboration de Paul Ricoeur), pp. 125-135. *Cahiers d'études pastorales 6.* Edited by Jean-Guy Nadeau. Montreal: Fides, 1989.

——. "Phenomenology and Hermeneutics." In *Hermeneutics and the Human Sciences*, pp. 101-130.

——. "Philosophical Hermeneutics and Biblical Hermeneutics." In *From Text to Action: Essays in Hermeneutics, II*, pp. 89-101. Translated by Kathleen Blamey and John B. Thompson. Evanston, Il: Northwestern University Press, 1991.

——. "Philosophical Hermeneutics and Theology." *Theology Digest*, 24/2 (1976): 154-164.

——. "Philosophy and Religious Language." In *Figuring the Sacred*, pp. 35-47. Reprinted from *Journal of Religion*, 54 (1974): 71-85.

——. "Preface to Bultmann." In *Essays on Biblical Interpretation*, pp. 49-72. Edited by Lewis S. Mudge. Philadelphia: Fortress Press, 1980. Originally published as Ricoeur's preface to Bultmann's *Jesus, mythologie et demythologisation*. Paris: Ed. du Seuil, 1968.

——. "Reply to David Detmer." The Library of Living Philosophers. Volume 22: *The Philosophy of Paul Ricoeur*, pp. 494-498.

——. "Science and Ideology." In *Hermeneutics and the Human Sciences*, pp. 222-246.

——. "Theonomy and/or Autonomy." In *The Future of Theology: Essays in Honor of Jürgen Moltmann*, pp. 284-298. Edited by Miroslav Volf, Carmen Kreig and Thomas Kucharz. Grand Rapids: Eerdmans, 1996.

——. "The Bible and the Imagination." In *The Bible as a Document of the University*, pp. 49-75. Edited by Hans Dieter Betz. Chico, CA: Scholars Press, 1981.

——. "The Canon between the Text and the Community." In *Philosophical Hermeneutics and Biblical Exegesis*, pp. 7-26. Edited by Petr Pokorny and Jan Roskovec. Tübingen: Mohr Siebeck, 2002.

Bibliography

——. "The Hermeneutical Function of Distanciation." In *Hermeneutics and the Human Sciences*, pp. 131-144. Modified and reprinted from *Philosophy Today*, 17 (1973): 129-143.

——. "The Hermeneutics of Testimony." In *Essays on Biblical Interpretation*, pp. 119-154. Originally appeared as "L'hermeneutique du temoignage," *Archivio di Filosophia (La Testimonianza)* 42 (1972): 35-61.

——. "The Narrative Function." *Semeia* 13 (1978): 177-202.

——. "The Sacred Text and The Community." In *Figuring the Sacred*, pp. 68-72. Reprinted from *The Critical Study of Sacred Texts*, pp. 271-76. Edited by Wendy D. O'Flaherty. Berkeley, CA: Graduate Theological Union, 1979.

——. "The Summoned Subject in the School of the Narratives of the Prophetic Vocation." In *Figuring the Sacred*, pp. 262-275. Originally published as "Le sujet convoqué: a l'école des récits de vocation prophétique." In *Revue de l'Institut Catholique de Paris*, 28 (1988): 83-99.

——. "Toward a Hermeneutic of the Idea of Revelation." In *Essays on Biblical Interpretation*, pp. 73-118. Reprinted from *Harvard Theological Review*, 70/1-2 (January-April 1977): 1-37.

——. "Toward a Narrative Theology: Its Necessity, Its Resources, Its Difficulties." In *Figuring the Sacred*, pp. 236-248. Originally published as "De moeilijke weg naar een narratieve theologie: Noodzaak, bronnen, problemen." In *Meedenken met Edward Schillebeeckx*, pp. 80-92. Edited by H. Haring. Baarn: H. Nielissen, 1983.

——. "Two Essays by Paul Ricoeur: The Critique of Religion and The Language of Faith." *Union Theological Quarterly Review*, 28/3 (Spring, 1973): 203-224.

——. "What is a Text?: Explanation and Understanding." In *Hermeneutics and the Human Sciences*, pp. 145-164. Originally published as "Qu'est-ce qu'un texte? expliquer et comprendre." In *Hermeneutik und Dialektik*. Volume 2. Edited by Rüdiger Bubner *et al.* Tubingen: J.C.B. Mohr, 1970.

Robinson, G.D. "Paul Ricoeur and the Hermeneutics of Suspicion: A Brief Overview and Critique." *Premise*, 2/8 (September, 1995): 12-21.

Schlatter, Adolf. "The Theology of the New Testament and Dogmatics." In *The Nature of New Testament Theology: The Contribution of William Wrede and Adolf Schlatter*. Edited and translated by R. Morgan. SBT 2/25. Naperville, IL: Allenson, 1973.

Sheppard, Gerald. "Barr on Canon and Childs: Can One Read the Bible as Scripture?" *Theological Students Fellowship Bulletin*,7/2 (1983): 45-47.

——. "Between Reformation and Modern Commentary: The Perception of the Scope of Biblical Books." In *William Perkins: A Commentary on Galations* (1617), pp. xlviii-lxxvii. Edited by Gerald Sheppard. New York: Pilgrims Press, 1989.

Smith, John E. "Freud, Philosophy, and Interpretation." The Library of Living Philosophers. Volume 22: *The Philosophy of Paul Ricoeur*, pp. 147-164. Edited by Lewis Edwin Hahn. Chicago: Open Court Press, 1995.

Steinmetz, David C. "Uncovering a Second Narrative: Detection Fiction and the Construction of Historical Method." In *The Art of Reading Scripture*, pp. 54-65. Edited by Ellen Davis and Richard Hays. Grand Rapids: Eerdmans, 2003.

Stell, Stephen L. "Hermeneutics in Theology and the Theology of Hermeneutics." *Journal of the American Academy of Religion*, 56/4 (1993): 679-703.

232 *Revelation, Holy Scripture and Church*

Stewart, David. "The Hermeneutics of Suspicion." *Journal of Literature and Theology*, 3/3 (November, 1989): 296-307.

Stout, Jeffrey. "Hans Frei and Anselmian Theology." In *Ten Year Commemoration of the Life of Hans Frei 1922–1988*, pp. 24-40. Edited by Giorgy Olegovich. New York: Semenenko Foundation, 1999.

——. "What is the Meaning of a Text?" *New Literary History*, 14 (1982): 1-12.

Tanner, Kathryn. "Theology and the Plain Sense." In *Scriptural Authority and Narrative Interpretation*, pp. 59-78. Edited by Garrett Green. Philadelphia: Fortress Press, 1987.

Thiemann, Ronald. "Response to George Lindbeck." *Theology Today*, 43 (1986): 377-382.

——. "Revelation and Imaginative Construction." *Journal of Religion*, 61/3 (July, 1981): 242-263.

Thiselton, Anthony C. "Barr on Barth and Natural Theology: A Plea for Hermeneutics in Historical Theology." *Scottish Journal of Theology*, 47 (1994): 519-539.

——. "Biblical Studies and Theoretical Hermeneutics." In *The Cambridge Companion to Biblical Interpretation*, pp. 95-113. Edited by John Barton. Cambridge: Cambridge University Press, 1998.

Vanhoozer, Kevin J. "Philosophical Antecedents to Ricoeur's Time and Narrative." In *On Paul Ricoeur: Narrative and Interpretation*, pp. 34-54. Edited by David Wood. New York: Routledge, 1991.

——. Review of *Text, Church and World: Biblical Interpretation in Theological Perspective* by Francis Watson. *Pro Ecclesia*, 7/3 (Summer, 1998): 365-367.

Wallace, Mark I. "Can God be Named Without Being Known?: The Problem of Revelation in Thiemann, Ogden and Ricoeur." *Journal of the American Academy of Religion*, 59/2 (Summer, 1991): 281-308.

——. "From Phenomenology to Scripture? Paul Ricoeur's Hermeneutical Philosophy of Religion." *Modern Theology*, 16/3 (July, 2000): 301-313.

——. "Introduction." *Figuring the Sacred: Religion, Narrative, and Imagination*, pp. 1-32. Translated by David Pellauer. Edited by Mark Wallace. Minneapolis: Fortress Press, 1995.

——. "Ricoeur, Rorty and the Question of Revelation." In *Meanings in Texts and Actions: Questioning Paul Ricoeur*, pp. 234-254. Edited by David E. Klemm and William Schweiker. Charlottesville, VA: University of Virginia Press, 1993.

——. "The World of the Text: Theological Hermeneutics in the Thought of Karl Barth and Paul Ricoeur." *Union Seminary Quarterly Review*, 41/1 (1986–87): 1-15.

Watson, Francis. "The Quest for the Real Jesus." In *The Cambridge Companion to Jesus*, pp. 156-169. Edited by Markus Bockmuehl. Cambridge: Cambridge University Press, 2001.

——. "The Scope of Hermeneutics." In *The Cambridge Companion to Christian Doctrine*, pp. 65-80. Edited by Colin E. Gunton. Cambridge: Cambridge University Press, 1997.

Webster, John B. "Confession and Confessions." In *Nicene Christianity: The Future for a New Ecumenism*, pp. 119-131. Edited by Christopher R. Seitz. Grand Rapids: Baker Book House, 2001.

——. "God and Conscience." *Calvin Theological Journal*, 33/1 (April, 1998): 104-124.

——. "Hermeneutics in Modern Theology: Some Doctrinal Reflections." *Scottish Journal of Theology*, 51/3 (1998): 307-341.

——. "Response to George Hunsinger." *Modern Theology*, 8/2 (April, 1992): 129-132.

Bibliography

——. "The Church as Theological Community." *Anglican Theological Review*, 75/1 (1993): 102-115.

White, Erin. "Between Suspicion and Hope: Paul Ricoeur's Vital Hermeneutic." *Journal of Literature and Theology*, 5/3 (November, 1991): 311-321.

Whitehouse, Glenn. "Ricoeur on Religious Selfhood: A Response to Mark Wallace." *Modern Theology*, 16/3 (July, 2000): 315-323.

Wilken, Robert Lewis. Review of *Thinking Biblically* by André LaCocque and Paul Ricoeur. *First Things*, 93 (May, 1999): 68-71.

Williams, Daniel D. "Comment." *The Christian Scholar*, 49 (1966): 311-312.

Williams, Rowan. "The Literal Sense of Scripture." *Modern Theology*, 7/2 (January, 1991): 121-134.

——. "Sacraments of the New Society." In *On Christian Theology*, pp. 209-221. Oxford: Blackwell, 2000. Reprinted from *Christ: The Sacramental Word*, pp. 89-102. Edited by David Brown and Ann Loades. London: SPCK, 1996.

——. "The Suspicion of Suspicion: Wittgenstein and Bonhoeffer." In *The Grammar of the Heart: New Essays in Moral Philosophy and Theology*, pp. 35-53. Edited by R.H. Bell. San Francisco: Harper and Row, 1988.

——. "Trinity and Revelation." In *On Christian Theology*, pp. 131-147. Reprinted from *Modern Theology*, 2/3 (1986): 197-212.

Wolterstorff, Nicholas. "Evidence, Entitled Belief, and the Gospels." *Faith and Philosophy*, 6/4 (October, 1989): 429-459.

——. "Inhabiting the World of the Text." In *Ten Year Commemoration of the Life of Hans Frei, 1922–1988*, pp. 66-80. Edited by Giorgy Olegovich. New York: Semenenko Foundation, 1999.

——. "The Importance of Hermeneutics for a Christian Worldview." In *Disciplining Hermeneutics: Interpretation in Christian Perspective*, pp. 25-48. Edited by Roger Lundin. Grand Rapids: Eerdmans, 1997.

Wood, Donald. "The Place of Theology in Theological Hermeneutics." *International Journal of Systematic Theology*, 4/2 (July, 2002): 156-171.

Yeago, David. "The New Testament and the Nicene Dogma: A Contribution to the Recovery of Theological Exegesis." In *The Theological Interpretation of Scripture: Classic and Contemporary Readings*, pp. 87-100. Edited by Stephen Fowl. Oxford: Blackwell, 1997.

Zachman, Randall C. "Gathering Meaning from the Context: Calvin's Exegetical Method." *Journal of Religion*, 82/1 (January, 2002): 1-26.

Index

allegory 84, 85, 111-114, 130-131
    Song of Songs 112, 113, 124, 125
Althaus, Paul 169
Ambrose, St, *De Sacramentis* 112
Aquinas, St Thomas 25, 44
    on revelation 44
Auerbach, Eric 141-143, 144, 151, 152
    Mimesis 140
Augustine, St 203

Balentine, Samuel 10-11, 93
Barr, James 1, 6, 9-31, 51-52
    on Bible and church role 158-167
        critique of 167-175
        hermeneutic convictions 158-159
        historical-critical analysis 158,
            160-162
        interpretive communities 162-165
        listening church 165-167
    on Bible as Holy Scripture 80-93
        allegory 84, 85
        authority of 89-93
            critique of 101-104
        canon 91, 92-93, 103
        Childs, review of 92
        Christology 86-87
            critique of 95-98
        critique of 93-104
        historical-critical inquiry 81-82
        interpretation 82
        Kelsey, review of 91-92
        typology unity, breakdown 82-86
            critique of 99-101
        unity of 87-89
    on biblical interpretation 10-11
    on divine agency 25
    on doctrine of God, critique of 26
    on the incarnation 13
    on inspiration 17-19, 29-30, 31, 80
    on revelation and the Bible 9-21, 24-25,
        79-80
        critique of 21-31

cumulative tradition 14-16, 21, 28
    historical-critical inquiry 14-17
revelational theologies, objections to
    12-14
works
    The Bible in the Modern World 27
    The Concept of Biblical Theology 27
    Holy Scripture 17fn52, 18fn56,
        19fn59, 83fn18, 89fn49, 51,
        90fn55, 92fn67, 94fn76, 158fn2,
        161fn12, 15, 163fn24, 29,
        165fn40, 169fn53
    Old and New in Interpretation 13,
        27, 83, 86, 87
Barth, Karl 10, 21, 24, 31, 61, 68, 104
    on biblical interpretation 22-24
    Frei on 72-74
    on intratextual interpretation 211
    Lindbeck on 74-75
    on prayer 72-73
    on revelation 52
    revelational theology 11
Barton, John 93
Berkhof, Hendrikus
    The Christian Faith 27
    on revelation 27-28
    on tradition 27-28
Berkouwer, G.C. 24, 96
Bible
    and The Church 4
    critical reading 157-158
    as cumulative tradition 14-16
    historical criticism 81-82
    kinds of reading 170, 176
    revelation in 12-13
    see also Barr; Frei; Ricoeur
Bible as Holy Scripture 2, 5, 79 *see also*
    Barr; Frei; Ricoeur
biblical interpretation
    approaches 1-7
    Barth on 22-24
    Calvin 132-134, 151

236 *Revelation, Scripture and Church*

Childs on 22
Christocentric 1, 2
church role 3, 213
classic mode 2
hermeneutic-poetic 1, 2, 3-4
historical-critical 1-2, 214
Sternberg on 3
and text 6-7
see also Barr; Frei; Ricoeur
Biblical Theology movement 83
Bultmann, Rudolf 43, 124

Calvin, John 25, 152-153, 154-155
biblical interpretation 132-134, 151
Campbell, Charles 60, 62
Childs, Brevard 10, 21, 24, 76-77, 99-100,
155
on biblical interpretation 22
Introduction to the Old Testament 92
Christocentrism 2
revelational theologies 13
Christology
Barr 86-87
Frei 65-67
Comstock, Gary 207
conscience
Luther on 53
O'Donovan on 53fn250
Ricoeur on 42-43
Webster on 53

Daley, Brian 99-100
Dawson, David 74
Deism 55, 134, 197
Demson, David 25
Detmer, David 184
divine agency 10, 19, 21, 25, 27, 30, 74, 75,
76, 119, 214
Donfried, Karl R. 174

exegesis, and tradition 16

Fodor, James 36, 127
Fowl, Stephen 173
Frei, Hans 2, 7
on Barth 72-74
on Bible and church role 196-205
critique of 205-212
Gospels, truth of 196-197

literal reading 199-205, 209
and extratextual reality 201-205
methodological space 196-199
on Bible as Holy Scripture 130-145
allegory 130-131
critique of 145-156
figural reading 2, 142, 146, 152, 154
critique 151-154
hermeneutic shift 134-138
literal reading 143-145, 146-151
Christology 148
critique of 151-156
meaning as reference 137
narrative integrity, breakdown 133-
138
post-critical retrieval 138-145
pre-critical frame 130-134
as realistic narrative 121-122,
140-142
Supernaturalist view 134-137
typology 133
on the Gospels 61
on Jesus 59
liberalism
alternative to 60-67
critique of 58-59
narrative, and Jesus' identity 121-122
on Old Testament 131-132
on parables 49, 50
on revelation and the Bible 55-67
Anselmian method 54-55, 64-65
Christology 55, 65-67
critique of 75-77
critique of 67-77
modern doctrine, formation 55-58
works
The Eclipse of Biblical Narrative
138, 139, 140, 151, 197, 202
The Identity of Jesus Christ 59, 60,
66, 69, 75, 76, 121, 139, 140,
151, 197, 207
Theology and Narrative 54fn255,
65fn309, 66fn316, 319, 320
Types of Christian Theology 62, 71,
139, 199

Geertz, Clifford 143, 144
God, doctrine of
Barr on, critique of 26

Index

as Holy Scripture 4
 referent 114-116
Gospels, Frei on 61
Green, Garrett 188-189

Henry, Carl F.H. 64
Higton, Mike 147, 148
Holy Scripture
 Bible as 2, 5, 79
 God as 4
 Schleiermacher on 55-57
 soteriological function 17-21
 see also Bible
Holy Spirit 18, 19
Homer 140
 Old Testament, comparison 141
Hunsinger, George 68

incarnation 13
inspiration
 Aquinas 44
 Barr on 17-19, 29-30, 31, 80
 doctrine 29, 31
 revelation as 32, 36, 44
 Ricoeur's rejection of 44-45
 Webster on 29
 see also 'insufflation'
'insufflation' 32, 36, 44, 45, 125 *see also* inspiration
Irenaeus 101

Jenson, Robert 98, 156, 208, 212, 214
Jesus Christ
 Frei on 59
 identity, in narrative 121-122
 and Jewish Scripture 155
 and revelation 13
Jewish Scripture, and Jesus Christ 155

Kelsey, David, *The Uses of Scripture in Recent Theology* 91
kerygma 42, 84, 95, 107, 111, 124, 193
King, Martin Luther 182-183

Lee, David 202-203
Levinas, Emmanuel, on Ricoeur 119-121, 127
liberalism, critique of 58-59
Lindbeck, George 76, 102, 103, 139,

203-204, 205, 211
 on Barth 74-75
Luther, Martin 150, 169
 on conscience 53

McCormack, Bruce 23
Macquarrie, John 99
manifestation, revelation as 43, 47-48
Melanchthon, Philip 53
Middletown, Conyers 137

New Criticism 69, 70, 143, 144, 151
New Testament 111
Niebuhr, H. Richard 28, 29

O'Donovan, Oliver
 on conscience 53fn250
 syneidesis 53
Old Testament 87
 appropriation 130-131
 Frei on 131-132
 Homer, comparison 141
 as revelation 13

parables 49, 50
paraenesis 85
Placher, William 25, 49, 66, 69
Plantinga, Alvin 173
poetic discourse, Ricoeur on 35-36
Poland, Lynn 68
prayer, Barth on 72-73
Preus, James 131

religion, revelation, distinction 11
revelation
 Barth on 52
 Berkhof on 27, 28
 beyond the Bible 15
 concept 12-13, 14
 doctrine 4
 historical-critical view 14-17
 as inspiration 32, 36, 44
 and Jesus Christ 13
 as manifestation 43, 47-48
 meaning, in the Bible 12-13
 as nonviolent appeal 34
 Old Testament as 13
 poetic nature of 44-50
 religion, distinction 11

through poetics 32-37
see also Barr; Frei; Ricoeur
revelational theologies
  Barr's objections 12-14
  Barth's 11
  Christocentrism 13
Ricoeur, Paul 2, 6
  on Bible and church role 176-185
    critique of 186-194
    distanciation 180
    preaching 184
    reading
      canonical 181
      kerygmatic 176-177, 181, 182,
        183, 185, 186, 193
      shared 180-183
      submissive 183-185, 188
      suspicious 176, 177-180, 186,
        187, 188-189
  on Bible as Holy Scripture 105-119
    allegory 111-114
      Song of Songs 112, 113, 124,
        125
    canon/authority 111, 117-119
      critique of 128-129
    Christology 116
    critique of 107, 119-130
    distanciation through writing
      110-114
    generic inscription 107-110
    God
      naming 36-37, 105-106, 115,
        126-128
      referent 114-116
    narrative theology, critique of 108
    regional hermeneutic 105-106
    testimony 108-109
  Gifford Lectures 191
  hermeneutics
    appropriation 38, 40
    conscience 42-43
      critique 53
    constitution of faith 37-43
      critique 51-53
    imagination, role 40-41
    theonomy 41, 51
  Levinas on 119-121, 127
  on revelation and Bible 31-37
    appeal, critique of 50-51

    critique of 43-53
    'insufflation' 32, 44, 45
    as manifestation 47-48
    misunderstanding of 50-51
    narrative discourse 32, 48-49
    as nonviolent appeal 34, 180
    parables 49-50
    poetic rearticulation 32-37, 43
      critique of 44-50
    in the text 34-39
  suneidesis 42
  works
    Critique and Conviction 31
    Figuring the Sacred 32fn132,
      42fn197, 107fn138, 108fn141,
      116fn190
    From Text to Action 32fn132,
      38fn163
    Hermeneutics and the Human
      Sciences 34fn140, 142, 37fn158,
      38fn160, 162
    Oneself as Another 42, 191
    'Philosophical Hermeneutics and
      Biblical Hermeneutics' 38
    Thinking Biblically (ed.) 33fn136,
      41fn188, 111fn160, 115fn186,
      118fn202, 180fn102, 181fn111

Schleiermacher, Friedrich, on Holy
  Scripture 55-57
Schneiders, Sandra 44
Scripture *see* Holy Scripture
Smart, James 99, 104
Sternberg, Meir 206-207
  on biblical interpretation 3
Stewart, David 179
Stout, Jeffrey 63
Strauss, David Friedrich 139
Swinburne, Richard 30
syneidesis (suneidesis) 42, 52-53

Tanner, Kathryn 30-31, 209-210
Tertullian 101
text
  and biblical interpretation 6-7
  revelation in 34-39
Thiemann, Ronald 25-26, 31, 75
Thiselton, Anthony C. 178, 192
  on intratextual interpretation 210-211

Index 239

Torrance, T.F. 153
tradition
    Barr on 15-17, 26-27
    Berkhof on 27-28
    Bible, as product of 14-16
    and exegesis 16

Vanhoozer, Kevin 26, 38, 149, 210

Wallace, Mark 42-43, 45, 47, 48, 109-110, 121
Ward, Timothy 97-98
Watson, Francis 103, 149, 152

Webster, John 46, 149, 170
    on conscience 53
    on inspiration 29
Wells, Paul 16-17, 26, 30
Wendel, François 152
Williams, Rowan 27, 190
Wolff, Christian 137
Wolterstorff, Nicholas 45, 123, 125, 148
Word of God 3, 18-19, 139, 166

Yeago, David 46

Zachman, Randall C. 152, 153